How India Became Democrati

How India Became Democratic explores the greatest experiment in democratic human history. It tells the untold story of the preparation of the electoral roll on the basis of universal adult franchise in the world's largest democracy. Ornit Shani offers a new view of the institutionalisation of democracy in India, and of the way democracy captured the political imagination of its diverse peoples. Turning all adult Indians into voters against the backdrop of the partition of India and Pakistan, and in anticipation of the drawing up of a constitution, was a staggering task. Indians became voters before they were citizens – by the time the constitution came into force in 1950, the abstract notion of universal franchise and electoral democracy were already grounded. Drawing on rich archival materials, Shani shows how the Indian people were a driving force in the making of democratic citizenship as they struggled for their voting rights.

AUTHOR BIO TO FOLLOW

How India Became Democratic

Citizenship and the Making of
the Universal Franchise

Ornit Shani

University of Haifa, Israel

CAMBRIDGE
UNIVERSITY PRESS

CAMBRIDGE
UNIVERSITY PRESS

University Printing House, Cambridge CB2 8BS, United Kingdom

One Liberty Plaza, 20th Floor, New York, NY 10006, USA

477 Williamstown Road, Port Melbourne, VIC 3207, Australia

4843/24, 2nd Floor, Ansari Road, Daryaganj, Delhi – 110002, India

79 Anson Road, #06-04/06, Singapore 079906

Cambridge University Press is part of the University of Cambridge.

It furthers the University's mission by disseminating knowledge in the pursuit of education, learning, and research at the highest international levels of excellence.

www.cambridge.org
Information on this title: www.cambridge.org/9781107068032
DOI: 10.1017/9781107705722

© 2017

First published 2017

Printed in <country> by <printer>

A catalogue record for this publication is available from the British Library.

Library of Congress Cataloging-in-Publication Data

ISBN 978-1-107-06803-2 Hardback
ISBN 978-1-107-67354-0 Paperback

For Fredrik

Contents

List of Figures   *page* viii
List of Maps   ix
Acknowledgements   x

Introduction   1

1   Designing for Democracy: Rewriting the Bureaucratic
    Colonial Imagination   21

2   The Pursuit of Citizenship in the Making of the Electoral
    Roll: Registering Partition Refugees   52

3   The Roll as 'Serialised Epic' and the Personalisation of the
    Universal Franchise   85

4   Disciplining the Federal Structure   122

5   Shaping the Constitution from Below and the Role of the
    Secretariat   160

6   The Limits of Inclusion   208

    Conclusion: A 17 Crore and 220 Yard Democracy   248

    Selected Bibliography   259
    Index   271

Figures

1 Postcard from the Election Commission of India Record
  Room files   *page* 114
2 B. N. Rau, the Constitutional Advisor of the Constituent
  Assembly of India. *Source*: courtesy of Dr Anil Seal.   199
3 S. N. Mukherjee, Joint Secretary, Constituent Assembly
  Secretariat. *Source*: *The Hindustan Times*, REPUBLIC DAY,
  Special Number, 26 January 1950.   201
4 K. V. Padmanabhan, Under Secretary, Constituent
  Assembly Secretariat. *Source*: courtesy of Geeta Doctor.   203
5 P. S. Subramanian, Secretary to the Election Commission
  of India (right), and Sukumar Sen, first Chief Election
  Commissioner (left). Previously Subramanian was Under
  Secretary, Constituent Assembly Secretariat. *Source*: Photo
  Division of India.   206

Maps

1 Provinces, states and districts prior to 15 August 1947. *Source*: Appendix I to the Government of India White Paper on the Indian States. Reproduced by permission of the British Library. *page* 120

2 Pre-Partition India, 1947   120

3 Post-Independence India and Pakistan   121

4 The progress of the political reorganisation of states according to integration and merger schemes up to 31 May 1948. *Source*: Appendix XX to the Government of India White Paper on the Indian States. Reproduced by permission of the British Library.   132

Acknowledgements

This book is about political hope. The story of the preparation of the first electoral roll in the world's largest democracy provided me with the inspiration that drove the long process of researching and writing this book. But this journey would have not been the same and as meaningful without the support and engagement that I received along the way from friends, colleagues, and family, and the help of a number of institutions.

I deeply thank Gordon Johnson, with whom I first shared the idea of the book. His feedback and encouragement helped me to turn what was at the time a rough plot in my head into a skeleton of a book. Roy Kreitner read parts of the work in the early stages. I am grateful to him for his sharp observations and to our discussions that helped to shape some of my ideas. I owe special thanks to Jennifer Davis, David Gilmartin, Gordon Johnson, Eleanor Newbigin, and Steven Wilkinson who read thoroughly parts of the work at different stages and made important and helpful comments. I am also thankful to Rohit De, Arvind Elangovan, William Gould, Stephen Legg, Eleanor Newbigin, Uditi Sen, and Taylor Sherman for the uniquely collaborative thinking during our two workshops on 'Law, Citizenship, and Democratic State Building in India, 1910s–1960', held at SOAS and the University of Nottingham. Ram Guha, a master chronicler of India's democracy, read the penultimate draft of the manuscript. I deeply thank Ram for his comprehensive engagement and for suggesting the title of this book. I will always be indebted to Raj Chandavarkar, who is sorely missed.

This is also a book about political imagination. I would like to thank Yaron Ezrahi and David Shulman, whose works on imagination, and the conversations I had with them at the beginning of this project inspired me. I thank historians Mushirul Hasan and Mahesh Rangarajan for providing me with important opportunities to present the work in India.

My periods of research in India were immensely rewarding. The most important primary materials for this book were obtained from the record room of the Election Commission of India. This book would not have been possible without them. I am beholden to former Chief Election Commissioners of India Jim Lyngdoh, T. S. Krishnamurthy, N. Gopalaswami, Navin Chawla, S. Y. Quraishi, and Nasim Zaidi for their support. Dr Zaidi took particular interest in the work, read parts of it and gave me a valuable opportunity to present it before election commissioners from across the world at a conference in Delhi. I also had the opportunity over the past fifteen years to meet these and other Election Commissioners at the annual Cambridge Conference on Electoral Democracy in the Commonwealth. I owe a debt of gratitude to their convener, Anil Seal, for inviting me to take part in these annual conferences.

My profound thanks also go to S. K. Mendiratta, Legal Advisor of the Election Commission but really a guru of election laws, practices, and procedures in India. Sharing with him my findings at the end of a day of reading the records, over a cup of tea, was a treasured ritual during my research. I had many questions and Mr Mendiratta was an inexhaustible fount of knowledge and experiences, patiently and generously sharing his wisdom. Moreover, witnessing his conduct and becoming aware of his disposition towards issues of the day brought to life the story of the dusty records and of the bureaucrats who managed the preparation of the first electoral roll on the basis of the universal franchise. It also made clearer the significance of what these unsung heroes of India's democracy bequeathed to its electoral system. Mr Mendiratta is one of its living heroes. At the Election Commission, I would also like to thank the kindness and help of the keeper of the records, R. S. Mahto, Ravinder Luthra, and Ravi Kumar, and to Umesh Sinha, Padma Angmo, and Aarti Aggarwal for their help towards the end of this project.

The book also draws on materials I researched at various archives and libraries. For their great help I would like to thank the librarians and staff of the National Archives of India, especially Jayaprabha Ravindran; the Nehru Memorial and Museum Library, in particular Deepa Bhatnagar and Neelam Vadsa, as well as Jyoti Luthra, Somaya, Mohanti, and D. S. Rawat; and the Maharashtra State Archives. In the UK I would like to thank the librarians and staff of the Asian & African Studies Reading Room at the British Library; the Cambridge University Library; St John's College Library, Cambridge; and the Centre of South Asian Studies library and archives, Cambridge, especially Kevin Greenbank, Barbara Roe, and Rachel Rowe. I obtained some rare research material from the collection of the late Shmuel N. Eisenstadt thanks to the generosity of his daughter Irit Meir. I am enormously grateful to Simrat Dugal and Ayesha Sheth who provided superb research assistance in collating and organising the newspaper materials for this project, and to Ayesha for collecting additional materials.

I presented parts of this book at conferences and seminars in Canberra, Cambridge, Jerusalem, Leeds, Lisbon, London, Madison, New Delhi, New Haven, Princeton, Sydney, Tel Aviv, and The Hague. I am grateful to the participants who pushed me to rethink my ideas. In particular to Pratap Bhanu Mehta, Keith Breckenridge, Arudra Burra, Urvashi Butalia, Joya Chatterji, Assa Doron, Roy Fischel, Niraja Gopal Jayal, Douglas Haynes, Robin Jeffrey, Tahir Kamran, Gyanesh Kudaisya, Kama Maclean, Karuna Mantena, Shail Mayaram, Nikhil Menon, Polly O'Hanlon, Francesca Orsini, Norbert Peabody, Jahnavi Phalkey, Gyan Prakash, Srinath Raghavan, Emilly Rook-Koepsel, Shabnum Tejani, Jyotirmaya Sharma, Benjamin Siegel, A. R. Venkatachalapathy, and David Washbrook.

I also benefitted from the discussions of the research group on 'Twentieth Century Partitions' in Haifa. I thank Eitan Bar-Yosef, Ayelet Ben-Yishai, Yael Berda, Arie Dubnov, Rotem Geva, Sandy Kedar, Moriel Ram, Ran Shauli, and Mahmoud Yazbak. For their financial support, I thank the Van Leer Jerusalem Institute and the Minerva Center for the Rule of Law Under Extreme Conditions Institute, at the University of Haifa.

I wrote the book during a sabbatical leave at Cambridge. I am grateful to the wonderful support I received from my dear friends and colleagues at the Department of Asian Studies at the University of Haifa, both during that time and earlier when I headed the Department, especially Nimrod Baranovich, Michal Daliot Bul, and Arik Moran. I am also thankful to Tamar Katriel. In Cambridge, I would like to thank the Master and Fellows of St John's College for their support and for the stimulating intellectual home they provided during my stay as an Overseas Visiting Fellow. My special thanks are to Robert Tombs who made this fellowship possible. I am also thankful to Duncan Dormor, the late Robert Hinde, Jacqueline Rose, Ulinka Rublack, Simon Szreter, and Christopher Warnes. I would like to thank the Centre for History and Economics, University of Cambridge, for welcoming me as a Visiting Scholar, especially to the directors, Emma Rothschild and Gareth Stedman Jones, and to Tim Harper and Inga Huld. The Centre of South Asian Studies in Cambridge, where I have been an Affiliated Scholar, has been a long-standing intellectual home. I am deeply grateful to the directors, the late Christopher Bayly, and Joya Chatterji. I also thank James Laidlaw and Bhasker Vira.

At Cambridge University Press, I greatly benefitted from working closely with Lucy Rhymer. Her comments always forced me to improve my arguments. I deeply thank her for that. I thank Melissa Shivers, Claire Sissen, and Martin Noble for their help in getting the book ready for publication. For their encouraging and useful comments I thank two anonymous reviewers.

Friends filled the journey of writing this book with support, warmth, hospitality, and love. I deeply thank Sheela Bhatt, Urvashi Butalia, Janti and Pepe Dugal, Mr Dugal, Ajit Ghose, Suzanne Goldenberg, Mushirul Hassan, Zoya Hassan, Horit Herman Peled, Faith Johnson, Roy Kreitner, Diane Leblond, Renaud Lejosne, Gideon Levy, Tony Munter, Neeru and Arun Nanda, Catrin Ormestad, Justin Pears, Yoav Peled, Mahesh Rangarajan, Puneeta Roy, Sanjoy Roy, Avina Sarna, Navtej Sarna, Jyotirmaya Sharma, Jen Simms, Mishka Sinha, John Slight, Isabelle Tombs, and Esther-Miriam Wagner. During the summer of 2014, when the war with Gaza struck, my work came to a complete halt. At that time of hopelessness, in the face of impossible dilemmas, the initiatives, activism, and friendship of Michal Barak, Fatan, Tami Kricheli-Katz, Maram Masarwi, Tali Regev, Maha Sakallah Tali, Samah Salaime Egbariya, and Anat Saragusti was a true source of hope, from which I later drew tremendous strength. I am indebted to these inspiring women. Through all this and far beyond, the love and friendship of Suchitra Balusubramaniam, Michal Barak, Jennifer Davis, Ruchira Ghose, Eleanor Newbigin, and Sunita Thakur have been very meaningful and strengthening. Michal has been there for me over the years in ways that my words of appreciation to her friendship cannot really convey.

I drew much joy and sustenance from the young people in my family: Ana, Maya, Michal, Noa, Roy, and Yoav, as well as from the grown-ups, Ami, Andreas, Fumi, Harald, Johan, Liv, Rafi, and Sally. My much-loved sisters, Ifat and Shimrit, have provided loving encouragement and an enduring support. Ana and Noa brought much love and joy into my life, for which I am indebted. The example my mother, Haya, set despite leaving us so young, has continued to be a source of much strength. My father, Hanan, has been exceptionally dedicated, supportive and loving. I owe them immense gratitude.

Rom has always been a source of abundant love, happiness, pride, and inner strength. It was in large measure thanks to his support that I was able to take the time away to write this book. Fredrik has been the closest witness to the long and demanding journey on which this book has been, and my constant source of support. His love and understanding made this book journey, and so much beyond, possible.

Introduction

All the great civilizations, and probably all human societies, have known that human beings are capable of imagining; India merely cultivated this art, or faculty, more boldly than most.[1]
(David Shulman, *More than Real. A History of the Imagination in South India*)

From November 1947 India embarked on the preparation of the first draft electoral roll on the basis of universal adult franchise. A handful of bureaucrats at the Secretariat of the Constituent Assembly initiated the undertaking. They did so in the midst of the partition of India and Pakistan that was tearing the territory and the people apart, and while 552 sovereign princely states had yet to be integrated into India. Turning all adult Indians into voters over the next two years against many odds, and before they became citizens with the commencement of the Constitution, required an immense power of imagination. Doing so was India's stark act of decolonisation. This was no legacy of colonial rule: Indians imagined the universal franchise for themselves, acted on this imaginary, and made it their political reality. By late 1949 India pushed through the frontiers of the world's democratic imagination, and gave birth to its largest democracy. This book explores the greatest experiment in democratic human history.

India's founding leaders were determined to create a democratic state when the country became independent in 1947. But becoming and remaining a democracy was by no means inevitable in the face of the mass killings and the displacement of millions of people unleashed by the subcontinent's partition on 15 August 1947. Partition led to a mass displacement of an estimated 18 million people, and the killing of approximately one million people.[2] Moreover, creation of a democracy had to be achieved in the face of myriad social divisions, widespread poverty,

---

[1] David Shulman, *More than Real. A History of the Imagination in South India*, Cambridge, Massachusetts: Harvard University Press, 2012, p. ix.
[2] The exact number of those killed in partition violence is unknown. The figure of one million is adopted in some studies. See, for example, Ian Talbot and Gurharpal Singh, *The Partition of India*, Cambridge: Cambridge University Press, 2009, pp. 61–2. For an

and low literacy levels, factors that have long been thought by scholars of democracy to be at odds with the supposedly requisite conditions for successful democratic nationhood.

How, against the context of partition, did democracy capture the political imagination of the diverse peoples of India, eliciting from them both a sense of 'Indianness' and a commitment to democratic nationhood? And how, in this process, did Indian democracy come to be entrenched? It was through the implementation of the universal franchise, I suggest, that electoral democracy came to life in India.

The adoption of universal adult suffrage, which was agreed on at the beginning of the constitutional debates in April 1947, was a significant departure from colonial practice.[3] Electoral institutions existed before independence. But these institutions were largely a means of coopting ruling elites and strengthening the colonial state.[4] The legal structures for elections under colonial rule stipulated the right of an individual to be an elector, and the provisions for inclusion on the electoral rolls were made on that basis.[5] But the representation was based on 'weightage' and separate electorates, wherein seats were allotted along religious, community and professional lines, and on a very limited franchise.[6] Rather than defining voters exclusively as individuals, the law defined them as

estimation of the scale of human displacement see, for example, Gyanesh Kudaisya, 'The Demographic Upheaval of Partition: Refugees and Agricultural Resettlement in India, 1947–67', *South Asia: Journal of South Asian Studies*, Vol. 18, Special Issue, 1995, p. 73. For the partition violence see, for example, Urvashi Bhutalia, *The Other Side of Silence: Voices from the Partition of India*, New Delhi: Penguin Books, 1998; Gyanendra Pandey, *Remembering Partition*, Cambridge: Cambridge University Press, 2001. Yasmin Khan, *The Great Partition: The Making of India and Pakistan*. New Delhi: Penguin Viking, 2007.

[3] *Interim Report of the Advisory Committee on the Subject of Fundamental Rights* (presented on 29 April 1947 – date of Report, 23 April 1947), Constituent Assembly of India, Reports of Committees (First Series) 1947 (from December 1946 to July 1947), New Delhi: The Manager, Government of India Press, 1947, p. 20. Accordingly, the Principles of the Model Provincial Constitution and the Union Constitutions both contained provisions for elections on the basis of adult suffrage.

[4] David Washbrook, 'The Rhetoric of Democracy and Development in Late Colonial India', in Sugata Bose and Ayesha Jalal (eds), *Nationalism, Democracy and Development: State and Politics in India*, Delhi: Oxford University Press, 1997, p. 36.

[5] Thus, provisions for franchise in the Government of India Act, 1935 repeatedly specified that: 'No *person* shall be included in the electoral roll ... unless he...' *Government of India Act, 1935*, Sixth Schedule, pp. 247–98 (emphasis added). Also see Article 291 of the 1935 Act. For a discussion of the designation of voters as individuals in colonial electoral law see David Gilmartin and Robert Moog, 'Introduction to "Election Law in India"', *Election Law Journal*, Vol. 11, no. 2, 2012, p. 137.

[6] See India Office Records, *Return Showing the Results of Elections in India 1937*, London: HMSO, 1937, pp. 5–13. Also see Reginald Coupland, *The Indian Problem, 1833–1935: Report on the Constitutional Problem in India, Submitted to the Warden and Fellows of Nuffield College, Oxford*. Part 1, London: Oxford University Press (Third Imprint), 1943;

members of communities and groups.[7] Thus, not only did the experience
and legacy of elections under colonialism offer restricted representation
without democracy, the electoral practices, which informed patterns of
political mobilisation, resulted in the deepening of sectarian nationalism and impeded unity.[8] British officials unfailingly argued that universal franchise was a bad fit for the people of India. The small and divided
electorate was based mainly on property, as well as education and gender qualifications. Under the last colonial legal framework for India, the
1935 Government of India Act, suffrage was extended to a little more
than 30 million people, about one-fifth of the adult population.[9]

The national movement had been committed to universal adult suffrage since the Nehru Report of 1928. Anti-colonial mass nationalism
after the First World War further strengthened that vision.[10] But there
remained a large gap to bridge in turning this aspiration into a reality,

B. Shiva Rao, *The Framing of India's Constitution: A Study*, Nashik: Government of India
Press, 1968, pp. 470–1.

[7] Indeed, as Gilmartin and Moog argue, the colonial legal structure of Indian elections
was based on contradictory principles. Gilmartin and Moog, 'Introduction to "Election
Law in India"', p. 137. For the structure of representation on the basis of communities
also see David Gilmartin, 'Election Law and the "People" in Colonial and Postcolonial
India', in Dipesh Chakrabarty, Rochona Majumdar and Andrew Sartori (eds), *From the
Colonial to the Postcolonial. India and Pakistan in Transition*, New Delhi: Oxford University
Press, 2007, pp. 70–1; David Gilmartin, 'A Magnificent Gift: Muslim Nationalism and
the Election Process in Colonial Punjab', *Comparative Studies in Society and History* 40,
no. 3, 1998, pp. 415–17.

[8] See James Chiriyankandath, '"Democracy" Under the Raj: Elections and Separate
Representation in British India', in Niraja Jayal Gopal (ed.), *Democracy in India*, New
Delhi: Oxford University Press, 2001, pp. 53–81. Also see Gilmartin, 'A Magnificent
Gift'; Sumit Sarkar, 'Indian Democracy: The Historical Inheritance', in Atul Kohli (ed.),
The Success of India's Democracy, Cambridge: Cambridge University Press, 2001, pp. 23–
46; Alistair McMillan, *Standing at the Margins: Representation and Electoral Reservation
in India*, New Delhi: Oxford University Press, 2005, 18–73; Uday S. Mehta, 'Indian
Constitutionalism: The Articulation of a Political Vision', in Dipesh Chakrabarty,
Rochona Majumdar, and Andrew Sartori (eds), *From the Colonial to the Postcolonial.
India and Pakistan in Transition*, New Delhi: Oxford University Press, 2007, p. 22.

[9] See India Office Records, *Return Showing the Results of Elections in India 1937*, p. 5;
F. O. Bell, 'Parliamentary Elections in Indian Provinces', *Parliamentary Affairs* 1, no. 2,
1948, p. 21; W. H. Morris Jones, 'The Indian Elections', *The Economic Weekly*, 28 June
1952, p. 654; Chiriyankandath, '"Democracy" Under the Raj', p. 51. The estimates
for the proportion of the adult population that could vote under the 1935 Act ranged
between 20% and 25% at most. The previous electorate to the Provincial Legislatures
under the *1919 Government of India Act* reached 2.8% of the population. See 'Summary
of Indian Franchise Report' (presented to Parliament, 2 June 1932), L/I/1/607, India
Office Collections, British Library, London (hereafter IOC).

[10] See Sarkar, 'Indian Democracy', p. 29. It is noteworthy that besides adult suffrage, the
Committee appointed by the All Parties Conference to determine the principles of the
Constitution for India, which resulted in the Nehru Report, discussed in detail three
main proposals with a more restricted franchise and their possible anomalies and implications for the representation of different communities. Their conclusion was that 'the
only solution is adult suffrage'. See Moti Lal Nehru, *Report of the All Parties Conference*

both institutionally and in terms of the notions of belonging that electoral democracy based on universal franchise would require. Throughout
the first half of the 1930s in the course of making inquiries 'into the
general problem of extending the franchise'[11] in the run-up to the 1935
Act, both colonial administrators and Indian representatives in the provincial legislatures across the country claimed that 'assuming adult suffrage' would be 'impracticable at present',[12] as well as 'administratively
unmanageable'.[13]

The preparation of the electoral roll on the basis of universal franchise
was a bold operation, wherein the newly born state set out to engage
with all its adult citizens, ultimately expanding the electorate more than
five fold to over 173 million people, 49 per cent of the country's population. Putting adult suffrage into practice and planning for the enrolment of over 173 million people, about 85 per cent of whom had never
voted for their political representatives in a legislative assembly and a vast
majority of whom were poor and illiterate, was a staggering bureaucratic
undertaking.

The first elections took place between 25 October 1951 and 21
February 1952. But the overwhelming and complex preparatory work
for the elections, in particular the preparation of the first draft electoral
roll on the basis of adult franchise, had begun in September 1947. Before
that 'stupendous'[14] administrative task was handed over in March 1950
to the first Chief Election Commissioner of India, it was designed and
managed by a small, newly formed interim bureaucratic body of the state
in the making: the Constituent Assembly Secretariat (hereafter CAS),
under the close guidance of the constitutional adviser, B. N. Rau.[15]

(*Together with a Summary of the Proceedings of the Conference Held at Lucknow*), General
Secretary, All India Congress Committee: Allahabad, August 1928, p. 93.

[11] Letter from Ramsay Macdonald to C. H. Lothian, 29 December 1931, Mss. Eur. f/138/
15, IOC. Emphasis added.

[12] *Reports of the United Provinces Government and Provincial Committee*, 1932, IOR/Q/IFC/
61, IOC.

[13] Bell, 'Parliamentary Elections in Indian Provinces', p. 21. In 1932 the Lothian
Committee estimated that adult franchise would mean an electorate of 130 millions. See
'Summary of Indian Franchise Report', L/I/1/607, IOC.

[14] Election Commission of India, *Report on the First General Elections in India 1951–52*, New
Delhi: Government of India Press, 1955, p. 10.

[15] The setting of the Constituent Assembly Secretariat to assist with the drafting of the
new Union Constitution began in May 1946. The Viceroy requested B. N. Rau to prepare a scheme for the secretariat, as well as with those of the Provinces and Groups. See
Rao, *The Framing*, Vol. 1, pp. 360–71. In a letter to Rajendra Prasad in early December
Rau stressed that: 'The whole organisation is non-political and non-party in character
and its services are equally available to every member, irrespective of party or creed.'
Ibid., p. 371. In a note to Nehru dated 7 September 1946, liaising the preparation for
the inaugural meeting of the Constituent Assembly, Rau mentioned the need to create

This book explores the making of the universal franchise in India between 1947 and 1950. It tells the story of the making of the Indian electorate through the preparation of the first draft electoral roll for the first elections under universal franchise. This work was done in anticipation of the Indian constitution. The book, therefore, focuses on the practical – rather than ideological – steps through which the nation and its democracy were built. In this process, during the extraordinary period of transition from colonial rule to independence, bureaucrats inserted the *people* (*demos*) into the administrative structure that would enable their state rule (*kratia*). This process of democratic state building transformed the meaning of social existence in India and became fundamental to the evolution of Indian democratic politics over the next decades.

In the process of making the universal franchise, people of modest means were a driving force in institutionalising democratic citizenship as they struggled for their voting rights and debated it with bureaucrats at various levels. I argue that in India the institutionalisation of electoral democracy preceded in significant ways the constitutional deliberative process, and that ordinary people had a significant role in establishing democracy in India at its inception. By the time the constitution came into force in January 1950, the abstract notion of the universal franchise and the principles and practices of electoral democracy were already grounded.

The first draft electoral roll on the basis of universal franchise was ready just before the enactment of the constitution. Indians became voters before they were citizens. This process produced engagement with shared democratic experiences that Indians became attached to and started to own. The institutionalisation of procedural equality for the purpose of authorising a government in as deeply a hierarchical and unequal society as India, ahead of the enactment of the constitution turned the idea of India's democracy into a meaningful and credible story for its people.

There is an ambiguity about the use and meaning of the term democracy. It both designates and describes empirical institutional structures, as well as a set of ideals about the power of the people by the people, and

---

forthwith a Reference and Research Section in the Constituent Assembly. H. V. Iengar, the Secretary of the CAS, recalled: 'it had been decided by the Viceroy that I would be the secretary of a new department, the object of which was to prepare the way, for all the administrative arrangements for the Constituent Assembly which was to meet in the month of December... Now, there were two people appointed. One was Sir B. N. Rau, a very fine man, he was made the Constitutional adviser; he was to prepare the ground for the constitution and the other was myself.' H. V. Iengar, *Oral History Transcript*, No. 303, p. 129, Nehru Memorial and Museum Library, New Delhi (hereafter NMML).

the will of the people. While analytically distinct, in practice the institutional and normative components always coexist.[16] The thrust of this
book lies in the structural makeup of democratic rule. It explores how
Indian bureaucrats departed from colonial administrative habits and
procedures of voter registration to make the universal franchise a reality.
In some ways, they were taking their cue from pre-independence local
Indian constitutional convictions about franchise such as the position of
the Nehru Report, which stated that '[a]ny artificial restriction on the
right to vote in a democratic constitution is an unwarranted restriction
on democracy itself' and that the colonial notion of 'keeping the number of votes within reasonable bound' for practical difficulty 'howsoever
great has to be faced'.[17] To do so, in the circumstances of independence,
Indian bureaucrats used imaginative power with which they ultimately
shaped their own democracy.

This book explains the relations between two key democratic state-
building processes – constitutional and institutional – that took place
against the backdrop of partition over the two and a half seam line years
of India's transition from dominionhood to becoming a republic. The
first was the process of constitution making, during which the ideals of
electoral democracy and the conceptions of the relations between the
state and its would-be citizens evolved. 'Who is an Indian?' was a contested issue and a constitutional challenge at independence.

The second process, which took place on the ground, was the preparation from November 1947 of the preliminary electoral roll. The preparation of the roll dealt in the most concrete way with the question of 'Who
is an Indian?', since a prospective voter had to be a citizen. The preparation of the preliminary roll for the first elections was principally based
on the anticipatory citizenship provisions in the draft Constitution. The
enrolment throughout the country, in anticipation of the Constitution
engendered, in turn, struggles over citizenship. This process provided the
opportunity for people and mid to lower level public officials to engage
with democratic institution building and to contest the various exclusivist
trends to be found at the margins of the Constituent Assembly debates.
The quality of the engagement and the responses to these contestations,
the suggestions and questions that arose in the process of making the
roll, and the language that these interactions produced, democratised
the political imagination. It was these contestations over membership

[16] There is a vast literature on that subject. For a brief analytical discussion see, for example,
Raymond Geuss, *History and Illusion in Politics*, Cambridge: Cambridge University Press,
2001, pp. 1–5.
[17] See Nehru, *Report of the All Parties Conference*, 93.

in the nation through the pursuit of a 'place on the roll', I argue, that grounded the conceptions and principles of democratic citizenship that were produced in the process of constitution making from above. For some key articles these contestations and the experience of roll making even shaped the constitution from below. Moreover, as a consequence of the process of implementing a universal franchise and the consequent citizenship making, the government at the centre was able to assert legitimate authority relatively smoothly over the changing political and territorial landscape of the subcontinent, giving meaning to the new federal structure.

The preparation of a joint electoral roll on the basis of universal franchise in anticipation of the constitution played a key role in making the Indian union. It contributed to forging a sense of national unity and national feeling, turned the notion of people's belonging to something tangible. They became the focus of the new state's leap of faith, in which they now had a stake.

The Archive

The archival materials that form the bedrock of this study are from the record room of the Election Commission of India. In addition, the book draws on a host of primary materials I researched at the National Archives of India, and the manuscript room of the Nehru Memorial and Museum Library, both in New Delhi, and briefly at the Maharashtra State Archives in Mumbai. Moreover, I was also able to gain copies of reports, parts of reports and documents prepared, in the main, in the context of the work of committees of the Constituent Assembly that are not available in the Constituent Assembly Debates, or in the collection of Select Documents in the *Framing of India's Constitution*.[18] In the UK I obtained supplementary materials from the India Office Collections (IOC) at the British Library, London, and from archival materials at the Centre of South Asian Studies, Cambridge.

The Election Commission of India Record Room was a true treasure trove. The materials on the preparation of the first electoral rolls on the basis of universal franchise that lay at the bottom of long shelves at the back of the cool basement of the building, held the tale of a staggering bureaucratic endeavour. The materials include 70 folders, containing more than 1,600 documents, among them correspondences between and among the Secretariat of the Constituent Assembly of

---

[18] Rao, *The Framing of India's Constitution: A Study*, Vols I–IV.

India in Delhi, high-, mid-, and low-level public officials and with a wide range of civic organisations and people from across the country. Between September 2010, when I sought permission to inspect the files dealing with the planning and preparation of the electoral roll for the first elections, and September 2012, I consulted all these records at the Election Commission record room. Thereafter, the files were transferred to the National Archives of India, where archivists catalogued them for the first time. The files became available for review there from December 2012.

What impelled me to search the early records of the Election Commission was a question I had been asking of senior election management officials for some time, and for which I could not get a satisfactory answer. I asked repeatedly how the first list of voters on the basis of universal franchise was prepared. How, under the conditions prevailing in the country at the time, did they actually enrol millions of men and women? The official *Report on the First General Elections in India* includes just over two pages on the 'preliminary steps taken by the Constituent Assembly' for the preparation of the electoral rolls.[19] It states, with reference to the Constituent Assembly, that it was 'decided that the work should be taken in hand immediately', and that in November 1947, the Secretariat of the Constituent Assembly addressed the state governments on the matter, and notes some steps that were taken thereafter.[20] I could not find a record of such a decision by the Assembly in 1947, nor of the work of the Secretariat. It was clear to me that behind these two pages there lay a much bigger story.

Once I began reading the records, I found myself drawn into an overwhelming story. I read the records in daily instalments; my schedule set by the opening hours of the record room, or by the working hours of its keeper, Mr Mahto. He suggested that I read the files upstairs in the air-conditioned library of the Commission. But I insisted on immersing myself in the files' home, quarrying through the solid dust that covered the files. Excavating my way through to the 'bottom of India's electoral democracy', I could gradually piece together the core plot. But there were manifold stories within the main story. On each issue or question raised there were a series of opinion notes prepared by members of the CAS, who each, in their turn, wrote a note on the previous note. The string of notes started from the junior staff, who usually presented the subject matter, and ended with comments and revisions made by the Joint Secretary of the CAS, and sometimes the Constitutional Advisor. These notes unravelled the thinking process

[19] Election Commission of India, *Report on the First General Elections in India 1951–52*, p. 20.
[20] Ibid., pp. 20–1.

that underlay the steps the CAS took for the preparation of rolls. From time to time, a member of the CAS prepared a note that recapped the 'story' of the preparation of rolls as it developed until that point. At the end of the working day I was left in great anticipation for the next, eager to find out how the CAS had replied to this person or that official. What were their decisions on the matters they were grappling with? I was like Padma, from Salman Rushdie's *Midnight's Children*, keen to know 'what happened next'.[21]

I began, I realised, to read the archive as a 'serialised epic': the epic of India's democracy. In particular, as I encountered letters from ordinary people and read the notes of members of the Secretariat on these letters, I grew eager to know what ultimately happened. I also grew in my admiration and appreciation of the real heroes of the making of the universal franchise in India: the staff of the Secretariat, under the leadership of B. N. Rau.[22]

There has been much theoretical discussion over the last few decades about politics and statecraft in the fashioning of archival knowledge, its structure, and control of what materials are preserved or 'lost', and the limits these impose on the discursive possibilities that the archive allows.[23] These, of course, caution against the excitement in the face of new archival discoveries. The story of the preparation of the rolls in this book also draws on a variety of other sources. Nonetheless, it has been truly impossible, as a reader of these records, not to be profoundly inspired by them. One striking omission in the archive of the preparation of the electoral rolls for the first elections, however, is that there was not a single letter from or to a woman.[24] It is also clear that some of the material is missing. I hope the following chapters will take the reader, as authentically as possible, with me along the archival trail.

Perspectives on Democracy and Modern Indian History

India's democracy and its survival has been a subject of major research interest over the last two decades. Previously, scholars of comparative politics and political theory considered India's democracy to be an

---

[21] 'But here is Padma at my elbow, bullying me back into the world of linear narrative, the universe of what happened next.' Salman Rushdie's *Midnight's Children*, London: Vintage Books, 2006, p. 44.

[22] On B. N. Rau and the staff of the Secretariat see Appendix 5.1.

[23] For an interesting discussion see Ian Almond, *The Thought of Nirad C. Chaudhuri. Islam, Empire and Loss*, Cambridge: Cambridge University Press, 2015, pp. 65–99. Also see Ann Laura Stoler, *Along the Archival Grain: Epistemic Anxieties and Colonial Common Sense*, Princeton, NJ: Princeton University Press, 2009.

[24] See a reference to that point in Chapter 3.

anomaly from which there was little to learn.[25] Yet, India's democracy has proved to be robust. A number of major challenges, which are currently being faced by other democracies – both old and new – such as the problem of managing democratic regimes in multicultural and multireligious societies, have already been debated and experimented with in India. Thus, comparativists and political theorists are no longer been able to ignore the contribution of the study of India to general democratic theory and practice.[26] As Sunil Khilnani pointed out, India represents 'the largest exercise of democratic election in human history; an index of what is in fact the largest reservoir of democratic experience within a single state, a resource for intellectual reflection that remains still underused'.[27] Indeed, since the 1990s, scholars of South Asia have 'highlighted the political and intellectual limitations of universalizing Western experiences of democratization by bringing to light the particular genealogies of postcolonial democracy in South Asia, many of which lie beyond the colonial state'.[28] This book about the institutionalisation of democracy in India aims to contribute to the study of democracy in three main ways.

[25] See, for example, Robert Dahl, *Democracy and Its Critics*, New Haven: Yale University Press, 1989; Dahl, *On Democracy*, New Haven, Yale University Press, 2000; Arend Lijphart, *Democracies: Patterns of Majoritarian and Consensus Governments in Twenty-One Countries*, New Haven, Yale University Press, 1984. India is not included in the classic study of the transition to democracy: Guillermo O'Donnell, Philippe C. Schmitter, and Laurence Whitehead (eds), *Transitions from Authoritarian Rule: Comparative Perspectives*, Baltimore and London, Johns Hopkins University Press, 1991 (first published in 1986).

[26] See, for example, Sunil Khilnani, *The Idea of India*, London, Hamish Hamilton, 1997; Khilnani, 'Arguing Democracy: Intellectuals and Politics in Modern India', Centre of the Advanced Study of India (CASI) Working Paper Series, University of Pennsylvania, 2009; John Keane, *The Life and Death of Democracy*, London: Simon & Schuster, 2009; Alfred C. Stepan, Juan Linz, and Yogendra Yadav, *Crafting State-Nations. India and Other Multinational Democracies*, Baltimore: Johns Hopkins University Press, 2011.

[27] Khilnani, 'Arguing Democracy', 2009, p. 4.

[28] Eleanor Newbigin, Ornit Shani, and Stephen Legg, 'Introduction: Constitutionalism and the Evolution of Democracy in India', *Comparative Studies of South Asia, Africa and the Middle East* 36, no. 1, 2016, p. 42. For the work of scholars who focus on the emergence of the Indian liberal subject and democratic ideas and politics as they emerged locally, from within India, in the context of anti-colonial struggle, see, for example, Partha Chatterjee, *The Nation and Its Fragments: Colonial and Postcolonial Histories*, Princeton, NJ: Princeton University Press, 1993; Chatterjee, *The Politics of the Governed: Reflections on Popular Politics in Most of the World*, New York: Columbia University Press, 2004; Uday Singh Mehta, *Liberalism and Empire: A Study in Nineteenth-Century British Liberal Thought*, Chicago: University of Chicago Press, 1999; Mrinalini Sinha, *Specters of Mother India: The Global Restructuring of an Empire*. Durham: Duke University Press, 2006; Sinha, 'Totaram Sanadhya's *Fiji Mein Mere Ekkis Varsh*: A History of Empire and Nation in a Minor Key', in Antoinette Burton and Isabel Hofmeyr (eds), *Ten Books that Shaped the British Empire: Creating an Imperial Commons*, Durham: Duke University Press, 2014, pp. 168–89; Anupama Rao, *The Caste Question: Dalit and Politics in Modern India*, Berkeley: University of California Press, 2009.

First, scholars have in the main studied how Indian democracy survives, despite profound divisions, by exploring a range of constitutional, institutional, and policy safeguards and mechanisms, which enabled it to manage its religious, ethnic and deep social diversity.[29] These explanations account for the endurance of democracy and democratic citizenship in India. But they offer little insight into its seemingly rapid and deep institutionalisation under the difficult conditions of independence. This book offers a fresh perspective on the embedding of democracy in India at the birth of the nation-state.

Second, theorists of democracy have conventionally seen the establishment of India's democracy as a product of elite decision-making and institutional design. In this view, popular democracy, and the constitution, were endowed from above by discerning nationalist leaders and intellectuals. The shared premise of many analyses stemming from this view is that ultimately democracy 'irreversibly entered the Indian political imagination'.[30] The universal franchise, accordingly, was destined to happen. One political theorist suggests that universal franchise came about because 'the idea of universal franchise lay securely within the

---

[29] Among others, see Sudipta Kaviraj, 'Democracy and Development in India', in Amiya Kumar Bagchi (ed.), *Democracy and Development. Proceedings of the IEA Conferences Held in Barcelona, Spain*, New York, Palgrave Macmillan, 1995, pp. 92–137; Arend Lijphart, 'The Puzzle of Indian Democracy: A Consociational Interpretation', *American Political Science Review* 90, no. 2, 1996, pp. 258–68; Khilnani, *The Idea of India*; Khilnani, 'Branding India', *Seminar*, 533, 2004; Khilnani, 'Arguing Democracy'; Ashutosh Varshney, 'Why Democracy Survives?', *Journal of Democracy* 9, no. 3, 1998, pp. 36–50; Varshney, *Battles Half Won. India's Improbable Democracy*, New Delhi: Penguin Viking, 2013; Alfred Stepan, 'Federalism and Democracy: Beyond the U.S. Model', *Journal of Democracy* 10, no. 4, 1999, pp. 19–34; Atul Kohli (ed.), *India's Democracy: An Analysis of Changing State–Society Relations*, Princeton, NJ: Princeton University Press; Kohli, *The Success of India's Democracy*; Susanne Hoeber Rudolph and Lloyd I. Rudolph, 'New Dimensions of Indian Democracy', *Journal of Democracy* 13, no. 1, 2002, pp. 52–67; Srirupa Roy, *Beyond Belief: India and the Politics of Postcolonial Nationalism*, Durham, Duke University Press, 2007; Ramachandra Guha, *India after Gandhi: The History of the World's Largest Democracy*, London, Pan Books, 2008 (first published, 2007); Stepan, Linz, and Yadav, *Crafting State-Nations*. These explanations examine, for example, the nature of federalism (Stepan 1999), consociational interpretations of power sharing (Lijphart 1996), the production of the state's image of itself as the authoritative entity that embraces diversity (Roy 2007). Khilnani explores the construction of the nation, the ideational sources for a logic of accommodation and the 'distinctive, layered character of Indianess' that is not defined as a singular identity (Khilnani, 1997: 153, 169, 175; 2009). Guha (2008) offers one of the seminal historical account of the forces, individuals and institutions that held India together against the 'axes of conflicts' that might have threatened its integrity, examining state support for certain forms of pluralism, in response to popular demands. Stepan, Linz, and Yadav (2011) analyse the formation of a 'state-nation', rather than nation-state – a polity with a number of diversity sustaining measures beyond federalism.

[30] See, for example, Khilnani, *The Idea of India*, p. 60; Khilnani, 'Arguing Democracy', p. 26. Also see Varshney, *Battles Half Won*, pp. 5, 39.

heart of nationalism' and that 'once the idea of a nation took root...
the idea of democratic self government could not but have followed'.[31]
Sumit Sarkar argued that there was a 'decisive linkage between anticolo-
nial mass nationalism and the coming of democracy', yet recognised that
the precise nature of the linkage has not been well explained.[32] Indeed,
how was universal franchise, the bedrock of democracy, institutionalised? The practical process of establishing universal franchise, that is the
enrolment of all adult would be citizens just after independence, and of
embedding the habit of an electoral democracy among India's gigantic
electorate was an enormously challenging task and it was not obvious
at all that India would succeed in doing so. Among the challenges that
Indian administrators confronted were the registration of millions of displaced refugees that were moving across the still open borders and that
their citizenship status was in question, and more generally, an electorate
that was 85 per cent illiterate, many of whom had no clear place of residence, which was required for enrolment. Even if the idea of universal
franchise was secured as a future constitutional provision, the question
of it coming into effect – its practicability and administrative feasibility –
was not preordained.

Third, many have viewed India's democracy as an inheritance of the
British Raj, an extension of its bureaucratic structures and legal framework, which the Government of India Act, 1935 had already established.[33]
The fact that other British colonies, with similar colonial constitutional
structures, did not evolve into robust democracies undermines this viewpoint. There is the example of Pakistan, which shares the same colonial
legacy as India but which has a deeply troubled history of democratic
practice despite its founder, Muhammad Ali Jinnah, stating at the beginning of the constitutional debates that Pakistan would have a liberal citizenship regime.[34]

---

[31] Rajeev Bhargava, 'Introduction', in Rajeev Bhargava (ed.), *Politics and Ethics of the Indian Constitution*, Delhi, Oxford University Press, 2008, pp. 17–18. In another study, for example, making universal franchise is described as something that happened almost by itself as a result of the constitutional provisions: 'with one stroke, not only were commu-nal constituencies abolished but also women got the voting right straightway via Articles 325 and 326 of the Indian Constitution'. M. L. Ahuja, *General Elections in India, Electoral Politics, Electoral Reforms and Political Parties*, New Delhi: Icon Publications, 2005, p. 17.

[32] Sarkar suggests that 'the connections between imperatives of united mass anti-colonial struggle and the specific ... form of Indian democracy in fact need to be explored much more than they have been so far'. See Sarkar, 'Indian Democracy', pp. 29–30.

[33] See, for example, Dahl, *Democracy and Its Critics, On Democracy*; Myron Weiner, *The Indian Paradox: Essays in Indian Politics*, Delhi, Sage, 1989. Also see discussion in Patrick Heller, 'Degrees of Democracy: Some Comparative Lessons from India', *World Politics*, 52, no. 4 (July 2000), pp. 484–519.

[34] Two recent important studies, which look into some political institutional aspects of why India, unlike Pakistan, democratised amidst the post-independence turmoil are Maya

In Pakistan the question of the nature of the franchise was the subject of controversy from the outset. The 1956 Constitution (subsequent to a second Constituent Assembly, after the first was dissolved by executive powers) provided for direct elections on the basis of universal franchise, and the electoral law provided for an ambiguous structure of separate electorates for West Pakistan and a joint electorate for East Pakistan.[35] The then Prime Minister, Huseyn Shaheed Suhrawardy, excused and bemoaned the lingering delay in holding elections, suggesting that the 'thorniest problem' in preparing for the process has been 'to relate the Moslem and non-Moslem portion of our population in the franchise'.[36] In the following four decades separate electorates were intermittently repealed and then reintroduced, mainly as an act of political expediency.[37] The altering nature of the franchise in Pakistan made it very difficult to compile electoral rolls. In Pakistan more than two decades passed before direct elections on the basis of universal franchise were held and electoral rolls were prepared in 1970.[38]

Tudor, *The Promise of Power: The Origins of Democracy in India and Autocracy in Pakistan*, Cambridge: Cambridge University Press, 2013; and Steven I. Wilkinson, *Army and Nation: The Military and Indian Democracy since Independence*, Cambridge, MA: Harvard University Press, 2015. Tudor examines the importance of a stable class alliance combined with the strength of the dominant Congress party in India for its democratic trajectory. Wilkinson explores the historical relationship between the Indian army and the nation, to show how India's new leaders succeeded in 'keeping the army out of politics and preserving its democracy'. Wilkinson, *Army and Nation*, p. 3.

[35] G. W. Choudhury, *Constitutional Development in Pakistan*, London: Longmans, 1959, p. 225. Adult franchise was introduced in Pakistan for the first time on the eve of Provincial Assembly elections in 1951 in Punjab and the North West Frontier Province, in 1953 in Sindh, and in 1954 in East Bengal. As Tahir Kamran argued, 'Those elections did not contribute in any tangible measure to bring about the development of political institutions in Pakistan.' Tahir Kamran, 'Electoral Politics in Pakistan 1955–1969', *Pakistan Vision* 10, no. 1, p. 82. The Electoral Reform Commission appointed in October 1955 ascribed the travesty of these elections to the fraud and mismanagement of the electoral rolls, which created doubts in democracy. See ibid., and Tahir Kamran, 'Early Phase of Electoral Politics in Pakistan: 1950s', *South Asian Studies* 24, no. 2, 2009, pp. 257–82.

[36] Huseyn Shaheed Suhrawardy, 'Political Stability and Democracy in Pakistan', *Foreign Affairs* 35, no. 3, 1957, p. 426.

[37] Under Ayub Khan's Basic Democracies system (1958–1965) elections were held under a joint electorate but the elections were indirect by an electoral college. Zia-ul-Haq imposed separate electorate in 1979 for political gains (on the basis of the political forecast at the time), and they remained intact until Pervez Musharraf abolished separate electorate after he took power in a military coup in 1999.

[38] Suhrawardy, 'Political Stability and Democracy in Pakistan', p. 426. The question of granting full legal citizenship and the right of franchise to the people of the Federally Administered Tribal Areas of Pakistan (the formerly North West Frontier Province) was still being considered by the Pakistani parliament in 2017, 70 years after independence. Manan Ahmed Asif, 'Half a Cheer for Democracy in Pakistan', *The New York Times*, 20 March 2017.

This book seeks to explain the institutionalisation of a democratic political imaginary in India, rather than taking it for granted. By demonstrating the ways in which Indians took part in the process of democracy building it suggests that democracy was not simply gifted from above. In doing so, I aim to contribute to our understanding of 'democratic deepening' that theorists have only recently started to explore, which is conceptually distinct from the democratic transition literature.[39] Showing how Indians made their own democracy will also indicate significant transformations and departures from the colonial legal framework and structures.

This is the first historical study of the preparations of India's first draft electoral roll on the basis of universal franchise. It will complement what is surprisingly a very limited scholarship on India's first elections, and an absence of research on the preparatory work for the first elections during the transition years from dominionhood to the establishment of the republic.[40] As such it offers scholars of democratic theory an important case on which to draw. Moreover, as the first study of the interrelationship between the making of universal franchise and the evolution of democratic Indian citizenship, which brings to light an important and previously untold part of modern Indian history, this book also aims to contribute in three main ways to current debates and new research on modern Indian history.

[39] See Heller, 'Degrees of Democracy', p. 484; Heller, 'Democratic Deepening in India and South Africa', *Journal of Asian and African Studies* 44, no. 1, 2009, pp. 123–49.

[40] Barring India's Election Commission report on the first election there is, to my knowledge, very little research on the actual preparatory work for the first elections. See Election Commission of India, *Report on the First General Elections in India 1951–52*. Also see Irene Celeste Tinker, 'Representation and Representative Government in The India Republic', PhD thesis, University of London, June, 1954, pp. 261–82. On the preparation for the elections in Hyderabad, see Taylor C. Sherman, *Muslim Belonging in Secular India. Negotiating Citizenship in Postcolonial Hyderabad*, New York: Cambridge University Press, 2015, pp. 132–3. For works on India's first elections see, for example, Richard Leonard Park, 'India's General Elections' *Far Eastern Survey* 21, no. 1, 1952, pp. 1–8; Park, 'Indian Democracy and the General Election', *Pacific Affairs* 25, no. 2, 1952, pp. 130–9; T. N. Z. and M. Z., 'The Indian General Elections', *The World Today*. 8, no. 5, 1952, pp. 181–91; Nagoji Vasudev Rajkumer, *The Pilgrimage and After. The Story of How the Congress Fought and Won the General Elections*, New Delhi: All India Congress Committee, 1952; Tinker, 'Representation and Representative Government in The India Republic'; Irene Tinker and Mil Walker, 'The First General Elections in India and Indonesia', *Far Eastern Survey* 25, no. 7, 1956, pp. 97–110; W. H. Morris Jones, 'The India Elections', *The Economic Weekly*, 28 June 1952; S. V. Kogekar and Richard L. Park, *Reports on The India General Elections 1951–52*, Bombay: Popular Book Depot, 1956; Margaret W. Fisher, and John V. Bondurant, *The Indian Experience with Democratic Elections*, Berkeley: University of California, 1956; Ramachandra Guha, 'Democracy's Biggest Gamble: India's First Free Elections in 1952'. *World Policy Journal* 19, no. 1, 2002, pp. 95–103; Guha, *India after Gandhi*, pp. 133–43.

The historian Sumit Sarkar, among others, called attention to a lack of historical research on the transition across the 1947 divide.[41] He also wrote that 'the constituting of democratic structures amidst the turmoil of the late 1940s' has not been addressed.[42] This book is part of what is now an emerging new body of work on that period.[43] Recent work on the Indian state, particularly as it was shaped during the transition from colonial rule to independence, tends to emphasise continuities.[44] While recognising important continuities, which such literature sheds light on, this book examines a key aspect of the rupture and discontinuity in the making of independent India, which was critical to its process of democratisation. In particular, it explores changes to the bureaucratic political imagination in the transition from colonial rule to independence, the actual creation of democratic citizenship, and the institutionalisation of electoral democracy that were enabled by the administrative undertaking of making the universal franchise.

Moreover, in the same way that theorists of the transition to democracy have focused for a long time on the role of elites in establishing and installing democratic institutions, scholars of India have often claimed that in India, social transformation and democratisation was not driven from within the society but through a state bureaucratic agency and a

---

[41] Sarkar, 'Indian Democracy', p. 23. Also see Guha, *India after Gandhi*, pp. xxii–xxiii.

[42] Sarkar, 'Indian Democracy', p. 23.

[43] See, for example, Sarah F. D. Ansari, *Life after Partition: Migration, Community and Strife in Sindh, 1947–1962*, Oxford: Oxford University Press, 2005; Joya Chatterji, *The Spoils of Partition: Bengal and India: 1947–1967*, Cambridge: Cambridge University Press, 2007; Chakrabarty, Majumdar, and Sartori (eds), *From the Colonial to the Postcolonial*; Taylor C. Sherman, William Gould and Sarah Ansari (eds), 'From Subjects to Citizens: Society and the Everyday State in India and Pakistan, 1947–1970'. *Modern Asian Studies*. 45, no. 1, Special issue, January 2011; William Gould, *Bureaucracy, Community and Influence: Society and the State in India, 1930s–1960s*, London: Routledge, 2011; Eleanor Newbigin, *The Hindu Family and the Emergence of Modern India. Law Citizenship and Community*, Cambridge: Cambridge University Press, 2013; Niraja Gopal Jayal, *Citizenship and Its Discontents. An Indian History*, Cambridge, MA: Harvard University Press, 2013; Wilkinson, *Army and Nation*; Sherman, *Muslim Belonging in Secular India*; Benjamin Siegel, '"Self-Help Which Ennobles a Nation": Development, Citizenship and the Obligations of Eating in India's Austerity Years', *Modern Asian Studies* 50, no. 3, 2016, pp. 975–1018; Gyan Prakash, Michael F. Laffan, and Nikhil Menon (eds), *The Postcolonial Moment in South and Southeast Asia*, New York: Bloomsbury (forthcoming); Rohit De, *The People's Constitution (1947–1964)*, Princeton: Princeton University Press (forthcoming).

[44] See, for example, Chakrabarty, Majumdar, and Sartori (eds), *From the Colonial to the Postcolonial*; Rajnarayan Chandavarkar, 'Customs of Governance: Colonialism and Democracy in Twentieth Century India', *Modern Asian Studies* 41, no. 3, 2007, pp. 441–70; Gould, *Bureaucracy, Community and Influence in India*; Sherman, Gould, and Ansari (eds), 'From Subjects to Citizens: Society and the Everyday State in India and Pakistan 1947–1970'.

'passive revolution'.[45] This book demonstrates how, in the process of making the universal franchise, ordinary people were a driving force in the institutionalisation of democratic citizenship – and that bureaucrats were responsive and engaging with these people. It provides a lens into the interaction between political processes and democratic institution building from above and from below. Recently, some scholars argued that in India it is ordinary Indians and particularly the poor who guard democracy and ensure its survivability.[46] I reveal the origins of this trait in India.

Over the last decade a new and important literature on citizenship in India has emerged.[47] Some of these studies focus on the legal formal articulation of citizenship, its history, and the ways in which the citizenship articles and future legislations were marked by the partition and the movement of population it wrought.[48] Jayal Gopal also examines citizenship in India beyond it being a legal status, looking at group struggles and their negotiation of rights and identity claims in the legal, social, and political spheres. Her study of the predicament of citizenship in India emphasises the ways India's democracy fell short of its constitutional promises, mainly to promote equality. Taylor Sherman studies the variety of ways Muslims of Hyderabad, who became particularly marginalised after partition, articulated and negotiated their belonging in the first decade of independence. Her examination of practices and performative aspects of citizenship, rather than its formal legal status, as these emerged in the local context of Hyderabad throw new light on the processes of Muslims' abstraction into the 'India-wide concept of the

---

[45] Partha Chatterjee, *Empire and Nation: Selected Essays*, New York: Columbia University Press, 2010, pp. 241–66; Sudipta Kaviraj, 'A Critique of the Passive Revolution', in Partha Chatterjee (ed.), *State and Politics in India*, New Delhi: Oxford University Press, 1998, pp. 45–87.

[46] See, in particular, Javeed Alam, *Who Wants Democracy?* New Delhi: Orient Longman, 2004. Also see, for example, Patrick Heller, 'Making Citizens from Below and Above. The Prospects and Challenges of Decentralization in India', in Sanjay Ruparelia, Sanjay Reddy, John Harriss, and Stuart Corbridge (eds), *Understanding India's New Political Economy. A Great Transformation?*, London: Routledge, 2011, pp. 157–171; Amit Ahuja and Pradeep Chhibber, 'Why the Poor Vote in India: "If I Don't Vote, I am Dead to the State"', *Studies in Comparative International Development*. 47, no. 4, 2012, pp. 389–410; Mukulika Banerjee, *Why India Votes?* New Delhi: Routledge, 2014.

[47] See Anupama Roy, *Mapping Citizenship in India*, New Delhi: Oxford University Press, 2010; Jayal Gopal, *Citizenship and Its Discontents*; Sherman, *Muslim Belonging in Secular India*; Vazira Fazila-Yacoobali Zamindar, *The Long Partition and the Making of Modern South Asia: Refugees, Boundaries, Histories*, New York: Columbia University Press, 2007; Joya Chatterji, 'South Asian Histories of Citizenship, 1946–1970', *The Historical Journal* 55, no. 4, 2012, pp. 1049–71; Haimanti Roy, *Partitioned Lives: Migrants, Refugees, Citizens in India and Pakistan*, New Delhi: Oxford University Press, 2012.

[48] Roy, *Mapping Citizenship*; Jayal Gopal, *Citizenship and Its Discontents*; Chatterji, 'South Asian Histories of Citizenship'.

Muslim Minority'.[49] Other studies have begun to look into issues relating to citizenship and to governance more broadly during that period of transition from colonial rule to independence.[50]

The struggles for citizenship that emerged in the context of the preparation of the electoral rolls on the basis of universal franchise turned the idea of democratic citizenship into a living practice prior to the Constitution being passed. As we will see, individuals and various groups fought for a place on the roll. Becoming voters turned them into equal right-bearing citizens for the purpose of authorising their government. They attained a position, albeit a limited one, of being equal in the public domain, while they were also members of a highly hierarchical society. This powerful aspect in the institutionalisation of democratic citizenship in India at its inception became, I suggest, a key to democracy's survival in the face of its enduring shortfalls and many unfulfilled constitutional promises.

While this book is not a study of India's Constitution, it offers a unique empirical lens into some of the ways in which people understood and reacted to the constitution in-the-making from below, and how they used the draft Constitution in their struggles for membership in the nation. There is no social history of the making of India's Constitution.[51] Commonly, studies of the drafting of the Constitution centre on the deliberations in the 'ivory tower' of the Constituent Assembly. The study of the preparation of the electoral rolls in anticipation of the Constitution shifts the focus onto the ways these deliberations were received on the ground by both officials and the people. I will show, in turn, how their inputs contributed to the shaping of the Constitution from below. India's Constitution, which is one of the longest in the world, has endured despite many predictions that it would not do so in the long run and that it would not succeed as a basis for a stable democracy. Indeed, India's ability to sustain its new democratic constitution was doubted even by some of its own makers. One of them commented at the end of the

---

[49] Sherman, *Muslim Belonging in Secular India*, p. 174. For a more general analysis of the ways in which Muslims who remained in India after partition negotiated their membership in the nation by intermittently drawing on different conceptions of citizenship see Ornit Shani, 'Conceptions of Citizenship in India and the "Muslim Question"', *Modern Asian Studies* 44, no. 1, 2010, pp. 145–73.

[50] See, for example, Gould, *Bureaucracy, Community and Influence;* Gould, 'From Subjects to Citizens? Rationing, Refugees and the Publicity of Corruption over Independence in UP', *Modern Asian Studies* 45, no. 1, 2011; William Gould, Taylor C. Sherman, and Sarah Ansari, 'The Flux of the Matter: Loyalty, Corruption and the "Everyday State" in the Post-Partition Government Services of India and Pakistan c. 1946–1952', *Past and Present* 219, no. 1 (1 May 2013), pp. 237–79.

[51] Also see Madhav Khosla, *The Indian Constitution*, New Delhi: Oxford University Press, 2012, pp. 38–43.

constitutional debates that 'this Constitution made as it is for regulating our daily life, would not prove suitable and would break down soon after being brought into operation'.[52] The study of the interrelationship between the preparation of the electoral rolls and constitution making offers a fresh perspective on its endurance.

How India Became Democratic

Chapter 1 analyses the process of designing the instructions for the electoral roll on the basis of universal franchise and examines its implications for fostering democratic dispositions among those individuals who made up and operated the administrative machinery around the country. I suggest that, in effect, this process became an all-India administrative exercise in guided democratic political imagination. The notion of universal suffrage came to be imbued within the administrative machinery around the country. The idea of equality for the purpose of voting was bureaucratised. By examining this process against colonial discourses on franchise and on preparation of electoral rolls, I explore key changes in the bureaucratic political imagination in the transition from colonial rule to independence that were enabled by the administrative undertaking of making the universal franchise.

Distinct forms of exclusionary practices on the ground in the preparation of the draft electoral roll, once the work started, generated struggles for citizenship. Chapter 2 examines how the anticipated constitutional citizenship provisions were acted upon in these struggles over membership of the new nation. I focus on the question of the registration of partition refugees as voters, an issue that was a constitutional challenge and that led to numerous contestations over citizenship in the early stages of the making of the electoral roll. In the context of these contestations, a wide range of organisations from across the country deliberated over and used the language of the draft Constitution. They also made resolutions on its basis and even enacted some draft-constitutional provisions in order to establish their democratic citizenship and voting rights. As a result of this process, democratic dispositions began to develop among both state officials and the people, as they were mentored into the principles of electoral democracy, and the abstract language and forms of the democratic constitution in the making started to strike roots among the population at large.

Chapter 3 explores how the principle and institution of universal franchise attained meaning and entered the political imagination of Indians.

---

[52] Lakshminarayan Sahu, *Constituent Assembly Debates*, Vol. XI, p. 613.

It argues that it was the way in which the preparation of the first electoral roll on the basis of adult franchise became part of popular narratives that played an essential role in connecting people to a popular democratic political imagination. The Constituent Assembly Secretariat communicated its directives for the preparation of electoral rolls as a story through press notes, subsequently discussed in the press. People could insert themselves into this narrative as its protagonists. This process, in turn, gave rise to a collective passion for democracy, contributing to the democratisation of feelings and imagination.

From its inception, the preparation of the electoral roll on the basis of universal franchise was an all-India administrative operation. It took place while 552 princely states were being dismantled and integrated into the new Union, and as the immediate consequences of partition were still unfolding. Chapter 4 explores how in the process of the preparation of the roll, and in dealing with the resulting contestations over citizenship, the centre disciplined the new federal structure. The constitutional and administrative challenges of welding the federation and of forging a common idea of Indianness manifested in the process of the preparation of the electoral roll. Yet, it was in the face of these challenges, I argue, that the preparation of electoral rolls became a key mechanism of integration, and of making a democratic federal structure.

The preparation for the first elections was inextricably linked to the process of constitution making. Both elections and citizenship lie at the heart of the democratic edifice. The outcomes of the preparatory work for the first elections, particularly the enrolment of voters, created facts on the ground and constrained the extent to which the work that was done over two years, in anticipation of the new constitution, could simply be reversed. Moreover, the experimentation with the draft constitution in the context of the making of the universal franchise, as well as the contestations over a place in the electoral roll and its relationship to citizenship, informed the making of India's constitution. Chapter 5 explores this shaping of the constitution from below.

Despite the Secretariat of the Constituent Assembly's imperative to be inclusive, and its efforts to redress breaches in the enrolment process, various forms of disenfranchisement occurred. Moreover, the work of the preparation of the rolls was done in anticipation of the constitution. The Secretariat took some inclusionary actions, such as the registration of partition refugees as voters, that were pending on finalising their citizenship status. The citizenship articles were only adopted in August 1949, when the rolls were largely ready. There were other late constitutional decisions that had an effect on the rolls. Chapter 6 explores the limits of inclusion in the making of the universal franchise, and the consequences of settling some constitutional decisions on the electoral rolls.

Making the draft electoral roll on the basis of universal franchise in the context of the unfolding grim tragedy of partition, ultimately enrolling 49 per cent of India's population, the vast majority of whom were poor and illiterate, in anticipation of the constitution, required a rich political imagination. The conclusion brings together and recapitulates how such a democratic political imaginary was made resonant as a result of the interrelationship between the preparation of the roll and citizenship and constitution making. The production of a gigantic registry of India's would be citizenry, through a qualitative engagement of officials at all levels with the people throughout the country, made the universal franchise a political and social fact that contributed to the creation and survival of a democratic collective imaginary in the world's largest democracy.

In *More than Real*, David Shulman shows that in the South Indian language Telugu of the fifteenth-century 'one gets exactly what one imagines', and that 'what is real is real because it is imagined'.[53] The kernel of making real the universal franchise began, as the next chapter explores, in an exercise in political imagination.

[53] Shulman, *More than Real*, p. 151.

1 Designing for Democracy
Rewriting the Bureaucratic Colonial Imagination

> It is suggested that we should initiate the preparations of Electoral rolls as a separate operation and address the Provincial Governments in the matter.[1]
>
> (K. V. Padmanabhan)

> I should then like [Under Secretary] to prepare a plan for India as a whole nation...[2]
>
> (B. N. Rau)

An electoral roll on the basis of universal franchise prepared and maintained as accurately and as up-to-date as possible, was the plinth upon which the institutions of electoral democracy would rest. Whereas legal provisions, administrative rules, and procedures for preparation of electoral rolls existed under the colonial framework of elections, neither a conceptual nor a practical institutional schema for universal adult franchise existed for India. Indeed, as already mentioned in the introduction, throughout the first half of the 1930s in the course of making inquiries 'into the general problem of extending the franchise'[3] in the run-up to the 1935 Act, both colonial administrators and Indian representatives in the provincial legislatures across the country asserted that 'assuming adult suffrage' would be 'impracticable at present',[4] and 'not administratively feasible'.[5]

---

[1] Note by the Under Secretary of the Constituent Assembly Secretariat, K.V. Padmanabhan, 18 October 1947, CA/I/FR/48-I, Election Commission of India Record Room (hereafter ECIR).

[2] Internal note by the Constitutional Advisor, B. N. Rau, 16 February 1948, CA/1/FR/48-I, ECIR.

[3] Letter from Ramsay Macdonald to C. H. Lothian, 29 December 1931, Mss. Eur. f/138/15, India Office Collections, British Library (hereafter IOC).

[4] Reports of the United Provinces Government and Provincial Committee, 1932, IOR/Q/IFC/61, IOC.

[5] 'Summary of Indian Franchise Report' (presented to Parliament, 2 June 1932), L/I/1/607, IOC. The Franchise (Lothian) Committee estimated at the time that adult franchise would mean an electorate of 130 millions.

The franchise provisions in the Government of India Act, 1935 (Sixth Schedule), with 12 parts spread over 51 pages, contained various qualifications for being a voter for a divided and restricted electorate in each of the 11 provinces.[6] The 'Table of Seats for the Provincial Legislative Assemblies' consisted of 17 columns, designating the different categories of seats, among them five distinct types of 'seats for women'.[7] Correspondingly, provisions for inclusion on the rolls read, for example: 'No person shall be included in the electoral roll for a Sikh constituency, a Mohammadan constituency or an Anglo-India constituency, a European constituency or an India Christian constituency unless he is a Sikh, a Mohammadan, an Anglo-India, a European or an India Christian, as the case may be.'[8] A District Magistrate of Dacca during the 1946 elections noted that 'there are entirely different electoral rolls for the different types of constituency, Hindus and Moslems having separate constituencies and separate rolls'.[9]

The proposal to institute universal franchise was founded on an entirely different concept of voter registration. It required a concrete practical method of rendering all eligible adults procedurally equal individuals on a joint electoral roll based on uniform qualifications. Producing the instructions for an electoral roll on the basis of adult franchise for India meant a conceptual and practical rewriting of the structures of colonial electoral rolls and the procedures on which they were compiled. This was essential because the institution of universal franchise did not exist in India until then – nor had it existed at the time on such a scale anywhere else. Moreover, the task of producing a joint electoral roll on an all-India scale in the context of immense territorial and administrative changes at the time of the integration of the princely states was also a critical test of the authority and administrative capacity of the centre. It was therefore necessary to produce instructions with a detailed description of the elementary features of the new electoral roll and the nature of the registration process. Because of the enormity of the task, which had no precedent, the portrayal had to be sufficiently comprehensive to allow administrators across the country to follow them.

---

[6] *Government of India Act, 1935*, Sixth Schedule, 247–98. For example, Part II Madras, contained sub-chapters on qualifications dependent on taxation, property, 'by reason of guardianship', literacy, Service in His Majesty's force, additional qualifications for women, applications necessary for enrolment in certain cases and general provisions as to joint property. Ibid., pp. 250–4. The Act also allowed for parts of the territory to be 'deem unsuitable for inclusion in any constituency.' Ibid., Fifth Schedule, Clause 5, p. 240.
[7] Ibid., Sixth Schedule, p. 245.
[8] Ibid., p. 247.
[9] F. O. Bell, 'Parliamentary Elections in Indian Provinces', *Parliamentary Affairs* 1, no. 2 (Spring 1948), p. 23.

This chapter centres on the process of devising the instructions for the preparation of the first draft electoral roll on the basis of adult franchise and its implications for the construction of democracy. It explores how Indian bureaucrats began to depart from colonial administrative habits and procedures of voter registration to make the universal franchise a reality. I suggest that in effect, the process of devising the instructions for the preparation of the preliminary draft electoral roll on the basis of adult franchise became an all-India administrative exercise in guided democratic political imagination, which imbibed the notion of universal franchise within the administrative machinery around the country ahead of the enactment of the constitution. The Constituent Assembly Secretariat (CAS) directed the process, which in turn informed deliberations about the practicalities of instituting adult franchise at the lower administrative levels. By examining this process and comparing it with colonial discourses on franchise and procedures for the preparation of electoral rolls, the chapter explores key changes in the bureaucratic political imagination in the transition from colonial rule to independence that were enabled by the administrative undertaking of making the universal franchise. This exercise, I argue, resulted in instituting and operationalising the procedural aspect of the idea of 'one woman/man, one vote'. It also set in motion the creation of a new national polity for India.

Devising the Instructions: An Exercise in Guided Democratic Imagination

It was somewhat by chance, and indeed unplanned, that the Constituent Assembly Secretariat undertook the colossal project of the preparation of the draft electoral roll on the basis of adult franchise in late September 1947. The practical implications of preparing the roll first arose in a detailed letter on the subject of 'Electoral Rolls and Census', which K. T. Shah, a member of the Fundamental Rights Committee of the Constituent Assembly, addressed to its President Rajendra Prasad on 27 August 1947. 'It has been decided', wrote Shah, 'that the elections to the Legislature under the new Constitution shall be by Adult Suffrage. The preparation of the Electoral Roll on this basis, in every Unit, as well as for the whole country, will be a prolonged and costly task. I, therefore, suggest that the occasion may be utilised to take a complete Census of the country about the same time.'[10] Shah stressed that there was a lack of

---

[10] Letter from K. T. Shah to Rajendra Prasad, 31 August 1947, CA/I/FR/48-I, ECIR. K. T. Shah's role in initiating the question of the practical implementation of full devolution is noteworthy in the light of his engagement with the question of self-rule and the ability of Indians to participate in it from the time of the 1919 constitutional reforms. See Stephen

statistics to underpin the work of the National Planning Committee that the Congress set up in 1938 and of which he was a member. The idea, Shah explained, would be to hold the decennial census two years earlier than originally planned.

Shah wrote that he did not know exactly to what Ministry he should address his suggestion. He explained that:

[t]he Constituent Assembly is the sovereign Legislature, to which the entire Ministry is now responsible; and as you are the President of that Legislature, I have deemed it most expedient to submit the suggestion, in the first instance to you, in the hope that you convey it to the proper quarters. I do not think it necessary to make a motion in the House for this purpose, even assuming it is a feasible course. I leave it, therefore, entirely to you to decide how to proceed, and get the best results.[11]

Prasad forwarded the letter for the Secretariat's consideration.

In late September 1947 the members of the Secretariat reviewed Shah's proposal.[12] In the notes of the discussions Shah's proposition to combine the preparation of the electoral roll with the census was viewed with scepticism. Someone remarked that merging the two exercises would risk bringing politics into the census, creating confusion for the public and thus affecting the accuracy of the two operations.[13] Before making a final decision they sought an expert opinion on Shah's proposal from K. B. Madhava, Professor of Mathematical Economics and Statistics at Mysore University.[14]

In his report Madhava advised not to combine the preparation of electoral rolls with the census. He explained that an electoral roll is a statutory document, while a census is a 'useful inventory', and the implications of the two tasks are very different. The former is done on the basis of particular qualifications for enfranchisement and requires a complete enumeration, while the latter covers demographic, sociological, and economic characteristics and can be done on the basis of sampling.[15] Madhava also mentioned that 'there has been much suspect [sic]' over

Legg, 'Dyarchy: Democracy, Autocracy, and the Scalar Sovereignty of Interwar India', *Comparative Studies of South Asia, Africa and the Middle East* 36, no. 1, 2016, pp. 44–65.

[11] Letter from K. T. Shah to Rajendra Prasad, 31 August 1947, CA/I/FR/48-I, ECIR.

[12] Internal notes, 29–30 September 1947, CA/I/FR/48-I, ECIR.

[13] Ibid.

[14] Professor K. B. Madhava introduced teaching of Statistics, Mathematical Economics and Social Measurements in the Graduate degree programme in Statistics, the first of its kind in India in 1924, at the Maharaja's College, University of Mysore. See http://ycm.uni-mysore.ac.in/statistics.php (accessed 24 December 2016). The Secretary of the CAS asked to also send Shah's proposal to Professor Mahalanobis, but he was engaged at the time with the UNO (United Nations Organisations).

[15] K. B. Madhava's Note (a five page report), 11 October 1947. CA/I/FR/48-I, ECIR.

the decennial censuses of 1921, 1931, and 1941.[16] He wrote that separate and adequate steps are due to be taken for repairing the lack of statistics for policy making, but that the importance of 'the maintenance of an accurate and up-to-date electoral roll' makes it 'worth while to concentrate attention' on it alone.[17]

Madhava wrote about the scope of the electoral roll on the basis of adult franchise, and the challenges that may arise in its preparation. He anticipated that 'Proofs of having attained "adult" age will turn out to be an insuperable problem since ignorance of precise age is almost universal in India', that 'citizenship and naturalization are also bound to throw up good many problems of interpretations', as would the 'case of migrant people'.[18] He also discussed the need to consider the particulars that should be in the voters' register, the drafting of suitable forms and instructions for filling them, and the process of districting.

Discussing Madhava's report, the Under Secretary of the CAS concluded that 'we should initiate the preparations of Electoral rolls as a separate operation and address the Provincial Governments in the matter'.[19] Subsequently, the Secretary of the CAS wrote to Rajendra Prasad with the recommendation not to mix up the preparation of electoral rolls with the census. He suggested that 'it is necessary that we should take steps to consult Provincial Governments about the ways and means of preparing electoral registers on the basis of adult franchise'. He noted that 'this is not an easy problem'.[20] Prasad agreed.

In its preliminary steps toward implementing the universal franchise the CAS recognised that preparing the electoral roll would require a new form of population counting and knowledge that would make a clean break from colonial practices of enumeration. The Secretary of the CAS emphasised that 'the last census was regarded as inaccurate on account of political and communal considerations having been allowed to come into play, and this criticism may become validated' if the census is combined with the registration of voters, 'in which, apart from individual interests, party interests may also be in action'.[21] In the view of the members of the Secretariat it was critical for the state to find a new way of seeing, to borrow James Scott's construction.[22] Their logic was informed

[16] Ibid.
[17] Ibid.
[18] Ibid.
[19] Note by Under Secretary, K. V. Padmanabhan, 18 October 1947, CA/I/FR/48-I, ECIR.
[20] Note from H. V. R. Iengar to Rajendra Prasad, 27 October 1947, CA/I/FR/48-I, ECIR.
[21] Letter from H. V. R. Iengar to Prof. K. T. Shah, 4 November 1947, CA/64/RR/47, ECIR. The 1941 census was adversely affected by the war.
[22] James C. Scott, *Seeing Like a State: How Certain Schemes to Improve the Human Condition Have Failed*, New Haven: Yale University Press, 1998.

by a new imperative of seeing like a people. Divorcing the preparation of the electoral rolls from the census operation meant designing for the enumeration and constitution of the people as citizens-sovereigns, not people as a population, subjects-targets of democratic governance.[23]

In November 1947 the Secretary of the CAS wrote to all the premiers of the provinces and states and the convenors of group states:

The draft of the new Constitution prepared on the basis of the decision taken by the Constituent Assembly provides adult franchise... The work involved in preparing electoral rolls on the basis of adult franchise is a colossal one, and it is necessary now to start examining the administrative problems involved. The President will be glad if you will undertake this in consultation with the other member States of the group of which you are acting as the Convener ... and let us know how you propose to prepare the rolls, what difficulties you anticipate and how you propose to meet them.[24]

In effect, this was an all-India administrative exercise in guided democratic political imagination. The CAS asked the premiers of provinces and states to imagine the making of a joint electoral roll. That meant they were asked to envision the whole adult population as capable equal voters, each carrying the same weight. They were asked to 'undertake this in consultation';[25] to envisage the difficulties, as well as to identify the possible solutions. The idea was, the letter stated, that 'after the views of the various Provincial and State governments have been received ... to evolve some uniform method for preparing the electoral rolls and also to enable a general exchange of ideas on the subject'.[26] The question before the premiers of provinces and states was how to operationalise the basic procedural aspect of the notion of equality. To address it they now had to engage concretely with making universal franchise in their local context.

Over the next few months the governments of the provinces and the states gradually took on the task. Some did so more conscientiously than others. The Jaipur Government, for example, appointed a committee to produce a report on the question of the 'administrative problems involved in preparing the electoral rolls on the basis of adult franchise'.[27]

---

[23] See Michel Foucault, 'Governmentality,' in Peter Miller, Colin Gordon, and Graham Burchell (eds), *The Foucault Effect: Studies in Governmentality*, Chicago: University of Chicago Press, 1991, pp. 87–104.

[24] Letter from the Secretary of the CAS to the Premiers of all the Provinces and States, 22 November 1947, CA/5/FR/48, ECIR. On 27 November 1947, the CAS sent the letter to an additional 11 states that were not on the list of addressees of the 22 November letter.

[25] Ibid. The letter only set the age limit of an elector to be no less than 21.

[26] Letter from the Secretary of the CAS to Conveners of the Groups of States Represented in the Constituent Assembly, 27 November 1947, CA/1/FR/48-I, ECIR.

[27] The Committee was set up on 16 December 1947 under the Chairmanship of the Development Minister. Other members of the committee included the Reforms

The Government of the United Provinces expanded the guided exercise in democratic political imagination, when it sent a detailed request to all District Officers asking for their views and proposals for the preparation of the roll. The letter laid out for the District Officers the differences between the nature of enrolment and franchise as it had been practised thus far, and enrolment on the basis of universal franchise, which they were asked to imagine. The letter stated, for example: 'the number of persons on the ... rolls will increase four times approximately [it actually increased 6.5 times], but the simplified qualification will to some extent at least make easier the preparation [sic]. There will be no need to refer to ... income tax, or revenue records, to judge a person's eligibility for being a voter nor will the roll for an area be prepared according to communities'.[28]

The Government of Madras considered some principle questions, for example, whether the onus of registering voters should rest on the voter or on the government. In doing so their note compared procedures for voters' registration in Ceylon, England and the USA. They also proposed, among other things, to set a date, which would be declared as a public holiday, on which a census of all adult voters would be taken throughout the province; to prepare fortnightly reports on the progress of the work; and to ensure sufficient publicity through the press and 'through propaganda vans'.[29]

The vast majority of the states and provinces that responded did 'not anticipate serious difficulties in the task stupendous as it is'.[30] 'So far as Patna State is concerned', wrote its Chief Minister, 'the work of the preparation of electoral rolls on the basis of adult franchise ... can be tackled with a tolerable degree of accuracy through the ... net-work [sic]

Adviser, the Law Secretary and the Revenue Secretary. A Statistical Officer was also invited to the discussions. See Report of the Jaipur Government on administrative problems involved in the preparation of the electoral rolls, 20 March 1948, CA/1/FR/48-I, ECIR.

[28] Letter from the Deputy Secretary to Government, United Provinces to All District Officers, United Provinces, 7 January 1948, CA/1/FR/48-I, ECIR.

[29] Letter from the Chief Secretary Government of Madras (Public (elections) Department) to CAS, 5 February 1948, CA/1/FR/48-I, ECIR. According to the proposal, the public holiday day could be declared under the Negotiable Instruments Act; all government officials, including pensioners and able-bodies could be mobilised for the task. The Chief Secretary suggested sending it to all Collectors of Districts, and Inspectors of Municipal Councils Commissioner for further remarks.

[30] Letter from the Raj Mandir, Danna C. I. to CAS, 7 December 1947, CA/1/FR/48-I, ECIR. The letter referred to preparation of electoral rolls for the States in Central India comprising of the Malwa States and Bundelkhand States. Also see letter from the Dewan, Baroda State to CAS, 2 January 1948; letter from the Secretary to the Government of His Highness the Maharaja of Mayurbhanj State, 17 December 1947, ibid.

of which the Patna government have got [sic] throughout the State'.[31] Similarly, Surguja State's letter laid out in detail their 'network of staff' that could 'prepare a list of all adults'.[32] Notably, Surguja, as in most princely states, had no experience with any form of democracy until that time, unlike the provinces of British India, where elections on a limited franchise were held. Some governments suggested that 'by the introduction of adult franchise preparation of electoral roll will be very much simplified'.[33] Bureaucrats in the states and provinces were quick to identify the officers who would be entrusted with the task. They even had notions of how much they would be paid for the additional work;[34] what the registration form should look like;[35] and who in, or which part of, the local administration would supply the forms.[36] Only in one state, Bhuj (Kutch) did the Dewan write that 'educationally and politically Kutch is a backward state … conditions are such as to make it very difficult in the immediate future to introduce adult franchise and to prepare electoral rolls based on such franchise'. [37] Some state governments suggested that

[31] Letter from the Chief Minister of Patna State to CAS, 8 December 1947, CA/1/FR/48-I, ECIR. Enrolment was envisioned to be conducted through the State's 700 circa Panchayats.

[32] See letter from the Chief Minister Surguja State, 2 December 1947, CA/1/FR/48-I, ECIR. The Chief Minister of the State explained: 'it will be possible for' the Patwaris, who have records of almost all residents of villages, 'to prepare a list of all adults'.

[33] Letter from Election Commissioner East Punjab to CAS, 13 January 1948, CA/1/FR/48-I, ECIR. Also see letter from the Deputy Secretary to Government, United Provinces to All District Officers, United Provinces, 7 January 1948, ibid.

[34] See, for example, letter from the Secretary to Government Law Department, Government of Mysore to CAS, 19 January 1948, CA/1/FR/48-I, ECIR.

[35] For example, the Mysore government suggested that the columns in the form include: s. no, name, age, father's/husband's name, occupation and address, and remarks. Ibid. The Madras Government proposed that the 'elector's form' would include: community, caste or sub-caste, literacy and occupation. Letter from the Chief Secretary Government of Madras (Public (elections) Department) to CAS, 5 February 1948, CA/1/FR/48-I, ECIR.

[36] Thus, the Rewa State laid out a comprehensive scheme for the process of enlistment, and passed in January 1948 two State Council resolutions regarding preparation of electoral rolls. The State's procedures set that 'printed forms will be supplied to the Revenue Minister by the Reforms Department within 15 days of the receipt of this resolution in the Reforms Department… The Revenue Minister will arrange to send the requisite number of forms to each Tahsil Headquarter within five days of the receipt of these forms … he will be provided with Motor Transport and Petrol coupons to facilitate the supply of forms'. The resolution further instructed that the work of enumeration would be done by the Patwaris in the Kothar areas, by the Forest Guards in the villages and illakedars (officers) in their respective (forest) areas. The Tahsildars will be responsible for the preparation of the electoral roll on the basis of the forms they will get from the enumerators within 25 days of receiving these forms; the roll will be in Hindi. 'The Reforms Department will supply instructions in simple Hindi.' See letter from the Chief Secretary Rewa State to CAS, 19 February 1948, CA/1/FR/48-I, ECIR.

[37] See letter from the Dewan of Bhuj (Kutch) to CAS, 6 December 1947, CA/1/FR/48-I, ECIR. The Dewan, however, noted that this question is seriously engaging the

the Indian Government should arrange for training courses for election officers to remedy lack of qualified personnel in this matter.[38]

It was perhaps because the request to 'imagine the roll' was not pinned to a grand nationalist dream about freedom and democracy, but was rather confined to the concrete technical venture of enlistment, that administrators of the states and provinces could envisage the fine details the process would entail in their local contexts. In the CAS's request of the provinces and states the idea of the universal franchise was not accorded with special moral weight or importance. The CAS asked them to 'start examining the administrative problems involved'[39] in preparing a list of all adults, as well as the difficulties that may arise in doing so. Their task was not to implement freedom, equality or the so-called 'will of the people'. The task was posited as ambitious and complex, but it was ultimately perceived to be a technical and administrative undertaking.

Indeed, the correspondences from administrators in the provinces and states demonstrated their pragmatic approach and problem-solving orientation to making universal franchise work. Administrators delved into the minutiae of the task. They described in detail and thus introduced before the CAS the local administrative structure and its capacities, as well as recent relevant legislation. The political, historical, or even symbolic significance of the universal franchise was completely absent from the correspondences. Accordingly, administrators made efforts to 'measure' the endeavour of the making of the universal franchise, breaking down the task into numbers.

Thus, the imagined difficulties were mostly logistical. A frequently expressed concern was an anticipated shortfall of paper for the roll and presses for printing because, for example, as the Election Commissioner East Punjab commented, 'all the big presses at which they [the rolls] used to be printed are in Lahore', which was now in Pakistan.[40] The Madras and Jaipur governments predicted a shortage of paper on the basis of estimated projections of their voter population under the adult franchise.[41]

consideration of His Highness Maharao Sahib Bhadur of Kutch, and asked to be informed 'how other important states of India propose to act in this behalf'. Ibid.

[38] See letter from Kotah State to CAS, 8 January 1948; S. no.63, 18 March 1948; S. no. 21–23 (on Bastar State), 2 January 1948, CA/1/FR/48-I, ECIR.

[39] Letter from the Secretary of the CAS to the Premiers of all the Provinces and States, 22 November 1947, CA/5/FR/48, ECIR.

[40] Letter from Election Commissioner East Punjab to CAS, 13 January 1948, CA/1/FR/48-I, ECIR.

[41] The Chief Secretary of the Madras government wrote: 'the voters list containing roughly 30 million voters (so far as the Madras Presidency is concerned) is not an easy job... There are four main regional languages... Finding paper for printing is another problem.' See letter from the Chief Secretary Government of Madras (Public (elections) Department) to CAS, 5 February 1948, CA/1/FR/48-I, ECIR.

The Jaipur Government calculated that 1,000 reams of paper would be needed, and that 'it may even be necessary to sponsor some legislation for commandeering private presses for the purpose'.[42] Another envisaged problem was the difficulty of determining the age of voters because of the general absence of birth records and certificates.[43] A few states also mentioned the difficult topographical conditions and the lack of means of communication as factors that might impede the work.[44]

In some of the states, for example, Cochin, Manipur, Mewar, Pudukkottai, and Travancore, adult franchise was already introduced at that time, or in the process of being introduced. These states, therefore, did not anticipate any special difficulty for preparing the electoral rolls.[45] The Government of Travancore was just preparing at the time for its first elections on the basis of adult franchise for an electorate of 2.95 million, which was to take place in early February 1948. The Secretary to the Government of Travancore shared with the CAS in great detail, over a six-page letter, the scheme that they had devised for the task, describing both the legal and administrative actions: how the enlisting of all adults was actually done; which personnel were in charge and how they were remunerated; what difficulties they encountered; what steps were taken to ensure as far as possible the accuracy of the work; and the methods for engaging the public in the process. Thus, they decided to conduct the registration 'on a house-to-house basis ... because it was thought that a voluntary or optional system of registration would hardly serve to achieve the desired object. For ensuring the collection of all relevant statistics relating to the adults of the State, a form (copy enclosed) was adopted for the registration of adults.'[46] The affixing of numbers

---

[42] Report of the Jaipur Government on administrative problems involved in the preparation of the electoral rolls, 20 March 1948, CA/1/FR/48-I, ECIR. On the anticipated shortage of paper for the roll also see letter from the Secretary to Government Law Department, Government of Mysore to CAS, 19 January 1948, letter from Kotah State to CAS, 8 January 1948, S. no.82, 23 April 1948, ibid.

[43] See letter from Bastar State, 8 December 1947, S. no. 21–23 (internal notes), 2 January 1948, letter from Bharatpur State, 12 January 1948, CA/1/FR/48-I, ECIR.

[44] See for example, letter from the Chief Secretary of the Tehri-Garhwal State to CAS, 26 January 1948, CA/1/FR/48-I, ECIR.

[45] See letter from the Chief Secretary Mewar Government Udaipur, 30 December 1947, letter from the Dewan of Pudukkottai, 5 December 1947, letter from the Secretary of Aundh State, 7 March 1948, letter from the Chief Minister of Manipur State, 15 March 1948, letter from the Chief Minister of Cooch Behar State, 27 January 1948, CA/1/FR/48-I, ECIR. The Bharatpur State informed that the rolls were prepared in this State just after the announcement of popular Ministry. See letter from Bharatpur State, 12 January 1948, ibid.

[46] Letter from the Secretary to the Government of Travancore to the Secretary, Constituent Assembly of India, 29 January 1948, CA/1/FR/48-I, ECIR. In Travancore, a Constitution Act of 7 April 1947 set that elections to their legislature should be on the basis of adult franchise. The registration in the State began on 18 August 1947 and was completed

to homes was part of the operation.[47] The letter of the government of Travancore expanded on the ways local bureaucrats were managed so as to prevent disenfranchisement. For example, for each registration unit two assessors of different communities were appointed in order to avoid communal bias.[48]

The Secretariat of the Constituent Assembly reviewed all the responses. After receiving and considering replies from most of the provinces and states, an 'analytical summary of the views expressed in their letters was prepared and placed for consideration' by the members of the CAS.[49] Ultimately, it was the Travancore plan for implementing adult suffrage that captured the political imagination of the CAS.

In a note to the Constitutional Advisor (CA), B. N. Rau, the Joint Secretary on 16 February 1948, asked that the 'CA may see the letter from the Travancore State ... containing the details of the steps taken by them for the registration of voters on the basis of adult franchise.'[50] On that same day Rau wrote: 'we must thank the Secretary of the Travancore Government for the full and detailed information given in the letter. I should then like [Under Secretary] *to prepare a plan for India as a whole nation* on the lines of the Travancore plan and bring up for discussion.'[51] Within a week this had been done. The Under Secretary added his own note: 'a revised note is placed below. I have drafted it in the form of a memorandum which can be sent to the States and Provinces'.[52]

During the four months of administrative deliberations within the CAS, in the provinces and the states, the question of implementing universal adult franchise was rendered into imagining a joint roll of all adults in the land as equal capable voters. Designing for that electoral roll began laying the groundwork for scaling up both a national polity for India, as well as the notion of procedural equality for its people.

---

on 16 September 1947. By 12 October 1947 the register of 29.5 Lakh (2.95 millions) voters was closed. Upon receiving this letter, the Under Secretary of the CAS asked the Travancore Government for further information and copies of the relevant Acts and forms.

[47] Registration was done on the basis of the house numbers given in the 1941 census, and new buildings were given supplementary numbers. Ibid.

[48] Ibid.

[49] See Summary note by Brij Bhushan, 19 January 1948, CA/1/FR/48-I, ECIR.

[50] Internal note, 16 February 1948, CA/1/FR/48-I, ECIR.

[51] Ibid. (emphasis added). This may throw more light on Robin Jeffrey's comment in his study of the first universal suffrage elections in Travancore in 1948 that 'not surprisingly, the electoral system retained a number of features of the princely legislature'. See Robin Jeffrey, 'The "Kerala Model" and Portents for Indian Politics: Inferences from the First Universal-Suffrage Elections, Travancore, 1948', unpublished paper, p. 17. I thank Robin Jeffrey for sharing his paper with me.

[52] Internal note, 20 February 1948, CA/1/FR/48-I, ECIR.

'A Plan for India as a Whole Nation'

By 15 March 1948 the Joint Secretary of the CAS issued a circular letter to all provinces, states, and convenors of group states containing instructions for the preparation of the draft electoral roll on the basis of adult franchise, and detailed directives for the actual enumeration, requesting that the work be carried out forthwith.[53] The rationale was that 'it is clearly desirable that the elections for the future Central and Provincial Legislatures (these latter are referred to in the new constitution as State Legislatures) should be completed as early as possible after the new constitution comes into operation'.[54]

The instructions for the compilation of the roll were issued in anticipation of the new constitution. But they were pegged to the Draft Constitution that was under consideration and were legitimated on that basis. The letter, which ran over six pages, included an introduction, general instructions, and explanations on the nature of the franchise, the order for preparing the rolls, the types of electoral rolls, the form of the electoral roll, directives for the revisions of the rolls, as well as an appendix with the 'provisions as to the disqualification of electors', based on articles from the draft constitution. General instructions, the letter stated, 'have been drawn up partly on the basis of the replies received from the various governments and partly on existing procedures in certain parts of India'.[55]

The instructions set out that every citizen, as defined in article 5 of the draft constitution, of or above 21 years of age who is not disqualified by reason of unsoundness of mind or of non-residence is entitled to registration on the electoral roll. A voter should have a place of residence in the electoral unit for a period of no less than 180 days in the year ending on 31 March 1948.[56]

---

[53] Letter No. CA/64/RR/47, 15 March 1948, CA/1/FR/48-I, ECIR.

[54] Ibid.

[55] Ibid.

[56] The appendix to the letter provided a copy of the draft citizenship article, and a definition of the notion of a 'place of residence' as set in the draft article in broad terms. For that purpose 'a person shall be deemed to reside in a place if he sometimes uses it as a sleeping place, and a person shall not be deemed to cease to reside in a place merely because he is absent from it or has another dwelling in which he resides, if he is at liberty to return to the place at any time and has not abandoned his intention of returning'. Ibid. (Appendix I). The requirements relating to disqualifications and residence qualifications of voters were based on the provisions of Part II of the Fourth Schedule to the Draft Constitution (as contained in the Schedules printed on 18 October 1947). These were based on the existing provisions of the Government of India Act, 1935, on the CAS's assumption that 'presumably the same provisions would be prescribed by the Electoral Law when enacted under the new Constitution'. See internal note by the Joint

While the qualifications for being a voter were uniform and were based on the draft constitution, the instructions for the preparation of the roll on the ground provided scope for adjustments and flexibility. The instruction letter stated that 'there is no intention to standardise the procedure, but only to indicate the general lines on which the work should proceed. Local variations may be found to be necessary and appropriate modifications may accordingly be made by the Governments concerned.'[57] The language of the roll was left to the discretion of each province and state, as was the method of ascertaining the age of a voter.[58]

At the same time, the elaborated description of the process of enumeration made it very concrete and easy to imagine: 'the registration should be on a house-to-house basis, that is to say, an officer should be deputed to visit each house for the purpose of preparing the register. The registration work may proceed on the basis of the house numbers given in the 1941 census. New buildings in electoral unit may be given supplementary numbers.'[59]

The instructions contrasted the pursuit of universal franchise with the state of franchise until that time:

Under the new constitution there will be no separate electorate for the different communities; but seats will be reserved in certain constituencies.... It is, therefore, not necessary to prepare separate rolls for the different communities: *one composite roll for all communities will suffice*... It may be pointed out that there will be no special constituencies under the new constitution as there are at present, for women, labour, commerce and industry etc.[60]

An illustrative Form of the Electoral Roll was attached in an appendix. These instructions and the new registration form essentially inverted the logic that underlay the colonial form of representation and principles of devolution.

Secretary, S. N. Mukerjee (note: his name is also sometimes spelt Mukherjee), 11 March 1948, CA/1/FR/48-I, ECIR.

[57] Letter No. CA/64/RR/47, 15 March 1948, CA/1/FR/48-I, ECIR.

[58] During the final discussions on the draft instructions both the under secretary and the joint secretary agreed that 'a rough-and ready method will have to be adopted for determining the age by the registering authorities'. See Internal note by the Joint Secretary, S. N. Mukerjee, 11 March 1948, CA/1/FR/48-I, ECIR.

[59] Letter No. CA/64/RR/47, 15 March 1948, CA/1/FR/48-I, ECIR.

[60] Ibid. (emphasis added). At that time, the draft constitution included provisions of reservations (reserved seats in the legislature) for Muslims, Scheduled Castes, Scheduled Tribes (except the Scheduled Tribes in the autonomous districts of Assam), as well as for Indian Christians in Madras and Bombay. The letter clarified that because it would be necessary to determine whether a candidate for a reserved seat is a voter belonging to one of these communities, the electoral roll should contain a column for this purpose.

Since the work was to be done in anticipation of the new constitution, the letter of instruction explained that for the present, until the constitution and an election law come into force, it would suffice if draft rolls were prepared under executive instructions, which each province and state should issue. Finally, the CAS requested a fortnightly report from all governments, giving details of the progress made and difficulties encountered.

The manner in which the instructions were formulated, in a collaborative consultation, as an exercise in guided democratic political imagination that went down to the smallest technical details, contributed to imbuing the notion and practical implications of universal franchise within the bureaucracy, which had been at the foundation of the colonial edifice. The almost four months of correspondences and consultations about the actual making of the universal franchise between the Secretariat and administrators across the country triggered a democratisation of the bureaucratic imagination. This did not mean that a new democratic bureaucracy simply emerged in India.[61] But this process produced a fundamentally new set of bureaucratic attitudes in relation to the notion and practice of procedural equality for voting. Moreover, devising the instructions for the preparation of electoral rolls on the basis of universal franchise fostered the sense of an administrative capacity for India as a whole nation, as bureaucrats embarked on making possible and practicable for India what was until then considered impossible.

The 15 March 1948 letter of instructions for the preparation of electoral rolls in anticipation of the new constitution constituted a common bureaucratic ground for democratisation on an all-India scale.[62] A day after the letter was issued B. N. Rau wrote a summary note on 'preparation of electoral rolls under the new constitution', which in effect set the instruction letter as a new bureaucratic precedent. Rau wrote in the margins of the note that this 'may be useful, if questions are asked as to what action we have taken'.[63]

---

[61] Indeed, at the time that some sections of the bureaucracy were dealing with devising instructions and preparing for making the universal franchise, other components of the bureaucracy were engaged in implementing structures and institutions that challenged the democratic path. Among these were, for example, the permit system and the Influx from West Pakistan Control (from 19 July 1948), the Influx from Pakistan both from East and West Pakistan (10 November 1948) and the Evacuee Property negotiations (January 1949).

[62] Along the process of the registration of voters administrators around the country made recurrent reference to 'letter No. CA/64/RR/47, dated 15 March 1948', in correspondences and discussions of questions and problems that arose.

[63] Note by B. N. Rau, 16 March 1948, CA/1/FR/48-I, ECIR.

The 15 March 1948 letter, and Rau's 'useful' note, turned the decisive moment of preparing a plan for the registration of voters on the basis of adult franchise *'for India as a whole nation'* – a task that was in essence revolutionary – into a convention. Subsequent to the process of devising the instructions for the preparation of the electoral roll, the grand abstract notion of the universal franchise became a concrete practicable administrative assignment for bureaucrats. The notion of universal franchise fundamentally went against the grain of the colonial mind.[64] At a stroke, designing the electoral roll for the registration of the entire adult population precipitated the emergence of new democratic dispositions within the bureaucracy and a rupture with its colonial past.

The issuing of executive instructions for the preparation of electoral rolls by the governments of the provinces and the states put into operation the making of the universal franchise, which officials at the local level were tasked with. Over the following months the CAS's instructions were translated into the breadth of the country's local contexts, and became more detailed and tangible. Provincial governments' instructions often spread over half a dozen pages or more, and included appendixes that explained relevant draft constitutional articles and a sample Form of Electoral Roll. They included hypothetical case illustrations, for example, for determining domicile and citizenship of a voter. Most governments sent more than one set of instructions. The first was followed up by clarifications in response to queries from district officers or comments from the CAS. The instructions sent to local level administrators were both in English and the vernacular.

The local instructions often contained a general background statement about the assignment. The Government of the Central Provinces and Berar, for example, wrote to all Deputy Commissioners in the province that: 'The draft Constitution of India is expected to be introduced in the Constituent Assembly in October next... As the basis of electoral qualification under the future Constitution is likely to be adult suffrage, the work of preparation of the electoral rolls will be a colossal one. The Provincial Government, therefore, desire that the preparation of these rolls should be undertaken forthwith in the districts.'[65] The Reforms Commissioner of Assam wrote with a seriousness of purpose:

---

[64] This is suggestive of Ann Laura Stoler's discussion of the emergence of dispositions out of a habitus that is rejected. See Ann Laura Stoler, *Along the Archival Grain: Epistemic Anxieties and Colonial Common Sense*, Princeton, NJ: Princeton University Press, 2009, pp. 38–40.

[65] Government of the Central Provinces and Berar Legislative Department, Memorandum No. 413/XVIII, 'Preparation of electoral rolls for elections to the future Central and Provincial Legislatures', 13 July 1948 – From Deputy Secretary to Government, Central Provinces and Berar, Legislative Department to All Deputy Commissioners

Government are fully alive to the fact that the task is a colossal one, but, it is expected that it should be tackled with determination and that it will be ungrudgingly carried out expeditiously, so that this Province may keep pace with the others in the matter... this does not mean that the work should be rushed... The interest of the Province very largely depends upon the accuracy of the electoral roll, unit by unit, in the preparation of which everyone concerned is expected to give the best of his ability.[66]

One of the first tasks was house numbering, which was prescribed in the form of the electoral roll. Provincial governments adopted the instructions for house numbering suggested at the time by the Census Commissioner.[67] Provincial governments elaborated and explained that house numbering in a village should start from the North-East and end in the South-East.[68] The Reforms Commissioner of Assam suggested

Centrals Provinces and Berar (5 pages), CA/1/FR/48-II, ECIR. Also see Home Department, Constitution and Elections, Memorandum No. 643(2) A.R., 'Preparation of Draft Electoral Rolls for Elections to the Lower Houses of the Central and Provincial Legislatures', from Joint Secretary to the Government of West Bengal to the Commissioner Burdwan/Presidency Division, Calcutta, 22 May 1948, CA/1/FR/48-II, ECIR.

[66] Letter from R. R. Khaund, Reforms Commissioner, Assam to All Deputy Commissioners of Plain Districts, 'Preparation of Draft Electoral Rolls under the new Constitution for Central and Provincial Legislators' (No. L.801/47/83), 3 May 1948, CA/1/FR/48-II, ECIR. Initially, the government of Assam forwarded the CAS's 15 March letter of instructions to all District Officers asking of them to take immediate steps for the preparation of the draft electoral rolls, and noted that further executive orders will be issued as soon as possible. See letter from Secretary to the Government of Assam in the Legislative Department to All District Officers and Political Officers including Superintendent, Lushai Hills, 'Preparation of electoral rolls under the new Constitution for Central and Provincial legislators', 23 March 1948, CA/1/FR/48-II. A month later they appointed a Reforms Commissioner to take charge of the work. By that time, district officers sent a variety of inquiries and suggestions regarding the preparation of the rolls. The Reforms Commissioner of Assam's instructions addressed the questions they raised.

[67] On 3 April 1948, the Census Commissioner for India sent a memorandum (No. 1316-278-II), to the provincial governments, suggesting that the preparation of the electoral rolls should be conducted along with the house numbering as instructed for the preparatory work on the future census, and that the rolls should be based on the house numbers so prepared. Provincial governments approved that. See, for example, Government of the Central Provinces and Berar Legislative Department, Memorandum No. 413/XVIII, 'Preparation of electoral rolls for elections to the future Central and Provincial Legislatures', 13 July 1948 – From Deputy Secretary to Government, Central Provinces and Berar, Legislative Department to All Deputy Commissioners Centrals Provinces and Berar, CA/1/FR/48-II, ECIR; letter from R. R. Khaund, Reforms Commissioner, Assam to All Deputy Commissioners of Plain Districts, 'Preparation of Draft Electoral Rolls under the new Constitution for Central and Provincial Legislators' (No. L.801/47/83), 3 May 1948, CA/1/FR/48-II, ECIR.

[68] See, for example, letter from R. R. Khaund, Reforms Commissioner, Assam to All District Officers (including Superintendent of Lushai Hills) (No. L.801/47/110), 'Preparation of electoral rolls under the new Constitution for Central and Provincial legislators', 3 May 1948, CA/1/FR/48-II. For similar instructions see Home Department, Constitution and Elections, Memorandum No. 643(2) A.R., 'Preparation of Draft Electoral Rolls for

that: 'Each house-holder is to be made personally responsible for pres-
ervation of the number affixed on the house.'[69] The Government of
West Bengal instructed that 'Numbering should be done in a readily
identifiable form' and that this 'may be done by etching on wood on
the door-piece or on a substantial tree near the house, or by hanging a
number-plate made of wood or bamboo or by painting, or in any locally
devised form'.[70]

Provincial governments instructed that a senior official, like an assistant
to the Deputy Commissioner or a 'capable Deputy Collector' should take
charge of overseeing the preparation of the rolls and supervise closely the
staff engaged in the work.[71] Moreover, the enumerators should be 'local
men of probity who know their area and who are generally respected
there'.[72] The instructions specified the staff that should conduct registration of voters and the compilation of the rolls in the rural and urban areas.
For example, in the Central Provinces and Berar it was the revenue staff
in rural areas and the municipal staff in urban areas, and in East Punjab
patwaris and registration muharrirs. Some of the executive instructions
depicted the compilation of the roll itself: 'once the period of registration of names has expired, all the patwaris shall assemble at their tehsil
head quarters with the list of each village arranged alphabetically. At the
tashsil headquarters the rolls will be compiled zailwise. Within each zail

Elections to the Lower Houses of the Central and Provincial Legislatures', from Joint
Secretary to the Government of West Bengal to the Commissioner Burdwan/Presidency
Division, Calcutta, 22 May 1948, CA/1/FR/48-II, ECIR.

[69] Letter from R. R. Khaund, Reforms Commissioner, Assam to All District Officers
(including Superintendent of Lushai Hills and Political Officers Balipara Frontier Tract)
(No. L.801/47), 'Preparation of electoral rolls under the new Constitution for Central
and Provincial legislators', 28 May 1948, CA/1/FR/48-II.

[70] Government of West Bengal Home Department (Constitution and Elections), Memo.
No. 780(2) A.R., 'Preparation of Draft Electoral Rolls for Elections to the Lower Houses
of the Central and Provincial Legislatures', from Joint Secretary to the Government
of West Bengal to the Commissioner Burdwan/Presidency Division, Calcutta, 26 June
1948, CA/1/FR/48-II, ECIR.

[71] Home Department, Constitution and Elections, Memorandum No. 643(2) A.R.,
'Preparation of Draft Electoral Rolls for Elections to the Lower Houses of the Central
and Provincial Legislatures', from Joint Secretary to the Government of West Bengal to
the Commissioner Burdwan/Presidency Division, Calcutta, 22 May 1948, CA/1/FR/
48-II, ECIR; Government of the Central Provinces and Berar Legislative Department,
Memorandum No. 413/XVIII, 'Preparation of electoral rolls for elections to the
future Central and Provincial Legislatures', 13 July 1948 – from Deputy Secretary
to Government, Central Provinces and Berar, Legislative Department to All Deputy
Commissioners Centrals Provinces and Berar, CA/1/FR/48-II, ECIR.

[72] Government of West Bengal Home Department (Constitution and Elections), Memo.
No. 780(2) A.R., 'Preparation of Draft Electoral Rolls for Elections to the Lower Houses
of the Central and Provincial Legislatures', from Joint Secretary to the Government
of West Bengal to the Commissioner Burdwan/Presidency Division, Calcutta, 26 June
1948, CA/1/FR/48-II, ECIR.

the villages should be arranged alphabetically'.[73] In urban areas the registration officials were instructed to 'go through every street systematically and make inquiries from house to house'.[74] The Central Provinces and Berar government clarified that 'Where there are more than adult persons than one in a house the names of all such persons should come one after another and the entry pertaining to the succeeding house number should follow after all such names.'[75]

Governments' instructions also described in detail how, for example, the names of voters should be arranged; what should be the unit for the preparation of the rolls – mainly village in rural areas and by ward in urban areas; and where and how essential stationery materials should be purchased. The West Bengal Government, for example, wrote that they requested of 'the Deputy Controller, Stationery', paper 'at the rate of 5 sheets half-foolscap for every 10 voters'.[76] Officials were asked to spell names of voters accurately, make sure the lists were legible and written neatly, in ink and on one side of paper. Moreover, governments' instructions provided very detailed technical explanations for each item on the form of the electoral roll, and for how to work out the residential and citizenship qualifications for enrolment. They also set the language of the rolls, and gave directives for the compilations of fortnightly reports on the progress of the work.[77]

[73] 'Instructions for the Preparation of Draft Electoral Rolls, 1948–49' (16 pages), attached to letter from M. R. Bhide, Election Commissioner East Punjab to CAS, 12 August 1948, CA/1/FR/48-II, ECIR.

[74] Ibid.

[75] Government of the Central Provinces and Berar Legislative Department, Memorandum No. 413/XVIII, 'Preparation of electoral rolls for elections to the future Central and Provincial Legislatures', 13 July 1948 – from Deputy Secretary to Government, Central Provinces and Berar, Legislative Department to All Deputy Commissioners Centrals Provinces and Berar, CA/1/FR/48-II, ECIR.

[76] Government of West Bengal Home Department (Constitution and Elections), Memo. No. 780(2) A.R., 'Preparation of Draft Electoral Rolls for Elections to the Lower Houses of the Central and Provincial Legislatures', from Joint Secretary to the Government of West Bengal to the Commissioner Burdwan/Presidency Division, Calcutta, 26 June 1948, CA/1/FR/48-II, ECIR.

[77] In Assam, for example, Assamese was prescribed for the Assam Valley Districts and Assamese in addition to Bengali in the Cachar District. See letter from R. R. Khaund, Reforms Commissioner, Assam to All Deputy Commissioners of Plain Districts, 'Preparation of Draft Electoral Rolls under the new Constitution for Central and Provincial Legislators' (No. L.801/47/83), 3 May 1948, CA/1/FR/48-II, ECIR. The West Bengal government instructed to prepare the rolls in Bengali, except for Calcutta and Darjeeling, where they were to be prepared in English. See Home Department, Constitution and Elections, Memorandum No. 643(2) A.R., 'Preparation of Draft Electoral Rolls for Elections to the Lower Houses of the Central and Provincial Legislatures', from Joint Secretary to the Government of West Bengal to the Commissioner Burdwan/Presidency Division, Calcutta, 22 May 1948, CA/1/FR/48-II, ECIR. In East Punjab, 'Three lac form of applications have been printed in Urdu, Hindi

The method of ascertaining the age of a voter was left to the discretion of each province and state. This was one of the expected challenges that arose in the process of the devising of the instructions. Governments suggested, for example, that a 'school certificate or a municipal certificate of birth or horoscope should be taken to be sufficient proof',[78] or checking birth registers at police stations and kotwar's books.[79] In Assam, one district officer suggested to 'intelligently frame' a questionnaire on historically important local and national events for each area, such as 'the floods of 1927, the freedom movement of 1930', and to ascertain the age qualification of voters by their ability to recall such events. The Reforms Commissioner of Assam's view, however, was that this method could not be applied in all cases, though it may be 'adopted to suit local conditions'. He suggested 'to leave this point for the district officers to decide for themselves as to the best method to be adopted to meet the need of each area'.[80] He anticipated, in particular, a difficulty in verifying the age of female voters. In case of doubt, and for the registration of 'purdahnashin' women he prescribed, on the basis of Rule 15 of Part I of the Assam Legislative Assembly Electoral Rules, 1936, a form for age certificate.[81]

Provincial governments noted the importance of the cooperation of the public for the success of the work. They asked that registering officials inform people in the village or ward about their planned visit to register names in that area a few days beforehand, and to come at a time people are likely to be home. Thus, muharrirs in East Punjab were instructed 'to make their house-to-house visits before 10 a.m. and from 4 p.m. to

and Gurmukhi.' Letter from M. R. Bhide, Election Commissioner East Punjab to CAS, 'Preparation of Draft Electoral Rolls under the New Constitution, 21 June 1948, CA/1/FR/48-II, ECIR.

[78] 'Instructions for the Preparation of Draft Electoral Rolls, 1948–49', attached to letter from M. R. Bhide, Election Commissioner East Punjab to CAS, 12 August 1948, CA/1/FR/48-II, ECIR.

[79] Government of the Central Provinces and Berar Legislative Department, Memorandum No. 413/XVIII, 'Preparation of electoral rolls for elections to the future Central and Provincial Legislatures', 13 July 1948 – from Deputy Secretary to Government, Central Provinces and Berar, Legislative Department to All Deputy Commissioners Centrals Provinces and Berar, CA/1/FR/48-II, ECIR. The government instructed that supervising officers should do percentage checking from birth registers at police stations and kotwar's books to find out if in each village or ward all persons eligible for registration have been rightly entered in the roll.

[80] Letter from R. R. Khaund, Reforms Commissioner, Assam to All Deputy Commissioners of Plain Districts, 'Preparation of Draft Electoral Rolls under the new Constitution for Central and Provincial Legislators' (No. L.801/47/83), 3 May 1948, CA/1/FR/48-II, ECIR.

[81] Purdahnashin means: women who observed rigid rules of seclusion. The certificate was to be signed by a government officer, or by a Mauzadar, or by the Sarpanch. See ibid.

7 p.m. During the day between 12 noon and 4 p.m. muharrirs and super-visors should be required to meet ... in order to exchange notes to avoid multiple entries of one name'.[82] An illustration was provided for that pro-cedure: 'Roshan lives in the Civil Station of Amritsar and also has a place of residence in Karmon Deorhi, which he may be using occasionally as his residence.' His name is thus likely to be entered in both places. 'When these muharrirs meet as suggested above and compare entries, they are bound to discover this.'[83] The Government of West Bengal suggested that enumerators may 'convene village or ward gathering, where the work can be explained and discussed, and data gathered for insertion in the Rolls', and that this may be completed by visiting individual houses.[84]

Local governments instructed to ensure wide and local publicity to the work of the preparation of electoral rolls. They asked officials to do so through press communiqués in the vernacular, or by other means.[85] For example, the East Punjab Government sent a copy of a press notice that announced the preparation of electoral rolls to the Director General of Public Relations 'for its adaptation for other means of publicity, such as Cinematograph slides, Radio, etc.'.[86] It was only with respect to the need to publicise the work that sometimes the plain administrative prose of the instructions was cut through by the sense of the gravity of the operations. 'For the first time', the Government of West Bengal stated, 'and under conditions of full self-government adult franchise is being worked out in the country. It is essential that everyone should come to know of this valuable political right which each adult wields.'[87]

---

[82] 'Instructions for the Preparation of Draft Electoral Rolls, 1948–49', attached to letter from M. R. Bhide, Election Commissioner East Punjab to CAS, 12 August 1948, CA/1/FR/48-II, ECIR.

[83] Ibid.

[84] Government of West Bengal Home Department (Constitution and Elections), Memo. No. 780(2) A.R., 'Preparation of Draft Electoral Rolls for Elections to the Lower Houses of the Central and Provincial Legislatures', from Joint Secretary to the Government of West Bengal to the Commissioner Burdwan/Presidency Division, Calcutta, 26 June 1948, CA/1/FR/48-II, ECIR.

[85] See, for example, Government of the Central Provinces and Berar Legislative Department, Memorandum No. 413/XVIII, 'Preparation of electoral rolls for elections to the future Central and Provincial Legislatures', 13 July 1948 – from Deputy Secretary to Government, Central Provinces and Berar, Legislative Department to All Deputy Commissioners Centrals Provinces and Berar, CA/1/FR/48-II, ECIR; letter from R. R. Khaund, Reforms Commissioner, Assam to All Deputy Commissioners of Plain Districts, 'Preparation of Draft Electoral Rolls under the new Constitution for Central and Provincial Legislators' (No. L.801/47/83), 3 May 1948, CA/1/FR/48-II, ECIR.

[86] Letter from M. R. Bhide, Election Commissioner East Punjab to CAS, 'Preparation of Draft Electoral Rolls under the New Constitution, 21 June 1948, CA/1/FR/48-II, ECIR.

[87] Home Department, Constitution and Elections, Memorandum No. 643(2) A.R., 'Preparation of Draft Electoral Rolls for Elections to the Lower Houses of the Central and Provincial Legislatures', from Joint Secretary to the Government of West Bengal to

Local instructions sometimes deviated from the CAS's guidelines, or were phrased in ways that were open to interpretation and potential breaches in the registration of all adults. Some governments made changes to the form that the CAS devised. For example, the Government of East Punjab added a column for occupation and omitted the column for house number and address. Some governments dwelled on colonial rules, for example, the age certificate form for women whose age was in doubt. Indeed, not every bureaucrat that was obstructionist in the 1930s suddenly turned into a non-obstructionist in 1947–1949. Once the registration started, distinct forms of exclusionary practices emerged among administrators on the ground. But, as the following chapters will show, the CAS and various citizen and social organisations took measures against such attempts on the basis of new parameters of governance, based on procedural equality, set by the universal franchise. The CAS unwearyingly oversaw local governments' instruction and their work on the ground, and redressed the breaches that came to its attention.[88]

Once the actual registration of voters started in anticipation of the constitution, the making of democracy on the ground sometimes outpaced the deliberative process of constitution making. The motion on the preparation of the electoral roll on the basis of universal franchise came up for discussion before the Constituent Assembly for the first time only in January 1949, when much of the preliminary work was already well under way.[89]

The democratic shift that took place in the bureaucratic bent and imagination could be illustrated, by looking briefly at the different attitudes and practices that were devised by colonial administrators while addressing the challenge of enrolling women and other groups at the margins of society during the expansion of the franchise in the 1930s. In particular, the next section looks at problems associated with the enlistment of women, which arose both in 1935 and in 1948–1949, but that were dealt with completely differently.

the Commissioner Burdwan/Presidency Division, Calcutta, 22 May 1948, CA/1/FR/48-II, ECIR.

[88] On 31 July 1948 the CAS asked of the provincial governments for copies of Provincial instructions in English. See letter from M. R. Bhide, Election Commissioner East Punjab to CAS, 12 August 1948, CA/1/FR/48-II, ECIR.

[89] The aim of the motion was 'that instructions be issued forth with to the authorities concerned for the preparation of electoral rolls'. See 'Motion Re Preparation of Electoral Rolls', *Constituent Assembly Debates* (hereafter *CAD*), 8 January 1949, (available on http://parliamentofindia.nic.in/ls/debates/debates.htm, accessed 28 June 2017). Members of the Assembly were informed during the discussion that the CAS under the direction of the President had 'already taken certain steps for the purpose'. Ibid.

Rewriting the Bureaucratic Colonial Imagination

In discussions on the expansion of the franchise in the early 1930s, provincial franchise committees regarded universal adult suffrage 'to be impracticable at present', in particular 'for administrative reasons'.[90] Colonial administrators' lack of imagination, or rather pursuit of bureaucratic expediency, went so far as to suggest that 'the size of the electorate should be determined by the number of polling officers available'.[91] There was an admission that

the difficulties relate, in our opinion, not to the incapacity of the voter to exercise his new power, nor to the inability of the candidate to handle a large electorate; but mainly to the administrative difficulty of enabling a large mass of the population to record its vote in a fair and satisfactory manner... But by far the most disturbing factor which makes the problem bristle with difficulties at the present moment is due to the colossal illiteracy of the people.[92]

When colonial administrators were asked ahead of the enactment of the Government of India Act, 1935 to make the leap in the expansion of franchise for elections to the Provincial legislatures from an electorate of approximately seven million to just under 32 million, they still expressed scepticism in some of the provinces, and found the work envisioned by that expansion of the franchise impossible or impracticable. But unlike the idea of universal suffrage, this modest expansion was thought to be 'generally administratively feasible'.[93]

---

[90] Reports of the United Provinces Government and Provincial Committee, 1932, IOR/Q/IFC/61, IOC. Also see Joint Secretaries' Notes, 1932, IOR/Q/IFC/88, IOC, 'Summary of Indian Franchise Report' (Presented to Parliament, 2 June 1932), L/I/1/607, IOC, and Reginald Coupland, *The Indian Problem 1833–1935: Report on the Constitutional Problem in India*. Part 1. London: Oxford University Press (Third Imprint), 1943, p. 129.

[91] Reports of the United Provinces Government and Provincial Committee, 1932, IOR/Q/IFC/61, IOC.

[92] Quoted from the Franchise Sub-Committee of the Round Table Conference in a letter to Lothian, 29 December 1931 in Joint Secretaries' Notes, 1932, IOR/Q/IFC/88, IOC. The Franchise (Lothian) Committee adopted this view. It rejected adult franchise as 'being immediately impracticable' on the grounds of, first, 'shortage of suitable electoral personnel, of police, of women officials necessary for dealing with the Purdah system and so on'. Second, the conditions of illiteracy 'coupled with the rudimentary stage which the organisation of political parties has reached make it undesirable at present'. See 'Summary of Indian Franchise Report' (presented to Parliament, 2 June 1932), L/I/1/607, IOC. For an excellent discussion on the way administrative and financial needs shaped devolution see Eleanor Newbigin, *The Hindu Family and the Emergence of Modern India. Law Citizenship and Community*. Cambridge: Cambridge University Press, 2013, pp. 110–27.

[93] Note by John Kerr, 16 October 1933, IOR/L/PJ/9/175, IOC. The expansion of the franchise was suggested on the basis of the recommendations of the white paper (and the Lothian Franchise Committee). Originally the expansion of franchise was planed to be ca. 36 million.

More fundamentally, the concept of an electoral roll that would bind all adults together as equal individuals was anathema to colonial administrators. They designed voter lists and registration forms that divided the electorate into at least three types of constituencies: general, European and Mohammadan. It contained qualifications such as 'Husband pays income tax, literacy'; and it included a 'Special provision regarding names of women'.[94] Indeed, the intention at the time to expand the franchise for women turned out to be a particularly difficult assignment for colonial bureaucrats.

The Government of India Bill, 1935 based on the White Paper and the Indian Franchise Committee envisioned, as part of the expansion of the franchise a growth of the female electorate. The Joint Parliamentary Select Committee was anxious that there should be a substantial increase in the number of women enfranchised.[95] But some provincial governments and administrators were at odds with that task. Early in the discussions of the 1935 constitution, the Government of Bihar and Orissa, for example, attempted to reduce the size of the electorate, and to disenfranchise women. The government had qualifications dependent on taxation for the right of franchise. They argued for an increase in the 'anna franchise' (from 9 to 12 anna), and even demanded a rupee franchise.[96] The Bihar and Orissa government threatened that otherwise there would be no guarantee that 'elections will be carried out with success and without grave disorder'.[97]

Already in 1933 Sir John Kerr, the Deputy Chairman of the Indian Franchise Committee, observed that some provinces, in particular

---

[94] See, for example, Assam, Reforms Officer, Assam Legislative Council electoral (preparation, revision and publication of electoral rolls) rules, 23 May 1936, IOR/V/27/111/10, IOC.

[95] See letter from Reforms Officer United Provinces to All District Officers United Province, 8 April 1935, IOR/L/PJ/9/153, IOC. Women in Britain obtained the franchise in 1928. For scholarship on women and political enfranchisement under colonialism see Jana Everett, *Women and Social Change in India*, New Delhi: Heritage, 1981, pp. 101–40, ' "All the Women Were Hindus and All the Muslims Were Men": State, Identity Politics and Gender', *Economic and Political Weekly* 36 no. 23, 2001, pp. 2071–80; Geraldine Forbes, *Women in Modern India*, Cambridge: Cambridge University Press, 1996; Mrinalini Sinha, 'Suffragism and Internationalism: The Enfranchisement of British and India Women under an Imperial State', *Indian Economic and Social History Review* 36, no. 4, 1999, pp. 461–84; Sinha, *Specters of Mother India: The Global Restructuring of an Empire*, Durham: Duke University Press, 2006; Wendy Singer, *A Constituency Suitable for Ladies and Other Social Histories of Indian Elections*. New Delhi: Oxford University Press, 2007, pp. 30–52.

[96] This was in reference to qualifications dependent on taxation for the right of franchise. Increasing the tax sum of the franchise requirement would thus reduce the number of voters.

[97] Note by John Kerr, 16 October 1933, IOR/L/PJ/9/175, IOC.

Punjab, Assam, Bihar and Orissa, were 'really after a reduction of the number of women votes'.[98] He explained that the landed oligarchy in the Legislative Council, who strengthened its power since the reforms of 1920, 'are now doing all they can to keep the franchise qualification for the tenant class as high as possible, and they are supported by the official element in the Government'.[99] The government of Assam wrote that 'they have already gone farther in extension of franchise [for women] than they really think is safe'.[100]

Moreover, various Reforms Officers in the provinces demanded to prescribe by local rules how 'their' women should be treated. The government of Bihar and Orissa, for example, was of the view that 'a woman's name should be removed from the electoral roll if she is divorced, or if her husband dies or loses his property'.[101] Indeed, a key criterion for franchise was property ownership. But when colonial administrators encountered a community where women generally held property they saw this as a pretext for an exception. Thus, at a conference of Reforms Officers in March 1935 in Delhi it was noted that 'A difficulty arises in the Khasi Hills where the Matriarchal system prevails, property being in the name of women, who will therefore have to appear on the roll. But since they do not ordinarily exercise any public function they will require to nominate some person to exercise the vote.'[102]

Another issue was the question of application for enrolment in relation to women.[103] After prolonged correspondences on the matter the Secretary of State ultimately agreed that in effect the provinces would make their own rules over women's registration.[104] Thus, the governments

---

[98] Ibid.

[99] Ibid.

[100] Letter from the Chief Secretary to the Government of Assam to the Secretary of State for India, 23 May 1935, in 'Public and Judicial Constitutional Series P& J(C) 3838 Franchise proposals for women in the White Paper: views of local governments', October 1933–June 1935, IOR/L/PJ/9/141, IOC. On similar attitudes towards the question of women's franchise in the run-up to the constitutional reforms of 1919 see Forbes, *Women in Modern India*, pp. 93–100. The 1919 Act allowed for the provincial legislatures to decide over the question of women's suffrage. See Everett, '"All the Women Were Hindus and All the Muslims Were Men"', p. 2072.

[101] 'Public and Judicial Constitutional Series P& J(C) 4763/Part IV Franchise Schedules', letter from Secretary to Government of Bihar and Orissa Reform Department to the Secretary to the Government of India Reform Department, 7 April 1935, IOR/L/PJ/9/175, IOC.

[102] 'Proceedings of the Conference of Reforms Officers held in New Delhi on 5 to 7 March 1935', IOR/M/1/19, IOC.

[103] According to the 'provisions as to franchise' in the 1935 Act, under certain qualifications for being a voter a person could be enrolled only by applications even if she/he fulfilled the qualifying criteria. Women were to be registered only on an application.

[104] 'Public and Judicial Constitutional Series P& J(C) 4763/Part IV Franchise Schedules', letter of 29 April 1935, IOR/L/PJ/9/175, IOC.

of Bengal, and Bihar and Orissa did not prescribe application requirement for women. In the United Provinces and Central Provinces applications by women were required 'in respect only of the qualification
arising from (a) literacy (b) being the pensioned widow or mother of
a soldier; or (c) being the wife of an ex-soldier or policeman'.[105] The
Madras, Bombay and Assam governments required applications from
women for all purposes. Governments of the provinces recognised that
the application requirement would have the effect of reducing the number of women enfranchised.[106]

The actual enrolment of women became a particularly contested matter. Officials in some provinces suggested that 'the recording of wom-
en's names present peculiar difficulties,' and 'is in any case a matter of
difficulty and delicacy and every care must be taken to avoid causing
offence'.[107] The problem was that women refused to be registered under
their own names. It was ultimately agreed that 'if a difficulty is experienced in finding out the names to be entered, there is no objection to
entering a women as the wife of "A B C"',[108] rather than being a free
enfranchised individual. An illustrative form for such a case was attached
to the letters for the District Officers.[109] Eventually, electoral rules for the
preparation of electoral rolls in the provinces included particular provisions regarding the registration of women, such as: 'Where for social or
religious reasons there is an objection to the entry of the actual name
of a woman in any electoral roll such women may be entered in the roll
as "the wife of A. B. (husband's name)" or, if she is unmarried, as "the
daughter of A. B. (father's name)".'[110]

---

[105] 'Public and Judicial Constitutional Series P& J(C) 3838 Franchise proposals for women
in the White Paper: views of local governments, October 1933–June 1935', letter from
the Chief Secretary to the Government of the United Provinces to the Secretary of
State for India, 23 May 1935, IOR/L/PJ/9/141, IOC.

[106] Thus, the Chief Secretary to the Government of the United Provinces admitted that
'in this province objection to abandonment of the application requirement due in [the]
main to administrative and financial difficulties'. Ibid.

[107] Letter from the Reforms Officer of the United Provinces to all District Officers in the
Province, 8 April 1935, IOR/L/PJ/9/153, IOC.

[108] Ibid.

[109] Ibid. Also see, for example, reference to the registration of female as a 'Wife of A.B.C.'
in Telegram from Secretary of State to Government of India, Reforms Department, 14
March 1934, (P.&J. (C) 4213/34, IOR L/PJ/9/175, IOC.

[110] 'Assam Legislative Council Electoral (Preparation, Revision and Publication of Electoral
Rolls) Rules, 23 May 1936', IOR/V/27/111/10, IOC. As another example: 'Preparation
of Electoral Rolls' (circular letter from Reform Officer United Province to all District
Officer), 8 April 1935, IOR/L/PJ/9/153, IOC. Female voters were also registered as
a 'widow of'. See 'Bombay Political and Reforms Department, Bombay Legislative
Assembly electoral (preparation, revision and publication of electoral rolls) rules 1936',
IOR/V/27/111/22, IOC.

Having to address the issue of women's franchise the colonial Government of India insisted that the matter of increasing the number of women on the register was 'intimately connected with the administrative feasibility of registering and polling larger numbers'.[111] But it really chose to shirk responsibility for that problem. The Government of India wrote to the Secretary of State for India: 'At the same time of second election this matter will concern responsible Provincial Governments not under your control. It would seem to be inappropriate now to determine finally what their administrative capacity will be, without giving them an opportunity of expressing their opinion.'[112]

From September 1947 to March 1948, during the process of devising instructions for the preparation of the electoral roll on the basis of adult franchise, not a single difficulty, administrative or otherwise, was envisioned in relation to the enrolment of women.[113] In fact, no doubts were expressed about the practicability of adult franchise at that time. However, a few months after the work on the preparation of the draft electoral roll began in 1948, several District Officers, for example, in the United Provinces, reported that 'difficulty is being experienced in ascertaining the names of lady voters who were unwilling to give out their names', and that 'they wish to be recorded as "wife of", "daughter of", "widow of", etc. of a male member of their family'.[114] Some District Officers did so. At this time, the United Provinces Government issued a letter to all District Officers to let them know that the difficulty with women electors was experienced in other districts. Contrary to earlier colonial practices, the Government made it clear that the practice of registering female voters as 'wife of' was not permissible, and

---

[111] Telegram from Government of India Reforms Department to Secretary State for India, 22 May 1935, IOR/L/PJ/9/141, IOC.

[112] Ibid.

[113] In fact, later on when provincial governments began issuing their executive instructions, the East Punjab government instructed explicitly that 'The actual name of a woman must be entered in the roll.' See 'Instructions for the Preparation of Draft Electoral Rolls, 1948–49' (16 pages), attached to letter from M. R. Bhide, Election Commissioner East Punjab to CAS, 12 August 1948, CA/1/FR/48-II, ECIR. The Government of the United Provinces instructed that 'No separate forms of electoral rolls for female voters are necessary.' See letter no. 1935/XVII-173/48 from M. K. Kidwai, Additional Deputy Secretary to the Government of the United Provinces to All District Officers, United Provinces, 11 August 1948, CA/1/FR/48-II, ECIR. Only the Reforms Commissioner of Assam anticipated difficulty in verifying the age of female voters. See n. 81 above.

[114] Fortnightly reports of progress of work in the preparation of electoral rolls from Government of the United Provinces, 1 October 1948, CA/1/FR/48-III, ECIR; Fortnightly report of progress of work in the preparation of electoral rolls for the fortnights ending 15 October 1948 and 30 October 1948, from the Additional Deputy Secretary to Government of the United Provinces, M. K. Kidwai, to CAS, 10 December 1948, CA/1/FR/48-IV, ECIR.

that they were to be registered as individual voters. It directed them to start propaganda work to encourage women to register by their names, suggesting that in addition to giving wide publicity through the press, 'platforms or beat of drums... you may enlist women workers for the purpose'.[115]

The Government also issued a press communiqué declaring that after a very careful consideration it decided that names of female voters must be given in the Draft Electoral Rolls. The press note encouraged the public to cooperate in giving names of women voters so as to avoid disenfranchisement. Addressing the people, the government explained:

The introduction of adult franchise is intended to confer on every adult, male or female, a right to participate in the establishment of a fully democratic system of Government in the country and the provincial Government is therefore anxious that the electoral Rolls are correctly prepared and no adult, male or female, is as far as possible left unrecorded in the Electoral Rolls.[116]

In contrast, in the 1930s colonial administrators made calculated efforts to reduce the size of the electorate. Thus, in August 1935, the Joint Secretary to the Government of India, Reforms Office, wrote with concern to the Bihar and Orissa government that it came to his notice that 'the number of persons entered on the rolls falls very considerably short of the numbers contemplated by the Indian Franchise Committee'.[117] The Bihar and Orissa government replied that, indeed, 'the total number of actual electors shows a net decrease of 1,118,511; *but then of course such a decrease was intentional, and the franchise was raised with the express purpose of producing a smaller electorate than the unmanageable one proposed*

[115] Letter from the Additional Deputy Secretary United Provinces Government to the District Officer of Agra, 19 November 1948, CA/1/FR/48-IV, ECIR. The letter stated, 'Copy forwarded to all District Officers in the Province'.
[116] Press Communiqué, Government of the United Provinces, 19 November 1948, CA/1/FR/48-IV, ECIR. It is noteworthy that despite these efforts a large number of women did not re-register as individuals, using their own name, and their initial enrolment as 'Wife of,' etc., remained on the final rolls. The Chief Election Commissioner of India at the time, Sukumar Sen, estimated that 'out of a total of nearly 80 million women voters in the country, nearly 2.8 million eventually failed to disclose their name, and the entries relating to them had to be deleted from the rolls'. Election Commission of India, *Report on the First General Election in India*, p. 73. The issue came before Sen before the elections, and he confirmed the decision taken on that matter by the CAS three years earlier that such registration was not permissible. 'Referring to the problem of those ladies whose names could not be enrolled properly in the voters list', on the eve of the first elections, 'Shri Sen assured that their names would be enrolled during the next elections of the country.' Directorate of Public Relations, Government of Rajasthan, press release following a press conference with Sukumar Sen at Bharatpur, 9 October 1951, 5/7/51-Elec, ECIR.
[117] Letter from the Joint Secretary to Government of India Reforms Office to Government of Bihar and Orissa Reform Department, 30 August 1935, IOR/L/PJ/9/175, IOC.

by the Lothian Committee.[118] The Committee recommended the enfranchisement of 350,000 women. At first, the Bihar and Orissa Government
estimated enrolment of only 54,976, and ultimately 232,140 women.
The government explained that the lower numbers of enrolled women
was 'simply due to the fact that women do not wish to have their names
enrolled... In many cases the husbands refuse to have them enrolled even
as "wife of".'[119] In other provinces, too, the electorate was ultimately
lower than anticipated.[120]

Moreover, colonial administrators avoided publicising their efforts,
which certainly did not contribute to the successful expansion of the
franchise. Several secret memorandums instructed Reforms and District
Officers that until the bill was approved in Parliament and received Royal
Assent, action had to be taken 'as a matter of administrative routine and
with the minimum of publicity for the preparation of a *provisional* roll'.[121]
The Government of India was explicitly asked 'to avoid any communiqué if possible and to deal with matters entirely informally'.[122]

In stark contrast, from 1948 onwards, publicity of the preparatory work
of the electoral roll became a prominent principle and a common practice. Paradoxically, the CAS did so by drawing on the same bureaucratic
colonial precedent, but with an inverted mind-set. The Joint Secretary
of the Constituent Assembly wrote at the outset of the operation that
'electoral rolls cannot be compiled without statutory authority. All that
we can do now is *to compile them in anticipation of such statutory authority*,
so that the draft rolls may be ready by the time the new Constitution and
electoral law thereunder are passed.'[123]

---

[118] Letter from the Government of Bihar and Orissa Reform Department to the Joint
Secretary to Government of India Reforms Office, 4 September 1935, IOR/L/PJ/9/175,
IOC (emphasis added).

[119] Ibid.

[120] In the United Province the total electorate reached 4,842,617, which came to just 11%
of the population. The Indian Franchise Committee envisioned an electorate of 13.5%,
6.5 million, out of which 1.5 million women. Only 520,000 women were ultimately
enrolled. See Election reports: United Provinces and North-West Frontier Province,
5 August 1937–29 September 1937, IOR/L/PJ/7/1319, IOC. In the 1952 first general
elections in independent India the size of the electorate in Uttar Pradesh (formerly the
United Provinces) was 31,770,309. See Election Commission of India, *Key Highlights
of General Elections, 1951 to the First Lok Sabha*, Election Commission of India, New
Delhi, p. 4.

[121] Letter of 18 April 1935, IOR/L/PJ/9/153, IOC (emphasis in the original). Also see
'Memorandum on delimitation and connected questions from India Office, 10 August
1934', IOR/L/PJ/9/175, IOC.

[122] Telegram from the Secretary of State to the Government of India, 24 May 1935, IOR/
M/1/19, IOC. The 1935 Act received a Royal Assent on 4 August 1935. It came to force
from 1 April 1937.

[123] Internal note by the Joint Secretary of CAS, S. N. Mukerjee, 11 March 1948, CA/
1/FR/48-I, ECIR (emphasis added). As for the instructions, 'presumably', the Joint

The notion of conferring the right to vote and bringing women genuinely onto the electoral roll was beyond the purview of the bureaucratic colonial imagination. It was, also, consistent with the colonial government's lack of faith in India's illiterate masses and their negative attitudes towards enfranchisement of people at the margins of the then franchise, such as the poor and rural, illiterate people. Thus, when it came to considering electoral matters and franchise in 'Backward Areas and Tribes', some provincial governments, like Orissa, suggested that the seats be filled by nomination rather than election 'because [of] the danger of introducing the election ferment among the excitable population of the Khondmals'.[124] The Reform Commissioner to the Government of India remarked that 'nomination should be resorted to only in the absence of any alternative. In the case of Khondmals, however, no alternative seemed to exist.'[125]

As another example, some provinces used coloured ballot boxes to enable rural illiterate people to vote. Each representative would be identified with a different colour. But in 1936 the United Province Government decided not to implement this. Instead, it devised a rule whereby local administrators, the presiding officer, or what they called, a 'literate friend', marked the ballot papers on behalf of illiterate voters. In response to an inquiry from the House of Commons in the matter, the United Province Government wrote that 'many illiterate persons have little sense of colour, with the result that many voters might find themselves bewildered in polling booths and might record their vote for a candidate they do not wish to support'.[126] It is noteworthy that during oral evidence before the Indian Delimitation Committee in 1935 some members of the Scheduled Castes stated that they 'preferred the coloured box system to a system of marked voting paper, since under the other method everybody would know that the scheduled caste voter had voted'.[127]

Secretary commented, 'the same provisions would be prescribed by the electoral law when enacted under the new constitution.' Ibid. In a note on the subject B. N. Rau wrote: 'We are proceeding on the assumption that the age qualification ... and the qualifications for enrolment ... will not be materially different from the existing provisions... For the time being, only draft rolls will be prepared under executive instruction.' See Note by B. N. Rau, 16 March 1948, ibid.

[124] Proceedings of the Conference of Reforms Officers held in New Delhi on 5 to 7 March 1935, IOR/M/1/19, IOC.

[125] Ibid.

[126] Telegram, 13 December 1936, IOR/L/PJ/9/257, IOC. The United Provinces Government explained that their practice of marking the paper on behalf of the voter was adopted on recommendation of the Hammond Committee (The Indian Delimitation Committee, 1936), paragraph 740.

[127] Oral evidence given before the Indian Delimitation Committee (evidence by Rev. B Das (Scheduled Castes)), Ranchi, 19 October 1935, Nehru Memorial and Museum Library (NMML), New Delhi.

As the following chapters will show, it was in relation to the task of enfranchising those at the margins of society – the subalterns – that the implications of the preparation for the first draft electoral roll on the basis of universal franchise for cultivating democratic dispositions among administrators, and for the rewriting of the bureaucratic colonial imagination was most strikingly demonstrated.

Conclusion

As a first step in devising the instructions for the preparation of the electoral rolls on the basis of full adult franchise the CAS consciously sought to break with colonial practices of enumeration. The correspondences and consultations about an action plan for preparing an electoral roll brought administrators around the country on board in the making of the universal franchise, and created a stake for them in the process. The universality of the franchise was not subject to question. It was posited as a premise. In the all-India exercise in guided democratic imagination administrators were not asked to submit their opinion on the merits or practicality of the idea of the rule of the people. They were asked to establish the institutional infrastructure in support of the notion that sovereignty resides with the people. That collaborative exercise in pursuit of creating a register of people that were bound together as equal citizens for the purpose of authorising their government also rendered existent the idea of 'the people'.

The bureaucrats who were asked to plan for and manage that new all-India project took part in setting a foundational bureaucratic precedent. It was new in a real sense: neither British bureaucrats, nor any other administration before them, had prepared for the enrolment of such a large electorate. The process of devising the instructions for the electoral roll produced a new form of population knowledge: the enumeration of all adults who have the right to vote. They were the sovereigns of the new state. Metaphorically, this list would represent the recipients of the 'transfer of power'.

In essence, the instructions provided a template for shaping democratic relations between the new Indian state, its bureaucrats at different levels, and the people. The plan to register voters on the basis of a house-to-house, village-by-village coverage would offer the opportunity for mid to lower level officials and ordinary people to engage with each other and with democratic institution building. This procedure for implementing the universal franchise created occasions for people to 'meet', 'see' and 'speak' with the state through the official representatives who showed up at their door to ensure their right to vote. And the plan for enrolment broke with prior colonial practices of counting, like the census. Roll making was not meant to simply *count* people for a 'useful inventory'. The people were also *taken into account* as the sovereigns of the new state.

In the process of devising the procedures for the preparation of the electoral roll, in anticipation of the constitution, the notion of procedural equality was bureaucratised. This experience gradually turned the notion of adult franchise for India's masses into a convention.

Initially, the design for India's democracy was still only on paper. It was not inevitable that the paper plan, as imaginative and bold as it was, would match the aspiration of making universal franchise in practice in the midst of the partition, at a moment when the basic question of 'who is an Indian' – the basic criterion for being a voter – was undecided and contested. The next chapter explores that first challenge to the making of the universal franchise.

2　The Pursuit of Citizenship in the Making of the Electoral Roll
Registering Partition Refugees

We should have *vision* first and *revision* afterwards.[1]
(A.C. Datta, President of the East Bengal Minority
Welfare Central Committee)

[W]e have to realise that democracy is not a mere political arrangement but a habit of mind. It is easy to acquire the forms of democracy but not so easy to get its spirit, that sensitive adjustment of the self to the infinitely varies demands of other persons.[2]

(S. Radhakrishnan)

With the division of India into Hindustan and Pakistan, the question of citizenship has been agitating the minds of several people. So far we were citizens of one country, viz., India; and our loyalty was to that country. Now a question is being put by those living in the seceding areas as to what will become of their citizenship... Several of them wish to continue their Indian citizenship. In case such an option is given and a person decides to continue his Indian citizenship, will it be necessary for him to leave Pakistan? Can he not continue to stay there as an alien?[3]

(Note by Ghanashyam J. Shivdasani, 30 June 1947)

The preparation of the draft electoral roll on the basis of universal franchise two years before the enactment of the constitution was entangled with the question of citizenship because being a citizen of India was a basic qualifying criterion for being an eligible voter. The preparation of

[1] Letter from the East Bengal Minority Welfare Central Committee, Calcutta, to Rajendra Prasad, 3 August 1948, CA/9/FR/48, ECIR (emphases in the original).

[2] S. Radhakrishnan, 'Democracy: A Habit of the Mind' (Presidential Address at the Annual Session of Andhra Mahasabha, Madras, September 1938), in *Education, Politics and War*, Poona: The International Book Service, 1944, p. 16.

[3] Note by Ghanashyam J. Shivdasani, 30 June 1947, in B. Shiva Rao, *The Framing of India's Constitution*, Vol. II, Nasik: The Manager, Government of India Press, 1968, p. 682. Similarly, the characters in Bhisham Sahni's 'We have Arrived in Amritsar' speculated 'whether Jinnah, the founding father of Pakistan, would relocate there or continue living in Bombay'. Quoted in Sanjib Baruah, 'Partition and the Politics of Citizenship in Assam', in Urvashi Butalia (ed.), *Partition: The Long Shadow*, Penguin: New Delhi, 2015, p. 81.

the preliminary roll for the first elections was principally based on the anticipatory citizenship provisions in the draft constitution of February 1948. The enrolment throughout the country in anticipation of the constitution engendered, in turn, struggles over citizenship. It was these contestations, I argue, over membership in the nation through the pursuit of a 'place in the roll' that gave a practical basis to the conceptions and principles of democratic citizenship that were debated at the time in the process of constitution making from above.

This chapter focuses on the question of the registration of partition refugees as voters, an issue that was a draft constitutional challenge and that led to numerous contestations over citizenship in the early stages of the making of the electoral roll. Refugees were on the fault line of 'who is an Indian' both in the citizenship draft article and in the preparation of the roll. The chapter examines the struggles for citizenship that arose in relation to the enrolment of the refugees. These struggles, in the main, were conducted through on-going correspondences between a wide range of civic organisations, the Constituent Assembly Secretariat (CAS) and administrators at the state and provincial levels. In that context, various organisations deliberated over the draft constitution and adopted its language. They also made resolutions on its basis and even enacted some draft-constitutional provisions in order to establish their democratic citizenship rights. As a result of this process, the abstract language and forms of the democratic constitution in the making began to strike roots among the population at large. People's struggles and claims of the state on the basis of the draft constitutional framework served, in turn, to entrench the Constitution. Moreover, in this process both the bureaucracy, at the provincial and local level, and the citizenry were tutored into adult franchise as a basis for democratic citizenship and into electoral democracy.

The first section examines the challenge that arose in relation to the registration of the refugees as voters and the way it was dealt with by both citizens' organisations and the CAS. The question of registering the refugees was particularly acute in the partitioned areas, namely, West Bengal, East Punjab, and Assam. But other parts of the country, such as Bihar, U.P., Delhi, and Bombay were also affected.[4] The second section explores the struggles for citizenship and franchise rights that emerged on the ground in the preparation of the draft electoral roll and that were informed by a variety of exclusionary practices in relation to refugees and immigrants. The third section looks at the ways the CAS dealt with

---

[4] Refugees reached various parts of the country. There were also internally displaced refugees, for example, from Hyderabad, and from other princely states.

these struggles. In doing so it analyses the implications of the struggles for franchise and citizenship rights in the context of the enrolment of the refugees and the responses to them for democratisation and democratic state building.

Registering Partition Refugees:
A Draft Constitutional Challenge

Although the evolving provisions for citizenship were still being drafted they were the basis for the preparation of the preliminary electoral roll.[5] The instructions for enrolment set out that every citizen of or above 21 years of age who is not otherwise disqualified by reason of non-residence, unsoundness of mind, crime, or corrupt practice shall be entitled to register on the electoral roll.[6] A voter should have a place of residence in the electoral unit for a period of no less than 180 days in the year ending on 31 March 1948 (i.e. no later than 30 September 1947).[7] As for citizenship, 'For the present', it was stated, 'the definition of citizen in article 5 of the Draft Constitution may be adopted'.[8]

The citizenship provisions, formulated and set in articles 5 and 6 of the Draft Constitution of February 1948, laid down birth, descent, and domicile as criteria for citizenship.[9] Article 5(a) set citizenship at the date of the commencement of the Constitution by birth and descent in the territory of the new state to everyone, barring those who left after 1 April 1947 to make their permanent abode in any foreign state.[10] Article 5(b) provided in very wide terms an Indian citizenship, by birth and descent (up to grandparents), to anyone who was born in the 'Greater

---

[5] The articles on citizenship came up for final discussions in the Constituent Assembly only in August 1949. The last time these provisions were presented briefly at the Assembly before that was on 21 July 1947, as part of the presentation of the Report on the Principles of the Union Constitution. That part, it was noted, was 'subjected to the decision of the ad hoc committee on the citizenship clause'. *Constituent Assembly Debates* (hereafter *CAD*), 21 July 1947, (available on http://parliamentofindia.nic.in/ls/debates/debates.htm, accessed 28 June 2017).

[6] Letter No. CA/64/RR/47, 15 March 1948, CA/1/FR/48-I, ECIR.

[7] Ibid., Appendix I. The appendix provided a definition of a 'place of residence'. For that purpose 'a person shall be deemed to reside in a place if he sometimes uses it as a sleeping place, and a person shall not be deemed to cease to reside in a place merely because he is absent from it or has another dwelling in which he resides, if he is at liberty to return to the place at any time and has not abandoned his intention of returning'. Ibid.

[8] Ibid.

[9] The guiding principle was that a citizen ought to have some kind of a territorial connection with India. See B. R. Ambedkar's cover letter to the 21 February 1948 draft Constitution, in The Drafting Committee, Constituent Assembly of India, *Draft Constitution of India*, New Delhi: The Manager Government of India Press, 1948, p. v.

[10] Ibid., p. 4.

colonial India' – India as defined in the Government of India Act, 1935 as long as they have their domicile in the newly constituted India.[11] The draft article made provisions for the needs of the large number of displaced persons from greater India, including Pakistan. It provided for them an 'easy mode' of acquiring domicile, and thereby citizenship. It was sufficient for a person to declare in the office of the District Magistrate that he desired such a domicile, provided that he has resided in the territory of India for at least one month before his declaration. Such declarations, however, could in practice only be made once the constitution came into force.[12]

Soon after the detailed instructions for the preparation of the rolls were disseminated, in mid-March 1948, and provincial governments began issuing their instructions to local administrators, letters began arriving at the CAS, asking whether and how refugees should be enrolled.[13] Indeed, refugees' citizenship and residential status – two key qualifying criteria for registration as voters – were unclear and soon became a contested matter. According to the prescribed residency qualification, a voter had to reside in the place where he would register from 30 September 1947 at the latest. But a large number of the refugees migrated after 30 September 1947. Moreover, waves of returnees from Pakistan who left during the violence in late 1947 were now coming back to India.[14]

The CAS acknowledged that '[t]he residential qualification of 180 days up to 31 March 1948, will cause hardship to refugees … for reason beyond their control… Some concession will have to be made for the

---

[11] The article referred to 'every person who or either of whose parents or any of whose grand-parents was born in India as defined in the Government of India Act, 1935 (as originally enacted), or in Burma, Ceylon or Malaya, and who has his domicile in the territory of India as defined in this Constitution'. Ibid.

[12] This was set in Explanation (ii) to Article 5 (b). Ibid. The explanation defined domicile for the purpose of the Article, as it was set under Part II of the Indian Succession Act, 1925.

[13] Letters were initially received from the governments of the United Provinces and East Punjab. See letter from the United Provinces Government to CAS, 10 April 1948, CA/I/FR/48-I, ECIR; internal note 82, 23–24 April 1948, and 27 April 1948, ibid. Also see letter from the Frontier Sabha Lucknow to the Prime Minister of India, 17 May 1948, CA/9/FR/48, ECIR. The Frontier Sabha asked of the Central Government 'to issue directive to the authorities concerned to include the names of evacuees from the NWFP in the Electoral Rolls'. Ibid. They copied their letter to the Ministry of Relief & Rehabilitation.

[14] From January 1948, there was a wave of returnees from Pakistan who left during the violence in late 1947 and were now coming back home. This became a critical issue in the development of exclusionary policies to delimit their return and their future prospect of becoming citizens. See Vazira Fazila-Yacoobali Zamindar, *The Long Partition and the Making of Modern South Asia: Refugees, Boundaries, Histories*, New York: Columbia University Press, 2007, chapter 3.

refugees otherwise a large number of persons will be left out'.[15] Seeking a solution to the question of refugees' registration, the Secretariat decided at the beginning of their discussions on the subject that 'the refugee problem will have to be tackled on an all-India basis'.[16] The Under Secretary of the CAS commented that 'there is also the question of their citizenship to be considered'.[17] From May to July 1948 the Secretariat engaged, among other things, with the task of 'finding a suitable formula regarding the residential qualifications of refugee voters'.[18] The Under Secretary directed the office 'to go into this problem with the help, if possible, of any precedents of other countries and put up a note as early as possible'.[19]

In the meantime, letters of complaint from a wide range of citizens' organisations and ordinary people began arriving at the Secretariat, indicating that the provisions and directions that they issued in the pursuit of universal franchise were challenged by evolving distinct exclusionary practices on the ground in the preparation of the roll. Many organisations raised questions and concerns over the refugees' registration and citizenship status.[20] There were also various queries from officials in the provinces about difficulties that surfaced.

[15] Internal notes, 24 April 1948, CA/1/FR/48-I, ECIR.
[16] S. no. 82, 27 April 1948, CA/1/FR/48-I, ECIR.
[17] Ibid.
[18] Internal note, 25 May 1948, CA/9/FR/48, ECIR.
[19] Ibid.
[20] From May to November 1948 citizen and professional organisations repeatedly wrote to the CAS inquiring about the registration of the refugees and the means of acquiring citizenship. They also sent complaint letters about abuses in the registration process of the refugees. Among these organisations were at least 19 citizens' organisations, five professional organisations, and three political organisations from Assam; five from West Bengal; and there were also letters from organisations in UP, East Punjab, and Bihar. Among these organisations were: the Assam Citizens Association Gauhati (established in 1935), Assam Citizens Association Mangaldai, Assam Citizens' Association Dhubri, Assam Citizens' Association Nowgong, Assam Bengalee Association, Assam Citizen Association Barpeta, The Bengali residents and settlers of Bilaripura, Assam Citizens' Association Goalpara, Tinsukia Bengali Association, Bengali Association Dibrugarh, Bengali Association, Margherita, Citizen Union Shillong (formed on 17 July 1948), Citizen Association Digboi, Citizens' Rights & Privileges Protection Committee, Karimganj Assam, Sapatgram Citizens' Association, Sonari Circle Bengali Association, Assam Prantiya Hindustani Sammelan Shillong, Lakhimpur Zilla Bengali Samity, Assam Refugees Association Shillong, Assam Railway Labour Association Sorbhog Branch, Silchar Local Board, District Bar Association Silchar, Muktsar Bar Association Silchar, Surma Upatyaka Cha-Sramik Union (INTUC) Cachar Branch, India Tea Employee's Union Silchar, Silchar Municipal Board, Congress East Bengal Minority Rehabilitation & Citizenship-Right Committee, Silchar-Cachar, Cachar District Congress Committee, Citizens of Calcutta and Refugees Eastern Pakistan, The Servants of Bengal Society (Non-Political Socio-Cultural-Economic association registered under Act XXI of

The President of the East Bengal Minority Welfare Central Committee, Calcutta, wrote that 'certain points mentioned in the Press reports regarding residence qualification and a few provisions in the Draft Constitution regarding citizenship, voting rights, etc. have created considerable apprehension among a large section of the people living in West Bengal and Assam but originally hailing from territories now in Pakistan'.[21] The Committee pointed out that because no arrangements were made as yet by the Government of India or by any provincial government for receiving declarations for citizenship as set in article 5 (b) of the Draft Constitution, 'any preparation of electoral rolls may be seriously prejudicial to the interests of the Immigrants'.[22] The Committee suggested that interim instructions for receiving declarations of domicile as envisaged in article 5 (b) of the Draft Constitution should be issued immediately. Additionally, they cautioned that unless new 'definite' directions were given with respect to the residential qualification of 180 days 'the immigrants from Pakistan are likely to be omitted from the Draft Electoral Rolls now to be prepared'.[23] The Committee suggested in this regard that the question of residence 'should be very leniently applied at least in the preparation of the first electoral rolls. Mere declaration as to intention of residence should be accepted as residential qualification'.[24] The Committee also reported that in some parts of Assam attempts were being made to leave out the immigrants from the electoral rolls.

Indeed, several letters referred to a circular that the Reforms Commissioner of Assam issued on 28 May 1948 to all district officers, containing detailed instructions for them and their staff regarding the preparation of the electoral roll.

The Government desires to draw your personal attention with regard to the floating and 'non-resident' population of the District. These people are not qualified to be registered as voters. They may be staying with friends, relatives or as refugees or labourers. Great caution will be necessary on the part of your staff to see

1860), The East Bengal Minority Welfare Central Committee, East Bengal Displaced Lawyers' Association Calcutta, All-India Marwari Federation, Calcutta, Frontier Sabha Lucknow, Committee for Acquiring Indian Citizenship, Jamshedpur, Bihar.

[21] 'Preparation of Electoral Rolls and Citizenship of the Immigrants from Pakistan': letter from the President of the East Bengal Minority Welfare Central Committee, Calcutta, to Rajendra Prasad [President of the Constituent Assembly], 12 May 1948, CA/9/FR/48, ECIR.

[22] Ibid. Also see, for example, letter from the Secretary of the Surma Sammilani, Assam, to CAS, 14 July 1948, CA/12/FR/48, ECIR.

[23] Letter from the President of the East Bengal Minority Welfare Central Committee, Calcutta, to Rajendra Prasad, 12 May 1948, CA/9/FR/48, ECIR.

[24] Ibid.

that not a single individual of this class manages to creep into the electoral roll by any chance.[25]

On his final note, the Reforms Commissioner asked that 'officers of all grades who may be entrusted with this work of national importance will devote their whole attention and care in the performance of their duties in this affair with patriotic zeal'.[26] In his following circular the Reforms Commissioner emphasised that the reference to 'residence' in the instructions for the preparation of the roll 'means residence of a citizen. Citizenship comes first and residence next... Citizenship will have to be first established before one can acquire franchise.'[27]

Angry letters about the Reforms Commissioner and Assam Government asked the CAS to 'appreciate it [this circular's] inherent defects which will vitally vitiate preparation of Electoral Roll', and demanded immediate rectification.[28] The letter added:

[25] Letter from the Reforms Commissioner of Assam to all District Officers, 28 May 1948 (circular No. L.801/47), CA/1/FR/48-II, ECIR.

[26] Ibid.

[27] Letter from the Reforms Commissioner of Assam to all District Officers, 2 June 1948, CA/9/FR/48, ECIR. The circular was attached to a letter from the Assam Citizens' Association Gauhati to Rajendra Prasad, 3 September 1948. It is noteworthy that in Assam there have been contestations over immigration, citizenship and who was a 'son of the soil' from the 1920s. This fight was largely driven by the quest to protect the Assamese-speaking inhabitants, mainly of the Assam Valley, in the face the growing share of Bengali-speaking population in Assam, as well as in government jobs, due to the rising influx of immigrants, both Muslims and Hindus, from Bengal (later East Bengal). The transfer of the Bengali speaking Sylhet to Pakistan with the partition was, therefore, endorsed in Assam. Yet with the post partition influx of (Bengali speaking) refugees from East Bengal and mainly Sylhet, immigrants and the question of their citizenship became an intensely contested issue. This is also the context for understanding the protracted ethnic and citizenship conflicts in Assam since independence (beginning with the promulgation of the Immigrants (Expulsion from Assam) Act 1950 (originally an Ordinance of 6 January 1950). For good discussions of this history see Amalendu Guha, *Planter-Raj to Swaraj: Freedom Struggle and Electoral Politics in Assam 1826–1947*, New Delhi: Indian Council of Historical Research, 1977, pp. 164–320; Myron Weiner, *Sons of the Soil: Migration and Ethnic Conflicts in India*, Princeton, NJ: Princeton University Press, 1978; Weiner, 'The Political Demography of Assam's Anti-Immigrant Movement', *Population and Development Review* 9, no. 2, 1983, pp. 279–92; Sanjib Baruah, 'Ethnic Conflicts as State–Society Struggle: The Poetics and Politics of Assamese Micro-Nationalism', *Modern Asian Studies* 28, no. 3, 1994, pp. 649–71; Baruah, 'Partition and the Politics of Citizenship in Assam', pp. 78–101. Also see Udayon Misra, 'Immigration and Identity Transformation in Assam', *Economic and Political Weekly* 34, no. 21, 1999, pp. 1264–71; Sujit Chaudhury, 'A God-Sent Opportunity', *Seminar* 510, 2002, pp. 61–7 (the quote from the Reforms Commissioner of Assam's circular of 28 May 1948 also appears in this article); Anupama Roy, *Mapping Citizenship in India*, New Delhi: Oxford University Press, 2010, pp. 92–134; and Government of Assam, Home and Political Department, *White Paper on Foreigners Issue*, 22.5.2015 http://assam.gov.in/web/home-and-political-department/white-paper1#1 (accessed 18 March 2016).

[28] Letter from the Chair of Cachar District Congress Committee to the Chairman of the Advisory Committee on Fundamental rights, 18 June 1948 CA/1/FR/48-II, ECIR. That letter was sent on behalf of ten organisations that were signatories to it.

The Constituent Assembly entrusted to draft the constitution should take note of the above to realise how simple provisions under the constitution could be misconstrued and how persons holding responsible positions may fail to implement the provisions of the constitution in accordance to its spirit and may even defeat its purpose by issuing directions that will lead to a negation of the fundamental conception of adult suffrage.[29]

'You will find', stated another letter, 'that attempts are being made to exclude all persons who were not born in Assam as constituted now.'[30]

Some organisations complained that they 'failed to have any definite form or direction either from the district authorities or provincial government in the matter of enrolment of voters under the new act', and requested to received 'all papers and forms so that people ... may correctly move to enlist themselves as voters'.[31]

The concerns and uncertainty over the citizenship and franchise rights of the refugees were also expressed in the press. An editorial entitled 'Confusing and Anomalous' in the *Amrita Bazar Patrika*, published in Bengal, suggested that 'impression has been sought to be created ... that unless an evacuee possesses immovable property in the Indian Union or gets himself registered with a refugee camp he cannot be treated as a citizen of India and as such is excluded from the franchise. This, however, is not confirmed by the existing law and on the whole it is a wrong approach to the problem.'[32]

Some provincial governments, for example East Punjab and West Bengal, sent reminders to the CAS, requesting orders in the matter of the refugees.[33] A member of the Constituent Assembly submitted a starred question with regard to the requirement of a fixed place of residence for

[29] Ibid. Also see letter from the Assam Refugees Association Shillong to CAS, 31 July 1948, CA/12/FR/48, ECIR.

[30] Letter from the Secretary of the Surma Sammilani, Assam, to CAS, 14 July 1948, CA/12/FR/48, ECIR. The Premier of West Bengal wrote personally in the matter of the instructions issued in Assam to the Constitutional Advisor and asked for clear instructions in the matter of refugees' registration. Letter from the Premier, West Bengal, to the Constitutional Advisor, 31 July 1948, CA/29/Const/48, CA/12/FR/48, ECIR.

[31] Letter from P. K. Sinha, Lakhimpur Zilla Bengali Samity to CAS, 27 July 1948, CA/12/FR/48, ECIR.

[32] 'Confusing and Anomalous', *Amrita Bazar Patrika*, 7 June 1948, CA/12/FR/48, ECIR. The article also explained that at the present 'there are no such things as "citizens" or "nationals" of India or of Pakistan... [A]ll that has been attempted so far is a formula recommended by the Drafting Committee set up by the Indian Constituent Assembly.' Ibid. It clarified that this formula is embodied in Article 5 of the Draft Constitution, and that birth and domicile are accepted as factors determining India citizenship. It discussed in detail the explanation to the Article, as well as the meaning of domicile and the means of acquiring it.

[33] The Government of East Punjab noted that '[t]he Government of India are aware that almost all refugees settled in the Indian Dominion after 1st October 1947' and therefore could not qualify for the residential qualification of six months up to 31 March 1948.

not less than 180 days in the financial year ending in March 1948, claiming that this will 'debar millions of voters'.[34]

Seeking an all-India solution to the question of the refugees' registration, members of the CAS initially explored international precedents. A member of the CAS looked at how European countries dealt with the refugee problem since the beginning of the First World War and in the wake of the partitioning of the Ottoman Empire.[35] His report concluded, however, that 'in the countries where automatic naturalization of the refugees took place, it could not be ascertained whether the residential qualifications for election purposes was also relaxed. There is no book or document available, which deals with this minute question.'[36] The Under Secretary pointed out that 'the refugees are always on the move, and, therefore, no residential qualification can be prescribed for them, if they are to be given the right of vote in the next elections'.[37] He also noted that 'the question of registration is linked up closely with that of citizenship'.[38]

The matter was forwarded to the Constitutional Advisor for his opinion. Rau's position was that:

The electoral rolls now under preparation are merely the preliminary rolls. Before a general election is held on the basis of these rolls, they will have to be ... published and revised under the electoral law. There should, therefore, be no objection to 'refugees' being registered in the rolls, for their province, on a mere declaration by them of their intention to reside permanently in the town or village concerned.[39]

Rau asked the Joint Secretary of the CAS to examine this suggestion.

In an attempt to assess the scope of the task and the means of identifying the refugees, the Joint Secretary instructed to inquire

Letter from the Chief Secretary to the Government of East Punjab to CAS, 28 June 1948, CA/1/FR/48-II, ECIR.

[34] A starred question to the Constituent Assembly submitted by Mr R. K. Sidhva, 12 July 1948, CA/64/RR/47, ECIR.

[35] Internal Report, 1 June 1948, CA/9/FR/48, ECIR. The Report looked into cases of en-masse naturalisation of refugees, such as the Greek refugees from Turkey, Russia, and Bulgaria who arrived in Greece between 1913 and 1922 and were granted Greek nationality. It reviewed the legal framework for doing so on the basis of the 1919 Neuilly Convention, and the 1923 Convention of Lausanne. The Report also looked into the cases of granting citizenship to Muslim refugees settling in Turkey without the ordinary residential qualifications, and the Armenian refugees in Syria and Lebanon.

[36] Ibid.

[37] Internal note, 8 June 1948, CA/9/FR/48, ECIR.

[38] Ibid. In making this point, the Under Secretary referred to the East Bengal Minority Welfare Central Committee letter. See n. 23 above.

[39] S. no. 3 (by B. N. Rau), 15 June 1948, CA/9/FR/48, ECIR. It is noteworthy that the East Bengal Minority Welfare Central Committee made a similar proposition. See letter from the President of the East Bengal Minority Welfare Central Committee, Calcutta, to Rajendra Prasad, 12 May 1948, CA/9/FR/48, ECIR. See n. 24 above.

whether there were any orders regarding the compulsory registration of refugees in the provinces.[40] According to the information gathered, the system of compulsory registration of refugees appeared to exist at the time only in Bombay and in the Central Provinces. In Delhi the compulsory registration 'recently discontinued ... as they do not want to encourage further ingress of refugees'.[41] In Assam and Orissa there was no system of registration; Madras informed that they were going to introduce the necessary legislation; and in Bihar the previously existing system was no longer in force. East Punjab and U.P. did not yet reply. The Under Secretary concluded that 'in the majority of cases it may not be possible to verify due to the absences of compulsory registration whether in a particular case the person is a refugee or not'.[42] But that 'this by itself need not perhaps stand in the way of the refugees being included on the preliminary rolls on the mere declaration given by them'.[43]

Upon further deliberations, the CAS decided by 13 July 1948 to register all refugees in the electoral rolls at this stage 'on mere declaration by them of their intention to reside permanently in the town or village concerned irrespective of the actual period of residence'.[44] Before issuing the instructions on the registration of the refugees, B. N. Rau wrote a detailed explanatory note to the President of the Constituent Assembly, Rajendra Prasad, giving the rationale for the decision.[45] Rau explained that 'before the time comes for the revision of these rolls, we may have to relax the residence qualification for refugees. How exactly the relaxation should be effected is a question whose consideration need not detain us just now. What is immediately needed is an instruction that for the

---

[40] S. no. 4, 2 July 1948, CA/9/FR/48, ECIR. The Under Secretary then instructed Mr Abidi, the CAS's Research Officer, to 'go over to the Relief & Rehabilitation Ministry and get authentic and complete details on the subject'. Ibid. On 6 July 1948 the CAS sent telegrams to all the Provincial Governments and the newly formed Unions of States and Chief Commissioners' Provinces asking for the information and for a copy of the relevant orders. Telegram, 6 July 1948, CA/9/FR/48, ECIR. Provincial Governments legislated an array of Refugees Registration and Movement Acts from early October 1947.

[41] Internal note, 13 July 1948, CA/9/FR/48, ECIR. (A four-page brief note by the Under Secretary, K. V. Padnamabhan.)

[42] Ibid.

[43] Ibid. The brief note also included a proposal for relaxing the prescribed period of residential qualification for refugees. It also examined and drew analogy from the Franchise Act of 1945, which enabled registration in the electoral roll to a person who was absent from his constituency on the grounds of being away on war service.

[44] Internal note (by the Joint Secretary, S. N. Mukerjee), 13 July 1948, CA/9/FR/48, ECIR. The Joint Secretary pointed out that 'we will have subsequently either to alter the qualifying period as mentioned above or to relax the residence qualification in the case of the refugees to enable them to be qualified for registration in the final electoral rolls'. Ibid.

[45] Internal note from B. N. Rau to Rajendra Prasad, 14 July 1948, CA/9/FR/48, ECIR.

present refugees should be registered as voters on a mere declaration...'[46] Prasad approved the proposal, but asked to clarify 'that such enrolment is subject to revision in due time in accordance with electoral laws'.[47] This point was made in the new directives on the enrolment of refugees, which the CAS sent to all provinces and states.[48] A detailed explanatory Press Note in the matter was issued on 15 July 1948.[49]

The new instructions, however, prompted further questions and uncertainties. The Government of West Bengal wrote to the CAS asking for a definition of who is a 'refugee'; whether the declaration to be made by a refugee should be oral or in writing; and whether 'such a declaration dispenses with the declaration required under clause (b) of article 5 of the Draft Constitution, or whether it is to be made independently of the latter.'[50]

In response, the Secretariat devised a uniform definition of a 'refugee'. For that purpose they reviewed the various Refugee Registration and Movement Acts of the provincial governments. The definition of a refugee in these acts differed mainly in relation to the date of migration to a province, which determined whether a person could be considered to be a refugee. The Constitutional Advisor expressed a preference for the definition given in the Central Provinces and Berar Act, precisely because it did not specify any date. He pointed out that 'any date that we may specify is bound to be more or less arbitrary; it may not suit all provinces; and rather than fix a date now and change it afterwards, it is better not to mention any date at all in the definition'.[51] The CAS decided that '"Refugee" with reference to any Province or State means a person who has migrated into the Province or State on account of disturbances in his usual place of residence.'[52]

On 26 July 1948 the CAS sent further instructions to all provinces and states, providing for the uniform definition of a 'refugee'. It clarified that a refugee declaration should be in writing before 'any responsible Officer' not necessarily before a district magistrate. These instructions moreover explained the distinction between a refugee declaration for registration as a voter and the declaration required under clause (ii) of the explanation to

[46] Ibid. Rau also clarified the distinction between the provision about one month residence in the Draft Constitution in relation to citizenship, and the prescribed residence rules in order to qualify as a voter.

[47] Internal note from Rajendra Prasad to B. N. Rau, 15 July 1948, CA/9/FR/48, ECIR.

[48] S. no. 4, Draft Telegram, 16 July 1948, CA/1/FR/48-III, ECIR.

[49] Press Note 15 July 1948. File No. CA/1/FR/48 1948-V, ECIR.

[50] Telegram from the Joint Secretary to the Government of West Bengal to CAS, 17 July 1948, CA/1/FR/48-II; Internal note, 23 July 1948, CA/9/FR/48, ECIR.

[51] Internal note (by B. N. Rau), 24 July 1948, CA/9/FR/48, ECIR.

[52] Ibid.

article 5 of the Draft Constitution, which related to citizenship, and which 'cannot be made until auxiliary action referred to in the footnote on page 4 of the Draft Constitution has been taken'.[53]

Despite the CAS's attempts at clarification, both officials and members of the public became confused. Many conflated the declaration for the registration of a refugee as a voter with the declaration that was required for acquiring domicile and thereby citizenship. In both the official and the public mind the two were sometimes believed to be synonymous. This mix-up, together with other distinct forms of exclusionary practices on the ground in the registration of refugees, generated struggles for democratic citizenship rights.

Citizenship Contests in Roll Making

This confusion between registration as a voter and registration for citizenship led the West Bengal Government, for example, to hastily initiate registration of refugees as citizens. On 20 July 1948 the Government of West Bengal issued an order that declarations under article 5 of the Draft Constitution should be made in the form of affidavits on an embossed stamp paper of Rs.2.[54] The CAS received several complaints against these orders. The Bengal Displaced Lawyers' Association, for example, claimed that this order 'cannot be legally supported'.[55] In their view, demanding of the refugees to file an affidavit and the court stamp fee will exclude a large number of persons entitled to vote and will thus frustrate the object of the preliminary preparation of the electoral rolls.[56]

Conversely, some organisations issued complaints against their local government for not registering citizens, and sought help in the matter from the CAS. 'The Government of Assam', wrote the Chairman of the Assam Refugees' Association, Shillong, unlike the Government of West Bengal, 'is doing nothing uptil [sic] now and pretending absence of instructions from the centre in regard to the declaration of acquiring

---

[53] Letter from CAS to All Provincial Governments, All Chief Commissioners Provinces and All Indian States and Unions, 26 July 1948, CA/9/FR/48, ECIR.

[54] Memo No. 938-AR, from Joint Secretary to the Government of West Bengal (Home Department) Constitution & Election to the Subdivisional Officer, Sadar (Hoogly), 20 July 1948, CA/1/FR/48-II, ECIR. It was noted that copies of these instructions were being forwarded to all District and Subdivisional officers, and that in Calcutta declarations will be deposited in the office of the Chief Presidency Magistrate.

[55] Letter from East Bengal Displaced Lawyers' Association to Rajendra Prasad, 28 July 1948, CA/9/FR/48, ECIR.

[56] Ibid. Also see, for example, letter from the Servants of Bengal Society to B. N. Rau, 12 August 1948; letter from the East Bengal Minority Welfare Central Committee to Rajendra Prasad, 14 August 1948, CA/9/FR/48, ECIR.

citizenship in Indian dominion... The time is too short ... we are afraid a majority of our people will fail to acquire citizenship... We in Assam are quite in the dark and we have no organisation to influence the central government in the matter until and unless you come forward to our help.'[57] The Chairman of the Assam Refugees' Association referred to the forms for registration of citizenship that were issued in Calcutta and asked whether they are to be accepted. Some organisations demanded to link voter's registration with the acquisition of citizenship. The Assam Citizens' Association Dhubri wrote to the CAS that 'in view of the fact that the work of enrolling voters is proceeding apace, this meeting urges on the government to immediately prescribe the procedure for making and depositing the declaration for citizenship'.[58] The Assam Citizens' Association Mangaldai decided 'to take a census of all persons entitled to citizenship and also to see that they submit the requisite declaration for citizenship'.[59]

Indeed, in the context of the preparation of the preliminary electoral rolls, securing citizenship and franchise rights became the raison d'être of bourgeoning citizens' organisations. For example, a public meeting held in Digboi, Assam, on 26 July 1948 resolved that:

An association to be called the 'Citizens' Association, Digboi' be formed with the following objects: (a) To acquire citizenship rights and to promote and protect the civil rights of citizens. (b) To safe-guard the right of franchise. (c) To promote omity [sic – amity], goodwill and cooperation among different communities.[60]

Likewise, the Assam Citizens' Association Mangaldai defined its main objectives as follows:

(1) To promote and protect the civic rights of all citizens and to safeguard their right of franchise as guaranteed by the new constitution. (2) To promote their general wellbeing. (3) To strive for the welfare of Assam. (4) To cultivate and maintain good feeling amongst all citizens.[61]

---

[57] Letter from the Assam Refugees' Association Shillong to CAS, 31 July 1948, CA/29/Const/48, CA/12/FR/48, ECIR.

[58] Letter from the Assam Citizens' Association Dhubri to CAS, 29 August 1948, CA/9/FR/48, ECIR. Also see their letter of 8 September 1948, ibid.

[59] Letter from the Assam Citizens' Association Mangaldai to CAS, 30 August 1948, CA/9/FR/48, ECIR. They copied their letter to the Reforms Commissioner of Assam, the Premier of Assam, Minister of Relief &Rehabilitation, and to the Constitutional Advisor.

[60] 'Resolution adopted in the public meeting held in Digboi Indian Club at 5.30 p.m. on Monday, the 26th July 1948', Appendix 'A' in: letter from the Joint Secretary to the Government of India Ministry of Labour to CAS, 16 November 1948, CA/12/FR/48, ECIR. The meeting resolved that membership in the Association will be open to adults of all communities.

[61] Letter from the Assam Citizens' Association Mangaldai to CAS, 30 August 1948, CA/9/FR/48, ECIR. As another example, the Assam Citizens' Association Goalpara stated

Many of these organisations sought affiliation with each other. They disseminated their 'constitutional opinions' about voter and citizenship rights of refugees and immigrants by sending copies of their letters to the CAS, the Constitutional Advisor, and even to the President of the Constituent Assembly and Nehru. Unsurprisingly, the contents of the letter of one citizens' organisation were sometimes reproduced verbatim by other organisations.[62]

Generally, citizens' organisations, determined to secure their right of franchise and citizenship, examined critically the CAS's solution for the registration of the refugees as voters. Thus, the East Bengal Minority Welfare Central Committee, Calcutta, wrote to the President of the Constituent Assembly, Rajendra Prasad:

We note with pleasure and gratitude that the 180 day's residential qualification has been dispensed with so far as preliminary rolls are concerned... But there is no guarantee that this inclusion will acquire for them the right of voting... The relief, therefore, is more illusionary than real... While feeling grateful to you ... allow us to say that we irresistible [sic] feel that this is no guarantee, but only a pious and kind wish... We are entitled to know what is the present intention of the government on this question ... an adult evacuee must be considered eligible to be a voter... We should have *vision* first and *revision* afterwards.[63]

that their 'main object is to look after and safeguard the civic and political rights of those residents in Assam who have come from outside the province but have settled in Assam and who are not regarded as "children of the soil" by the administration'. Letter from the Assam Citizens' Association Goalpara to Rajendra Prasad, 2 September 1948, CA/9/FR/48, ECIR. Some citizens' organisations in Assam, for example the Assam Citizen Associations of Dhubri and Gauhati, were originally established in the 1930s by Bengali-speaking immigrants who struggled for equal citizenship rights in the context of policies that restricted land settlement by immigrants. They later became inactive. See Guha, *Planter-Raj to Swaraj*, pp. 207–11, 260–2. In the face of the influx of partition refugees from East Bengal, some of these organisations were re-established.

[62] For example, the Bengali Residents and Settlers Bilasipura sent on 12 September 1948 a (handwritten) resolution, which reiterated word for word the letter from the Assam Citizens' Association Dhubri to CAS, 8 September 1948, CA/9/FR/48, ECIR. The Assam Citizens' Association Goalpara sent a copy of their resolutions to the Assam Citizens' Associations of Dhubri and Gauhati. Letter from Assam Citizens' Association Goalpara to Rajendra Prasad, 30 August 1948, CA/9/FR/48, ECIR. The Citizens' Association Digboi officially sought an affiliation with the Citizen Union Shillong. See 'Resolution adopted in the public meeting held in Digboi Indian Club at 5.30 p.m. on Monday, the 26th July 1948', Appendix 'A' in: letter from the Joint Secretary to the Government of India Ministry of Labour to the CAS, 16 November 1948, CA/12/FR/48, ECIR. The Secretary of the Sonari Circle Bengali Association requested of 'the "Tinsukia Bengali Associations" and the "Citizens" Union, Shillong to keep the association informed of any new changes or new rules coming into the constitution and advise accordingly'. Letter from the Sonari Circle Bengali Association to CAS, 23 September 1948, CA/9/FR/48, ECIR.

[63] Letter from the East Bengal Minority Welfare Central Committee, Calcutta, to Rajendra Prasad, 3 August 1948, CA/9/FR/48, ECIR (emphases in the original).

It was the vision embedded in the anticipated new constitution that citizens' organisations now vigorously pursued in their struggles for franchise and citizenship rights. Various organisations deliberated and used the language of the draft constitution. They also made resolutions on its basis and even enacted some draft-constitutional provisions in order to establish their citizenship.

Thus, the Servants of Bengal Society, who were keen advocates of citizenship and voting rights for the refugees in their midst, objected to the fee the West Bengal Government charged for the declarations for citizenship. They took the initiative of issuing their own forms for that purpose instead. They sent a sample form to the Constitutional Advisor, explaining that they devised the form on the basis of article 5 (b) of the Draft Constitution 'read with the instruction of the Secretariat of the Constituent Assembly supported by the public statement of Dr. Rajendra Prasad'.[64] They stated that '[m]ore than a lakh [100,000] of East Bengal refugees anxious to acquire Indian citizenship' applied with this form to the District Magistrates of West Bengal.[65] They asked Rau to 'please consider the matter from the point of view of the West Bengal refugees who have already filed their declarations in the attached form and *inform us immediately if the declaration is in order*'.[66]

Similarly, the Committee for Acquiring Indian Citizenship Jamshedpur, Bihar, wrote to the CAS that after 'much persuasion the District Magistrate kindly agreed to receive Declarations [of citizenship] and kept it pending in the file but [he] could not give any guarantee regarding its acceptance'.[67] They asked for the CAS to provide instructions.

Citizens' organisations also rehearsed the draft constitutional citizenship provisions with the object of safeguarding the citizenship and franchise rights of persons whose domicile of origin was in Pakistan, but who had long been residents in a province of the Dominion of India. There was an abundant correspondence on this issue, from organisations

---

[64] Letter from the Servants of Bengal Society to B. N. Rau, 12 August 1948, CA/9/FR/48, ECIR.

[65] Ibid.

[66] Ibid. (Emphasis in original.) The form of declaration for registration of citizenship the organisation issued was attached to the letter. Notwithstanding the CAS's repeated clarifications that declarations for citizenship could not yet be made and that magistrates had no legal authority to receive or retain them, the Servants of Bengal Society persistently asked for recognition of the citizenship declarations that refugees already submitted. See letter from the General Secretary, Servants of Bengal Society to CAS, 14 October 1948, CA/9/FR/48, ECIR; letter from the General Secretary, Servants of Bengal Society to Hon'ble Sardar Ballav Bhai Patel [sic], Minister for Home Department, 24 October 1948, CA/9/FR/48, ECIR.

[67] Letter from the Committee for Acquiring Indian Citizenship Jamshedpur, Bihar, to CAS, 25 September 1948, CA/9/FR/48, ECIR.

in Assam and West Bengal in particular.[68] These were immigrants who were not partition refugees, but in the context of the preparation of the electoral rolls were sometimes put on the same wagon as the refugees.[69] The West Bengal Government instructed that in the case of such persons no refugee declaration is necessary for the purpose of enrolment.[70] In Assam, however, citizens' organisations complained that such persons are 'not regarded as "children of the soil" by the administration', and that 'according to the opinion publicly expressed by the Reforms Commissioner, Assam, of these people those who fulfil the condition of the 180 days' residence will be enrolled as voters but whether they can or will acquire the status of "citizens" will be decided later on'.[71]

Citizens' organisations in Assam wrote to the CAS to protest about the Reforms Commissioner's policies. One organisation suggested that he was 'both legally and constitutionally wrong', and that the cases of people born outside the present Indian territory but long settled in Assam are covered by article 5(B) 'read with the Explanation (i)) of the Draft Constitution. As such they are to be regarded as citizens at the date of the commencement of the constitution'.[72] They added that:

It is not understood on what ground the reform Commissioner thinks that the citizenship of such persons should remain in abeyance and will be decided later... Such an attitude definitely engenders civic and political status of a very large number of residents in Assam who are very eager to have their status as citizens of Indian Dominion confirmed during the course of enrolments votes. Our Association thinks that enrolment as voters, ipso facto invests the person so enrolled with the status of a citizen.[73]

---

[68] There were similar cases with regards to people who migrated to a province or a state from another part of the country. For example, the Government of Travancore refused initially to enrol Tamils who migrated to the State many years earlier, but were not Travancore subjects.

[69] Numerous letters on the matter referred, for example, to '*the resident non-indigenous non-refugees* of the Province'. Letter from the Congress East Bengal Minority Rehabilitation & Citizenship-Right Committee Silchar-Cachar to the Reforms Commissioner of Assam, 29 August 1948, CA/9/FR/48, ECIR (emphasis in original). Also see Telegram from the Citizen Association Silchar to Rajendra Prasad, 9 September 1948; letter from the Assam Citizens' Association Gauhati to Rajendra Prasad, 3 September 1948, CA/9/FR/48, ECIR. For the historical context of the struggles of this group of immigrants see n. 27 above.

[70] See ibid.

[71] Letter from the Assam Citizens' Association Goalpara to Rajendra Prasad, 2 September 1948, CA/9/FR/48, ECIR.

[72] Ibid. That part of the Explanation to Article 5 referred to the Indian Succession Act.

[73] Letter from Secretary Assam Citizens' Association (including Domiciles & Settlers Goalpara Branch), to the President, Constituent Assembly of India, 2 September 1948, CA/9/FR/48, ECIR. For similar arguments see letter from the Citizens' Rights & Privileges Protection Committee Karimganj to CAS, 2 September 1948; letter from the Sonari Circle Bengali Association to CAS, 23 September 1948; letters from the Assam

The struggles for citizenship and franchise rights were furthermore informed by the instructions for the registration of refugees that provincial governments issued to their staff. The Government of Assam, for example, set a court-fee stamp of the value of eight annas to be affixed on the declarations to be filled by refugees for inclusion in the preliminary electoral rolls, even though no fee was stipulated to the order to relax refugees' registration on the roll.[74] It also set that such declarations should be made in writing before the Circle Sub-Deputy Collector before 30 September 1948.[75] In his confidential instructions on the enrolment of the refugees, the Reforms Commissioner of Assam directed officers to 'verify that the declarant is actually a refugee'.[76] Thus, on the refugee declaration form that he devised, the declarant was required to provide information about the province, district and thana from where he arrived, and the month of arrival, in order to ascertain 'as far as possible the actual happening of the disturbing event or events as the cause or probable cause of migration'.[77]

Numerous citizens' organisations across Assam held emergency meetings upon the publication of these instructions. They submitted their resolutions, complaints and suggestions to the CAS. Generally, citizens' associations were of the view that the Government of Assam's instructions 'will have the inevitable affect [sic] of disenfranchising the majority of the refugees, though it is very complacently said that the intention is to give the refugees all possible facilities for enrolment as voters'.[78] The Assam Bengalee Association warned that unless modified, the Assam procedure for the registration of refugees will 'nullify the intent and purpose of the declared object of the Govt. of India for granting citizenship right to the refugees in an easier method'.[79] The *Hindustan Standard* wrote that the Reforms Commissioner 'issued instructions in flagrant violation

---

Citizens' Association Dhubri to CAS, 29 August 1948, and letter of 8 September 1948; and letter from the Bengali Residents and Settlers Bilasipura to CAS, 12 September 1948, CA/9/FR/48, ECIR.

[74] Assam Information and Publicity Department Press Communiqué, 'Enrolment of Refugees on Electoral Rolls', 12 August 1948. Also see *The Assam Gazette*, 18 August 1948, p. 595, CA/9/FR/48, ECIR.

[75] Confidential letter No.LRE.530/48/7 from the Reforms Commissioner of Assam to All District Officers (Including Superintendent, Lushai Hills), Subdivisional Officers and Political Officers of Frontiers Tract, 9 August 1948, CA/1/FR/48-III, ECIR.

[76] Ibid. The letter stated that '*These instructions are intended for the guidance of officers only and should not in nay case be printed along with the form.*' (Emphasis in original.)

[77] Ibid.

[78] Letter from the Assam Citizens' Association Nowgong to CAS, 26 August 1948, CA/9/FR/48, ECIR. Also see a copy of a Telegram from the Assam Citizens Association Gauhati to CAS, 17 August 1948, CA/9/FR/48, ECIR.

[79] 'Resolution No. 2', Assam Bengalee Association, in Internal discussions, CAS, 28 August 1948, CA/9/FR/48, ECIR.

of the principle and procedure ... and has not hesitated even to indulge in sheer nonsense in order to prevent what any officer of average intelligence might otherwise do in fulfilment of his duties as an enumerator'.[80]

Specifically, citizens' organisations demanded, first, the cancellation of the court-fee charge, claiming that it was an economic blow for the refugees. Second, they asked that the male head of household be allowed to file a declaration on behalf of his wife and other women in the family, explaining that a large number of women were purdanashin, and that it was impossible for a pregnant woman to appear in person.[81] Third, citizens' organisations demanded to extend the time limit for the submission of declarations. 'It is apprehended', wrote the Assam Bengalee Association, 'that most innocent refugees who *have not adequate sense of civic duties* and who might have settled in out of the way places are still in the dark and may be deprived of the chance of becoming citizens of India.'[82]

Citizens' organisations in Assam suggested concrete ways of expediting the registration of the refugees. For example, they asked to be officially allowed to collect and submit the declaration forms filed by the refugees.[83] One organisation suggested that issuing receipts to the refugees declarations is necessary 'in order to generate a feeling of confidence in the minds of the refugees, specially because, nearer home, the West Bengal Government have already made such arrangements'.[84] Several organisations emphasised the need for adequate publicity, and proposed 'to adopt effective measures to receive the declarations by fixing the receiving Centres in such suitable places

[80] 'A Sinister Move', *Hindustan Standard*, Calcutta, 14 August 1948, CA/5/FR/48, ECIR. This newspaper was published and read in Bengal.
[81] Letter from The Assam Citizens Association Gauhati to CAS, 18 August 1948, CA/9/FR/48, ECIR. Purdanashin (pardanashin) means: women who observed rigid rules of seclusion. Also see letter from the Assam Citizens' Association Nowgong to CAS, 26 August 1948; 'Resolution No. 2', Assam Bengalee Association, in Internal discussions, CAS, 28 August 1948; letter from Tinsukia Bengali Association to CAS, 5 September 1948; letter from the Bengali Association Dibrugarh to CAS, 9 September 1948; letter from the Assam Citizens' Association Dhubri to CAS, 8 September 1948; letter from the Bengali Residents and Settlers of Bilasipura, 12 September 1948; and letter from the Sonari Circle Bengali Association to CAS, 23 September 1948, CA/9/FR/48, ECIR.
[82] 'Resolution No. 2', Assam Bengalee Association, in Internal discussions, CAS, 28 August 1948, CA/9/FR/48, ECIR (emphasis added).
[83] See letter from the Assam Citizens' Association Nowgong to CAS, 26 August 1948; 'Resolution No. 2', Assam Bengalee Association, in Internal discussions, CAS, 28 August 1948; letter from the Assam Citizens' Association Dhubri to CAS, 8 September 1948, CA/9/FR/48, ECIR.
[84] Letter from the Congress East Bengal Minority Rehabilitation & Citizenship-Right Committee Silchar-Cachar to the Reforms Commissioner of Assam, 29 August 1948, CA/9/FR/48, ECIR.

where Thanas & Post Offices are situated and all important villages & business places within the District & to grant receipt for the declarations received'.[85]

While in Assam citizens' organisations fought for the registration of the refugees in order to secure their franchise and citizenship rights, in East Punjab refugees refused to give any declaration as regards their intention to reside permanently in the electoral unit for the purpose of their registration in the roll because they 'are constantly on the move'.[86] Some refugees' organisations in East Punjab demanded that 'the refugees should be enrolled as voters where-ever they are now settled'.[87] Indeed, as the work of enrolment progressed in East Punjab, the main difficulties that were encountered were connected with the transfers of refugees between camps within and outside districts as part of their rehabilitation, rather than by disenfranchisement attempts. This was indicative of the differences between the partition of Punjab and Bengal, particularly in relation to the government policy towards the rehabilitation of the refugees.[88] Thus, the Deputy Commissioner of Karnal reported that 'thousands already registered left the district while thousands registered in other district came to the district. These transfers have thus resulted in change of tents and camps recorded in the original list.'[89] Moreover, he informed that 'refugees from the Bahawalpur State at present settled in Refugee Camp No. 1 at Kurukhshetra were not offering themselves for registration unless they were assured that

---

[85] Letter from Sapatgram Citizens' Association Assam to Rajendra Prasad, 17 September 1948, CA/9/FR/48, ECIR. Also see letter from the Assam Citizens' Association Nowgong to CAS, 26 August 1948; and letter from the Assam Citizens' Association Dhubri to CAS, 8 September 1948, CA/9/FR/48, ECIR.

[86] Summary of discussions between Mr S. N. Mukherjee, Joint Secretary, Constituent Assembly of India and Mr Luthra, Personal Assistant to the Election Commissioner, East Punjab, 8 September 1948, CA/9/FR/48, ECIR.

[87] Letter from the Liaison Officer, East Punjab Government (with U.P. Government) to Jawaharlal Nehru, 21 August 1948, CA/9/FR/48, ECIR. He wrote the letter after being approached in the matter by some refugees' organisations.

[88] See, for example, Joya Chatterji, 'Right or Charity? The Debate over Relief and Rehabilitation in West Bengal, 1947–50', in Suvir Kaul (ed.), The Partitions of Memory: The Afterlife of the Division of India, Delhi: Permanent Black, 2001, pp. 74–110; Chatterji, The Spoils of Partition: Bengal and India: 1947–1967, Cambridge: Cambridge University Press, 2007. It is noteworthy that the archive of the preparation of the rolls does not contain direct representations from refugees in East Punjab or Sindh, two areas where refugees came from.

[89] The Election Commissioner of East Punjab informed the Deputy Commissioner that these refugees should not be registered again and that 'at the time of claims and objections it will be possible to solve [these] difficulties'. Fortnightly Report on the progress made and difficulties encountered in the preparation of electoral rolls, for the second fortnight of September 1948, from M. R. Bhide, Election Commissioner, East Punjab to the Joint Secretary, CAS, 16 October 1948, CA/1/FR/48-III, ECIR.

they would be resettled in East Punjab and would not be shifted to some other Province'.[90]

Struggles for a place in the roll were also driven by infringements in the actual registration of the refugees. Citizens' organisations reported in detail about the misconduct of specific local officials. Thus, the Tinsukia Bengali Association complained that although the Deputy Commissioner's directives specified that declarations were to be accepted on 4 September 1948 until 3 pm, the Sub Divisional Commissioner (SDC), who was authorised to receive declarations, stopped working at 1.15 pm. A few hundred refugees, 'including about a hundred ladies' were waiting to file declarations 'in the scorching sun for hours'.[91] In Hojai, wrote the Assam Citizens Association Nowgong, the Sub-Deputy Collector Kampur, who set to receive declarations on 24 September 1948 did not show up. As a result, '[a]bout 500 Refugees including females, who had come from distant villages ... had to go back disappointed'.[92]

When unexpected problems arose, citizens' organisations sometimes tried to negotiate with various local authorities to facilitate the refugees' registration. For example, in Lakhimpur on one occasion the Executive Engineer compelled the SDC to stop receiving refugees' declarations, fearing of the collapse of the building due to the large number of refugees who congregated in it. The Secretary of the Bengali Association Margherita then proposed that the SDC might accept declarations in the Assam Railways & Trading Co., or some schools 'in order to avoid a great risk of life'.[93] The SDC said he would agree if the Deputy Commissioner would direct him to do so. The Secretary of the Association then wrote

---

[90] Ibid.

[91] Letter from Tinsukia Bengali Association to the Deputy Commissioner Lakhimpur District, Assam, 4 September 1948, CA/9/FR/48, ECIR. They sent a copy of the letter to the Reforms Commissioner of Assam, the Premier of Assam, the CAS, as well as to four other citizens' organisations. Similar complaints about specific officers arrived, for example, from Gauhati, Hojai and Lakhimpur. See, respectively, Telegram from the Assam Citizens Association Gauhati to CAS, 6 September 1948; letter of the Assam Citizens Association Nowgong to the District Magistrate Nowgong, Assam, 30 September 1948; and letter from the Secretary of the Bengali Association Margherita to the Deputy Commissioner Lakhimpur, 20 September 1948, CA/9/FR/48, ECIR.

[92] Letter of the Assam Citizens Association Nowgong to the District Magistrate Nowgong, Assam, 30 September 1948, CA/9/FR/48, ECIR. They also reported that the Sub-Deputy Collector cancelled his scheduled programme to receive declarations at Lumding without notifying in advance. Instead, he asked the refugees to go to Hojai or to Kampur, which were 27 and 44 miles away respectively. The Association estimated at the time that there were about 25,000 refugees at Lumding, and 60,000 in Nowgong, out of which only 10,000 submitted declarations.

[93] Letter from the Secretary of the Bengali Association Margherita to the Deputy Commissioner Lakhimpur, 20 September 1948, CA/9/FR/48, ECIR.

to the Deputy Commissioner of the District with a request to direct the SDC accordingly.

In some cases, local authorities raised difficulties and refused to register refugees by devising ad hoc, sometimes capricious, procedures and definitions of a 'refugee'. Thus, for example, according to a complaint of the Assam Citizen Association Nowgong, in both Hojai and Dabeka, Assam, the Sub-Deputy Collector refused to receive the declaration forms from refugees because in his view, 'those who live under a shed cannot be called refugees, and that refugees were only those who had to live under the trees or on the road ... or in the station platforms'.[94] The Sub-Deputy Collector's other contentions were that the 'Government is not a charitable institution that it should maintain people from Eastern Pakistan' and 'that the Hindus from Eastern Pakistan have come here to convert Assam into a "BANGAKISTAN"'.[95] The Assam Citizen's Association Mangaldai, as another example, reported that the Sub-Deputy Collector 'refused to accept declaration of a female refugee ... aged 22 years (mother of 3 children), presented by her husband on 5.10.48, on the ground of non-production of horoscope in support of her age'.[96] They also reported that the Sub-Deputy Collector of Kalaigaon Circle 'rejected wholesale declarations of female refugees ... unless the females themselves appeared before him for his satisfactions as to the age of the declarants'.[97]

In the contestations over the refugees' place on the electoral roll, rivalling conceptions of membership in the nation surfaced. In Assam, for example, ethno nationalist attitudes manifested particularly towards the non-Assamese 'floating population', many of whom were Bengali speaking Hindus from East Pakistan. Local authorities expressed a view of membership in the state that was defined by a descent group and delimited to the 'children of the soil', who were eligible to have full rights.[98] Thus, ethno nationalist conceptions were not necessarily on the basis

---

[94] Letter of the Assam Citizens Association Nowgong to the District Magistrate Nowgong, Assam, 30 September 1948, CA/9/FR/48, ECIR.

[95] Ibid. (emphasis in original).

[96] Letter from the Assam Citizen's Association Mangaldai to CAS, 25 October 1948, CA/9/FR/48, ECIR.

[97] Ibid. They reported that this happened on 19 October 1948 at the Sub-Deputy Collector's camp centre at Tangla, and on 20 October 1948 at Kalaigaon.

[98] In Assam, as already mentioned, these attitudes were linked with anti-immigration policies that arose already in the 1920s, and that attained new life in the context of the influx of partition refugees. See n. 27 above. But there were similar attitudes elsewhere in India. For example, the Government of Travancore, as already mentioned, refused for a long time to register Tamils who resided in the State for many decades on the grounds that they were not subjects of Travancore.

of religion.[99] By contrast, in West Bengal, as far as the preparation of the preliminary roll was concerned, 'any person who would state that he has domicile in the Indian Union was to be straightaway included in the roll'.[100] At the same time, the notion of a unitary all-Indian citizenship across the forging new territory was not yet clearly understood. Indeed, some citizen organisations asked of the CAS to clarify whether people who had come to a province from other provinces of the Indian Dominion and had made their abode there were required to submit declaration for citizenship rights.[101]

In these struggles, citizens' organisations fought for and defended their future democratic franchise and citizenship rights with great passion. They debated and adopted the draft form of the constitution, particularly its articles on citizenship; they rehearsed its language, and sometimes even, albeit without legal basis, enacted its provisions. They inspected vigilantly their government's instructions for enrolment, compared them with those issued by the CAS and other governments and consciously strove to cultivate a 'good feeling amongst all citizens',[102] and a 'sense of civic duties'[103] among the people. In this process, a wide range of organisations entered into on-going discussions on democratic Indian citizenship with the CAS, as well as with their local authorities. They sought remedial actions from the CAS. In making the universal franchise, democratic citizenship became a subject of discussion, which administrators at various levels now had to contend with, and were consequently mentored into by the CAS.

Democratising Citizenship: Mentoring into an Electoral Democracy

Confronted with disparate exclusionary practices in the registration of the refugees on the ground, the Secretariat of the Constituent Assembly

---

[99] Different ethno-nationalist trends emerged, for example, in Delhi, where letters from various Gurdwaras (a Sikh's place of worship) complained that Sikhs were forcibly entered into the electoral rolls as Hindus. This is discussed in Chapter 6.

[100] Summary of discussions between Mr S. N. Mukherjee, Joint Secretary, Constituent Assembly of India and Mr M. A. T. Iyengar, Joint Secretary to the Government of West Bengal, Home Department, 14 September 1948, CA/9/FR/48, ECIR.

[101] See for example, letter from the Assam Prantiya Hindustani Sammelan Shillong to CAS, 27 September 1948, CA/9/FR/48, ECIR.

[102] Letter from the Assam Citizens' Association Mangaldai to CAS, 30 August 1948, CA/9/FR/48, ECIR. Also see, for example, 'Resolution adopted in the public meeting held in Digboi Indian Club at 5.30 p.m. on Monday, the 26th July 1948', Appendix 'A' in: letter from the Joint Secretary to the Government of India Ministry of Labour to the CAS, 16 November 1948, CA/12/FR/48, ECIR.

[103] 'Resolution No. 2', Assam Bengalee Association, in Internal discussions, CAS, 28 August 1948, CA/9/FR/48, ECIR.

became the principal guarantor of an inclusive conception of member-ship in the process of the making of the electoral roll. In the provisions the Secretariat devised, particularly for refugees, everyone was granted equal membership. Although these provisions were tentative, enacted in anticipation of the relevant laws, and were therefore liable to revision. The conception of citizenship and equality of membership that underlay the relaxed provisions for refugees' enrolment, on the basis of their mere declaration, went beyond traditional liberalism. It was a concept of mem-bership and equality that allowed for differential treatment in order to address the special situation of some prospective members of the nation, thus reflecting the values and common good intended by universal fran-chise. In this spirit, the CAS extended its activity to ensure the capability of the prospective citizens to become voters and legitimately authorise their government.

The staff of the CAS acted with accountability. They acknowledged the receipt of all letters and responded, often in great detail, to explain the procedures and the actions that were taken or that already took place. Before replying, they considered each and every letter.[104] They acted rap-idly to rectify faulty procedures. In doing so, they can be said to have mentored bureaucrats and the public in the institutional and procedural principles of an electoral democracy.

Thus, upon receiving information that the Government of West Bengal issued an order that declarations for citizenship should be made in the form of affidavits, the Secretariat sent forthwith an explanatory letter about their misconstrued instructions.[105] The Government of West Bengal issued an amendment to its order. While stating that 'such affi-davits are not necessary to establish any claim to citizenship at this stage and as such have no legal value' it, in effect, continued to facilitate the receipt of declarations for citizenship.[106] Indeed, the rest of the letter explained that 'District Magistrates and other Magistrates empowered to receive affidavits have, however, no option but to receive declarations if they are made in the manner of other affidavits'; and although these declarations have no value at present 'they may at best provide a means to the declarer of proving to others his intention regarding domicile'.[107]

---

[104] See Internal discussion, 13–28 August 1948, CA/9/FR/48, ECIR.
[105] Express letter from CAS to the Joint Secretary to the Government of West Bengal, 24 July 1948 CA/1/FR/48-II, ECIR.
[106] West Bengal Government Home Department, Memorandum No. 1103- A.R., 'Constitution and Elections: Preparation of Draft Electoral Rolls', 9 August 1948, CA/1/FR/48-II, ECIR.
[107] Ibid. In an additional follow-up letter the West Bengal Government even suggested that to 'minimise the work in offices and allow greater facility to persons desirous of mak-ing such declarations… Declarations may be made on ordinary paper, if accompanied

The CAS thereupon invited the Joint Secretary to the Government of West Bengal for discussions in Delhi, noting, that 'There is apparently a lot of confusion and misunderstanding on this point [declarations under article 5 of the Draft Constitution] and it is essential that we should explain our policy to you so that you can give clear instructions to the local officers.'[108] Subsequently, the Government of West Bengal cancelled and replaced its order, explaining that such declaration could not be made until auxiliary action is taken, and directed that 'Affidavits hitherto filled by persons ostensibly in terms of Explanation (ii) to article 5 (b) of the Draft Constitution [should be] returned to them free of charge whenever asked for.'[109]

In the face of the growing confusion between the declarations for the registration of refugees as voters and the declarations for acquiring citizenship, and attempts to enact the draft constitutional citizenship provisions, the CAS produced an explanatory reply note on the question of citizenship. It wrote to citizens' organisations, that the declaration under clause (ii) of the Explanation to article 5 of the Draft Constitution cannot be made until auxiliary action has been taken; that all persons who want to benefit from such declarations will get an opportunity to do so before the commencement of the Constitution and the revisions of the rolls; and that the declarations of domicile referred to in article 5 relate to the acquisition of the rights of citizenship of the Indian Union and are distinct from the declarations that refugees are required to make for getting themselves registered as voters in the Draft electoral rolls which were under preparation.[110] In

by a Treasury Challan showing payment of rupees two in lieu of Court Fee Stamps or they may be filed on non-judicial paper of the value of two rupees.' Letter from Joint Secretary to the Government of West Bengal to the Commissioner Presidency/Burdwan Division, 11 August 1948, CA/1/FR/48-II, ECIR. The West Bengal Government even set a procedure for the declarer to get a certificate of submission of the declaration, and for the District Magistrates to 'maintain an up-to date Register'. Ibid.

108 Letter from the Joint Secretary, CAS, to M. A. T. Iyengar, Joint Secretary to the Government of West Bengal Home Department (Constitution & Elections), 2 September 1948, CA/1/FR/48-II, ECIR.

109 West Bengal Government Home Department, Constitution and Elections, Memorandum No. 1513- A.R. 'Draft Electoral Rolls', 30 September 1948 (from M. M. Basu, Deputy Secretary to the Government of West Bengal to The Commissioner, Presidency/Burdwan Division), CA/1/FR/48-III, ECIR. These dynamics of events throw more light on Haimanti Roy's discussion on 'refugees or citizens', particularly as it was discussed in the press in July 1948. Haimanti Roy, *Partitioned Lives: Migrants, Refugees, Citizens in India and Pakistan*, New Delhi: Oxford University Press, 2012, pp. 14, 130–3.

110 See copy of a letter from CAS to the Secretary, Citizens' Union Shillong, 1 September 1948, CA/12/FR/48, ECIR. The letter mentioned that: 'These instructions will also apply to the residence of Assam who originally belonged to Sylhet and who are not refugees.' Ibid. Also see letter from CAS to Assam Refugees' Association, Nowgong, 2 September 1948, CA/12/FR/48, ECIR; letters from CAS to the East Bengal Displaced

practice, the CAS became the authority on the constitutional position of 'who is an Indian'.[111]

The CAS reacted swiftly and thoroughly to abuses of authority in relation to refugees' registration. It redressed problems that arose with local governments' directives and forms for the registration of the refugees, and indeed oversaw that corrective actions were taken. The CAS even summoned senior officials who breached or bent the CAS's instructions to Delhi for meetings.[112] These officials were given the opportunity to explain their actions. After the meeting, the CAS would issue minutes of these meetings with clarifications, corrections and adjustments that were mutually agreed upon. For example, at a meeting with the Reforms Commissioner of Assam, who was summoned following several complaints from citizens' organisations in Assam, he was asked to withdraw the court-fee charge he imposed on refugee declarations. He agreed to extend the deadline for the declarations of refugees to 31 October 1948 and to give due publicity to this extension. He also agreed that 'in the case of women it would be enough if their husbands or parents sign the declarations on their behalf', as suggested by the CAS and as was requested by numerous citizens' organisations on behalf of the women.[113] The CAS asked for a report on the actions agreed at their meeting.[114] Accordingly, within a fortnight the Reforms Commissioner of Assam

Lawyers' Association Calcutta; to the Servants of Bengal Society; and to the East Bengal Minority Welfare Central Committee, 20 September 1948; letters from CAS to the Assam Citizens' Associations Gauhati, Assam Citizens' Associations Mangaldai, Assam Citizens' Associations Nowgong, Assam Citizens' Associations Dhubri, Assam Citizens' Associations Goalpara and Assam Citizens' Associations Dibrugarh, 1 October 1948, CA/9/FR/48, ECIR. In their reply to the latter six organisations in Assam the CAS acknowledged the receipt of their letters and telegrams of 17 August 1948, 18 August 1948, 3 September 1948, 4 September 1948, 24 August 1948, 30 August 1948, 26 August 1948, 26 August 1948, 29 August 1948, 8 September 1948, 30 August 1948, 2 September 1948, 7 September 1948.

[111] Indeed, Government Ministries also sought the CAS's opinion in the wake of confusions over the declarations for citizenship. For example, letter from the Home Ministry to B. N. Rau, 2 September 1948, CA/9/FR/48, ECIR.

[112] In mid-September the CAS invited the Reforms Commissioner of Assam, the Election Commissioner of East Punjab and, as already mentioned, the Joint Secretary Home Department of West Bengal for discussions in Delhi.

[113] Summary of discussions between Mr S. N. Mukherjee, Joint Secretary, Constituent Assembly of India and Mr R. R. Khaund, Reforms Commissioner, Assam, 10 September 1948, CA/9/FR/48, ECIR. It was also agreed that persons whose domicile of origin was outside the Union territory but who have been long residing in Assam but were not refugees could be provisionally enrolled if they filed a statement to the effect that they intend to become citizens of India and in due course to deposit the requisite declarations under clause (ii) of the Explanation to article 5.

[114] Telegram from CAS to Reforms Commissioner of Assam, 20 September 1948, CA/9/FR/48, ECIR.

issued new revised instructions to all District Officers, and a new form for a refugee declaration.[115]

Similarly, the CAS criticised and qualified the West Bengal Government's 'Questions for the Guidance of Enumerators' procedure, which they subsequently revised.[116] Moreover, following the discussions held with the CAS at Delhi, the Government of West Bengal prepared a comprehensive seven-page note on what they understood 'to be correct procedure intended to be observed in the preparation of the Draft Electoral Rolls ... as well as on the implications of the distinction meant to be drawn between a citizen as defined in article 5 of the draft Constitution and a voter for the purpose of such elections'.[117] They asked for the CAS's opinion on the note, so that the enumerators and other supervision officers could be instructed 'on the proper lines'.[118]

The Government of the Central Provinces and Berar, as another example, wrote to the CAS saying that 'refugees living in Relief Camps should not be enrolled merely on the strength of their declaration. Their residence in Camps will not be compatible with their declaration indicating their intention to reside permanently in the locality to which the electoral roll relates.'[119] Following the CAS's reply the Government of the Central Provinces and Berar revised their instructions and directed their Deputy Commissioners to receive declarations from refugees in camps.[120]

[115] The revised instructions were issued on 23 September 1948 and on 24 September 1948, CA/9/FR/48-III, ECIR. The new form was issued in: letter from the Reforms Commissioner of Assam to All District Officers (including Superintendent, Lushai Hill), Sub-Divisional Officers and Political Officers of Frontier Tracts, 30 September 1948, CA/9/FR/48-III, ECIR. The new declaration form provided for the declarant to make a declaration on behalf of himself/his wife/his daughter. It no longer contained information on the place in Pakistan the refugee arrived from. See nn. 76–7 above. Moreover, at the beginning of November 1948 the Reforms Commissioner of Assam reported to the CAS that he gave the 'widest possible publicity' to the extension of time for refugees' registration to the instructions for filing their declarations. Fortnightly report in connection with the preparation of electoral rolls under the new Constitution, from the Reforms Commissioner of Assam to the Joint Secretary, Constituent Assembly of India, 2 November 1948, CA/1/FR/48-IV, ECIR.
[116] Summary of discussions between Mr S. N. Mukherjee, Joint Secretary, Constituent Assembly of India and Mr M. A. T. Iyengar, Joint Secretary to the Government of West Bengal, Home Department, 14 September 1948, CA/9/FR/48, ECIR.
[117] Letter from M. M. Basu, Deputy Secretary to the Government of West Bengal Secretariat Home Department to Joint Secretary CAS, 28 September 1948, CA/1/FR/48-III. A seven-page note was attached to the letter.
[118] Ibid. This was ahead of enumeration in the area of Calcutta.
[119] Letter from the Secretary to Government of Central Provinces and Berar to CAS, 13 September 1948, CA/1/FR/48, ECIR. They noted that refugees who have settles in towns should however be enrolled.
[120] Memorandum 737/XVIII, 'Enrolment of refugees as voters in the electoral rolls', from the T. C. Shrivasta, Deputy Secretary to Government of Central Provinces and Berar, Legislative Department to the Deputy Commissioner, Jubbulpore, Raipur, Bilaspur Saugor, Bhandara, 25 November 1948, CA/1/FR/48-IV, ECIR.

The Government of Madras instructed its officials to exclude from enrolment those refugees who have migrated from Hyderabad, because, in their view, 'the Hyderabad deadlock cannot last long and the refugees will return to their normal places of residence in that State before long'.[121] The CAS asked the Government of Madras to register the refugees from Hyderabad State, explaining that they 'apparently come under the definition of the term "refugees" which we have adopted for the purpose of registration of refugees in the electoral rolls. We do not know when they will be able to return to their places in the State. We can therefore hardly exclude them at this stage from the preliminary electoral rolls under preparation.'[122]

Finally, the CAS also made inquiries into complaints about specific incidents of abuse in the registration of the refugees. It thus asked the Reforms Commissioner of Assam to account for such occurrences, for example when Sub-Deputy Collectors did not show up according to the published schedule to register refugees.[123] The Reforms Commissioner investigated the complaints with his District Officers, Deputy Commissioners and Sub-Deputy Collectors. He sent a detailed report to the CAS, and assured them that remedial actions were taken.[124]

---

[121] S. no. 24, 3 September 1948, CA/1/FR/48, ECIR.

[122] Letter from CAS to the Additional Secretary to the Government of Madras, 13 September 1948, CA/1/FR/48, ECIR. The CAS suggested that 'instructions should accordingly be issued to the registering authorities to put a distinguishing mark against the name of all persons who are registered ... as "refugees" to enable the residential and citizenship qualifications of such persons to be verified at a later stage'. Ibid.

[123] See nn. 87–9 above.

[124] Letter from the Reforms Commissioner Assam to the CAS, 4 November 1948, and letter dated 10 November 1948, CA/9/FR/48, ECIR. In the matter of the complaints of the Bengali Association Tinsukia, the Reforms Commissioner wrote to the CAS that 'the Government [of Assam] do not think that there were reasonable grounds for making these allegations against the Sub-Deputy Collector'. He attached a copy of a memo prepared by the Deputy Commissioner Lakhimpur dated 28 October 1948, claiming that the allegations made by the organisation 'misrepresented the whole facts'. Letter from the Reforms Commissioner Assam to the CAS, 4 November 1948, CA/9/FR/48, ECIR. Upon inquiry with the Deputy Commissioner Nowgong, the Reforms Commissioner of Assam wrote to the Secretariat that the 'changes in the programme made were due to unavoidable reasons and there is now no reason for complaint as stated by the Deputy Commissioner. The Government do not think that any further action is necessary in the matter and observe that the figures of refugees given are highly exaggerated.' The letter of the Deputy Commissioner Nowgong stated: 'It is a fact that due to sudden out-break of Cholera in certain areas of the district the programme which was drawn up by the sub-deputy collectors for the month of September 1948 had to be changed in a few centres. But as the time for filing declarations was extended ... a fresh programme was drawn up opening 19 different centres in the district fixing dates and hours'. See letter from the Reforms Commissioner of Assam to the CAS, 10 November 1948 (referring to their letter of 13 October 1948, CA/9/FR/48, ECIR).

The CAS also made the public aware of their activities. On 25 September 1948 the CAS published a detailed explanatory press note that clarified for the sake of 'ensuring uniformity' the definition of a 'refugee' and their registration.[125] The press note explained the distinction between the declaration for the purpose of citizenship under article 5 in the draft Constitution, which awaited auxiliary legislation and could therefore not yet be made, and the registration as voter. It also referred to the misleading orders of the West Bengal and Assam Governments, and emphasised that it was never intended that a fee should be imposed on refugee registration, and that these orders were therefore withdrawn. Thereafter, the CAS sent a batch of detailed response letters to the numerous citizens' organisations that awaited a reply, answering their queries, and informing them about the decisions that were taken in the wake of their inquiries and complaints.[126]

Henceforth, the CAS regularly asked provincial authorities to respond to written inquiries from citizens' organisations. It forwarded these letters to local authorities with a proposed draft reply, and asked to be endorsed with a copy. In doing so, the Secretariat delegated authority to provincial officials and strengthened their competence; it also created a mechanism for overseeing their activities while endeavouring to achieve as much uniformity in the implementation of the procedures for the preparation of the rolls as possible. The CAS did not simply issue orders. Instead, it tended to offer advice. Thus, for example, when asking the Government of Bihar to reply to a letter from the Committee for Acquiring Indian Citizenship, Jamshedpur, the CAS wrote: 'the Committee may also be told that...'[127] Provincial governments often copied the CAS's proposed draft reply in their responses.

Moreover, the all-inclusive practices and conception of membership that the CAS developed around the registration of refugees in the preliminary electoral roll offered an alternative discourse to the ethno nationalist political language, and institutional practices and policies that were also being enforced in relation to refugees at that time beyond the process of roll making. Among these ordinances were, for example, the permit system (Permit Ordinances, 14 July 1948), the Influx from West Pakistan Control Act from 19 July 1948. Additional policies were, for example, the evacuee property laws.[128] The political vocabulary of

---

[125] Press Note 25 September 1948, CA/1/FR/48 1948-V, ECIR.
[126] See n. 110 above.
[127] Letter from CAS to the Government of Bihar Appointment Department Reforms and Election Branch, 7 October 1948, CA/9/FR/48, ECIR.
[128] See Zamindar, *The Long Partition and the Making of Modern South Asia*, pp. 126–40; Joya Chatterji, 'South Asian Histories of Citizenship, 1946–1970', *The Historical Journal* 55,

these exclusionary ordinances and policies distinguished between a displaced person, an evacuee and an intending evacuee, by implication creating categories of 'good' and 'bad' refugees.[129] In contrast, in the enrolment process all were simply 'refugees' on the basis of a uniform definition.

Notwithstanding the CAS's inclusionary efforts, clarifying press notes, substantial correspondence with citizens' organisations, and its remedial measures, struggles for citizenship and a place in the roll, and infringements in the registration of the refugees did occur. In some cases, the initial instructions of provincial governments continued to be used on the ground, despite having been revoked and replaced with new orders. Revised instructions sometimes took time to trickle down.[130] The CAS continued to look into directives issued in the provinces and the states, which citizens' organisations reported on. It asked of administrators for clarifications and corrective actions.[131] The CAS's supervision through repeated correspondences with local authorities did not always yield immediate success. Yet this on-going dialogical process between the CAS, administrators at the local level, and the prospective citizen-electorate became a key factor in instituting democratic citizenship and stimulated a process of building electoral democracy.

4, 2012, pp. 1049–71; Roy, *Partitioned Lives*; Antara Datta, *Refugees and Borders in South Asia: The Great Exodus of 1971*, London: Routledge, 2013, pp. 49–56. Many of these ordinances resulted in the dispossession of masses of India's Muslim population.

[129] See Chatterji, 'Right or Charity? The Debate over Relief and Rehabilitation in West Bengal, 1947–50', p. 82. Also see Roy, *Partitioned Lives*, p. 195.

[130] Thus, for example, the Reforms Commissioner of Assam's circular of May 1948, which instructed enumerators to exclude from the roll the 'floating and "non-resident" population', attained a new lease of life and triggered renewed protests from October 1948 onward when both citizens' organisations and local officials interpreted it as an intention to exclude the labour from the voters list. See letter from the Assam Citizens' Association Digboi to the Labour Minister, 6 October 1948, CA/12/FR/48, ECIR. Also see letter from the Assam Prantiya Hindustani Sammelan Shillong to CAS, 27 September 1948; letter from the Assam Citizens' Association Gauhati to Rajendra Prasad, 3 September 1948; letter from Joint Secretary to the Government of India Ministry of Labour to the CAS, 16 November 1948, CA/12/FR/48, ECIR.

[131] The CAS, for example, asked the Reforms Commissioner of Assam to clarify his 'floating and "non-resident"' population category. Letter from CAS to the Reforms Commissioner of Assam, 22 October 1948, CA/12/FR/48, ECIR. The Reforms Commissioner argued that he was merely working within his interpretation of the rules at the time (May 1948). He explained that these instructions were issued 'when the question of "refugees" being given special treatment was not considered by this Government. The term "floating population" seemed at the time to apply to persons of this category, but as they have since been treated as "refugees" …

Citizens' organisations continued writing to the CAS in pursuit of their place on the electoral roll. As the deadline for submitting refugee declarations approached, various citizens' organisations in Assam asked to extend it to 31 December 1948 from 31 October 1948.[132] They blamed their local government for the failure of many refugees to file declarations on time, claiming that:

owing to the shortage of Officers competent to receive such declarations it was not possible to carry on work simultaneously in several centres... Besides these, a great confusion has been created in the public mind due to very frequent changes introduced by the Government from time to time, in the form and method of declaration – a confusion which is rather difficult to remove... If this is not done a large number of refugees in the interior of the District are bound to remain unenlisted [sic] for no fault of theirs.[133]

In support of their case, citizens' organisations sent lists of houses and homesteads that were not numbered and left out of enumeration in both towns and villages.[134]

---

they do not now fall within the term'. Letter from the Reforms Commissioner of Assam to CAS, 5 November 1948, CA/12/FR/48, ECIR. Earlier in October when the renewed complaints arose, he wrote to the relevant Deputy Commissioner, clarifying that: 'Labourers working in the Tea gardens ... could by no stretch of imagination be said to be "non-resident" or "floating population"'. Copy of a letter from the Reforms Commissioner of Assam to the Deputy Commissioner Lakhimpur Dibrugarh (in charge of Digboi), 13 October 1948, CA/12/FR/48, ECIR. The Reforms Commissioner of Assam attached it to his letter to CAS. Nonetheless, the Reforms Commissioner of Assam continued directing officers that were authorised to receive refugees' declaration to 'exercise the greatest care before passing orders for inclusion of refugees in Electoral Rolls'. Letter from The Reforms Commissioner of Assam to All District Officers (including Superintendent, Lushai Hills), Political Officers of Frontier Tracts and Sub-divisional Officers, 'Registration of names of refugees in electoral rolls', 4 November 1948, CA/1/FR/48-IV, ECIR.

132 For example, letter from the Assam Citizen's Association Mangaldai to CAS, 25 October 1948, CA/9/FR/48, ECIR. The Assam Citizens' Associations Gauhati and the Assam Bengali Association sent similar requests. The CAS forwarded these letters for disposal to the Government of Assam. Also see letter from Sapatgram Citizens' Association to the President of the Constituent Assembly, 17 September 1948; letter from the Assam Citizens Association Nowgong to the Reforms Commissioner of Assam, 26 October 1948; letter from the Assam Citizen Association Barpeta to the Reforms Commissioner of Assam, 29 October 1948, CA/9/FR/48, ECIR. They copied the letters to the CAS.

133 Letter from the Congress East Bengal Minority Rehabilitation & Citizenship-right Committee Silchar-Cachar to the Reforms Commissioner Assam, 23 October 1948, CA/9/FR/48, ECIR. They also suggested that inadequate publicity and lack of transport facilities stood in the way of the work.

134 See letter from the Assam Citizens' Association Mangaldai to CAS, 25 October 1948; letter from the Assam Citizen Association Barpeta to the Reforms Commissioner Assam, 29 October 1948, CA/9/FR/48, ECIR. The latter organisation reported that 'in villages, enumerators are only registering the names of the head-man of the family excluding all other adult member whether male or female, entitled to vote' and that

Conclusion

Citizens' organisations articulated a range of arguments, including constitutional ones, in their pursuit of securing citizenship and franchise rights for refugees. The set of instructions for the relaxation of the residential qualification for the refugees, on the one hand, and the subsequent directives that some provincial governments issued, based on their interpretation of the CAS's instructions, on the other hand, fed into the struggles over citizenship. In conducting these struggles, numerous citizens' organisations followed closely the CAS's and local governments' instructions, press notes, and gazette reports. They monitored the directives and actions of their local government, paying attention to small details, and were quick to demand remedies when they thought their rights or the CAS's instructions were infringed. Significantly, these citizens' organisations were aware of each other, and made continuous efforts to coordinate their resolutions and actions. They compared notes, sent copies of their letters to the CAS to other citizens' organisations and sought affiliation with one another.[135] As already mentioned, sometimes the content of a letter from one citizen organisation was repeated verbatim by another. The efforts to liaise and work together meant that struggles for citizenship were persistent and not simply sporadic initiatives. In doing so, people engaged in overseeing the way they were governed.

Thus, while the citizenship article at that time was discussed behind the closed door of the Constitution Drafting Committee and the Special Committee, citizenship was also made and contested on the ground.[136] The dynamics of struggles around roll making had, in effect, established temporal citizenship. As the illustrations above suggest, people expressed growing and passionate interest in their franchise and citizenship rights. As part of collectives they debated their future citizenship, but essentially already acted as engaged citizens. The responsiveness of the CAS in

'enumerators exclude "those who came to Assam after January 1938", and are either living with others or in their own houses'. The organisation also pointed that although the number of immigrant settlers is very large, 'still no immigrant enumerator has been appointed in this Sub Division. This looked unfair and raised doubt in the minds of many about proper enumeration. This may kindly be enquired into.' *Ibid.*

[135] See n. 62 above.
[136] These Constituent Assembly Committees discussed comments and suggestions on the draft article on citizenship, and worked on its redrafting while the Draft Constitution of February 1948 was under review until a reprint with amendments was published in October 1948.

dealing with the problem of the registration of the refugees empowered them to do so.

Finding a solution for the registration of the refugees on an all-India basis was a first test to the making of the universal franchise. The absence of legal precedents in relation to the 'minute question' of refugees' residential qualifications for the purpose of election rendered significant the need for a creative yet principled approach. The way the Secretariat solved problems under conditions of great uncertainty, against the backdrop of a draft constitution and in the absence of even a draft election law exhibited flexibility, but it was not ad-hoc or arbitrary. They were continuously in pursuit of precedents or ensured to set new ones. They drafted templates of principled and detailed explanatory answers to queries from local governments and citizens' organisations, which were based on the draft Constitution. Thus, even before the enactment of the constitution, the Secretariat demonstrated through their daily practices the value and meaning of the constitution, and the potential quality of democratic power. Indeed, people at the margins – like the refugees – successfully made claims of the state, and were taken into account. The CAS also strengthened provincial authority by mentoring administrators and delegating responsibility.

It was in dealing with citizens' organisations and their struggles for citizenship and franchise that the CAS fostered what S. Radhakrishnan referred to a decade earlier as electoral democracy's 'habit of mind'.[137] Not merely the form of democracy, but its spirit. This was not simply a result of the CAS's impressive responsiveness to citizens' organisations' letters. It was rather related to the terms and style of engagement, which the CAS developed. For a start, the CAS took seriously citizens' organisations grievances, queries, and suggestions. Indeed, some of its decisions in redressing problems were aligned with proposals that organisations put forward. Moreover, the CAS was authentic and transparent in their correspondences, repeating, sometimes word for word, their internal notes or content of letters they sent to provincial authorities. The internal office notes, the official letters to provincial and state authorities, and replies to letters from the public were entirely consistent and based on identical wording. These correspondences formed the

---

[137] S. Radhakrishnan, 'Democracy: A Habit of the Mind' (Presidential Address at the Annual Session of Andhra Mahasabha, Madras, September 1938) in *Education, Politics and War*, Poona: The International Book Service, 1944, p. 16.

beginning of democratic dialogues between people and the CAS. The principles and practices that the CAS developed and instilled in administering the first steps of making the universal franchise, particularly the way it tackled the question of the refugees' registration, contributed to institutionalising electoral democracy in India from its inception. For the universal franchise to become a meaningful political order and a political reality, however, it also had to enter the political imagination of Indians.

3   The Roll as 'Serialised Epic' and the Personalisation of the Universal Franchise

Once understood in the context of the narratives that give it meaning, law becomes not merely a system of rules to be observed, but a world in which we live.[1]

(Robert M. Cover, 'Nomos and Narrative')

The people exist as a narrative, a collection of stories, rather than a fixed voting bloc.[2]

(Pierre Rosanvallon, *Democratic Legitimacy.*
Impartiality, Reflexivity, Proximity)

...Will you tell the postman it's Amal who sits by the window here?

What's the good of that?

In case there's a letter for me.

A letter for you! Whoever's going to write to you?

If the King does.[3]

(Rabindranath Tagore, *The Post Office (Daak Ghar)*)

The design of the instructions for the preparation of electoral rolls on the basis of universal franchise began cultivating among administrators the democratic dispositions and imagination that was needed in order to build the institutional infrastructure for the notion of procedural equality in relation to electoral voting. The struggles for citizenship that arose in the context of the registration of partition refugees as voters, and the way the challenge of their enrolment was resolved triggered the beginnings of democratic dialogues between people and the Constituent Assembly Secretariat (CAS). These struggles became a driving force in the dem-ocratisation of the popular political imagination. But it would not have

---

[1] Robert M., Cover, 'Foreword: Nomos and Narrative in the Supreme Court, 1982 Term', *Harvard Law Review* 97, no.1, 1983, pp. 4–5.
[2] Pierre Rosanvallon, *Democratic Legitimacy. Impartiality, Reflexivity, Proximity.* Translated by Arthur Goldhammer. Princeton: Princeton University Press, 2011, p. 70.
[3] Rabindranath Tagore, *The Post Office (Daak Ghar).* Translated by Devabrata Mukerjea. 1914.

sufficed for a democratic vision based on adult franchise to become embedded merely in the institution of electoral democracy. It needed to become a meaningful political order in which ordinary Indians would believe and to which they would become committed. As we already saw in the previous chapter, while people struggled for a place in the roll, they sometimes also expressed suspicion about the registration process and the government's intentions. How, then, did the principle and institution of universal franchise attain meaning and enter the political imagination of Indians?

This chapter suggests that it was the way in which the preparation of the first electoral roll on the basis of adult franchise became part of popular narratives that played an essential role in connecting people to a popular democratic political imagination. In pursuing this proposition, I draw on Robert Cover's contention that 'No set of legal institutions or prescriptions exist apart from the narratives that locate it and give it meaning.'[4] Cover argued that 'Once understood in the context of the narratives that give it meaning, law becomes not merely a system of rules to be observed, but a world in which we live.'[5] Thus, the rules and institutions that would constitute the normative universe ('nomos') of universal franchise would not be sufficient for people to truly inhabit it. This normative world is also composed of the stories individuals make of it for themselves. This chapter explores this process of the concretisation and personalisation of the universal franchise. It examines narratives of how the preparation of rolls and adult franchise came to be, and how Indians began to own the principle of adult franchise, and to conceive of themselves as the protagonists of the story.[6]

The indispensability of narrative as a way of shaping our understanding of the world is a cornerstone of works in literary theory.[7] The notion that norms, institutions, and law have no substance other than their meaning

---

[4] Robert M. Cover, 'Forward: Nomos and Narrative' in 'The Supreme Court, 1982 Term', *Harvard Law Review* 97, no.1, November 1983, p. 4.

[5] Ibid., pp. 4–5.

[6] Cover argued that the 'objectification of the norms to which one is committed frequently, perhaps always, entails a narrative – a story of how the law, now object, came to be, and more importantly, how it came to be one's own'. Ibid., p. 45.

[7] For a comprehensive discussion of fundamental debates about the value and nature of narrative see 'On Narrative', *Critical Inquiry* 7, no. 1, 1980, particularly: W. J. T. Mitchell, 'Editor's Note: On Narrative', *Critical Inquiry* 7, no. 1, 1980, pp. 1–4; Hayden White, 'The Value of Narrativity in Representation of Reality', *Critical Inquiry* 7, no. 1, 1980, pp. 5–27. Also see Peter Boxall, *The Value of the Novel*, Cambridge: Cambridge University Press, 2015. Frank Kermode, *The Sense of an Ending: Studies in the Theory of Fiction (The Mary Flexner Lectures, 1965)*, Oxford: Oxford University Press, 1967; Marco Caracciolo, *The Experientiality of Narrative*, Berlin: De Gruyter, 2014; Genese Grill, *The*

within a particular narrative logic is suggestive of Ken Hirschkop's inspiring work on *Mikhail Bakhtin: An Aesthetic for Democracy*.[8] In his discussion of narrative and the constitution of the self, Hirschkop argued that for Bakhtin 'narratives have to embody "becoming" not in order to represent an external history, but to make possible an inner one'.[9] This chapter aims to shed light on the way in which narratives of the preparation of the electoral roll made imaginable and personal the definitive historical transformation that the universal franchise wrought. To do so, the chapter studies key press notes, newspaper coverage and a range of letters on the preparation of the rolls that Indians and some social and political organisations sent to the CAS. The chapter focuses on narratives that preceded the motion on the preparation of electoral roll in the Constituent Assembly.[10] As well as gripping Indians' political imagination, these narratives grounded the constitutional principle of adult franchise, making it a convention ahead of the enactment of the constitution.

The 15 March 1948 letter of instructions of the CAS for the preparation of the draft electoral rolls became a common bureaucratic ground for the making of the universal franchise.[11] Once the preparatory work started and questions about it arose, the instructions letter became a basis for a press note on the 'preparation of electoral rolls under the new Constitution', which the Secretariat composed in a form of a narrative-story, recognising the need to share their actions with the public. As we saw in Chapter 2, the Secretariat continuously communicated with various social and political organisations and with administrators across the country over difficulties that emerged in the preparation of the rolls. The CAS's press notes opened a channel of communication with the public at large.

World as Metaphor in Robert Musil's The Man Without Qualities: *Possibility as Reality*, New York: Camden House, 2012.

[8] Ken Hirschkop, *Mikhail Bakhtin: An Aesthetic for Democracy*, Oxford: Oxford University Press, 1999 (2011 online). Also see Peter Boxall's discussion on the value of the novel as such that allows us 'to form pictures of bodies living collectively in spaces under the authority of the law'. Boxall, *The Value of the Novel*, p. 143.

[9] Hirschkop, *Mikhail Bakhtin: An Aesthetic for Democracy*, p. 229. Hirschkop's discussion is built on Bakhtin's suggestion (in 'Epic and Novel', 1941) that the novel 'is the only genre which is in a state of becoming' and 'reflects the becoming of actuality itself', ibid. p. 12.

[10] Accordingly, my discussion of narratives of the preparation of the rolls and of correspondences about it does not go beyond 8 January 1949, when the motion on the preparation of electoral rolls was moved in the Constituent Assembly, ten months after the work began.

[11] Indeed, all fortnightly reports on the preparation of the roll began: 'with reference to your letter of 15 March, 1948 I have the honour to say that'.

Moreover, the CAS in its press notes fashioned a bureaucratic narrative genre, which spoke directly to the people. The CAS described in a sequential order the preparation of the rolls, and conveyed the thoughts and intentions that underlay its actions. As it said in their first press note, it was 'giving full publicity in order to educate the public on the subject'.[12] In the same way that an 'intimate address allows the novel to conjure a uniquely vivid experience of presence',[13] the CAS's story of the preparation of the rolls allowed people to imagine and make a picture of the world adult franchise would shape. Stories about the preparation of rolls appeared regularly in the press. The reporting in the press also expanded the channels of communication with the public, lending visibility to the Secretariat's work. It is noteworthy that high rates of illiteracy at the time did not necessarily preclude public access to these modes of communication thanks to a widespread custom of 'listening' to newspapers in public readings. As some works on the practices and the culture of reading in India have suggested, at that time and even today, daily newspapers are customarily kept in, for example, teashops, both in rural and urban areas, and are often read out aloud.[14] Thus, even illiterate people 'were getting news through papers read to them'.[15] Moreover, although the CAS composed and published its press notes exclusively in English, these materials also reappeared in vernacular languages.[16]

---

[12] Press Note, 'Electoral Rolls Under the New Constitution', 15 July 1948, CA/1/FR/48-V. Also see in CA/1/FR/48-III, ECIR.

[13] Boxall, *The Value of the Novel*, 12.

[14] A. R. Venkatachalapathy, 'Reading Practices and Modes of Reading in Colonial Tamil Nadu', *Studies in History* 10, no. 2, 1994, p. 290. Venkatachalapathy's important work focuses on the popular consumption of literature in Tamil Nadu. It relates in particular to the *Dina Thanthi*, a Tamil daily newspaper founded in 1942. Robin Jeffrey describes in his work on newspapers how 'People in offices, or even agricultural labourers, will congregate around a communal newspapers in their free time.' Robin Jeffrey, 'Culture of Daily Newspapers in India: How it's Grown, What it Means?' *Economic and Political Weekly* 22, no. 14, 1987, p. 608. Francis Cody's recent study further supports these works. Moreover, Cody shows that the newspaper even 'acts as a spark of conversation without prompting explicit reference back to the paper itself' and has argued that 'To read the paper is to talk about the news'. Francis Cody, 'Daily Wires and Daily Blossoms: Cultivating Regimes of Circulation in Tamil India's Newspaper Revolution', *Journal of Linguistic Anthropology*, Vol. 19, Issue 2, 2009, p. 290.

[15] K. E. Eapen, 'Daily Newspapers in India: Their Status and Problems', *Journalism Quarterly* XLIV (1967), p. 523.

[16] From time to time the CAS received translations of newspapers articles in vernacular languages. For example: A summarised translation of an article from the *Kesari*, the Marathi bi-weekly, 27 July 1948, sent from Secretary to the Government of Bombay Home Department to CAS, 11 August 1948, CA/12/FR/48, ECIR. Provincial governments sometimes mentioned in their letters that they published press notes in the vernacular language. Certainly the instructions for the preparation of rolls were published in the provinces and the states both in English and in the vernaculars. In a letter of 31 July 1948, CA/1/FR/48-II, the CAS asked of the provinces and the states to sent

The preparation of rolls generated a kind of narrative that communicated substantially, and therefore convincingly, India's movement to becoming a democracy. Accounts about the actualisation of the universal franchise – the registration of voters – connected with the lives of ordinary Indians. The persons described in the press notes and the press were like them; and the narratives did not simply represent the order of actions of making adult franchise, but also implied its meaning. In this sense, the dynamics of narrations by the CAS and in the press had the effect of turning the story of the preparation of the rolls into an epic, which, in turn, stimulated the engagement of people and various organisations with the making of adult franchise.[17] Storytelling the preparation of the electoral roll not only made it more meaningful and conceivable to India's would-be citizens who individually experienced its making, it also gave rise to a collective passion for democracy, thus contributing to the democratisation of feelings and imagination.

The first section discusses the way in which the CAS's narration of the preparation of electoral roll through its key press notes had a storytelling effect. The second part shows how the reporting in the press turned the story of the making of the roll into a series of episodes, or a prolonged episodic narrative, which generated discussions of and interest in the meaning of the right to vote and democratic citizenship. This process deepened as people began to incorporate the story of the preparation of rolls into their personal lives and to show a growing interest and commitment to it. The contents of letters that people and social and political organisations wrote to the CAS evidenced this. The third section discusses this correspondence.

Press Notes: Narrating the Preparation of the Electoral Roll

It was at the beginning of the CAS's discussions of the question of the enrolment of the refugees in early June 1948, that a member of the Secretariat suggested the issuing of a press note 'to allay the fears of

---

copies of the instructions that they issued in English for the preparation of draft electoral rolls. Moreover, it has been shown that materials from English newspapers 'reappeared in some forms in the vernaculars and in the traditional idiom which allowed otherwise alien ideas to attract a broader response'. See Milton Israel, *Communications and Power: Propaganda and the Press in the Indian Nationalist Struggle, 1920–1947*, Cambridge: Cambridge University Press, 1994, p. 21. Also see Gyanendra Pandey, 'Mobilization in a Mass Movement: Congress "Propaganda" in the United Provinces (India) 1930–1934, *Modern Asian Studies* 9, no. 2, 1975, pp. 205–26.

[17] This is suggestive of Boxall's suggestion that 'It is the novel that allowed us to narrate to ourselves the passage of modern democracy.' Boxall, *The Value of the Novel*, p. 11.

the refugees in general and to clarify the position, after final decision has been taken in the matter'.[18] A fortnight later the need for a press note came up again when members of the CAS reviewed an editorial in *Amrita Bazar Patrika*, a newspaper, which stated that if the report about the preparation of electoral rolls is true, 'the Governments concerned owe it to themselves and to the public to take the latter into their confidence and publish the rules and directives which may have been or may be addressed to their officers'.[19] The discussion note mentioned that 'a detailed note has recently been put up to J.S. [joint secretary]' and that '[i]t has also been contended that the rules etc. on the basis of which the provincial governments are preparing the preliminary rolls may also be given in the Press for the information of the public'.[20]

On 8 July 1948 a draft press note regarding the preparation of electoral rolls was placed before the Joint Secretary of the CAS for approval. The drafters commented that 'the note reproduces, almost in full the general instructions which have been issued to the Provincial and State Governments. A new para relating to the position of refugees has been added and a summary is given of the work so far done by Provinces and States.'[21] At the bottom of a series of comments on the draft press note, the Constitutional Advisor, B. N. Rau commented that this is 'a useful summary. I have revised slightly in places. H.P. [Rajendra Prasad] should see before the press note issued.'[22]

Upon its approval, the CAS sent one hundred copies of the five-page press note, 'Electoral Rolls under the new Constitution', to the Press Information Bureau of the Government of India 'for immediate release'. It requested that 'in view of the importance of the subject-matter... we are anxious that it should receive the widest possible publicity throughout India and we shall therefore be grateful if you will kindly make

[18] Internal discussions, 3 June 1948, CA/9/FR/48, ECIR.
[19] 'Confusing and Anomalous', *Amrita Bazar Patrika*, 7 June 1948, CA/12/FR/48, ECIR (in Internal note, 17 June 1948, CA/12/FR/48, ECIR. From time to time the CAS received and discussed newspaper reports related to the preparation of the electoral rolls from the Public Information Bureau. See, for example, a series of two long articles on 'Method of Voting', *Harijan*, 25 April 1948, pp. 74–5, and 2 May 1948, pp. 85–6, CA/12/FR/48, ECIR.
[20] Internal note, 17 June 1948, CA/12/FR/48, ECIR.
[21] Internal note, 8 July 1948, CA/12/FR/48, ECIR.
[22] Internal note (by B. N. Rau), 12 July 1948, CA/12/FR/48, ECIR. 'We are proposing', the CAS wrote to Prasad, 'to issue a detailed press communiqué regarding the preliminary work on the electoral rolls which we have undertaken. We have added a paragraph specifically dealing with the question of refugees, which, it is hoped, would allay some of the apprehension which have been expressed on their behalf.' Internal note (by the Under Secretary K. V. Padmanabhan), 13 July 1948, CA/9/FR/48, ECIR.

arrangements accordingly'.[23] The CAS also sent copies directly to election and reform commissioners across India.

The press note, as its drafters commented, reproduced 'almost in full' the 15 March 1948 instructions letter for the preparation of electoral rolls that the CAS issued to the Provincial and State Governments.[24] But what was written originally as general instructions, as a common bureaucratic ground for the preparation of electoral rolls on the basis of adult franchise was now redrafted and presented as a kind of storytelling, narrating the preparation of the rolls from its beginning, as reproduced here.

Constituent Assembly of India

Press Note

Electoral Rolls under the New Constitution

The Secretariat of the Constituent Assembly has received from time to time enquiries regarding the preparation of electoral rolls under the new Constitution and there have also been references in the press to the same subject. In order to remove any misapprehensions that may exist in the minds of the public on the matter, it has been considered useful to issue the following Press Note:

Recognising the need for holding fresh general elections as early as possible after the new Constitution comes into force, the Constituent Assembly Secretariat first addressed the Provincial and States Governments on the subject in November last. Subsequently, in March, certain general instructions for the preparation of the electoral rolls were issued to these Governments, allowing for local variations by the Governments concerned where necessary.

The Draft Constitution provides that elections to the Lower House of the Central and Provincial Legislatures should be held on the basis of adult suffrage. The age limit is fixed in birth cases at 21, and every citizen who is not otherwise disqualified under the new Constitution or under any law made by the Central or Provincial Legislature on the ground of non-residence, unsoundness of mind, crime or corrupt practice, is entitled to be registered as a voter. It is assumed that the new electoral law in respect to these disqualifications will not be materially different from the existing provisions.

As a preliminary step the Government of each Province or State has been asked to issue executive instructions to District Officers and other appropriate authorities to prepare draft electoral rolls for each village or other electoral unit. These instructions will prescribe January 1, 1949, as the date with reference to

---

[23] Letter from CAS (Under Secretary) to V. R. Bhatt, Deputy Principal Information Officer, Press Information Bureau, Government of India, 15 July 1948, CA/12/FR/ 48, ECIR.

[24] Internal note, 8 July 1948, CA/12/FR/48, ECIR.

which the electoral rolls are to be prepared. For instance, the age of the electors will be calculated with reference to that date.

Under the new Constitution, there will be no separate electorates for the different communities; but seats will be reserved in certain constituencies for Muslims, the Scheduled Castes, most of the Scheduled Tribes, and in Madras and Bombay for Indian Christians as well. It will thus be seen that one composite roll for all communities will suffice. As, however, it will be necessary to determine whether a candidate for a reserved seat is a voter belonging to the particular community for which the seat is reserved, a column has been inserted in the form of the electoral roll for recording this information.

As already mentioned, the electoral rolls are to be prepared by villages or other convenient units. When ultimately constituencies are delimited whether for Central or Provincial or State elections, a number of these unitary rolls will form the electoral roll for each constituency. The constituencies for Provincial or State elections will of course be smaller than for Central elections and will, therefore, comprise a smaller number of the component units; but since the qualifications and disqualifications for the franchise are likely to be the same, the same unitary rolls, though in different combinations, can be utilised for all elections.

The electoral roll for each electoral unit is to be prepared in the following form: -

FORM OF ELECTORAL ROLL

1. Province or State...................
2. Constituency.............(To be filled when constituencies have been delimited).
3. Town or Village and Post Office...................
4. Ward......................(To be filled in the case of municipalities divided into wards).

1	3	3	4	5	6	7
Sl. No.	House Number and address	Name	Father's or Husband's name	Male Or Female	Whether Muslim, or Scheduled Caste or Scheduled Tribe or (in Madras and Bombay) Indian Christian	Age

The language in which the roll is to be prepared for each area will be prescribed by each Province or State. The registration is to be on a house to house basis, that is to say, an officer will be deputed to visit each house for the purpose of preparing the register.

For the purpose of general elections, it is necessary to provide for the publications of the draft rolls, for the granting of time for filing claims and objections, and for the revision of the rolls after hearing the claims and objections. Provisions for all these purposes will doubtless be made by an election law after the new

Constitution comes into force. The draft rolls prepared under executive instructions in the manner explained above can be published and revised under the new electoral law when that law is enacted.

Since the issue of these instructions, it has been pointed out that some difficulty is being experienced in regard to the fulfilment of the residential qualification by refugees or displaced persons. This is a problem which does not admit of any easy or ready solution and will therefore have to be reviewed constantly as the resettlement of refugees progresses. In view, however, of the fact that the rolls now under preparation are merely the preliminary rolls and these will have to be duly published and revised under the relevant law before holding a general election, there need to be no objection to refugees being registered in the rolls, for the present, on a mere declaration by them of their intention to reside permanently in the town or village concerned. If, when the time comes for revision of the rolls, they have not actually resided in the area for the prescribed period, and if the lack of this qualification comes, or is brought, to the notice of the revising authority, the necessary corrections can be made at that stage.

A summary, based on information so far received in the Constituent Assembly Secretariat, of the steps taken by various Provinces and States in regard to the preparations of these rolls is given below:

Provinces:

Most of the Provincial Governments have already issued the necessary executive instructions to their District Officers and have already appointed or are appointing Election Officers and the requisite staff to carry out the work. In the United Provinces, the preparation of the rolls for the rural areas has been entrusted to Tahsildars who have already started work through patwaris, and in regard to the urban areas the work is being done through Municipal and other urban local bodies. In Assam, the numbering of houses and registration of voters is already in progress. In East Punjab, the registration of voters will commence on August 1, 1948; in the meantime the Government is giving full publicity in order to educate the public on the subject. In Bihar, the numbering of houses has already started; so too in Coorg where the electoral rolls are expected to be completed by November.

States:

In Manipur and Travancore, the preparation of the electoral rolls for elections to their respective State Legislatures has already been completed. In Cochin, a preliminary list of voters is ready. Reports of good progress have also been received from Baroda, Jodhpur, Kolhapur and Cooch-Behar. In Mysore, the rolls are being prepared progressively and the manuscript rolls for the State Legislature are expected to be ready shortly.

The Constituent Assembly Secretariat is in constant communication with the various Governments and any difficulties reported are at once looked into and remedies suggested. There is every reason to believe that if the present progress in the work is maintained, the general elections need not be unduly delayed after the passing of the new Constitution.

New Delhi
July 15, 1948[25]

The press note provided a coherent account of the preparation of electoral rolls in a sequential order, chronicling what happened first, what happened next, where things stood, and what should be expected at the later phases. The account was posited as a response to inquiries from the public, as part of a dialogue. The CAS recounted for the people the backstory of the decision to start preparing the rolls. It established the legal basis, the source of authority of their actions. The plot laid out how the people were to become the holders of the universal franchise. The 'need for holding fresh general elections as early as possible after the new Constitution comes into force'[26] provided a clear 'sense of an ending' to the narrative.[27] The CAS interwove into the narrative the content of the instructions it sent three months earlier to the Provincial and States Governments, including the Form of Electoral Roll, making it authentic.

Moreover, the CAS's narrative depicted a preparation of rolls that enabled the reader to conceptualise India as a unitary space. India was divided into manifold electoral units, marked by village, town, ward, and local post offices. These spatial markers lay within the immediate imagination of people. These electoral units and the unitary rolls prepared for them were ultimately to be reassembled into territorial constituencies, constituting the body of voters to the central and state legislatures. Such a portrayal evoked a concrete image of the voter-citizen of the new Indian democratic republic.[28] The descriptions of the steps that had already been taken and the progress that was made in some of the provinces and the states, like the 'Tahsildars who have already started work through patwaris', and 'the numbering of houses', gave credence to that spatial visualisation of the rolls as a basis for India's electoral democracy.

Addressing the public directly, speaking to it intimately, the CAS shared in all openness the difficulty that arose with regards to the registration of the refugees. In doing so, the CAS rehearsed the same formulations its

---

[25] Press Note, 'Electoral Rolls Under the New Constitution', 15 July 1948, CA/1/FR/48-V, ECIR.

[26] Ibid.

[27] Kermode, *The Sense of an Ending*.

[28] Peter Boxall suggests that the novel allows us 'to form pictures of bodies living collectively in spaces under the authority of the law'. Boxall, *The Value of the Novel*, p. 143.

members used during internal discussions on the subject, describing this as 'a problem which does not admit of any easy or ready solution', and that it 'will have to be reviewed constantly'.[29] The CAS explained how the solution to the challenge of registering refugees came to be and the rationale that underlay it.

The CAS's style and language of recounting the preparation of rolls was reminiscent of Robert Musil's concept of a narrative as 'the simple order that allows one to say: "First this happened and then that happened..." It is the simple sequence of events in which the overwhelmingly manifold nature of things is represented, in a unidimensional order... Stringing all that has occurred in space and time on a single thread, which calms us.'[30] A month after the publication of the press note, the Under Secretary of the CAS suggested that 'we should now collect the material for another press note on the work of preparing electoral rolls. We should keep the public informed that the work is going ahead... Our recent instructions regarding refugee registration may also be published'.[31] The Secretariat had begun thinking about the importance of continuing the narration of 'what happened-next'.[32]

The discussions about the next press note continued in the following weeks. Bit by bit the latest information gleaned from the on-going summary overviews of the progress made in the work of the preparation of electoral rolls was added to the new draft press note. Thus, an updated comment in an internal note suggested that the 'fortnightly reports received, during the interval after the issue of our previous Press Note indicates that the work of numbering houses and registration of voters in some of the Provinces and States is progressing well, whereas from some of them no progress has been reported. It will be observed ... that except from Panth-Piploda where electoral rolls have been completed, no detailed or appreciable progress has been reported from any other place, and as such a detailed account of the progress ... was not included in the draft Press Note now under preparation'.[33] By the third week of

---

[29] Press Note, 'Electoral Rolls Under the New Constitution', 15 July 1948, CA/1/FR/48-V, ECIR.

[30] Robert Musil, *The Man Without Qualities* (1995), pp. 708–9, quoted in Caracciolo, *The Experientiality of Narrative*, pp. 52–3. Also see Grill, *The World as Metaphor in Robert Musil's* The Man Without Qualities, p. 61.

[31] Internal discussion, 11 August 1948, CA/12/FR/48, ECIR. The under secretary's comment referred to the CAS's instructions of 26 July 1948, which provided for a uniform definition of a refugee.

[32] The curiosity to know what happened next is part of the dynamics of a serialisation of a story. The 'pressures of what happened-nextism' is a motif in Salman Rushdie, *Midnight's Children*, London: Vintage Books, 2006 (first published in 1981), pp. 44–5.

[33] Internal discussion, 25 August 1948, CA/12/FR/48, ECIR.

September the draft press note was finalised when the particulars about the confusion that arose between citizenship and refugee registration and declarations, and a detailed account of the complaints against the orders of the West Bengal and Assam Governments in the matter of the registration of refugees and the corrective measures that were taken in this regard, were added to the draft press note.

On 25 September 1948 the CAS published a second comprehensive press note. That 'next chapter' recapped the story of the preparation of electoral rolls so far, and then recounted what had happened subsequent to the previous press note. The CAS introduced the uniform definition of a 'refugee'. It told about the decision that a husband of a female refugee could make the refugee declaration for inclusion in the roll on her behalf, and that 'in the case of other women the head of the family might be permitted to sign the declarations on their behalf'.[34] The CAS then recounted the various confusions that arose over the declaration of a refugees and the one that was required for citizenship under article 5 of the Draft Constitution, and explained the distinction between the two. It also described the complaints that it received against the order of the Government of West Bengal, requiring that declarations relating to citizenship should be made in the form of an affidavit on embossed stamp paper of two rupees. The CAS clarified that these orders 'were apparently issued under some misapprehension' and that the 'Government of West Bengal has since withdrawn their original orders and issued fresh orders making it clear that such affidavits are not necessary at this stage'.[35] The Secretariat also shared with the public the complaints against the order of the Government of Assam to affix a court-fee stamp on the refugee declarations. The Secretariat's authentic voice as the narrator of the story surfaced when it remarked: 'It was never intended that such a fee should be imposed.'[36]

---

[34] Constituent Assembly of India Press Note, 25 September 1948, CA/12/FR/48, ECIR. See full text of the press note Chapter 3, Appendix 3.1. The explanation for that was that 'as the wife's domicile would follow the domicile of her husband'.

[35] Ibid.

[36] The Secretariat also reported that the Government of Assam have extended the deadline for making a refugee declaration from 30 September 1948 to 31 October 1948 in response to representations from the public. In this Press Note the Secretariat also dispelled a misconception that arose at that time in the wake of a Press Note of the Ministry of Relief & Rehabilitation of 2 July 1948, which was erroneously understood as suggesting that persons who have migrated or might migrate from Pakistan to India before 30 September 1948 could claim Indian domicile. The Secretariat clarified that this 'has no bearing at all on the general question of the citizenship of the Indian Union or of a person's eligibility for enrolment in the provisional electoral roll'. The Press Note of the Ministry of Relief & Rehabilitation of 2 July 1948 was corrected and replaced by a new Press Note on 24 September 1948. See ibid.

At a very basic level, these public narratives formed a source of knowledge about the preparation of rolls and made the Secretariat's work visible to the people.[37] The CAS, however, did not only register chronologically their actions but narrated the passage of events 'as possessing a structure, an order of meaning, which they [did] not possess as mere sequence'.[38] The detailed account in the second press note about problems over the registration of refugees was related to the reality people experienced around them in different ways at the time. The story also drew links between these experiences, the sentiments associated with them – migration as a result of 'fear of disturbances', 'intention to reside permanently' and to belong – and the draft Constitution, which was the basis for adult franchise, thus grasping the story in its fullness. The Secretariat became the omniscient narrator of the preparation of the electoral roll, though not omnipotent. It openly shared drawbacks, complaints and representations from the public, as well as the way these were redressed. In that sense, the CAS's story created a real place for people in it. The press notes' narratives and the storytelling effect that they had infused the universal franchise with meaning. Moreover, the release of the press notes began a process of serialisation of the story. Newspapers covered the enrolment with their own stories. This was complemented by further press notes issued by the provincial and state governments.[39] Consequently, the story of the preparation of the rolls turned into a series of episodes and connected events that augmented the core story of the making of the universal franchise, like an epic of India's democracy.

[37] Many letters that arrived at the CAS from individuals and organisations began with a reference to the press notes.

[38] See Hayden White's discussion of what makes a narrative. White, 'The Value of Narrativity in Representation of Reality', p. 9.

[39] As one example, the Government of Bihar published a detailed Press Note informing that: Steps have been taken for the preparation of electoral rolls based on adult suffrage for the Legislatures under the forthcoming new Constitution of India... Under the new constitution there will be no separate communal electorates... All communities and interests residing in a particular constituency will go into a single composite roll... The registration ... at the preliminary stage will be done on a house to house basis, that is to say that an officer such as the Chowkidari, Sarpanch, or the Municipal Tax Daroga, etc. will be deputed to visit each house for the purpose of preparing the register... The electoral roll will be prepared in rural areas, village by village and in urban areas, ward by ward. The post office serving the village and the ward will be noted against the name of each village and the name or the number of each ward... The electoral roll will be prepared in Hindi in Devanagri script throughout the provinces. Electoral rolls should be prepared in Bengali as well as Hindi, for the ... district, for which electoral rolls were prepared in Bengali in 1936... The co-operation of every citizen of Bihar in this colossal task in invited. Government of Bihar, Press Note (undated), CA/1/FR/48-III, ECIR.

Press Reports: Information, Narratives and a Passion for Democracy

Stories about the preparation of the rolls in the press contributed to the process that enabled Indians to conceive of adult franchise as the concrete basis for the evolving political world, which they inhabited in three main ways. The press formed a channel of communication that provided information about the work, continued to give it visibility, and from time to time was also a means of provincial and state governments to reach out to their people with various notifications. Newspaper accounts of the preparation of rolls in the provinces and the princely states also fostered a sense of interconnectedness between the disparate territorial parts of the country. The repetition of similar stories about the preparation of rolls from different places created a temporal and spatial unity of the making of adult franchise, as well as a new way of imagining the unified territory.[40] Moreover, press reports generated opinion pieces and discussions about the meaning of the right to vote and of democratic citizenship.

Early reports about the preparation of electoral rolls for 'Free India's First Elections', which were thought at the time to take place in the spring of 1949, appeared in the press in March 1948.[41] Just before the CAS sent its letter of instructions for the preparation of rolls to the provinces and the states *The Times of India* reported that:

In the meantime the gigantic task of preparing electoral rolls for the three-hundred million people of India on the basis of adult suffrage will have been set in motion. In fact, the Constituent Assembly Secretariat is already in correspondence with the Provincial and State Governments in regard to the commencement of the work of electoral rolls... Since this work has to be started practically from scratch, it is anticipated that it will take at least eight months before electoral rolls are completed.[42]

In April Rajendra Prasad was reported to have said that 'they had already written to different provinces to take up preliminaries in connection with the preparation of electoral rolls'.[43]

Thereafter accounts about the preparation of rolls in the provinces and the states began appearing in the Press. Some of these stories provided detailed accounts of the operation, iterating large parts of the instructions

---

[40] On the effect of repetition on the temporal and spatial unity of the novel see Boxall, *The Value of the Novel*, p. 54.

[41] 'Free India's First Elections Likely in Spring of 1949', *Times of India* (henceforth *TOI*), 3 March 1948, p. 1.

[42] Ibid.

[43] 'New Constitution of India: Adoption Expected by End of June. Provinces asked to Get Ready for Elections', *TOI*, 15 April 1948, p. 1.

that were issued by the CAS, or locally by the provinces and the states. Thus, it was reported from Surat that:

[S]teps to prepare tentative electoral rolls for the purpose of elections to Central and State legislatures immediately after the new Constitution is passed ... are being taken place... Orders have been issued by Provincial governments to Collectors to register electors on a house-to-house basis... Following the abolition of separate electorate and special constituencies, one composite roll for all communities will be prepared though the roll will contain necessary information as to what community the voter belongs... The roll will be prepared for each town and village with a post office. Villages without post offices will be grouped conveniently... No person will be included in the roll who is not a citizen of India. 'Citizen' had been defined as... No person shall be included in the electoral roll ... unless he has a place of residence in that unit and has resided in such a place for a period of no less than 180 days in the financial year ending March 31, 1948.[44]

Often, news stories gave short glimpses of the developments in the preparation of rolls in different parts of the country, like the report from Surat above. One news article reported that the West Bengal Government had taken up the task of preparing draft electoral rolls for elections to the Lower House of the Central and Provincial Legislatures. The article produced excerpts from the government's circular to all divisional commissioners.[45] Another story suggested that the general elections may not be delayed as the work of preparation of electoral rolls under adult franchise in the provinces and states has already commenced.[46] A report from East Punjab announced that the 'preparation of Electoral rolls on the basis of adult franchise ... will begin on August 1 and the registration of names will conclude on 30 September'.[47]

With the publication of the CAS's press note of 15 July 1948, the story about the preparation of the rolls made the front page's main headlines: 'General Elections On Adult Suffrage Basis';[48] 'Preparation For Elections';[49] 'General Elections in India Under New Constitution: Directive on Preparation of Voters' List'.[50] The latter article stated: 'The progress made regarding the holding of general

[44] 'New Electoral Rolls: Tentative Steps for Preparation', *TOI*, 20 April 1948, p. 5.
[45] 'Draft Electoral Rolls: West Bengal Move', *TOI*, 9 June 1948, p. 8.
[46] 'General Elections in India', *TOI*, 30 June 1948, p. 7.
[47] *TOI*, 7 July 1948, p. 8.
[48] *The Hindustan Times* (Delhi Edition) (henceforth *HT*), 18 July 1948, p. 9.
[49] *The Hindu* (Madras Edition), 17 July 1948, p. 5. On the same page there was a report on the Return of Muslims to India, the imposition of a permit system, and a report that 'the immediate introduction by the Pakistan Government of the permit system to limit the entry of Indian nationals, particularly Hindus and Sikhs ... is anticipated as a retaliatory measure to the Government's of India's recent decision'.
[50] *TOI*, 17 July 1948, p. 1.

elections after the new constitution has come into force is reviewed in an announcement issued by the Secretariat of the Constituent Assembly.'[51] It emphasised in a subtitle the 'Unitary Rolls'. These articles reproduced and re-narrated the Secretariat's press note and gave it publicity. Over the next months, reports in the press continued to carry the story.

In Madras 'Collectors of Districts have been, it is understood, addressed to collet statistics as to the number of voters likely to be enrolled on the basis of adult franchise and send them on to the Government before the end of the month.'[52] Two months later it was reported that the Government of Madras issued directives to all authorities and municipal panchayat boards in the province to prepare draft electoral rolls on the basis of adult franchise.[53] In Nagpur, it was reported, the rolls were to be prepared by 1 January 1949.[54] Newspapers also published stories about disputes and difficulties that arose in the preparation of rolls. One report suggested that in Assam 'the intention seems to be to exclude [from the roll] those whose homes are in another province though they may have been living in Assam for a number of years. Bengal interprets this move as a blow aimed at disenfranchising the Bengali population of Assam. The Assamese ... would argue that ... care should be taken by a province to safeguard the interests of the "sons of the soil"'.[55] This action was reported to have fuelled the 'heart-burning between Assam and Bengal'.[56]

The CAS's 25 September press note also received wide coverage in the newspapers. It covered in detail 'Refugees Rights as Electors', and the instructions for their inclusion on the electoral rolls.[57] The press continued to bring stories from across the country under the occasional title: 'Progress In Preparation of Electoral Rolls'.[58] It reported, for example, that the East Punjab Government extended the final date for the completion of electoral rolls to 31 October 1948 'since a large number had not got themselves registered... The public are requested to help in the preparation of rolls by submitting their forms on or before that date.'[59] In U.P., it was reported, electoral rolls on the basis of adult

[51] Ibid.
[52] 'Electoral Rolls in Madras', *The Hindu*, 17 July 1948, p. 5. The Daily also reported about the holding of 'General Elections on Cochin', *The Hindu* (Madras Edition), ibid., p. 6.
[53] 'The Rest of the News', *TOI*, 10 September 1948, p. 5.
[54] 'Provincial News in Brief', *HT*, 26 July 1948, p. 6.
[55] 'The Indian Background: Unhappy Border Regions', *TOI*, 26 August 1948, p. 6.
[56] Ibid.
[57] 'Refugees Rights as Electors (Enrolment on Declaration of Domicile to be Valid)', *HT*, 26 September 1948, p. 12. The article reproduced large parts of the Press Note. Also see 'Indian Electoral Rolls', *TOI*, 26 September 1948, p. 3.
[58] For example, 'Progress In Preparation of Electoral Rolls', *HT*, 17 October 1948, p. 11.
[59] 'East Punjab Electoral Rolls', *HT*, 5 October 1948, p. 6.

franchise for Allahabad Municipality were compiled as part of the progress of the preparation of the rolls;[60] in Calcutta the 'preparations for the draft rolls ... for both the provincial and Central elections is in full swing. It is estimated that about a quarter of the City's eligible voters have been enumerated.'[61] By mid-October 1948 newspaper accounts reported that the preparation of electoral rolls was expected to be completed by March 1949, suggesting that: 'Reports from provinces show that good progress has been made in the compilation of the electoral rolls.'[62]

As the work of the preparation of the rolls progressed and in some places the actual enlistment started, reports were more detailed, and the scale and significance of the undertaking began to be appreciated. Thus, a story from Bombay noted: 'These being the first general elections in free India held under the Constitution drafted by Indians themselves, it is of utmost importance that they should be completed successfully.'[63] A few weeks later, reports suggested that the preparation of electoral rolls in greater Bombay was 'in full swing'.[64] The story noted that a staff of 400, including 350 enumerators and 40 inspectors, assisted the Electoral Roll Officer (H. K. Sheikh); that for the enumeration in Bombay the city was divided into 38 sections and the suburbs into eight sections. 'These sections have again been divided into circles, and a certain number of buildings in each circle has been assigned to each enumerator who will visit the buildings from 7:30 a.m. to 6:30 p.m. every day.'[65] From East Punjab, it was reported that according to the fresh electoral rolls prepared for elections the total number of adult voters is estimated to be around six million.[66]

Newspaper articles portrayed the evolving experiences of making adult franchise and electoral democracy across the country, weaving into the narrative democratic developments in the states, which were in the process of integration into the Union. The ruler of Baroda, as recounted in

[60] *HT*, 19 October 1948, p. 4.
[61] *HT*, 30 October 1948, p. 5. Also see 'The Rest of the News', *TOI*, 25 October 1948, p. 8.
[62] 'New Electoral Rolls', *TOI*, 19 October 1948, p. 5. Also see 'Progress in the Preparation of Electoral Rolls', *HT*, 17 October 1948, p. 11.
[63] 'First Elections in Free India: Preparations Afoot', *TOI*, 27 November 1948, p. 10. The article reported in detail that the Government of Bombay issued the necessary instructions and the work relating to the preparation of the electoral rolls in this Province has already commenced. The report rehearsed the instructions, affirming that refugees should make their declaration regarding residence in writing before an officer not below the rank of a Mamlatdar in the mofussil and before the Presidency Magistrate or a Justice of the Peace in Bombay City.
[64] 'Preparation of New Electoral Rolls: Bombay Measures', *TOI*, 19 December 1948, p. 3. The report anticipated that the enumeration would be completed by the end of March 1949 and the rolls would be compiled and ready by May 1949.
[65] 'Ibid.
[66] *TOI*, 6 December 1948, p. 5.

one such story, announced new reforms towards granting full responsible government to the people of the state.[67] A few months later the
press reported that the Government of Baroda 'ordered preparation of
election on the basis of adult franchise: "Bahivatdars and Mahalkaris
have ... been asked to prepare before September 30 preliminary electoral
rolls for each village, town and city'.[68] A voter had to be 21 years old on
1 August 1948, of sound mind and domiciled in Baroda according to the
Baroda Domicile Act. Further notification affirmed that: 'Active measures are being taken by local officers in Baroda in preparing the electoral
roll on the basis of adult franchise'.[69]

'Full Responsible Government' was reported from Cochin, as the
'Maharaja of Cochin has transferred power to the administrative controls
of popular ministers ... thus completing the phase of full responsible
government in the state'.[70] A press communiqué of the State of Bhopal
announced that the Nawab agreed to hold elections in the state at the
earliest possible opportunity on the basis of adult franchise, joint electorate and direct voting for the constitution-making body of the state.[71]
There were additional brief reports on the holding of elections for constituent assemblies in Saurashtra and Malwa; on the delay in holding the
planned elections in Patiala and the East Punjab States; and on the anticipated first general elections on the basis of adult franchise in Baroda.[72]

Once the Indian Army invaded to Hyderabad, and the press could
announce that 'Hyderabad Issue Virtually Settled', newspapers followed
closely the preparation of the election for the Constituent Assembly in
the state.[73] It reported in detail on the appointment of the former Home
Minister of Mysore, M. Seshadri, as an Election Commissioner for
Hyderabad. His duty was 'to prepare electoral rolls, conduct free elections
and convene a Constituent Assembly which will be charged with the task

---

[67] *TOI*, 12 April 1948, p. 7.
[68] 'Constituent Body for Baroda: Preparing electoral rolls', *TOI*, 5 July 1948, p. 7.
[69] *TOI*, 25 July 1948, p. 13.
[70] 'Full Responsible Government in Cochin', *HT*, 1 October 1948, p. 8.
[71] 'Elections Soon in Bhopal: Constitution-Making Body to Be Set-Up', *HT*, 23 January
    1949, p. 9. It was reported that elections were expected to be held by April 1949.
[72] 'Saurashtra C.A. Elections', *HT*, 31 October 1948, p. 12; 'Malwa Elections to C.A.',
    ibid; 'No Election to C.A. from Patiala Yet', *HT*, 3 November 1948, p. 9; 'General
    Elections in Baroda Next Month', *HT*, 3 January 1949, p. 5.
[73] 'Hyderabad Issue Virtually Settled', *HT*, 1 October 1948, front page. Already in July
    1948, before the Indian Army invasion to Hyderabad, the *TOI* reported that 'arrange-
    ments are under way for the setting up of a Constituent Assembly for Hyderabad'
    on the basis of adult franchise. *TOI*, 23 July 1948, p. 7. In mid-September 1948 the
    Government of India sent Indian Army troops into Hyderabad. Upon the Nizam's sur-
    render within the 4 days of 'Operation Polo', a military Government was established
    with Major-General J. N. Chaudhuri at its head. See, for example, Srinath Raghavan,
    War and Peace in Modern India, Basingstoke: Palgrave Macmillan, 2010, pp. 65–100.

of determining the future of the state'.[74] Later accounts suggested that 'Side by side with the efforts to restore peace and order in Hyderabad, steps are also being taken to speed up setting up of popular and democratic institutions.'[75] For that purpose, 'the State Assembly Department has been converted into the Election Department and the entire staff placed under Mr. Seshadri, Election Commissioner'.[76] A vivid follow-up account suggested that: 'an idea of the magnitude of the undertaking was given yesterday by official sources who said that electoral rolls, ballot papers and other matters to be printed would consume 180 tons of paper'.[77] Subsequent stories described in great detail the estimated costs of preparing the rolls in the State; suggested that over 400,000 electoral forms were printed in English, Kanarese, Marathi, Telugu, and Urdu and were distributed in all towns and villages of the State; that each form had space for over 50 names; and projected that no more than ten million adults may be finally qualified to vote.[78] The government of India ultimately decided not to hold separate elections for a Constituent Assembly in Hyderabad, but to hold elections in the state along side the first national general elections.[79] Yet, the recounting in detail of the preparation of rolls in Hyderabad, and in the states more generally, was part of what fashioned a new way of imagining the unified territory.

The press, moreover, provided a channel of communication for provincial and state governments to reach out to the public with regard to the preparation of rolls. A classified ad in the *Times of India* invited applications for temporary posts under the Collector of Bombay for the preparation of electoral rolls for the Bombay Assembly for the City of Bombay and the Bombay Suburban District. 275 Surveyors and

---

[74] 'Hyderabad's Election Commissioner', *HT*, 4 October 1948, p. 6.

[75] 'Hyderabad C.A. (Electoral Rolls to be Prepared)', *HT*, 19 October 1948, p. 8. Also see 'Compiling Electoral Rolls for Hyderabad: Preliminary Steps to Be Taken This Month', *TOI*, 21 October 1948, p. 1.

[76] 'Hyderabad C.A. (Electoral Rolls to be Prepared)', *HT*, 19 October 1948, p. 8. Also see on the preparation of rolls for election to Hyderabad constituent assembly: Taylor C. Sherman, *Muslim Belonging in Secular India. Negotiating Citizenship in Postcolonial Hyderabad*, Cambridge: Cambridge University Press, 2015, pp. 93, 132–3.

[77] 'Election Budget', *HT*, 29 October 1948, p. 5. The estimated budget was 30–40 lakh. Also see 'People's Raj for Hyderabad', *HT*, 31 October 1948, p. 12.

[78] 'Hyderabad C.A. Elections: Rule Framed', *HT*, 10 January 1949, p. 6. The rolls were expected to be ready by February.

[79] 'Hyderabad Elections Postponed', *HT*, 21 February 1950, p. 9. 'Hyderabad Legislature to Function as C.A.', *HT*, 11 March 1950, Front page. During question hour in Parliament on 11 March 1950 Sardar Patel stated that 'the delay so far in holding elections was the result of recent exchange of territories between the State and the former provinces of Madras and Bombay. Suitable changes had thus to be made in the electoral rolls resulting in an inevitable postponement of the elections. The approach of the general elections all over the country then made it necessary to revise the timing of the election to avoid duplication with the elections to the State Legislature on adult franchise.'

750 Checkers were among the job openings.[80] Another news article reported that the Delhi Municipality issued a press note, announcing that staff had been appointed to prepare the electoral rolls, emphasising the need for public cooperation to give 'necessary information' in order to complete the preparation of the roll accurately and in time.[81] In a note to the press two months later, the Chief Commissioner of Delhi asked the public once more to cooperate with the officials in charge of the preparation of the rolls because: 'It has been brought to the notice of the Chief Commissioner of Delhi ... that the staff of the various local bodies who are deputed to number the houses ... are not getting the co-operation of the public and in some cases they are not even allowed to enter the premises of the main buildings to obtain necessary information required by them ... without their co-operation they will be depriving themselves of the right of exercising franchise and the necessary information sought for the purpose will also remain incomplete'.[82]

It was indeed through the press and reports on governments' press communiqués that the wider public became aware of problems that arose in the preparation of rolls. Thus, the press reported, as already mentioned in Chapter 1, that 'in view of the reluctance of Indian women to give their names, the Government [of U.P] have issued a warning that failure to state names by women will mean their disenfranchisement'.[83] Another related short story informed that in Jullundur, the General Secretary of the Provincial Branch of the All-India Women's Conference, Shrimati Seeta Devi, 'appealed to women to get themselves registered as

---

Ibid. For an examination of the first elections in Hyderabad (from October 1951) see Sherman, *Muslim Belonging in Secular India*, pp. 133–46.

[80] 'Classified Ad', *TOI*, 4 September 1948, p. 12. The Ad noted that: 'Enumerators applicants for these jobs should preferably be graduates' and that the post was for 3 months. Ibid.

[81] 'New Electoral Rolls for Delhi', *HT*, 12 September 1948, p. 10.

[82] 'Preparation of New Electoral Rolls', *HT*, 22 December 1948, p. 3. It is noteworthy that the compilation of rolls in Delhi was a prolonged and unsteady process. Ultimately, in May 1950 the Delhi Administration decided to prepare fresh electoral rolls, stating that 'whether full or supplementary, the enumerators would have to go from house to house' to compile fresh lists on the basis of adult franchise. The reasons given by the authorities were the fluctuation in population; that 'when enumeration is done now, there would be no classification under heads of religion and sub-sect'; that there were complaints that many persons, who were qualified to be voters, were not included in the previous enumeration; and that '[m]any people were out of their homes when enumerators called and the women-folk invariably wanted the enumerators to come again instead of cooperating with them and giving the details'. 'New Voters' List For New Delhi', *HT*, 13 May 1950, p. 10. Also see 'Fresh Electoral Rolls for Delhi by June 10', *HT*, 19 May 1950, p. 3. The enumeration was set to take place from 17 May until 31 May 1950.

[83] 'Preparation of Allahabad Municipal Electoral Rolls', *HT*, 19 October 1948, p. 4.

voters so that they could send their representatives to legislatures to safe-guard the interest of women'.[84]

Newspaper stories about the preparation of electoral rolls elicited public engagement with the anticipated universal adult franchise. Indeed, through the press, as Pierre Rosanvallon has suggested, members of the public could experience 'the right to give advice' and to have 'a constitutive voice in public affairs'.[85] Newspaper editorials, op-eds, interviews and letters to the editor offered meditations on the meaning and implications of the right to vote, its connection to democratic citizenship and with responsible government, and democracy more broadly.

A passionate article on 'The Power of Your Vote', published shortly after the publication of the CAS's press note on the preparation of electoral rolls, implored readers to think about the 'precious possession' they have got in their vote.[86] 'By your vote', the author explained, 'you have a voice in your Government. It empowers you directly or through a representative of your choice to be a party to the framing of the law.'[87] The author made the connection between an individual's vote and the cabinet ministers that would ultimately constitute their government. It conveyed the momentous character of the vote as one that could 'help materially to transform the structure and the quality of your Government and consequently also the nature of society of which you are not an insignificant part'.[88]

The importance of people's thoughtful use of their right of franchise was also emphasised by writers and political figures at the time and reported in the press. For example, the Maharani of Scindia warned that: 'On the correct exercise of franchise depends the welfare of the future generation, our country, our relations with the different nations, because we should and will be leaving these factors in the hands of those whom we empower to rule.'[89]

---

[84] 'Women Urged to Enlist as Voters', *HT*, 19 October 1948, p. 8.

[85] Rosanvallon, *Democratic Legitimacy*, p. 212. In that sense Rosanvallon also suggests that: 'Election matter not as expressions of the people's will but as one element of a much larger system for the generation and circulation of information and opinion'. Ibid.

[86] N. B. Parulekar, 'The Power of Your Vote', *HT* (Sunday Magazine), 1 August 1948. Parulekar was the founding Editor of the Marathi daily newspaper *Sakal* in January 1932.

[87] Ibid.

[88] Ibid. 'We must, therefore, see', the article concluded, 'that no voter fails to register his vote.' Newspapers published occasionally at that time articles about the meaning of 'responsible government'. See, for example, 'Parliament, Cabinet and Party', *HT* (Sunday Magazine), 21 August 1948.

[89] '"Use Franchise Wisely": Maharani's Call', *TOI*, 13 November 1948, p. 5. The Maharani made that statement while presiding the seventeenth annual session of the Gwalior Mahila Madal, held at the Kamala Raja's Girls.

There were also public expressions of doubt about the granting of the universal franchise. For example, early on in the preparation of rolls A. D. Shroff was reported to have said that 'the country was not prepared for adult franchise, which, he said, should be introduced gradually'.[90] Moreover, actual experiences with elections to constituent assemblies in some states or newly formed Unions of States also exposed genuine problems. Thus, following the elections for a Constituent Assembly in Saurashtra, there were reports of 250 cases of impersonation during the election, and of the secrecy of the ballot being violated in many places.[91] After the first municipal elections in Sambhar Lake, Rajputana, the Secretary of the Salt Merchants' Association complained the electoral roll was full of mistakes, that the names of some mohallas were omitted and that wrong details of voters have been recorded. He concluded by stating that 'the forthcoming [general] election, if held under these circumstances, will not represent the true wishes and aspirations of the people of Sambhar'.[92]

As the preparation of the rolls progressed, even the President of the Constituent Assembly, Rajendra Prasad, who was the senior most political figure who approved and oversaw the steps taken by the CAS regarding the preparation of the rolls, had misgivings about adult franchise. Prasad was quoted to have said at a public address that the adoption of adult franchise 'was causing him and his colleagues grave anxiety... Unless properly exercised, adult franchise was fraught with grave dangers. It would mean putting educated and ignorant and honest and dishonest persons on the same footing.'[93]

Just before the draft constitution was brought for consideration before the Constituent Assembly in November 1948, the *Times of India* editorial stated:

Certain principles embodied in the draft constitution have been called into question since their adoption by the Constituent Assembly or its committees. One of these is adult franchise. Although the leadership of the Congress is committed to this principle, there is growing evidence of anxiety lest in the present state of the masses' education the vesting of this powerful political weapon in the entire adult population should lead to abuse of the democratic system. No less than Dr

---

[90] '"Break with Empire Suicidal": Mr. A. D. Shroff's Plea to India', *TOI*, 29 July 1948, p. 17.

[91] 'Saurashtra C.A. Elections', *HT*, 9 November 1948, p. 6.

[92] Secretary of the Salt Merchants' Association, 'Elections in Sambhar Lake (Rajputana)', *HT* (Letters to the Editor), 17 November 1948, p. 6.

[93] 'Adult Franchise Principles: Dr Prasad's View', *TOI*, 30 October 1948, p. 5. Prasad spoke at the Rotary Club Jubbulpore. The article reported that he 'had nothing to say against the principle of adult suffrage, but he could not say how they could provide against possible abuse of that democratic system'. Ibid.

Rajendra Prasad has given expression to hesitancy in this behalf. A similar feeling was voiced in the Madras legislature when that body discussed the draft constitution six months ago. Constitutional pundits ask. 'Are we going to be governed by the ignorant, the unwise, "the thriftless"?' It may be a trifle late in the day to go back on the principle of universal suffrage, but the Constituent Assembly might profitably consider devices which would minimise the danger of unrestricted political power in the hands of millions not yet sufficiently trained in the art of democratic government.[94]

A *Hindustan Times* editorial noted that 'the question of adult franchise has lately exercised the minds of many thinkers. It is too late, we feel, to go back on decisions already taken twice by the Assembly on the subject but the doubts to which Dr. Rajendra Prasad recently gave expression suggest that for at least ten years elections to the Lower House of the Indian Parliament should be through electoral colleges totalling in membership about a million of the elect [sic] of the people.'[95]

A reader's response to the *Times of India* editorial suggested that the 'real danger lies in entrusting the precious right to vote to our raw young men, swayed by temptations deliberately placed in their way by those who seek their suffrage during the hectic days of electioneering'.[96] The reader proposed raising the age of voters to 28 instead of 21, the age level 'where young men and women are faced with the cruel realities of life and are expected to get a little more sober'.[97]

Opinion pieces in the press, and the ongoing reporting about various aspects of the preparation of electoral rolls and its effects continued the process of narrating the roll, capturing the story's components and its whole. Thus, reporting in the press, despite its fragmented nature, provided the narrative of the preparation of rolls with some sustained coherence. The reproduction of parallel stories from different parts of the country also provided a new way of thinking about *an* India. The prolonged serialisation of the story, the narrations about the preparation of rolls in relatively regular instalments in the press, ultimately recounted the ambitious journey of India's transition to democracy. It was a story of monumental historical significance, grand in scope, and therefore, as suggested earlier, like an epic of India becoming a democracy.

The public, as already indicated by the reader's response above, were not passive readers of the CAS's press notes or of the stories that appeared in the press about the preparation of rolls. In fact, they engaged with the preparation of rolls in detail. As the future bearers of the right

---

[94] 'Constitution: Task before the Assembly', *TOI*, 1 November 1948, p. 8.
[95] 'Constituent Assembly', *HT*, 4 November 1948, p. 5.
[96] 'Adult Franchise', *TOI* ('Readers' Views' section), 10 November 1948, p. 6.
[97] Ibid.

to vote, people thought about adult franchise and their place in the roll from their personal perspective, as well as from the grand viewpoint of the nation. As the next section will show, they wrote to the CAS with a variety of suggestions and complaints. Their letters manifested a kind of inventiveness, which suggested that they were busy imagining their place in the new Indian polity, based on universal franchise. I reproduce below a few of these letters in full in order to convey the sentiments and passionate engagement with democracy they expressed. One prevalent concern was indeed the age of voters.

The Correspondences: Democratising Feelings and Imagination

'Your excellency', wrote Mr Vora from Bombay to Rajendra Prasad in a cursive handwritten letter:

The recent press announcement by the Secretariat about the enrolment of voters for the General Elections, to be held under the new constitution ... has given me a great shock. Your Excellency will notice ... that January 1st 1949 is to be the date of reference for the calculation of the age for the voter. I learn from well informed quarters that the General Elections are only possible at the beginning of 1950. This means, your Excellency, that voter should be a year older than the prescribed age limit of 21. I forward my own case before your excellency; that I come to the limit only in May 1949. Under the announcement I will not be qualified as a voter only because I happened to have born two or three months later... These elections for the Provincial and Central assemblies are as a normal course, to be held after every four or five years. This means that I, and thousands of others like me, are not to take active part in the Country's task because I and they happen to fall short of the age limit by 2 or 3 months. I request your excellency, that your excellency will direct the Secretariat to modify the date of reference. The voters' roll will have no effect at all by the announcement, since persons like me can be asked to forward a special application.[98]

'Why 21 Yrs adults have been chosen', questioned another letter rhetorically.[99] 'Because they have been chosen on the presumption they on that age can understand things well of the world, men and leaders. But there are some villagers though even at the age of 40 or 50 yrs they are

[98] Letter from Mr Kanaiyalal G. Vora, 467-A King's Circle, Matunga (G.I.P.), Bombay to the President of the Constituent Assembly, 17 July 1948, CA/12/FR/48, ECIR. The letter arrived at the CAS's Franchise Section on 21 July 1948. Less than a fortnight after Mr Vora sent his letter, the Under Secretary of the CAS sent him a reply, acknowledging the receipt of his letter, 'containing suggestions regarding the preparation of electoral rolls'. Draft letter from CAS to Mr Kanaiyalal G. Vora, 29 July 1948, CA/12/FR/48, ECIR.

[99] 'Open letter to the Constituent Assembly Regarding Elections', 21 September 1948, CA/12/FR/48, ECIR. The name of the author of the letter could not be deciphered.

simply innocent and vote as per money demands. Then what action you are going to take to stop such kind of atrocities... It is not the age that determines the man's intelligence or general knowledge but the actual experience he has got in the world. This is the time in which all the required things should be set right.'[100]

Mr Sreenivasan, from Poona, expressed a great deal of creativity over the age of voters and its implications for the electoral system. He wrote to Rajendra Prasad a four-page handwritten letter entitled 'Suggestions for adult franchise code':

Sir,

The definition of adult ideally requires revision. The present age limit of 21 goes for both the sexes is arbitrary and has no psychological basis behind it. It should rather be 25 for men and 20 for women. These are considered to be the proper ages for marriage and it may as well serve as the age for voting. After all there is not much of a difference between choosing mate and choosing a legislator.[101]

Moreover, Mr Sreenivasan worked out and proposed an alternative scheme for the future electorate:

[T]here ought to be two groups of voters one more responsible than the other and hence having greater weightage than the other. The former (let us call them A and B group voters respectively) are those who have had their share of responsibilities and hence are credited to be the wiser than the latter. Hence all householders who are managing or have managed a separate family of their own should be A group voters. The wife also in such a case shares with her husband the privilege of being an A group voter. All other adults who are staying with this family and who have not yet set up a separate establishment (adult sons, daughters etc.) of their own are all B group voters except when it can be proved that they are holding some responsible post in government or in business or that they are managing or have managed some private institution or other. This arrangement is more important than the age limit since in exceptional cases even the age limit may be relaxed as when a non adult member is a bread-winner. In such a case he is entitled to be an A group voter and if married his wife is also entitled to the A vote. Selection: A candidate to be selected must obtain a majority in both the groups or (ii) must poll 60% of the total votes cast in case he proves to be in a minority among the A group voters.[102]

---

[100] Ibid. The writer suggested that students who have passed matriculation standard 'got originality, statesman-ship and general knowledge even at a lower age'.

[101] Letter from Mr T. Sreenivasan, 'Suggestions for Adult Franchise Code', 2 November 1948, CA/8/Fr/48 in CA/12/FR/48, ECIR. The letter arrived at the CAS on 8 November 1948, and to its Franchise Section on 9 November 1948.

[102] Ibid. The Under Secretary sent a reply to Mr Sreenivasan within 11 days after he sent his letter, noting the receipt of his letter 'addressed to the Hon'ble Dr. Rajendra Prasad'. S. no 70, Draft letter from P. S. Subramanian, Under Secretary of CAS to Shri T. Sreenivasan, 13 November 1948, CA/12/FR/48, ECIR.

A man named Baljit Singh Shergill from Patiala wrote to suggest, or rather demand, an alternative scheme for elections based on divisions into voting areas and constituencies. 'Dear Mr Nehru, I have got a suggestion to make which <u>must</u> be followed up before the next general elections.'[103] Drawing on the last general elections in Britain he claimed that 'the representation in parliament is not proportional to the votes cast in favour of the various parties ... which is very unfair to the cityzens [sic]', and that it is not the most able members of a party that get into parliament, but 'the most richer who were able to pour money in their election campaigns. Thus politics become complicated, dirty, expensive and unfair. Candidates acquire political power for the sake of their personal power and not for the sake of their Party ideals about which they pretend to be sincere.'[104] Baljit Singh also proposed a solution, suggesting that 'a Bill be *immediately* introduced by which the *election by units should be abolished*. The votes should be *counted in the centre* and seats allotted to the various parties *in ration of the grand total of votes they get*.'[105] He suggested to Nehru that such a Bill 'will raise your esteem in the eyes of all educated people', and signed the letter: 'Yours sincerely, Baljit'.[106]

The preparation of rolls on the basis of adult franchise also fostered engagement with and recognition of the need to cultivate the spirit and ethics of democracy. Representatives of different organisation and various individuals raised concerns about the necessity of dealing with the question of education and caste in order to secure the democratic future of the nation. 'The success of Democracy and the development of the nation depends on the Civic and the patriotic sense of the voters well educated and dutiful', wrote the Secretary of the East Khandesh District Congress Committee to the CAS.[107] He explained at length the importance of making the voters literate and that they should 'understand the rights and the duties of a voter'. He informed the CAS that he, therefore, 'approached the Premier and Education Minister, Government of Bombay with a scheme of "Voters Education and Voter Test Examination"', and asked the CAS 'to

---

[103] Letter from Baljit Singh Shergill to Nehru, 5 May 1948, CA/12/FR/48, ECIR. Emphasis in original.
[104] Ibid. He also discussed the problem of uneven number of voters in different constituencies.
[105] Ibid.
[106] Ibid. Articles on electoral systems appeared from time to time in the Press. For example, in April and May 1948, a series of two articles were published on 'Method of Voting' in the *Harijan*. *Harijan*, 25 April 1948, pp. 74–5, and 2 May, 1948, pp. 85–6, CA/12/FR/48, ECIR.
[107] Letter from K. G. Lele, Secretary of the East Khandesh District Congress Committee to the Secretary of CAS, 21 July 1948, CA/12/FR/48, ECIR.

provide for the machinery to chalk out carriculumn [sic] and text books and make arrangements for offer for "the Voter Test examination"'.[108]

Mr Jagan Nath, a Member of the Communal Harmony Board from Ambala District in East Punjab, wrote to the CAS, asking of them, firstly, to consider adding to the electoral rolls a column 'literate or illiterate', because it would help the education authorities with the task of educating the masses. Secondly, he suggested that the column of caste should be deleted. He argued:

The monster of caste requires to be grappled with from all quarters before the Indian Union becomes one Indianised whole. The very idea of 'votes for all' connotes horizontal distribution of society and not a vertical one. Hence if the column of caste disappears from the electoral roll it will not remain easy for contending candidates to make caste appeals and affect the purity of election by introducing extraneous considerations.[109]

Mr Gagan Dev Bhandari of Ludhiana also urged: 'Now when joint electorate has been enforced these columns [mentioning religion and caste] are meaningless and will not only impede the progress of the nation but will possibly hamper it. They will cause Communal dissention and disharmony.'[110] He asked to delete this column and 'to get the list prepared on National lines'.[111] The CAS's reply explained that 'information regarding "communities", "caste", and "religion" is not to be included in the electoral rolls now under preparation except in the case of a person who is a Muslim, a member of a Scheduled Caste or of a Scheduled

[108] Ibid. Mr Lele referred to the experience of the small State of Aundh (deccan), the model constitution of which was framed in consultation with Mahatma Gandhi. In Aundh there was a state-wide campaign against illiteracy for more than six months before the franchise was brought into being. The Under Secretary of the CAS drafted the reply letter, acknowledging the receipt of his letter 'regarding the preparation of Electoral Rolls under the new Constitution' on 5 August 1948. S. no 22, Draft letter from CAS to Secretary of the East Khandesh District Congress Committee, 5 August 1948, CA/12/FR/48, ECIR.

[109] 'Electoral Rolls', letter from Mr Jagan Nath, Member of the Communal Harmony Board, Ambala District East Punjab to CAS, 20 July 1948, CA/12/FR/48, ECIR. Mr Nath noted that 'Of course the column of Harijans shall have to be retained for the present.' This was a handwritten letter, ending with the following sentence: 'Begging to be excused for my inability to get myself typed and requesting the favour of your kind reply.' The letter arrived at the CAS on 21 July 1948. The Under Secretary of the CAS drafted the reply letter acknowledging the receipt of his letter, 'containing suggestions regarding the preparation of electoral rolls' on 29 July 1948. Draft letter from CAS to Mr Jagan Nath, Member Communal Harmony Board Distt Ambala, 29 July 1948, CA/12/FR/48, ECIR.

[110] Letter from Gagan Dev Bhandari, Ludhiana, to the President of the Constitution Committee, 4 September 1948, CA/12/FR/48, ECIR. This was a handwritten letter. As already mentioned in Chapter 1, at that time there was a column for religion, SCs and STs in the preliminary rolls because the issue of reservations for minorities was still under consideration.

[111] Ibid.

tribe, or is in the Province of Madras or the Province of Bombay and is Christian, and for whom seats are reserved'.[112] Mr S. Balbir Singh Uppal suggested that by eliminating the caste and religion column 'except in the case of the depressed classes and that too for the first decade only... By adopting it into practice the secular state would automatically move a step forward in removing the religious propaganda from the political sphere of our free mother land.'[113]

For some individuals, the context of enumeration as voters provided an opportunity to appeal for communal harmony in the midst of partition. Mr D. V. Narasimha Rau, Headmaster of Board Secondary School at Duddukur, officially changed his name to Franklin Ram Mahomed. He did so as part of an initiative he started to promote – a 'world amity path' – to transcend religious conflicts. He suggested that the best method for India under the present circumstances would be for its people 'to adopt new names formed by conventionally combining three small names pertaining to the three "Major" "communities" ... one from Hindu, one from Muslim, and one from Christian'.[114] He explained that this idea 'has been very strongly agitating my mind... But Mahatmaji's [M. K. Gandhi] tragic demise has aggravated the agitation to its highest pitch, and I now find myself unable to resist ... the putting into action'. He wrote to the CAS complaining that while he was enumerated 'in Agraharam Ward Guntur Municipality Area, on 9.10.1948', the enumerator entered his name in the electoral roll as 'Franklin Ram Mahomed alias D. V. Narashimha Rau'.[115] He asked that this enumeration of his name should be ignored, and that his name 'may kindly be included in the Electoral Roll as given below: Franklin Ram Mahomed'.[116]

Most significantly, people began recognising their power in ensuring the success of the operation. The Government of Madras planned to

---

[112] Draft letter from CAS to Gagan Dev Bhandari, Ludhiana, 13 September 1948, CA/12/FR/48, ECIR. For a discussion of caste in relation to the electoral roll see Chapter 6.

[113] Letter from S. Balbir Singh Uppal to the President of the Constituent Assembly 19 November 1948, CA/12/FR/48, ECIR.

[114] 'Statement: World Amity Path', 4 April 1948, attached to a letter from Franklin Ram Mahomed, Alias D. V. Narashimha Rau, to CAS, 17 October 1948, CA/12/FR/48, ECIR. He also sent this statement to newspapers and news agencies for publication and comments.

[115] Letter from Franklin Ram Mahomed, Alias D. V. Narashimha Rau, to CAS, 17 October 1948, CA/12/FR/48, ECIR.

[116] Ibid. Within a week the Under Secretary of the CAS drafted the reply letter, acknowledging the receipt of his letter 'regarding the inclusion of your name in the preliminary electoral roll now under preparation'. Draft letter from CAS to Franklin Ram Mahomed, Alias D. V. Narashimha Rau, 25 October 1948, CA/12/FR/48, ECIR.

conduct the enumeration on 8 and 9 October 1948, and declared these two days as public holidays under the Negotiable Instruments Act.[117] It appealed to the people to stay in their homes on these days until they were enumerated. But some firms, as well as the Madras Chamber of Commerce, notified their employees that these dates would not be observed as public holidays. Some labour unions protested and wrote in the matter to their employers, the Premier of Madras and to the President of the Constituent Assembly, claiming that this is 'against the spirit of the Press Note published by the Government and the principle of adult suffrage enunciated by the Constituent Assembly of India'.[118] One union wrote:

It will be a waste to the Government both financially and politically if we do not actively extend our co-operation in their attempt for preparation of electoral rolls based on Adult Franchise on which depends the fate of toiling millions... We request you to declare both the days [of enumeration] as holidays to enable us to enlist all the members in our families as voters lest we should forfeit our citizenship.[119]

The union's letter explained that the cancellation of the enumeration holiday 'will prevent us from actively participating in the Enumeration, as female members in our families will be greatly handicapped by our absence for the following reasons: (1) Female members in our families will not furnish the names of their husbands ... in accordance with the prevailing custom; (2) There will not be any response from female members ... in our absence...'[120] This (letter) may throw some light on the notable fact that I could not find any letters from women in the records of the CAS's franchise branch.

The contents of the various correspondences, which were stimulated by narratives of the preparation of the rolls, suggest that people became active and creative readers of the CAS's press notes and the stories in the press. These stories elicited in them a sense of purpose in making adult franchise. People wrote to the CAS with their personal cases

[117] It is noteworthy that the Negotiable Instruments Act (1881) is still in existence and on its basis the Election Commission of India declares public holidays for elections. See, for example, Election Commission of India Press Note ECI/PN/54/2014, 'Schedule for General Elections to the Legislative Assemblies of Jharkhand and Jammu & Kashmir', 26.10.2014.

[118] Letter from Volkart Brothers Employees' Union Madras to the Chief Secretary, Government of Madras, 30 September 1948, CA/12/FR/48, ECIR. They requested that the government 'takes immediate steps' to ensure that all people working in commercial houses will be enumerated.

[119] Letter from the Madras Port Trust Employees' Union to Madras Port Trust, 6 October 1948, CA/12/FR/48, ECIR.

[120] Ibid.

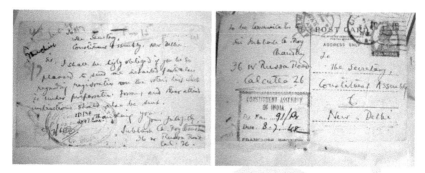

Figure 1 Postcard from the Election Commission of India Record Room files

and suggestions, which demonstrated that they made a place for themselves in the new Indian constitutional polity based on adult franchise. They also recognised their potential power to shape this world. Indeed, people's sense of stake in the successful preparation of rolls also manifested in their requests for information about 'what happened next' in the preparation of rolls. A few postcards arrived at the CAS asking for detailed information regarding the registration of the voters' list, requesting that 'forms and other allied information should also be sent'.[121] (See Figure 1.)

Typically, people's letters arrived at the CAS within less than five days from the date they were written, or posted. The CAS replied within at most two weeks from the day it received a letter, but usually even sooner.[122] The experience of having a direct and relatively quick contact with the Secretariat of the Constituent Assembly was, at least technically, enabled by the postal system.[123] It is symbolic that the post office serving

---

[121] Postcard from S. C. Roy Choudhry, Calcutta, to Secretary of the CAS, CA/12/FR/48, ECIR (date unclear; it was received on 8 July 1948). Also see Postcard from the Editor, *Nateshwar*, Bomaby, to CAS, 19 July 1948, CA/12/FR/48, ECIR. A reply from the CAS was drafted on 5 August 1948. The Secretary of the East Khandesh District Congress Committee wrote to the CAS that he hoped 'the Government will publish it widely throughout the villages before they start their work of collecting the required information about the voter from house to house'. Letter from K. G. Lele, Secretary of the East Khandesh District Congress Committee to the Secretary of CAS, 21 July 1948, CA/12/FR/48, ECIR.

[122] This is also based on the extensive correspondences between citizens' organisations and the CAS, which I discussed in Chapter 2.

[123] For an important work on the way postal networks created a national connectedness and became an actualisation of a federal government see David M. Henkin, *The Postal Age: The Emergence of Modern Communication in Nineteenth-Century America*, Chicago: The University of Chicago Press, 2006. For discussions on the history of the postal system in India see Geoffrey Clarke, *The Post Office of India and Its Story*, London: John Lane

a village was noted against the name of each village in the Form of the Electoral Roll.[124] The exchange of letters between people and the CAS contributed to connecting the personal and local with the national.[125] The fact that the CAS replied relatively promptly to people's letters was even more significant. From the perspective of ordinary people, getting a letter with a printed heading and an inscribed symbol of the Constituent Assembly of India was not, it can be safely assumed, an ordinary matter. It was likely as meaningful and as 'splendid to have a letter from the king'.[126] Moreover, the CAS's responsiveness to people's letters, which was also demonstrated in their correspondences with numerous citizens' organisations over the question of the registration of refugees and citizenship discussed in Chapter 2, fostered a sense of personal proximity and of being taken into account. People's experience of having, in effect, no degree of separation from the Secretariat of the Constituent Assembly intensified and personalised the sense of interconnectedness. The resulting collective passion over adult franchise was indispensible for the democratic imagination to resonate in the minds of Indians.

From the viewpoint of the Secretariat, while the devising of the instruction for the preparation of rolls rendered the people abstract individuals, their correspondences turned them into living subjects. The people now began to exist 'as a narrative, a collection of stories'.[127]

Conclusion

Storytelling the preparation of the rolls contributed to embedding the abstract principle of universal franchise in the imagination of people and thus to creating a legal meaning for it in three main ways. First, the iterative stories about how the preparation of the electoral roll came to be, and more importantly, as the chapter has shown, how it came to be owned by people, concretised the vision of adult franchise. It was now understood, to borrow Robert Cover's construction, 'in the context of the narratives that [gave] it meaning'.[128] Cover argued that for 'every constitution there

The Bodley Head, 1921; C. A. Bayly, *Empire and Information: Intelligence Gathering and Social Communication in India, 1780–1870*, Cambridge: Cambridge University Press, 1997, pp. 58–66; Devyani Gupta, *The Postal System of British India, c. 1830–1920*, Unpublished PhD thesis, University of Cambridge, 2016.

[124] Letter No. CA/64/RR/47, 15 March 1948, CA/1/Fr/48-I, ECIR. (Letter of instructions for the preparation of electoral rolls.)

[125] This point is suggestive of Henkin's discussion of the role of postal networks in annihilating time and space. Henkin, *The Postal Age*, p. 8.

[126] Rabindranath Tagore, *The Post Office (Daak Ghar)*, 1914.

[127] Rosanvallon, *Democratic Legitimacy*, p. 70.

[128] Cover, 'Forward: Nomos and Narrative', pp. 4–5.

is an epic'.[129] The dynamics of narrating the roll produced in some sense an epic for India's constitution, which was in the making.

Second, accounts of the preparation of rolls did not simply allow Indians to narrate the passage of the universal franchise. These narratives fostered among people a sense of commitment to the normative vision that universal franchise entailed. As evidenced by the contents of their letters, people began to show dedication and a will to protect it. Their name in the voters' list was not just a procedural site that marked a right. They began identifying with it and conveyed a sense that it belonged to them. A place in the roll became their title deed for democracy. Indeed, the subjects of democracy, as Ken Hirschkop suggested, 'are not just bearers of rights and duties, but also "heroes" of narratives, and their desire for a good life embraces not only material goods ... but also a narrative which endows all these features [of a good life] with a symbolic meaning'.[130]

Third, the CAS's storytelling of the preparation of the electoral roll, and the ensuing narratives in the press from across the country contributed to connecting the local, regional, and the national into a single coherent story, epitomised in the joint list of voters. In the same way that the repetition of similar stories about the preparation of rolls from across India created a temporal and spatial unity of the story of making adult franchise, the correspondences compressed time and space. In doing so, storytelling the roll enabled the possibility of imagining a new spatial set up for India.

It was not a straightforward task to make of India a unified territory, or to make sense of its territory after partition and in the midst of the process of the integration of the princely states. While recognising that the accession of the rulers of the states by 15 August 1947 'was only the prelude to a final solution of the States problem',[131] V. P. Menon, the architect of the integration of the Indian states, explained in reference to the moment of independence that 'By the policy of accession we had ensured the fundamental unity of the country. India had become one federation, with the provinces and the states as integral parts.'[132] But accession did not commit the ruler of a state in any way to acceptance of any future constitution of India or to 'fetter his discretion to enter into arrangements with the Government of

---

[129] Ibid., p. 4.
[130] Hirschkop, *Mikhail Bakhtin: An Aesthetic for Democracy*, p. 245.
[131] V. P. Menon, *The Story of the Integration of the Indian States*, New Delhi: Orient Longmans, 1961, p. 119.
[132] Ibid., p. 116.

India under any such future constitution'.[133] Under the Instrument of Accession the rulers retained their full autonomy and sovereignty except on three subjects: defence, external affairs, and communications. Only these were transferred to the central government of the new dominion.[134]

Indeed, the Indian Supreme Court ruled years later that 'whatever measure of sovereignty they [rulers] had when paramountcy lapsed, less the portion given to the Indian Dominion by their Instruments of Accession in 1947; they lost none of it during the interlude when they toyed with the experiment of integration'.[135] The rulers of the states ceded their sovereignty only with the signing of an Instrument of Merger, which in some cases materialised just before the new Constitution came into force in 1950. The preparation of electoral rolls on the basis of adult franchise for India as a whole nation, I suggest, played an important part in bringing to fruition the integration and the making of the new federal structure. The next chapter explores this process.

Appendix 3.I

Constituent Assembly of India

Press Note

The following Press Note is issued by the Secretariat of the Constituent Assembly of India on the progress of the work connected with the preparation of electoral rolls under the new Constitution:

As already announced in the Press Note dated the 15th July 1948, instructions have been issued to the Provincial and State Governments that for the present refugees should be registered in the roll on the mere declaration by them of their intention to reside permanently in the locality to which the electoral roll relates, irrespective of the actual period of residence, that such enrolment is liable to revision in due time in accordance with the new electoral law when enacted, and that the question of *relaxing the residential qualification* would be considered when the electoral law is under examination.

---

[133] AIR 1961 Guj 151, (1961) 2 GLR 343. This was set in Clause 7 of the Instrument of Accession. Also see a discussion of this clause in D. N. Banerjee, 'Indian States and the Future Constitution of India', *The Indian Journal of Political Science* 10, no. 1/2, 1949, pp. 94–100.

[134] The Indian Supreme Court established this position in AIR 1954 SC 447 and in AIR 1958 SC 816.

[135] AIR 1954 SC 447.

For ensuring uniformity, a 'refugee' has been defined as a person who has migrated into a Province or a State on account of disturbances or fear of disturbances in his usual place of residence. It has also been decided that the declaration which a refugee has to make regarding his intention to reside permanently in a town or village should be in writing, that a separate declaration should be filled in respect of each adult member of a family except in the case of a wife, in whose case the husband's declaration would serve the purpose as the wife 's domicile would follow the domicile of her husband, and that in the case of other women the head of the family might be permitted to sign the declarations on their behalf. These declarations should be made before any responsible officer to be specified in this behalf by the Provincial or State Government, and nor necessarily the District Magistrate, the intention being that a person who desires to make the declaration should not find it difficult to get at the officer.

This declaration is quite different from and does not dispense with that required under clause (ii) of the explanation to article 5 of the Draft Constitution, which related to citizenship and which cannot be made until auxiliary action referred to in the foot-note on page 4 of the Draft Constitution has been taken. Refugees are being enrolled for the present on the strength of declarations made by them indicating their intention to reside permanently in the locality to which the electoral roll relates, *the verification regarding their citizenship being left to a later stage.*

Attention in this connection is invited to the Press Note issued by the Government of India Ministry of Relief and Rehabilitation on September 24, that their earlier press note dated 2nd July which was misconstrued in some quarters as purporting to announce that persons who have migrated or might migrate from Pakistan to India before 30th September 1948 could claim India domicile has no bearing at all on the general question of the citizenship of the Indian Union or of a person eligibility for enrolment in the provisional electoral rolls now under preparation.

Several complaints have been received in the Secretariat of the Constituent Assembly against the order of the Government of West Bengal requiring that declarations under clause (ii) of the Explanation to article 5 of the Draft Constitution, relating to citizenship, to be made in the form of an affidavits on embossed stamp paper of Rs 2/-. These orders were apparently issued under some misapprehension since as stated in the previous paragraph the declaration about citizenship cannot be made at this stage. The Government of West Bengal has since withdrawn their original orders and issued fresh orders making it clear that such affidavits are not necessary at this stage and that the refugees are now only required to make a declaration in writing, *free of charge,* indicating their intention to reside permanently in the locality for which the electoral roll is being prepared.

Complaints have also been received against the order of the Government of Assam in requiring a court-fee stamp of value of annas eight to be affixed on the declarations to be filled by refugees for inclusion in the preliminary electoral rolls now under preparation. It was never intended that such a fee should be imposed[136] and the Government of Assam too have since withdrawn that order.

Representations have also been received to the effect that the period between now and the 30th September 1948, the date fixed by the Government of Assam as the date on or before which the declarations are to be filled is too short, that large numbers of refugees in Assam would not be able to file their declarations before that date and that this period should be extended. In response to these representations the Government of Assam have extended the period and have fixed the 31st October 1948 as the date on or before which the declarations for enrolment should be filed.

From the reports received in this Secretariat the work on the preparation of the preliminary rolls seems to be progressing well in most of the Provinces and States

New Delhi,
September 25, 1948.[137]

---

[136] This sentence from internal discussions on the matter in the Secretariat was reproduced in the Press Note. This is indicative of the authenticity of the CAS's Press Notes, which in turn evoked a sense of trustworthiness – a virtue that lay at the heart of a successful electoral process and system.
[137] Constituent Assembly of India Press Note, 25 September 1948, CA/12/FR/48.

Map 1 Provinces, states and districts prior to 15 August 1947

Map 2 Pre-Partition India, 1947

Map 3 Post-Independence India and Pakistan

4   Disciplining the Federal Structure

The big thing before India is now Federation. I have spent, off and on, over a dozen years in the study of constitutional law in general and the India Constitution in particular; and within the limits permitted to me, I have had some share in the working out of the details of the federal scheme now taking shape.... I should like to stay on here until Federation, in whatever form it ultimately comes, is an accomplished fact.

(B.N. Rau to the Private Secretary of the Viceroy,
Lord Wavell, ca. June 1945)[1]

Those who claim 'India' do not know what its limits really are... The Indian Independence Act, whatever else it may have done, has not rendered India one. For the matter of that, it cannot.

(R. K. Ranadive)[2]

India is trying an experiment of planting parliamentary democracy on the stem of federalism and its success depends upon creating an enlightened electorate.

(N. V. Gadgil)[3]

The joint electoral roll, comprised of all India's adult citizens, would need to cover the entire territory over which the Indian state exercised authority. But after independence, the question of what constituted the limits of 'India' remained a challenge and was in flux. The Union did not yet exist. India was trying to integrate 552 princely states that covered about 40 per cent of the subcontinent's territory, with

---

[1] Letter from B. N. Rau to the Private Secretary of the Viceroy, Lord Wavell ca. June 1945, in B. N. Rau, edited by B. Shiva Rao, *India's Constitution in the Making*, Madras: Orient Longmans, 1960, p. xix.

[2] R. K. Ranadive, *The Legal Rights of the Indian States and of Their Subjects or The Truth about the India States*, Baroda: The Good Companions, 1950, p. 125.

[3] N. V. Gadgil, in 'Gadgil Praises India's Constitution', *The Hindustan Times*, 3 January 1950, p. 5.

a population of nearly 90 million people.[4] Making the federation was indeed the 'big thing before India'.[5]

'By any standards "integration"', as Ian Copland argued, 'represented a major watershed.'[6] Indeed, contrary to a previously prevalent view that the destruction of the princely states was inevitable, historical works in recent decades argue that no empirical evidence 'suggests that the states were about to self-destruct'[7] in the 1940s, and that the states' 'relatively quick and smooth integration was not foreseen'.[8] On the whole, studies of the integration of the princely states conclude their historical investigations with the signing of the Instrument of Accession (hereafter IOA) at independence.[9] But the states possessed various degrees of sovereignty

---

[4] See Ian Copland, *The Princes of India in the Endgame of Empire, 1917–1947*, Cambridge: Cambridge University Press, 1997, p. 1; V. P. Menon, *The Story of the Integration of the Indian States*, Bombay: Orient Longmans, 1961 (first edition 1956), p. 468.

[5] Letter from B. N. Rau to the Private Secretary of the Viceroy, Lord Wavell ca. June 1945, in Rau, *India's Constitution in the Making*, p. xix.

[6] Copland, *The Princes of India in the Endgame of Empire*, p. 1. Sardar Patel who headed the Ministry of States during the process of integration described the process during a debate at the Constituent Assembly as 'a bloodless revolution, an achievement unparalleled in the history of any country at any time'. *Constituent Assembly Debates* (hereafter *CAD*), 13 October 1949, (available on http://parliamentofindia.nic.in/ls/debates/debates.htm, accessed 28 June 2017). All references to the *CAD* hereunder are taken from this source.

[7] Copland, *The Princes of India in the Endgame of Empire*, p. 270. Also see his discussion on pp. 13–14, 217–28 and 270–87.

[8] Barbara Ramusack, *The Indian Princes and Their States*, Cambridge: Cambridge University Press, 2004, p. 8. Also see pp. 9–12, 245–74. For earlier important collection of studies on the princely Indian states see Robin Jeffrey (ed.), *People, Princes and Paramount Power. Society and Politics in the Indian Princely States*, Delhi: Oxford University Press, 1978. Ramusack and Copland aim in particular to understand the rapid changes that led to integration. These works began to open for further investigation what has been one of the authoritative narratives of the *Story of Integration*, written by V. P. Menon, who was one of the prime architects of the process and who conducted the prolonged negotiations over the mergers of the state between 1947–1950. For illuminating discussions of the sovereign status of the princely states see Stephen Legg, 'An International Anomaly? Sovereignty, the League of Nations and India's Princely Geographies', *Journal of Historical Geography* 43, 2014, pp. 96–110; Sarath Pillai, 'Fragmenting the Nation: Divisible Sovereignty and Travancore's Quest for Federal Independence', *Law and History Review* 34, no. 3, 2016, pp. 743–82. Also see Eric Lewis Beverley, *Hyderabad, British India, and the World. Muslim Networks and Minor Sovereignty c. 1850–1950*, Cambridge: Cambridge University Press, 2015. For a broader review of the historiography of the princely states see Fiona Groenhout, 'The History of the Indian Princely States: Bringing the Puppets Back onto Centre Stage', *History Compass*, 4, no. 4, 2006, pp. 629–44. For recent literature on various aspects of political modernisation in the princely states see, for example, Waltraud Ernst and Biswamoy Pati (eds), *India's Princely States. People, Princes and Colonialism*, London: Routledge, 2007; Janaki Nair, *Mysore Modern: Rethinking the Region under Princely Rule*, Minneapolis: University of Minneapolis Press, 2011.

[9] For some recent important detailed studies of specific princely states during the period of transition from independence to the early 1950s see Taylor C. Sherman,

even after their rulers signed the IOA by 15 August 1947.[10] As these studies recognise, the actual amalgamation of the states into the new Indian Union, was a piecemeal process carried out during 1947–1950.

Contemporaneous accounts of the mergers that took place between 1948 and 1950 presented, in the main, descriptions of the number and names of units, as well as total area, that was brought into the jurisdiction of the Government in Delhi. These studies reviewed the different forms of amalgamation that took place: the absorption of small states into the provinces, the formation of covenants of Unions of States, and the takeover of some single princely states by the central administration.[11] *The Story of the Integration* told by one of its key architects, V. P. Menon, provides to date the most detailed account of the negotiations of mergers with the rulers as these transpired from the months preceding independence until just after the constitution came into force.[12] The various accounts, however, did not examine the immediate implications of the long process of integration for the operation of state making on the ground. Indeed, some of the merger agreements were finalised just

---

Muslim Belonging in Secular India. Negotiating Citizenship in Postcolonial Hyderabad, Cambridge: Cambridge University Press, 2015; Srinath Raghavan, *War and Peach in Modern India*, Basingstoke: Palgrave Macmillan, 2010, for a study of Junagadh, Hyderabad, and Kashmir; to date, V. P. Menon's *The Story of Integration* forms the most detailed account of the process of integration as it transpired from the months preceding independence until just after the constitution came into force.

[10] Government of India, Ministry of States, *White Paper on Indian States*, Delhi: The Manger of Publications, 1950, p. 58, V/27/272/21, India Office Collections, British Library, London (hereafter IOC). Notably, while the majority of states signed the Instrument of Accession (hereafter IOA) by 15 August 1947, 52 states signed it between then and 2 November 1948. Only by 19 November 1947 the seven Regional Commissioners were appointed for a total of 250 states. See All India States' People Congress (AISPC) papers, f. 277, Nehru Memorial and Museum Library, New Delhi (hereafter NMML).

[11] See, for example, 'India: An Enigmatic Future', *The Round Table: The Commonwealth Journal of International Affairs*, 38: 151, 1948, pp. 690–5; 'India: First Year of Freedom', *The Round Table: The Commonwealth Journal of International Affairs*, 38: 152, 1948, 793–7; 'The Revolution of the Indian States', *The Round Table: The Commonwealth Journal of International Affairs*, 39: 153–6, 1948, pp. 36–43. (No author name is mentioned for these articles.) For a comprehensive review see Holden Furber, 'The Unification of India, 1947–1951', *Pacific Affairs*. 24, no. 4, 1951, pp. 352–71. Also see Government of India, *White Paper on Indian States*, Delhi: The Manger of Publications, July 1948, V/27/272/20, IOC; and Government of India, Ministry of States, *White Paper on Indian States*, 1950.

[12] Menon, *The Story of the Integration*. The integration process ultimately resembled Ambedkar's proposition a decade earlier: 'To pension off a prince and to annex his territory is a legal way and can fall under the principles with which we are familiar under the Land Acquisition Act which allows private rights and properties to be acquired for political purposes.' B. R. Ambedkar, *Federation versus Freedom*, Jullundur: Bheem Patrika Publications, 1977, p. 115. ('Kale Memorial Lecture', Gokhale Institute of Politics and Economics, Pune, 29 January 1939).

before the enactment of the constitution in January 1950.[13] How, then, did the administrative machinery, both at the Centre and in the provinces, assume authority over the integrated territories? And how did the people of the states make the change from state subjects into subject-citizens of India? Moreover, how would the bureaucratic apparatus of hitherto autocratic princely states adapt to democracy?

The task of welding a federation, that would bring the princely states and the provinces into a new unitary polity, and of establishing the authority of the Centre over it, presented both a constitutional and an administrative trial. Moreover, moulding the notion of all-India subjects, belonging to 'India', out of the state subjects and the subjects of British India was not guaranteed to become a self-realised category that would be inevitably derived from draft laws or merger agreements.

From a constitutional viewpoint, the IOA in effect secured in the immediate the rulers' sovereignty. Under the IOA the rulers ceded to the government of the new dominion control only over defence, external affairs and communication. The rulers or the State governments even retained exclusive authority over the States Forces because these armed forces were 'excluded from the scope of "defence"'.[14] The IOA, contained a clause, which stated that 'nothing in the Instrument of Accession shall be deemed to commit the Ruler of the State in any way to acceptance of any future constitution of India or to fetter his discretion to enter into arrangements with the Government of India under any such future constitution'.[15] Some rulers of the states evoked this clause from time to time.[16] The scope of the accession of the states in August 1947 was therefore very limited.

---

[13] The fiscal integration agreements, which would enable the Government of India to extract revenue from across the new polity, a basic state function, were executed only in April 1950. See Menon, *The Story of the Integration*, pp. 438–41.

[14] This was the case barring when the State Forces were operating with any of the armed forces of the Dominion. See Menon, *The Story of the Integration*, p. 429.

[15] AIR 1961 Guj 151, (1961) 2 GLR 343. This was clause 7 of the IOA. Also see a discussion of this clause in D. N. Banerjee, 'Indian States and the Future Constitution of India', *The Indian Journal of Political Science* 10, no. 1/2, 1949, pp. 94–100.

[16] For example, in April 1948 the ruler of Bikaner based his criticism of the Draft Constitution on this clause while noting that 'While the Maharaja of Bikaner strongly advocated the accession of the States in regard to the three subjects ... he is naturally keen to safeguard the sovereignty of the States and to protect them against any encroachment by the Centre except to the extent that the sovereignty has already been surrendered by agreement.' 'Note containing the views of the Bikaner State in regard to the Draft Constitution of the Indian Union', in a letter from Jaswant Singh, Prime Minister of Bikaner to the Joint Secretary to the Constituent Assembly of India, 9 April 1948, Ministry of States (hereafter MoS), f. 414(I)-P, National Archives of India, New Delhi (hereafter NAI). Also see, as another example, letter from the Government of Patiala and East Punjab States Union to the Secretary to the Government of India,

Moreover, the Constituent Assembly of India had no power of framing any constitution for the territories comprised of the Indian states. The Draft Constitution did not contain any provision for the acceptance of the Constitution as finally approved by the Constituent Assembly by the states specified in Part III of the First Schedule.[17] The covenants of mergers for the creation of the Union of States during 1948 were 'an act of State', entered into by rulers of independent states.[18] These covenants made provisions for the creation of a constituent Assembly for the new Unions of States that would frame a constitution for them. Some of these Unions were in the process of establishing constitution-making bodies for themselves until late in 1949.[19] Thus, between 1947 and 1950, many of the states and Unions of States enjoyed internal sovereignty and remained uncommitted to the new draft Constitution.

For mergers to become fully effective they required on-going revisions and adaptations of laws and administrative procedures, both at the provincial level and at the centre. Until such legislation came into effect, the rulers' policies and obligations had legal standing despite the mergers.[20] Legal disputes that arose across several areas of law in the 1950s between former subjects of the states or commercial entities and state governments demonstrated that such constitutional gaps and challenges that the integration of the states wrought, sometimes lived longer than

Ministry of States, 18 January 1948, CA/1/FR/49-I, ECIR. The letter dealt with the formation of the Constituent Assembly of the Patiala and East Punjab States Union.

[17] This issue and the question of the relations between the Union and the Princely States more broadly elicited many comments and suggestions on the Draft Constitution. See, for example, V. T. Krishnamachari, Jai Dev Singh, B. H. Zaidi, and Sardar Singh of Khetbi (members of the CA), *Memorandum on the Draft Constitution of India*, 22 March 1948, pp. 12–13, 17–18, NAI, MoS, f. 414(I)-P. Also see *Report of the Committee for the Drafting of a Model Constitution for the Indian States*, New Delhi: Manager Government of India Press, 22 March 1949, MoS, f. 414-P, NAI.

[18] AIR 1960 Raj 138. Also see AIR 1954 SC 447. Thus, despite covenants which the rulers of some states signed, after they already signed the Instrument of Accession and under negotiations with the Government of India, to unite themselves into one State, like the covenant that formed in March 1948 the United States of Vindhya Pradesh, or the covenant of eight Indian States in East Punjab in May 1948 for the merger of their territories into one State called the Patiala and East Punjab States, the rulers' sovereignty was not lost to the Dominion of India.

[19] *White Paper on Indian States*, 1950, pp. 108–10.

[20] For example, the Indian Income-tax Act, 1922, did not automatically repeal taxation laws in the merged states. They were revoked by the Taxation Laws (Extension to Merged States and Amendment) Act 67 of 1949. The Governor General of India issued the Taxation Laws (Extension to Merged States) Ordinance 21 of 1949 to make certain taxation laws applicable to the merged States. This Ordinance was repealed by the Taxation Laws (Extension to Merged States and Amendment) Act 67 of 1949. See 1968 AIR 579, 168 SCR (2) 1. Also see Government of India, Ministry of States, Report of the Indian States Finance Enquiry Committee 1948–49, Part I, New Delhi: Manager of Government of India Press, 1949.

the merger agreements. For example, in legal disputes over tax liabilities, or suits over the age of retirement, the Indian Supreme Court held that the existing laws in the states and the Union of States that acceded to the Dominion of India continued until they were repealed. Sometimes the revocation of laws took place long after accession.[21]

Creating the federation lay at the heart of the process of the integration of the states. The Government of India Act, 1935, on which the draft constitution was mainly based, provided for a Federation of India comprised of the provinces, Chief Commissioner's provinces and the Indian states. But that part of the Act required the accession of the Indian states in sufficient numbers for this federation to come into effect. That threshold was never reached.[22]

The making of the new Indian federation was also consequential for the provinces, which were soon to be states. From 1919 onwards, and especially under the 1935 Act, provincial governments enjoyed a high degree of autonomy.[23] For example, provinces could set their own rules

---

[21] For example: under the rules of the Wadhwan State the retirement age of civil servants was 60. The state's administration was made over to the Saurashtra Government as part of the covenant entered into by the rulers of the Kathiawar States on 16 March 1948. In a case of a suit by a former subject of the Wadhwan State for compensation against the Saurashtra State for forced premature retirement from service at the age of 55, in June 1948, the Supreme Court of India held that 'the terms of the Covenant showed that the existing laws were to continue and whatever the rights of the Appellant were under the existing laws were available for enforcement to the Appellant'. The Court held that 'When the Wadhwan State merged with the Saurashtra State and again when it acceded to the Dominion of India all the existing laws continued until repealed.' *Bholanath J. Thaker vs State Of Saurashtra* on 4 May 1954 (Appeal (civil) 170 of 1954). This set a precedent for other cases on a variety of matters. See, for example, *The State of Madhya Bharat vs Behramji Dungaji And Co.* on 6 September, 1957.

[22] See 'The Parliamentary System of Government in India' (an address delivered by B. N. Rau to I.A.S. probationers in New Delhi in June 1948), in Rau, *India's Constitution in the Making*, p. 327. Nevertheless, it was doubtful whether the 1935 federal scheme could at all provide a good basis for the integration of the states, and the democratisation of India. Ambedkar, for example, argued that 'the Federal scheme does not help, indeed hinders British India from setting up in motion processes which would result in the democratization of the Indian States. On the other hand it helps the Indian States to destroy democracy in British India.' Ambedkar, *Federation Versus Freedom*, p. 82. To argue this, Ambedkar presented an analysis of sections 34(1), 380 and 40 of the Act. See ibid, pp. 75–82. For the federal vision of the Indian states see Pillai, 'Fragmenting the Nation: Divisible Sovereignty and Travancore's Quest for Federal Independence'.

[23] For a recent discussion of that process see Eleanor Newbigin, Ornit Shani, and Stephen Legg, 'Introduction: Constitutionalism and the Evolution of Democracy in India', *Comparative Studies of South Asia, Africa and the Middle East* 36, no. 1, 2016, pp. 42–3; Stephen Legg, 'Dyarchy: Democracy, Autocracy, and the Scalar Sovereignty of Interwar India', *Comparative Studies of South Asia, Africa and the Middle East* 36, no. 1, 2016, pp. 44–65; Arvind Elangovan, 'Provincial Autonomy, Sir Benegal Narsing Rau, and an Improbable Imagination of Constitutionalism in India, 1935–38', *Comparative Studies of South Asia, Africa and the Middle East* 36, no. 1, 2016, pp. 66–82. Under the 1935 Act the legislatures of the provinces, in six of the eleven of the lower chamber, consisted of wholly elected representatives.

for franchise qualifications and election management.[24] The federal scheme that the Union Power Committee of the Constituent Assembly submitted to the Assembly on 20 August 1947 introduced a federation with a strong centre.[25] This was a radical departure from the federal scheme put forward in the cabinet mission's statement of 16 May 1946, which envisioned serious limitations on the scope of central authority, and which the Union Power Committee originally worked with. Thus, it was not just the princely states that had to be integrated into the new union. To some extent the provinces also had to be brought in. Moreover, mergers also posited administrative challenges. The gradual merger of states with provinces, ultimately an amalgamation of 216 of the 552 states with provinces, required administrative adaptations and integration procedures. For a start, district-level administrative units did not exist in the states.[26]

Finally, while the constitutional and administrative boundaries of the dominion's sovereignty were negotiated and changing India was yet to become a nation. It had to be both 'physically and emotionally integrated … and the national sentiment strengthened'.[27] Ambedkar's view, ahead of the 1935 Act, was that 'the most vital need of the day is to create a mong the mass of the people of India the sense of a common nationality, the feeling … that they are Indians first and Indians last'.[28] His position was that the 1935 federal scheme did not forge a common citizenship for all member units, nor did it create a common nationality. Under the Act, the people of the states remained subjects of the states.[29] In 1948 some members of the Constituent Assembly, as well as rulers and governments of states, envisioned a dual citizenship in India: union citizenship and state citizenship.[30]

The constitutional and administrative challenges of welding the federation and the need to forge a common idea of Indianness, manifested in

[24] See, for example, the discussion on the registration of women as voters under the 1935 Act in Chapter 1.

[25] Appendix 'A', No. CA/23/Com./47, 'Constituent Assembly of India Report of the Union Powers Committee', *CAD*, 20 August 1947. This was a supplementary report to the Committees' first Report to the Assembly on 28 April 1947.

[26] Government of India, *White Paper on Indian States*.

[27] Constituent Assembly of India, *Report of the Linguistic Provinces Commission*, New Delhi: The Manager Government of India Press, 1948 (10 December 1948), p. 31. The Commission concluded that only then the planning for linguistic re-organisation could take place.

[28] Quoted in D. R. Gadgil (Dhananjaya Ramchandra), *Federating India*, Vol. 13. Poona: Gokhale Institute of Politics and Economics, 1945, p. 11.

[29] Ambedkar, *Federation versus Freedom*, pp. 21, 64, 75.

[30] See, for example, V. T. Krishnamachari, Jai Dev Singh, B. H. Zaidi, and Sardar Singh of Khetbi, *Memorandum on the Draft Constitution of India*, pp. 12–13; and 'Note containing the views of the Bikaner State in regard to the Draft Constitution of the Indian Union'.

the process of the preparation of the electoral roll. Yet, it was in the face of these challenges, I argue, that the preparation of electoral rolls on the basis of universal franchise became a key mechanism of integration, and of making a democratic federal structure. The preparation of the preliminary electoral roll comprising of all India's adult citizens was inherently tied to its territory. A voter had to be a citizen, and to have a place of residence in the electoral unit where he or she would register.[31] The preparation of rolls was a state building project of the largest possible scale in terms of its population and territorial reach. Thus, at a time when 'who is an Indian' was in question, and 'where is India' was in flux, the preparation of the roll became an important factor in the actual binding of the territories of the provinces and the states, and the people into a unified democratic order.

First, the preparation of electoral rolls rendered the integration of the states into the newly emerging federal structure concrete, sometimes even before their mergers were completed. It required of administrators across the country at the same point in time to penetrate its territories up to the lowest local level, to reach every adult, and to implement an all-India plan. The Constituent Assembly Secretariat (CAS) directed this mega bureaucratic project from Delhi. By engaging the states and provinces in the preparation of the electoral rolls, the CAS brought all the units of the evolving federation within the ambit of the new draft Constitution. In doing so it demonstrated the institutional capacity of the centre to penetrate its territories and implement the Constituent Assembly's decision to adopt universal franchise.[32]

Second, the preparation of the electoral rolls set in motion the relations between the centre and the states under the newly envisioned constitutional federal scheme. The preparation of rolls involved basic matters of federal (Centre-State) relations, as well as of state building. It entailed significant expenditures. It required, for example, the sanctioning of budgets for enumerators, large amounts of paper for printing,

---

[31] Moreover, an underlying principle of the draft constitutional citizenship provisions was that a citizen ought to have some kind of a territorial connection with India. See B. R. Ambedkar's cover letter to the 21 February 1948 draft Constitution in: The Drafting Committee, Constituent Assembly of India, *Draft Constitution of India*, New Delhi: The Manager Government of India Press, 1948, p. v. Also see B. Shiva Rao, *The Framing of India's Constitution: A Study*, Vol. III, Nasik: The Manager, Government of India Press, 1968, p. 511; Vol. I, pp. 157–8, 161–2.

[32] This point is suggestive of Matthew G. Hannah's discussion of institutional capacity. See Matthew G. Hannah, *Governmentality and the Mastery of Territory in Nineteenth-Century America*, Cambridge: Cambridge University Press, 2000, pp. 38–9. Hannah bases his discussion on Michael Mann, *The Sources of Social Power*, Vol. II, Cambridge: Cambridge University Press, 1998, p. 59.

among other costs. The question of the apportionment of the costs of the preparation and printing of rolls between the Centre and the states became a subject of prolonged correspondence between the CAS and the provinces and the states. State governments' demands that the centre should share the costs of the preparation of rolls lent recognition to its authority. The way this question was dealt with became a means of disciplining the federation.

Third, the decision to print the preliminary rolls entrenched spatially the universal franchise and electoral democracy upon India's forming territory. The printed registry of all adult voters, and therefore the universal franchise, turned India into a *pucca* democracy. The design and the form of printing produced a democratic cartography for India, and constructed its unity.

The chapter explores these three influences of the preparation of the roll in the throes of national integration and in making a democratic federal order. The first section examines the dynamics of bringing the integrating states and the provinces in, within the forming Union, through the preparation of the electoral rolls. The second part focuses on the question of the cost of the preparation of the rolls and its implications for the disciplining of the new federation. The third section examines the implications of the design and the form of the printing of the preliminary rolls for the spatial democratisation of India and its unity.

Bringing the States and Provinces in

In November 1947 the CAS sent a circular letter to the Premiers of all the provinces, the states, and the Convenors of group states, asking them to examine the administrative problems involved in the 'colossal' project of preparing electoral rolls on the basis of adult franchise.[33] Reaching out to the governments or rulers of the states, however, was not a simple task. A member of the CAS noted that 'a great difficulty was experienced in issuing letters to the individual states and the States Ministry was informally approached and a list showing designations of Regional Commissioners and the states with whom they are concerned ... has been procured'.[34] Yet, they found that the lists of states, and the relevant addresses for correspondences became dated very quickly.

---

[33] Letters from CAS to Premiers of all the Provinces, the States, and the Convenors of group States, 22 November 1947 and 27 November 1947, CA/1/FR/48-I, and CA/5/FR/48, ECIR. For a detailed discussion see Chapter 1.

[34] S. no. 46, 18–20 March 1948, CA/I/FR/48-I, ECIR. In November 1947 the Ministry of States sent a letter to all the Chief Secretaries of the provinces, Chief Commissioners of provinces, all government of India ministries and other governmental bodies on

When the CAS reviewed replies from the states and the provinces to the November 1947 letter in mid-January, the political landscape already began to change. For example, a member of the CAS noted that since November the Bastar and Surguja states had merged with the Central Provinces & Berar, and that Patna, Kalahandi and Keonjhar states had merged with Orissa Province. He noted that the Secretariat already received replies from the Patna, Surguja, and Baster states. But since they had merged, there was no need to send a letter of reminder in the matter to the Kalahandi and Keonjhar states.[35]

By the time the CAS issued the instructions for the preparation of rolls on 15 March 1948, 59 states merged with provinces and 217 states covenanted to form the Union of Saurashtra.[36] At that time, the Under Secretary of the CAS sent an instruction letter to the Regional Commissioners concerned 'with as many spare copies as there are states under their charge'.[37] But calculating the number of copies that were needed for that purpose was not a straightforward enterprise. A member of the CAS observed that some of the states to which the Secretariat already issued the 15 March letter have since come under Regional Commissioners. 'It is not known', he wrote, 'whether the states which have since merged with the Provinces or have formed them-selves into unions, still continue to be under charge of the Regional Commissioners.'[38] Moreover, some of the minor states did not appear in the list obtained from the Ministry of States and it was not clear whether they were under the charge of the Regional Commissioner. Indeed, the position of states was in such a flux that between 15 March and 10 April 1948, while the CAS had prepared copies of the letter of instructions to the Regional Commissioners, one state merged into a province, 35 states formed the United States of Vindhya Pradesh, and four states formed the Union of Matsya. Ultimately, on top of the letters they had already

'Correspondences with Indian States'. The Ministry informed that they have appointed Regional Commissioners for states, and instructed that 'all correspondence on non-controversial matters and not involving a question of policy intended for the States may be addressed to the Regional Commissioners concerned direct. Correspondence in respect of other matters may continue to be addressed through this Ministry as before.' Letter from the Under Secretary to the Government of India, Ministry of States, 10 November 1947, CA/I/FR/48-I, ECIR. Initially, the CAS worked with a list of 574 Indian States in the 'Statistical Hand Book No. 1 (revised)'.

[35] S. no. 24–26, 12 January 1948, CA/I/FR/48-I, ECIR. A list of 34 States and of 11 rulers of states was attached to this note. On 1 January 1948, 23 States ceded to Orissa, and 14 to C.P. & Berar.
[36] Government of India, *White Paper on Indian States*, 1948; *White Paper on Indian States*, 1950.
[37] Internal note, 20 March 1948, CA/I/FR/48-I, ECIR.
[38] Internal note (by A. A. Abidi), 6 April 1948, CA/I/FR/48-I, ECIR.

Map 4 The progress of the political reorganisation of states according
to integration and merger schemes up to 31 May 1948

sent, a further 229 copies of the 15 March instruction letter were sent
to seven Regional Commissioners 'for transmission to the various states
with which you are concerned, with a view to enable them to take immediate steps for the preparation of the electoral rolls, where that work has
not been taken up so far'.[39]

The 15 March instruction letter became the main reference against
which to align administratively and constitutionally the evolving parts
of the Union.[40] Moreover, the letter inaugurated officially the new ter-
minology of the forming federal structure comprised of the Centre and
states. The letter specified: 'It is clearly desirable that the elections for

---

[39] S. no. 69, Draft letter from CAS to Regional Commissioners for States, 10 April 1949,
CA/I/FR/48-I, ECIR.
[40] Indeed, as already mentioned in Chapter 1, reports on the progress of the work from
across the country repeatedly stated: 'with reference to your letter No. CA/64/RR/
47, dated 15th March, 1948'. See, for example, Fortnightly Report from East Punjab
Government, 16 October 1948, CA/1/FR/48-III, ECIR; letter from the Deputy
Secretary to the Government of West Bengal, M. M. Basu, to the Joint Secretary of the
Constituent Assembly of India, 14 December 1948, CA/1/FR/48-IV, ECIR.

the future Central and Provincial Legislatures *(these latter are referred to in the new Constitution as State Legislatures)* should be completed as early as possible after the new Constitution comes into operation.'[41]

Between March 1948 and October 1949 the CAS sent 13 circular letters to all the forming parts of the Union with regard to different aspects of the preparation of the electoral rolls.[42] These letters and the ensuing correspondences they prompted, sustained the bureaucratic dialogues on the making of the universal franchise between the CAS and the states and provinces that began in November 1947. Subsequently, administrators from all parts of the future federation began to engage substantially with the operation. Their reports on their progress of work provided the CAS with the opportunity to keep all the units of the forming federation in line while taking major steps towards democratisation.

The successful preparation of the electoral rolls hinged on the cooperation of the states and the provinces. A majority of states responded positively to the letter of November 1947 on the feasibility of preparing electoral rolls on the basis of adult franchise. Some rulers, however, pointed out that while this may be practicable it appeared to them premature to undertake this work.[43] The Secretary of the External Affairs Department of Bhopal wrote that the State 'has not yet participated in the work of preparation of India Union Constitution so far. In terms of its instrument of Accession it would prefer to exercise its option when the complete constitutional picture is filled up in its entirety. It would be appreciated therefore that this State could not at this stage ... participate in the consideration of one item connected with the preparation of constitution'.[44] Despite these reservations, he wrote that the Bhopal

---

[41] Letter No. CA/64/RR/47,15 March 1948, CA/1/FR/48-I, ECIR. Emphasis added.
[42] See letters: 16 July 1948, CA/9/FR/48 (Telegram); 26 July 1948, CA/1/FR/48 (Express letter); 24 August 1948, CA/1/FR/48-III (Telegram); 8 October 1948, CA/1/FR/48-III; 30 November 1948, CA/1/FR/48-IV (Express letter); 21 December 1948, CA/1/FR/48-IV; 11 February 1949, CA/11/FR/49; 28 February 1949, CA/1/FR/49-I; 10 March 1949, CA/1/FR/49; 28 August 1949, CA/1/49-Elec; 5 October 1949, CA/1/FR/49-III; 12 October 1949, CA/1/FR/49-III; 9 November 1949, CA/2/FR/49. The list and letters were attached to Draft letter from CAS to the Chief Secretary to the Government of Hyderabad, 16 December 1949, CA/1/FR/49-IV, ECIR.
[43] This was particularly the case with the states that had individual representation in the Constituent Assembly of India and were treated as 'viable units'. For the list of these states see Government of India, *White Paper on Indian States*, 1948, p. 101.
[44] Letter from the Secretary of the External Affairs Department, Bhopal State, to CAS, 8 January 1948, CA/I/FR/48-I, ECIR. The ruler of Bhopal tried from the outset to maintain his State intact. The Nawab did not attend the meeting of the rulers and States' representatives, which discussed the question of their accession on 25 July 1947 in Delhi. 'He felt, as he put it, that they [rulers] are being "invited like the Oysters to attend the tea party with the Walrus and the carpenter". He though it was impossible for the State to "become an organic part of either dominion".' Menon, *The Story of*

Constitution already provides for adult franchise as the basis for election to the State Legislature.[45]

For some rulers, the question of the preparation of rolls may have been an occasion to gain leverage in the face of pressures to cede fully into the Union. For example, the Maharaja of Mayurbhanj wrote to the CAS that his government already introduced a Bill, which provided for adult franchise at the village panchayat level. He suggested that the electoral rolls that would be prepared for that purpose in due course 'will be used for elector's to the [Federal] Alderal [sic] Legislature'.[46] Two days earlier, at a conference held in Cuttack with the rulers of the Orissa states, the Maharaja avoided discussing the merger of his State with Orissa province on the ground that he had already granted responsible government. He explained that a ministry was functioning in his State, and so he could not make any commitment without consulting his ministers.[47]

Once fortnightly reports on the preparation of rolls started to arrive at the CAS from July 1948 onwards, the way the integration of the states took shape became more palpable. The Government of Orissa, for example, reported in July 1948, in response to the CAS's letter of 16

the Integration, p. 113. The ruler entered negotiations on the merger of the State only in January 1949. Despite pressures to merge with Madhya Pradesh, Bhopal became a Chief Commissioner Province (a Centrally administered area) on 1 June 1949. The Indian Government committed to retain the State's identity for five years and the ruler received high Privy Purse. See ibid., pp. 289–90.

[45] Letter from the Secretary, Ministry of External Affairs, Government of Bhopal to Secretary of CAS ('Note on Electoral Rolls'), 16 April 1949, CA/1/FR/49-II, ECIR. The letter stated that electoral rolls on the basis of adult franchise were prepared in June 1946 for the Village Panchayat Elections. Electoral rolls for the Notified Areas (towns with a population of 2,000 or more) were prepared in December 1947 for elections in January–February 1948. In November 1947 the Bhopal Government ordered preparation of rolls for Bhopal city and Sehore on the basis of adult franchise. In the CAS's discussion of the letter it was noted that 'these rolls have evidently become out of date and will require considerable modifications before they could be used for elections to the House of the People. We may therefore inform the Govt. of Bhopal to undertake revisions of these rolls in the light of our instructions issued from time to time.' S. no. 52, 21 April 1949, CA/1/FR/49-II, ECIR.

[46] Letter from the Secretary to the Government of his Highness the Maharaja of Mayurbhanj to CAS, 17 December 1947, CA/I/FR/48-I, ECIR.

[47] The conference at Cuttack was held on 14–15 December 1947. See Menon, The Story of the Integration, pp. 157, 165. Mayurbhanj merged in November 1948, and a Chief Commissioner was appointed. While the Orissa States merged with Orissa Province on 1 January 1948, Mayurbhanj kept its identity as a unit for another year. It merged with Orissa only on 1 January 1949. Government of India, White Paper on Indian States, 1950, p. 294. As another example, the ruler of Rewa, who also opposed strongly the loss of his State's identity, sent to the CAS a detailed legal and administrative scheme for the preparation of electoral rolls on the basis of adult franchise, thus demonstrating the viability of self-government in his State. Despite its resistance, Rewa entered into the covenant forming the Union of Vindhya Pradesh on 2 April 1948. See Menon, The Story of the Integration of the Indian States, p. 202.

July, that 'preparation of electoral rolls under the new Constitution has already been taken up in the States integrated to this Province under orders of the Provincial Government'.[48] The report from 'Orissa and the States ceded to it' of November stated that:

House numbering in the major parts of the province is completed. In few cases the house numbering was delayed due to the circumstancial [sic] difficulties. Verification of the Preliminary Electoral Rolls in respect of units is being made by the special staff and the district staffs. An appreciable progress in fair copying of electoral rolls has also been made. The preparation of the final copy of the electoral rolls for the press will be taken up as soon as the constituencies are delimited...[49]

In early December the Orissa government reported that:

Women electors of the province have not so far taken any special interest in the election work but they are found consenting parties to enrolment as voters. Scheduled castes and scheduled tribe are gradually getting election-minded. Arrangements have been made for wide propaganda among the illiterate mass to create in them interest in election work... On the whole the preparation of electoral rolls is smoothly proceeding and it is expected to be completed in time.[50]

By the end of the month the Orissa Government reported that the copying work of the rolls was 'in full swing', and that the 'press copies of the rolls which were kept in abeyance will be made ready as per instructions received subsequently from the Constituent Assembly of India in their letter ... dated 21st December, 1948'.[51] They also mentioned that they were rectifying certain errors and omissions relating to the house numbering. The attached table of the progress of work in Orissa and the states ceded to it by the end of November 1948 showed that they completed the work in 2,688,828 houses; 2,358,771 houses were checked; and for 15,823 houses the work was still in progress.[52]

---

[48] Preparation of electoral rolls under the new Constitution, letter from the Additional Secretary to the Government of Orissa, to the Secretary of CAS, 21 July 1948, CA/1/FR/48-II, ECIR.

[49] Return of Progress Fortnightly report of progress of work in the preparation of electoral rolls, from the Additional Secretary to the Government of Orissa, to the Secretary of CAS, 12 November 1948, CA/1/FR/48-IV, ECIR. This report was in continuation of their report of 8 October 1948.

[50] Return of Progress Fortnightly report of progress of work in the preparation of electoral rolls, from the Additional Secretary to the Government of Orissa (Home (Election) Department), to the Secretary of CAS, 2 December 1948, CA/1/FR/48-IV, ECIR.

[51] Submission of return of progress ending 30.11.48, from the Additional Secretary to the Government of Orissa (Home (Election) Department), to the Secretary of CAS, 31 December 1948, CA/1/FR/49-I, ECIR.

[52] Ibid. According to the Census of 1941 there were 2,614,835 houses in Orissa.

In August 1948 the Chief Commissioner of Himachal Pradesh, which was formed on 15 April 1948 out of a merger of the 21 Punjab hill states, sent a detailed report of the work in various districts from mid-June to mid-July. Over that period, 16,274 houses were numbered and 31,235 voters were recorded in 54 Parganas.[53] The Chief Commissioner explained that the Regional Commissioner sent a copy of the CAS's instructions letter of 15 March 1948 to Districts Deputy Commissioners in mid-April, and that he had to then send further reminder letters.

The Chief Commissioner of Himachal Pradesh attached to his report letters from the districts and tehsils on the progress of work.[54] These letters reflected the evolving process of merger at the local level in the midst of the preparation of rolls. Thus, the Deputy Commissioner of Sirmur district wrote that reports from the tehsildar of Paonta 'revealed that out of 170 villages in that tehsil the work of the preparation of electoral rolls has been completed in 66 villages'.[55] The tehsildar of Pachhad reported that 'the work in 175 villages out of 402 villages has been completed'.[56] The Chief Commissioner sent a few express reminder letters to the Deputy Commissioner of Mandi. The latter wrote back: 'Before Mandi State was included in the Himachal Pradesh, orders had been issued to prepare Electoral Rolls on the basis of Adult Franchise. These Rolls are being prepared and no difficulty has so far been reported by any of the Tehsildars who have been charged with this work. It is hoped that the work will be completed by the end of August, 1948.'[57]

The figures of houses that were numbered and enumerated and of the voters that were enrolled, as well as other related 'sum-totals', became a concrete expression of the integration of the states into the new federation. One of the final reports from the government of Kolhapur State, just three months before it merged with Bombay province, illustrates this: 'From the number of voters so far enumerated', the Kolhapur government wrote, 'it is found that more than 50% of the population are recorded as voters. Based on this calculation there will be about 16000

---

[53] Preparation of Electoral Rolls, letter from the Chief Commissioner, Himachal Pradesh to the Under Secretary, CAS, 7 August 1948, CA/1/FR/48-II, ECIR. The report provided the breakdown of the date for each Pargana. Pargana: an administrative (revenue) unit under British administration (in land surveys, village identification), consisting of a few villages. For example, the northern part of the Bhagat State comprised of three parganas, covering an area of 2.2 square miles. See *Census of India 2011*, Himachal Pradesh, District Census Handbook: Sloan, Series-03 Part XII-B, p. 10.

[54] A tehsil is an administrative region of India. A tehsildar is a person who administers a tehsil.

[55] Preparation of Electoral Rolls, letter from the Chief Commissioner, Himachal Pradesh to the Under Secretary, CAS, 7 August 1948, CA/1/FR/48-II, ECIR.

[56] Ibid.

[57] Ibid.

pages of the roll of the State; each page containing 40 names. The estimated costs of printing excluding the cost of paper will, therefore, be RS.
1,28,000/-.'[58]

Early fortnightly reports from the provinces revealed administrative
and constitutional discrepancies between the CAS's instructions and
their implementation on the ground. At the same time, these reports
presented an opportunity for immediate correction, and therefore a way
of bringing the provinces into the Union. For example, the government
of East Punjab made changes in the form of electoral roll suggested by
the CAS. It added three columns: a serial number for Scheduled Castes
(SCs), a serial number for Muslims, and a column for the occupation
of the voter. Moreover, the government also considered excluding from
the roll persons disqualified from voting on account of corruption and
other illegal practices, on the basis of the rules for elections under the
Government of India Act, 1935.

The CAS invited the Election Commissioner of East Punjab to Delhi
to discuss the matter. At the meeting, the Personal Assistant to the
Election Commissioner of East Punjab, Mr Luthra, explained that the
columns for serial number of the SCs and Muslims were added to ascertain their population in the province. He clarified that these columns will
appear only in the manuscript copy of the roll, but will be omitted in the
printed copies.[59] The Joint Secretary of the CAS accepted that explanation. As for the additional column on the occupation of the elector, Mr.
Luthra explained that it was included 'mainly to identity the voters as
there was a possibility of having more than one voter in a village answering to same description as respects his own name and that of his father'.[60]
The Joint Secretary explained that 'it should be possible to differentiate
the voters with reference to the house number', and asked that 'the East
Punjab Government should, for the sake of uniformity, follow the prescribed form'.[61]

---

[58] Letter from the Government of Kolhapur (Administrator's Office, Legal & Legislative
Department), to CAS, 23 November 1948, CA/18/FR/49, ECIR. A fortnight later the
state's chief secretary reported that the Election Officer toured in six local administrative units (Petas and Jaghirs), 'checked house numbering & voters in 64 villages on
representative sample basis, correcting errors on the spot, after verification'. Letter from
the Chief Secretary to the Government of Kolhapur to the Under Secretary of CAS, 2
December 1948, CA/1/FR/48-V, ECIR.

[59] Summary of discussions between Mr S. N. Mukherjee, Joint Secretary, Constituent
Assembly of India and Mr Luthra, Personal Assistant to the Election Commissioner,
East Punjab, 8 September 1948, CA/9/FR/48, ECIR. The CAS wrote to the Elections
Commissioner of East Punjab in regard to these changes in the Form of the electoral roll
on 3 September 1948.

[60] Ibid.

[61] Ibid.

Mr Luthra then explained that 'the Provincial Government have not taken a "house census" and that in villages there was no numbering of houses'.[62] The Joint Secretary drew his attention to the CAS's instruction letter, which emphasised that a 'house-to-house census was quite essential'.[63] Mr Luthra committed to take up immediately the work relating to the house census. The Joint Secretary also asked that 'pending the passing of the necessary electoral law', the government of East Punjab should not exclude from the electoral rolls for the first elections under the new Constitution persons who were disqualified on the basis of corrupt practices in past elections.[64] A month later, in October 1948, the Election Commissioner of East Punjab reported that 'In deference to the wishes of the public and due to the fact that the addition of a column for house numbers involved considerable additional time and labour to enable the muharrirs to make the necessary entries, the period for the registration of names in electoral rolls has been extended till the 31st October, 1948.'[65]

The sequence of fortnightly reports on the progress of work and on the problems that were encountered brought in the Centre, particularly when the CAS's intervention was required. These accounts also drove a process of connecting administrators at all levels. In October 1948 the government of the United Provinces, for example, reported that 'most of the district officers have made considerable headway in the preparation of rolls', however, in the districts of Kheri, Mirazpur, and Banaras the work was 'considerably hampered due to excessive rains and floods'.[66] In other places it was impeded due to the outbreak of cholera. In November, the government still reported that in Banaras and Ballia 'havoc caused by recent floods in these districts and consequent engagement of officials in relief work very much dislocated the arrangements for preparation of electoral rolls and no progress could therefore be made during the fortnight under review'.[67] The United Provinces

---

[62] Ibid.

[63] Ibid.

[64] Ibid.

[65] Fortnightly Report on the progress made and difficulties encountered in the preparation of electoral rolls, for the second fortnight of September 1948, from M. R. Bhide, Election Commissioner, East Punjab to the Joint Secretary, CAS, 16 October 1948, CA/1/FR/48-III, ECIR. Muharrirs are registration clerks/officers.

[66] Fortnightly report of progress of work in the preparation of electoral rolls, from the Additional Deputy Secretary to Government of the United Provinces, M. K. Kidwai, to CAS, 1 October 1948, CA/1/FR/48-III, ECIR. This was in continuation of their fortnightly report of 21 September 1948. One of the main problems reported at the time in the United Provinces concerned the registration of woman, which is discussed in Chapter 1.

[67] Fortnightly report of progress of work in the preparation of electoral rolls for the fortnights ending 15 September 1948 and 30 September 1948, from the Additional Deputy

Government asked for the CAS's intervention in 'moving the Ministry of Defence of the Government of India to issue a directive to the cantonment boards [authorities] in the United Provinces for extending all practicable facilities and help to the district authorities' with the preparation of rolls.[68] The CAS requested of the Ministry of Defence to do so on the grounds that the rolls were 'being prepared by the Provincial and States Government under instructions from the Constituent Assembly of India'.[69] The Ministry of Defence issued the necessary instructions.[70]

The government of the United Provinces also reported that they did not receive fortnightly reports regularly from some districts. They reminded the district officers concerned and asked of them 'to state the reasons for non-submission of such reports'.[71] In early December the government reported that 'some district officers have still not sent their reports for the fortnights under review and they are being asked to be strictly regular in the submission of the reports in future'.[72] In turn, the Election Commissioner of East Punjab reported that he received complaints from many districts that 'Harijans were being coerced into getting themselves registered in electoral rolls as Sikhs'.[73] He instructed the Deputy Commissioners to 'examine all such complaints and take strong action when the complaints were found to be true. A press note

Secretary to Government of the United Provinces, M. K. Kidwai, to CAS, 9 November, 1948, CA/1/FR/48-IV, ECIR.

[68] Ibid. In the past, during elections under colonial rule, Cantonment Boards helped with the preparation of electoral rolls. The payment for their services was calculated on the basis of the number of voters enrolled for the area. In the Central Provinces the Saugor cantonment authorities appointed some extra staff for the purpose of preparing the electoral roll in 1948–1949. See S. no. 11, 11 February 1949, CA/17/FR/49, ECIR.

[69] Letter from the Under Secretary of the CAS to the Ministry of Defence, 19 November 1948, CA/1/FR/48-IV, ECIR.

[70] Letter from the Director, Military Lands and Cantonments, Ministry of Defence, to the General Officer Commanding-in-Chief, Eastern Command, 2 December 1948, CA/18/FR/49, ECIR.

[71] Fortnightly report of progress of work in the preparation of electoral rolls for the fortnights ending 15 September 1948 and 30 September 1948, from the Additional Deputy Secretary to Government of the United Provinces, M. K. Kidwai, to CAS, 9 November 1948, CA/1/FR/48-IV, ECIR.

[72] Fortnightly report of progress of work in the preparation of electoral rolls for the fortnights ending 15 October 1948 and 30 October 1948, from the Additional Deputy Secretary to Government of the United Provinces, M. K. Kidwai, to CAS, 10 December, 1948, CA/1/FR/48-IV, ECIR. The report noted, however, that the reports received thus far suggested that further progress was made in the preparation of rolls both for the rural and urban areas, with the exception of a few districts 'where due to some unforeseen causes, such as the recent floods, the work has been delayed'. Ibid.

[73] Fortnightly Report on the progress made and difficulties encountered in the preparation of electoral rolls, for the second fortnight of September 1948, from M. R. Bhide, Election Commissioner, East Punjab to the Joint Secretary, CAS, 16 October 1948, CA/1/FR/48-III, ECIR. Additional problem reported at the time concerned the registration of the refugees, which is discussed in Chapter 2.

was also issued asking the public to bring all such cases to the notice of Government to enable it to take suitable action.'[74]

Indeed, as a result of regular correspondences between local governments and district officers on the preparation of rolls, the disciplining of the Union was trickling down. Local governments updated district officers on new directives of the CAS. In these correspondences they made reference to their previous letters, as well as to the CAS's instructions. Thus, in his letter to all district officers in late November, the Reforms Commissioner of Assam referred them to paragraph 8 of the CAS's 15 March 1948 letter of instructions.[75] In a follow up letter, while reiterating that the rolls needed to be written '*unit by unit*' he noted: 'In this connection your particular attention is drawn to paragraph 6 of this Department letter No.L.801/47/83 dated 3rd May, 1948 and paras 6 & 8 of the Constituent Assembly's letter No. CA/64/RR/47 dated 15th March, 1948 (a copy of which was forwarded to you with this Department letter No.L.801/47 dated 23rd March, 1948).'[76] This bureaucratic paper trail connected the CAS's decisions on the preparation of rolls for the Central and State legislatures under the new Constitution to the decisions and actions provincial and state government took as they embarked on implementing the instructions.

The CAS, in turn, took periodic stock of the 'state of the States'. The CAS produced at the end of December 1948 a bird's-eye view of the progress made in the preparation of electoral rolls in 37 units of the forming federation. It accounted for the progress in 9 Governor's provinces, 8 Chief Commissioner's provinces, 6 Unions of States and 14 individual states.[77] At that point, 241 states had merged with the provinces or with the centre, and 294 states covenanted to form 6 Unions of States.[78]

In Assam about 10 lakh electors were recorded by the end of November 1948, and its government expected to complete the draft electoral roll

---

[74] Ibid.

[75] Letter from the Reforms Commissioner of Assam to All District Officers (Including Superintendent, Lushai Hills) Sub-Divisional Officers and Political Officer of Frontier Tracts, 30 November 1948, CA/1/FR/48-IV, ECIR.

[76] Letter from the Reforms Commissioner of Assam to All District Officers, 14 December 1948, CA/1/FR/48-IV, ECIR.

[77] 'The progress made by the various provincial and States Governments in the preparation of electoral rolls under the new Constitution, as on 31st December 1948', CA/1/FR/49-II, ECIR. The CAS conducted an earlier overview in September 1948. See copy of notes from f. no. CA/6/FR/49, 29 September 1948, CA/1/FR/49-II.

[78] The numbers are taken from the Government of India, *White Paper on Indian States*, 1948, pp. 97–101. Ultimately, by 1950, after changes in the administrative designation of some of the merged states, 216 states merged with provinces, 61 constituted seven Centrally Administered Areas, and 275 constituted five Unions. Government of India, *White Paper on Indian States*, 1950, pp. 294–6.

by the end of January 1949. In Orissa province and the 23 states that ceded to it, the preparation of electoral rolls was completed in respect of about 27 lakhs houses by the end of November 1948, and the copying of the rolls was 'in full swing'.[79] In Bihar 'out of 11 thousand units, rolls have been prepared in respect of about 7 thousand units',[80] and the government expected to complete the work by the end of January 1949. In the United Provinces 'work in rural and urban areas is nearing completion except in a few places which were affected by floods etc.',[81] and the government expected to complete the work shortly. In East Punjab the compilation of rolls was completed in almost all districts, 'except a few, due to the strike of the patwaris,[82] and the rolls were ready for printing. In Madras the preliminary electoral rolls were ready for printing. In Bombay, West Bengal, and C.P. & Berar 'Executive instructions for the preparation of electoral rolls have been issued and the work is progressing well. However, no specific progress reports have so far been received.'[83]

As for the position in the Chief Commissioner's Provinces: in Panth Piploda the rolls were ready. In Coorg, Himachal Pradesh, and Mayurbhanj the work was nearing completion, as well as in the Municipal areas of Ajmer-Merwara. In its rural areas it was progressing well. No progress was reported for the Andamans and Nicobars, Delhi and Cutch. In the Unions of States: preliminary steps for the preparation of the rolls were taken in Saurashtra. In Rajasthan 'the preparation of electoral rolls for the House of the People has been taken up from the House Register'.[84] In Madhya-Bharat, Matsya, and Patiala & East Punjab States Union 'necessary steps have been taken. No progress reported.'[85] No progress was reported for Vindhya Pradesh.

Finally, as far as the individual states were concerned, in Mysore, Travancore, Cochin, Manipur and Baroda the manuscript rolls for elections to the State Legislature on the basis of adult franchise were completed. In Kolhapur the rolls were ready for printing. In Tripura the work was 'expected to be finished in time'.[86] In Cooch-Behar the work was progressing well. In Benares the manuscript rolls were ready. In Jodhpur

---

[79] 'The progress made by the various provincial and States Governments in the preparation of electoral rolls under the new Constitution, as on 31st December 1948', CA/1/FR/49-II, ECIR.
[80] Ibid.
[81] Ibid.
[82] Ibid.
[83] Ibid.
[84] Ibid.
[85] Ibid.
[86] Ibid.

'only the preliminary spade work has been done'.[87] Bhopal did not yet take up the work of the preparation of electoral rolls. No progress was reported from Bikaner, Jaipur, and Rampur.

This overview of the state of the preparation of electoral rolls by the end of 1948, shortly before the motion on the preparation of rolls was brought before the Constituent Assembly for the first time, grounded the forming federation. This account produced a picture of the federal contours. The preparation of rolls contributed to gradually turning what began in November 1947 as an administrative exercise in democratic political imagination into 'a reality unto itself'.[88] Beyond making real the abstract notion of the universal franchise, it was also the Indian federation that was slowly created in this process. As we will see later in the chapter, its evolution deepened with the continual progress in the preparation of rolls. The initial bringing together of the states and the provinces, through the preparation of the rolls, began answering the question of what constituted the limits of India. It also provided the centre with an opportunity to exercise its new sovereignty and authority.[89]

The preparation of rolls in the midst of the integration engendered on-going substantial interactions between the CAS and all the units of the forming federation. Occasionally, the CAS sent new directives, or sought the opinion of the provincial and states governments, in particular on matters of great administrative and financial consequence. One such issue, which embodied basic elements of the federal state building process, revolved around the question of the apportionment of costs in connection with the preparation and the printing of the electoral rolls for the House of the People, between the government of India and the provincial and states governments. This became the subject of all-India administrative dialogues, which brought to light differences of opinion between the CAS at the centre, and the governments of the states and the

---

[87] Ibid.

[88] Yaron Ezrahi, *Imagined Democracies: Necessary Political Fictions*, Cambridge: Cambridge University Press, 2012, p. 170. Ezrahi discusses the political imagination as 'a reality unto itself, a self-creating reality that can supersede other realities'. Ibid.

[89] Indeed, even beyond the integration of the states, this was not a straightforward matter. The CAS's (Franchise Section) file on 'Preparation of electoral rolls under the new constitution in the Governors Provinces & the centrally administered areas' contained a 'List of Districts of the various provinces which now fall in the Dominion of Pakistan' (undated), CA/1/FR/49-I, ECIR. Even the list was not simple and clear cut. For example, for seven out of the 19 districts of East Bengal Province that fell under the Dominion of Pakistan there were many qualifications. Thus, in respect to Nadia district: 'comprising of Kushtia Subdivision except the portion of Daulatpur Thana which has been awarded to the Dominion of India'. Similarly in respect to Jessore district: 'except the Thanas of Bongaon and Gaighata'. 'List of Districts of the various provinces which now fall in the Dominion of Pakistan'. Ibid.

provinces. It also unravelled some constitutional discrepancies between some provisions in the Indian draft constitution and their counterpart stipulations in the merging states. This occurred while some of the states or Unions of States, which had not yet completed their integration, were also preparing elections for their own constitution making bodies. The bureaucratic dialogues on the question of costs, in the midst of mergers, set in motion centre–state relations. Resolving the disagreements and constitutional challenges that emerged in that context became, in effect, a means of disciplining the federation, and of legitimating the authority of the centre. In that context, the CAS, as the de facto election management body at that time, asserted effective autonomy over the preparation of elections. It did so in the absence of authorisation, and in anticipation of the constitution and the electoral laws.

Setting in Motion Federal Relations: The Question of Costs

When the CAS asked the governments of the provinces and the states in November 1947 how they proposed to prepare the electoral rolls and what difficulties they anticipated, some the states' governments raised the matter of costs. Some governments wrote that the centre should cover the costs involved in the preparation of rolls.[90] At that point, the CAS decided that 'this is a matter in which we need not express any opinion now, as it is not free from controversy'.[91] It is noteworthy, as already mentioned in Chapter 1, that the provincial and state governments did not have any statutory authority to order the preparation of the rolls. To start the work, the governments issued executive instructions to district officers and other appropriate authorities. Moreover, the draft constitution did not make any provisions for the constitution of legislatures in the princely states. The question of costs came up again when the CAS issued the 15 March letter of instructions. Its members considered the matter, but decided yet again not to address the matter with the governments of the provinces and the states.

By the end of November 1948, however, the CAS was compelled to deal with the question of costs. In some places the preparation of rolls was nearing completion and manuscript copies of the rolls were prepared for printing. The printing would entail significant costs. Some state and

---

[90] See, for example, letter from the Chief Minister of Patna State, 8 December 1947; letter from Bikaner State to CAS, 16 December 1947, CA/1/FR/48-I, ECIR.

[91] S. no. 21–23, 2–3 January 1948, CA/1/FR/48-I, ECIR. Also see Internal note, 29 November 1948, CA/17/FR/49, ECIR.

provincial governments submitted reimbursement claims for the expenditures they incurred on the preparation of the rolls, and asked for an advance on the printing costs. The government of Kolhapur, for example, wrote that 'tenders were called for from local Press keepers', and asked for a retainer of Rs.125,000 for the printing of the rolls for the 'Lower House of the Dominion Parliament'.[92] The Government of Orissa submitted a claim for Rs.196,399 for the year 1948–49, and of Rs.485,560 for the year 1949–50 on account of expenditure 'incurred or likely to be incurred in connection with elections to the Central Legislature'.[93] The Orissa Government based its request for the recovery of costs on article 235(3) of the Draft Constitution.[94] This article was set in chapter II of Part IX of the draft Constitution, which dealt with administrative relations between the Union and the states. It stated that 'Where by virtue of this article powers and duties have been conferred or imposed upon a State or officers or authorities thereof, there shall be paid by the Government of India to the State such sum as may be agreed or, in default of agreement, as may be determined by an arbitrator appointed by the Chief Justice of India in respect of any extra costs of administration incurred by the State in connection with the exercise of those powers and duties.'[95]

At this point, the question of costs had not yet been submitted to the Government of India. The Under Secretary of the CAS noted that the matter for decision in the immediate was, therefore, whether 'we should allow the Provincial and State Governments to continue with the work connected with the preparation of electoral rolls; and the nature of reply to be given to the various Governments in regard to the incidence of expenditure'.[96] Until a decision on these two questions would be taken,

---

[92] Letter from the Government of Kolhapur (Administrator's Office, Legal & Legislative Department), to CAS, 23 November 1948, CA/18/FR/49, ECIR. In June 1948, some states, for example, Patna, Bikaner, Jaipur and Phalton raised the matter of costs generally with the CAS. The Under Secretary thought then that 'it was too early to take up this question and address the Government of India in this matter'. Internal note, 29 November 1948, CA/17/FR/49, ECIR. The Chief Commissioner of Ajmer-Merwara, as another example, requested a reimbursement of Rs.13,346 on account of the preparation of rolls. Letter from the Secretary to the Chief Commissioner, Ajmer-Merwara, to the Joint Secretary, CAS, 7 January 1949, CA/18/FR/49, ECIR.

[93] 'Recovery of costs incurred in connection with the preparation of Electoral rolls for, and elections to, the Central Legislatures', letter from the Additional Secretary to the Government of Orissa to the Secretary to the Government of India, Ministry of Law, 25 November 1948, CA/18/FR/49, ECIR.

[94] Ibid. The Additional Secretary to the Government of Orissa noted that this article corresponded to section 124(3) of the Government of India Act, 1935.

[95] The Drafting Committee, Constituent Assembly of India, *Draft Constitution of India*, p. 108.

[96] S. no. 1, 30 November 1948, CA/17/FR/49, ECIR (note by P. S. Subramanian).

the CAS asked of the provinces and the states to defer the printing of the electoral rolls.[97] The Joint Secretary concluded that because the question of costs involved a large expenditure from the revenues of India it should be immediately brought to the notice of the Prime Minister and 'his orders obtained'.[98] Rajendra Prasad, the President of the Constituent Assembly, wrote to Nehru in the matter.

This was the first time, since the CAS embarked on the preparation of electoral rolls on the basis of adult franchise under the new Constitution, that it addressed the government of India. In his letter to Nehru, Prasad described the work done thus far. He asked 'whether the Government of India approve our going a head with the printing of electoral rolls under preparation'.[99] Nehru replied only a month later. He wrote that 'It is for the province or State concerned to write directly to the Government of India on this subject. I am having this matter enquired into.'[100]

In the meantime, the CAS sent on 21 December 1948 a circular letter to the governments of all provinces and states suggesting that they should proceed with the printing of the electoral rolls if they agreed to leave the question of the expenditure on the preparation of these rolls open. The Joint Secretary explained:

Our aim is to hold the general elections under the new Constitution in the winter of 1949–1950 if possible, and accordingly, we should like the preparation of the electoral rolls completed as early as possible. The printing, however, had to be temporarily suspended, since the Governments of certain Provinces and Indian States raised the question as to who should bear the expenditure incurred in connection with the preparation of the rolls. This question is now under the consideration of the Government of India and there is likely to be some delay in arriving at a decision. Some Provinces and States which have completed the manuscript of their rolls are, however, anxious to get these rolls printed. The printing of the rolls can be proceeded with if the Governments ... are willing to get on with the work leaving the question of expenditure open.[101]

---

[97] Telegram No. CA/1/FR-IV, 30 November 1948.

[98] S. no. 1, 3 December 1948, CA/17/FR/49, ECIR (note by the Joint Secretary, S. N. Mukerjee).

[99] S. no. 4, copy of letter from Rajendra Prasad to the Prime Minister, 13 December 1948, CA/18/FR/49, ECIR. The two-page letter began: 'As you are aware the Secretariat ... requested all the Provincial and State Governments to undertake the preparation of electoral rolls'.

[100] Letter from Jawaharlal Nehru to Rajendra Prasad, 16 January 1949, CA/1/FR/49-I, ECIR. This query with Nehru led, over the next two months, to discussions between Nehru, the Law Ministry and Prasad on the role of the CAS in the preparation of the electoral rolls, which became somewhat disputed. See discussion in Chapter 5.

[101] Letter from the Joint Secretary of the CAS (to all the provinces and the states), 21 December 1948, CA/1/FR/48-IV, ECIR. At that point it was expected that the draft of the new Constitution would be introduced before the Constituent Assembly in May 1948.

Following the pattern the CAS set from the beginning of the work, the Joint Secretary explained:

We cannot anticipate the decision of the Government of India but it is not difficult to guess how they are likely to view the problem. The preparation of electoral rolls for the Lower House of the Central Legislature is, no doubt, a function of the Government of India and if this function is entrusted to the Government of any State, then, in accordance with the principle embodied in article 235(3) of the draft Constitution, the latter Government may properly claim payment of any extra cost incurred in connection with the discharge of that function. This extra cost is almost negligible, for the States would need the same electoral rolls for their own Legislative Assemblies. At most, they might have to print some extra copies for the Centre, and they can therefore claim only the cost of printing the extra copies, and not the entire cost of preparing the rolls.[102]

But many governments of the provinces and the states contested the CAS's views, or its draft constitutional interpretations, from a variety of perspectives. Over the following six months the question of the costs became a subject of abundant correspondence between the governments of the provinces and the states and the CAS. Thus, the Government of West Bengal wrote:

It was as a result of the specific direction contained in the Constituent Assembly's letter No. CA/64/RR/47 dated the 15th March, 1948 that the Provincial Government took the work on behalf of the Government of India... *The fact remains that the Provincial Government were specifically asked to take up work in which the Government of India had an original and independent interest.* In a case, therefore, were entirely new staff and services are especially brought into being for execution of work which the Government of India ask the Province to do on their behalf and for which expenditure is also incurred on materials and equipment, the entire cost on that account becomes the 'extra cost of administration' incurred by the Province within the meeting of Article 235(3) [of the Draft Constitution] or Section 124(4) [of the Government of India Act, 1935] which, it is felt, the Government of India should legitimately pay.[103]

The Government of West Bengal was prepared to go ahead with the printing, but notified that 'if any heavy extra cost be incurred by reason of the printed rolls being materially affected later on, necessitating substantial

[102] Ibid. The Constituent Assembly debated Article 235(3) six months later, on 13 June 1949 and on 13 October 1949.
[103] Letter from the Deputy Secretary to the Government of West Bengal to CAS, 21 January 1949 (in reference to CAS's letter of 21 December 1948), CA/18/FR/49, ECIR. Emphasis added. The governments of Assam and of Madras expressed a similar view and reasoning. See letter from the Reforms Commissioner of Assam to CAS, 4 March 1949, CA/18/FR/49, ECIR; letter from the Additional Secretary to the Government of Madras to the Secretary to the Government of India, Ministry of Law, 25 May 1949, CA/18/FR/49, ECIR.

reprinting, it should in all fairness be borne by the Government of India'.[104]

The Government of Bihar adopted the CAS's reasoning in the matter of costs, but inverted its conclusion:

It has been argued that the States would need the same electoral rolls for their own Legislative Assemblies; *it may be argued with equal force that the Union would need the same electoral rolls for its own House of the People, and the States may request the Union to print a few extra copies at a negligible cost for their own use.*[105]

It also claimed that 'the extra costs incurred in connection with the preparation of the electoral rolls for the House of the People of the Union of India will not be "almost negligible" as has been stated in the [CAS's] letter'.[106] The Government of Bihar suggested that the cost of preparation and printing of the rolls should be shared equally between the Union and the State. It agreed, however, that the question of apportionment of the expenditure between the Union and the State should not stand in the way of the preparation and printing of the electoral rolls. Other provincial, as well as states, governments also held the view that the costs should be equally shared between the Indian government and the states, and similarly agreed, in the meanwhile, to make the necessary arrangements for the printing.[107] Indeed, some governments asked

---

[104] Letter from the Deputy Secretary to the Government of West Bengal to CAS, 21 January 1949 (in reference to CAS's letter of 21 December 1948), CA/18/FR/49, ECIR.

[105] Letter from the Chief Secretary, Government of Bihar (Appointment Department, Reforms and Elections Branch) to the Joint Secretary, CAS, 9 February 1949, CA/18/FR/49, ECIR. Emphasis added.

[106] Letter from the Chief Secretary, Government of Bihar (Appointment Department, Reforms and Elections Branch) to the Joint Secretary, CAS, 9 February 1949, CA/18/FR/49, ECIR. The Chief Secretary to the Government of Bihar explained that a constituency for the House of the People will cover a much larger area than a constituency of the State of Bihar Legislative Assembly, therefore, the names of constituencies and number of pages in the rolls will be different. This will effect printing costs because printed copies of the electoral rolls for the State will have to be re-arranged and re-edited 'by changing the names of constituencies and numbers of pages to serve as manuscript for the printing of rolls for the House of the People'. Ibid.

[107] See, for example, letter from the Additional Secretary to the Government of Madras to CAS, 26 January 1949, CA/18/FR/49, and letter from the Additional Secretary to the Government of Madras to the Secretary to the Government of India, Ministry of Law, 25 May 1949, CA/18/FR/49; letter from the Deputy Secretary to the Government of the Central Provinces and Berar to CAS, 15 February 1949, CA/18/FR/49; letter from Additional Deputy Secretary to Government of United Provinces to CAS, 23 April 1949, CA/1/FR/49-III, ECIR. The government of Assam was of the same opinion upon consultation with the district officers in the province on the matter. Letter from the Reforms Commissioner of Assam to CAS, 4 March 1949, CA/18/FR/49, ECIR. Also see letter from the Joint Secretary, Assembly Department, United State of Saurashtra to the Under Secretary of the Government of India, 8 March 1949, CA/18/FR/49, ECIR. Also see s. no. 25 & 26, 12 March 1949, CA/17/FR/49, ECIR.

for immediate supply of paper. The government of Assam, for example, placed a request for 3,000 reams of paper from the Central Stationery Office in Calcutta.[108]

Although no decision was yet made on the question of the costs, the CAS arranged through the Ministry of Works, Mines and Power of the Government of India, that paper in connection with the preparation of the electoral rolls under the new Constitution could be placed with the Controller of Printing and Stationery in New Delhi.[109] By that time, the CAS's determination to continue with the work of the preparation for the first elections under the new constitution was reinforced by the resolution, for the first time, of the Constituent Assembly that 'instructions be issued forthwith to the authorities concerned for the preparation of electoral rolls and for taking all necessary steps so that elections to the Legislatures under the new Constitution may be held as early as possible in the year 1950'.[110] Hereafter, the CAS often referred to this resolution, or attached a copy of it, in its correspondence with governments of the provinces and the states, while reiterating its request that they proceed with the printing if they agree to leave open the question of costs.[111]

In the case of the merging states, the question of costs brought to the fore broader constitutional discrepancies within the federation. In some cases it became apparent that the qualifications for enrolment as a voter for the states' legislatures were different than the qualifications set for the preparation of rolls to the House of the People. Thus, the Chief Minister of Cooch Behar State wrote that:

The State's electoral rolls ... are substantially different... As our residential quali-fication is 10 years, the number of voters will be substantially more to the Lower House of the Parliament of India. The Cooch Behar Darbar desires to point out that the cost of printing the Electoral Rolls for the Lower House ... is estimated at about Rs.1,00,000 and that the burden of printing them is much too heavy for

---

[108] Letter from the Reforms Commissioner of Assam to CAS, 11 February 1949, CA/1/FR/49-I, ECIR. Also see, for example, letter from the Chief Minister, Cooch Behar State to CAS, 28 June 1949, CA/1/FR/49-II, ECIR.

[109] Letter from CAS to all provinces and states, 11 February 1949, CA/1/FR/49-I, ECIR.

[110] 'Motion moved by the Hon'ble Pandit Jawaharlal Nehru and adopted on the 8th January 1949', CA/1/FR/49-I, ECIR.

[111] The Joint Secretary of the CAS noted, while discussing recurring queries from pro-vincial governments about the costs: 'I think we should go by the resolution recently adopted by the Constituent Assembly which directs the issue of instructions for the preparation of electoral rolls and for taking all necessary steps so that elections to the legislatures under the new Constitution may be held as early as possible in the year 1950. Even if the elections are held towards the end of 1950, we must keep up to the programme that the draft rolls should be printed ... by the end of 1949'. S. no. 31, 18 March 1949, CA/17/FR/49, ECIR. B. N. Rau agreed with this view. S. no. 31, 4 April 1949, CA/17/FR/49, ECIR.

the Darbar to bear after they have already spent over Rs. 50,000 on the publication of the Electoral Rolls for the Legislative Council of the State. The Darbar also are unable to supply the vast quantity of paper that will be required.[112]

The Chief Secretary to the Government of Madhyabharat, as another example, wrote that they 'hitherto considered it unnecessary to raise any question as to the responsibility of the cost for the Dominion rolls, since they felt that the Government of India would themselves bear the whole cost'.[113] He explained that the state's position is unlike that of the provinces.

This Government is engaged in the preparation of two rolls, one for its own Constituent Assembly ... and the other the Dominion rolls. Unlike the Provinces where the same franchise as for the Dominion Parliament would apply for provincial elections by virtue of the decision of the Constituent Assembly of India, the franchise for future Madhyabharat Assembly would be a matter for the Constituent Assembly of Madhyabharat to determine and the decision cannot be anticipated at this stage. The deliberations of the Madhyabharat Constituent Assembly are likely to take some time and the Dominion rolls may not be useful for the future Madhyabharat Assembly.[114]

The Government estimated the cost of preparing the two rolls at about Rs.8 lakhs (800,000). They were willing to proceed with the printing 'on the presumption that the whole of the cost ... would be borne by the Government of India'.[115]

While recognising the legal rights of the merging states at that point, to determine the qualifications for enrolment for their own legislatures, the CAS explained to the governments of the states that ultimately 'there will be the same franchise qualifications and disqualifications throughout India'.[116] The CAS noted, for example, that although the

[112] Letter from the Chief Minister, Cooch Behar, to CAS, 11 February 1949, CA/18/FR/49, ECIR.
[113] Letter from the Chief Secretary to the Government of Madhyabharat to the Joint Secretary, CAS, 5 April 1949, CA/18/FR/49, ECIR.
[114] Ibid.
[115] Ibid. Similar constitutional disparities arose in other states, for example, Ajmer-Merwara, Bhopal, Baroda and Manipur. See S. no. 23, 9 March 1949, CA/17/FR/49; letter from the Secretary to the Chief Commissioner, Ajmer-Merwara to CAS, 22 February 1949, CA/18/FR/49; letter from the Secretary, Ministry of External Affairs, Government of Bhopal to Secretary of the Constituent Assembly of India ('Note on Electoral Rolls'), 16 April 1949, CA/1/FR/49-II; letter from the Chief Secretary to the Government of Baroda to CAS, 5 April 1949, CA/1/FR/49-II, ECIR. The Dewan of Manipur produced a table, which surmised the differences between the Indian constitution and the Manipur state constitution with regard to franchise qualification of the state legislature and of the House of the People. Letter from the Dewan of Manipur State to the Joint Secretary of the Constituent Assembly, 30 July 1949, CA/1/FR/49-II, ECIR.
[116] S. no. 101, 18 August 1949, CA/1/FR/49-II, ECIR. Also see letter from the Joint Secretary, CAS, to the Dewan of Manipur, 24 September 1949, CA/1/FR/49-II, ECIR.

franchise qualifications in Madhyabharat are to be determined by the State Constituent Assembly, 'which has itself not coming into being as yet', its Government should be informed that 'eventually elections to the State Legislature will be on the basis of adult suffrage and instead of preparing fresh rolls for those elections the present rolls could be conveniently utilised with whatever modifications and alterations that become necessary'.[117]

Provincial and state governments persistently demanded that the government of India should share equally with them the expenditure on the preparation of rolls. They also continued sending reimbursement claims for the expenditures they incurred. The CAS responded to all letters, repeatedly stating that the matter of costs is still under the consideration of the Government of India, and asked the governments to proceed with the printing if they are prepared to keep open the question of cost.[118] In doing so, the governments of the provinces and the states lent recognition and authorised the legitimacy of the Union. At the same time, by proceeding with the work, while claiming an even share of the costs with the Union, the states reserved their standing as co-equals with the Union with respect to the primary source of their legitimate autonomy.[119] In effect, by continuing the preparation of rolls, they also recognised the authority of the CAS as the election management body at the time. A decision to apportion the costs of the preparation of rolls between the Indian government and the states on an equal basis was taken only in December 1949.[120] By then, the work on the printing of the preliminary rolls was in full swing.

Printing the Rolls: A Pucca Democracy and the Unity of India

The cost, however, was not the only concern that arose when the work on the preliminary rolls was nearing completion in some parts of the country, and manuscript copies were prepared for printing. The timing

---

[117] S. no. 73, 17–18 May 1949, CA/1/FR/49-II, ECIR. Also see draft letter from CAS to the Law Secretary to the Government of Madhyabharat, 20 June 1949, CA/1/FR/49-II, ECIR.

[118] See, for example, Draft letter from CAS to the Chief Minister, Cooch Behar, 28 February 1949, CA/18/FR/49, ECIR; letter from CAS to the Chief Secretary to the Government of Madhyabharat, 9 May 1949, CA/18/FR/49, ECIR.

[119] See for this point the analysis of India's federalism in Madhav Khosla, *The Indian Constitution*, New Delhi: Oxford University Press, 2012, p. 46.

[120] See, for example, s. no. 46, draft letter from CAS to the Deputy Secretary Government of Central Provinces and Berar, December 1949, CA/1/FR/49-IV, ECIR. Also see Ministry of Law, Justice and Company Affairs, f. 2/1950/c Vol. II, NAI.

of the printing of the rolls was also questioned. In December 1948 the Chief Secretary to the Government of West Bengal, for example, advised against it. He argued that 'As far as is possible to judge at present, the rolls as now being prepared are likely to undergo considerable change', which will ultimately require for entire pages to be reprinted before printing for the final publication of the rolls could be taken.[121] Therefore, 'whatever printing is made now would be materially wasted'.[122] Some other senior bureaucrats also suggested that the printing could not be undertaken because the constituencies were not yet delimited, and the polling stations were not known.[123]

The CAS, however, did not plan to print the rolls again for final publication. The Under Secretary explained in his reply that the 'printed copies of the preliminary rolls with necessary corrections for the purpose of omitting names therefrom [sic] together with a supplementary list of names to be included on the rolls may be published as final copies of the rolls under the electoral law to be enacted'.[124]

On 28 February 1949 the CAS sent to all the provinces and the states a follow-up letter (to their 21 December 1948 circular), regarding the printing of the preliminary rolls stating that:

in view of the time that will be taken in printing the electoral rolls as revised after the hearing of claims and objections and the consequent delay in the holding of

---

[121] Letter from the Deputy Secretary to the Government of West Bengal, M. M. Basu, to the Joint Secretary of CAS, 14 December 1948, CA/1/FR/48-IV, ECIR. He referred, in the main, to changes resulting from the very large number of refugees that will have to be brought on the roll 'in their appropriate places' after the citizenship provisions will be finalised, which may have affects beyond the refugees. Moreover, a delay in the passing of the constitution would lead to a change in the date with reference to the age of voters and will result in many additions; and finally, even after the constitutions will be passed, dealing with claims and objections will take a few months before printing for final publication could be taken.

[122] Ibid. The Government of Bengal brought this matter again in a letter from the Deputy Secretary to the Government of West Bengal to CAS, 25 February 1949, CA/18/FR/49, ECIR. Also see, for example, letter from the Reforms Commissioner of Assam to All District Officers, 14 December 1948, CA/1/FR/48-IV, ECIR.

[123] See, for example, letter from the Deputy Secretary to the Government of the United Provinces to CAS, 12 February 1949, CA/18/FR/49, ECIR; and letter from the Chief Secretary to the Government of Bihar to the Secretary of the Constituent Assembly, 5 November 1948, CA/1/FR/48-IV, ECIR. The Government of Bihar also pointed out that there was an uncertainty about the availability of paper required for printing. Also see letter from the Deputy Secretary to the Government of West Bengal, M. M. Basu, to the Joint Secretary of CAS, 14 December 1948, CA/1/FR/48-IV, ECIR.

[124] Letter from the Under Secretary (P. S. Subramanian), CAS to the Deputy Secretary to the Government of West Bengal, 21 January 1949, CA/1/FR/48-IV, ECIR. The CAS engaged at the time in similar correspondence with the Governments of Assam and Bihar. It wrote to the Government of Bihar that the names of polling booths, polling stations and constituencies could be left blank and filled in hand when constituencies

elections *it is not intended that the rolls should be reprinted at that stage.* The printed preliminary rolls will be published in due course and claims and objections invited. They will then be revised. *The printed rolls with any necessary omissions together with the supplementary list of any necessary additions will form the final rolls.*[125]

The CAS asked the governments whether they had any objections to that suggestion, as well as for an estimation of the number of copies of the preliminary rolls that should be printed if there is no reprinting, and the justification thereof.[126]

The CAS's decision to print the preliminary electoral rolls and use them, together with supplementary list of any necessary additions, as the final rolls made the universal franchise for the people of India *pucca*. These registries of all adults would be open to public scrutiny before being finalised. The questions the CAS posed to bureaucrats across the country invited them, in effect, to commit to deliver on the work. These requests also compelled them to imagine the scale of their output.

As a result of the CAS's design for the form of printing of the draft rolls, in the absence of delimited constituencies, India's national space acquired a reality as a democracy. The CAS asked that the governments not defer the printing until after the delimitation of the constituencies. It suggested and explained instead that:

Each village should be treated as a unit for preparing the register and all the names belonging to a particular village should be printed on sheets which could be separated from similar other sheets. When the delimitation of constituencies is completed, the sheets referring to villages coming within a particular constituency could be put together to form the electoral roll for that constituency.[127]

---

are delimited. S. no. 16, 15 November 1948, CA/1/FR/48-IV, ECIR. Also see S. no. 81, draft letter from the Joint Secretary, CAS, to the Reforms Commissioner of Assam, 26 January 1949, CA/1/FR/48-IV, ECIR.

[125] Letter No. CA/1/FR/49/I from the Under Secretary (P. S. Subramanian), CAS, 28 February 1949, CA/1/FR/49-III, ECIR. Emphasis added. The letter was sent to 9 provinces, 6 Chief Commissioners' Provinces, 6 Unions of States and 11 individual States. Reminder letters were sent on 14 April 1949. Provincial governments estimated that the printing would take at least six to seven months. See, for example, letter from the Reforms Commissioner of Assam to CAS, 11 February 1949, CA/1/FR/49-I, ECIR. The Government of Bihar estimated in early February 1949 that the printing would be completed by the end of August 1950. Letter from the Chief Secretary, Government of Bihar, (Appointment Department, Reforms and Elections Branch) to the Joint Secretary, CAS, 9 February 1949, CA/18/FR/49, ECIR.

[126] Ibid.

[127] S. no. 24, draft letter from CAS to the Additional Secretary to the Government of the United Provinces, 1 March 1949, CA/18/FR/49, ECIR. Also see, for example, draft letter from CAS to the Chief Secretary to the Government of Bihar, 11 March 1949, CA/1/FR/49-I, ECIR; draft letter from CAS to the Chief Minister, Cooch Behar State, 9 July 1949, CA/1/FR/49-II, ECIR. This instruction accorded with the CAS's vision for the preparation of rolls in its 15 March 1948 letter of instructions. Letter No. CA/64/RR/47, 15 March 1948, CA/1/FR/48-V, ECIR.

That design for the printing meant that at first, the whole territory of India would be broken-up into villages and town wards. Subsequently, these units would be re-assembled and amalgamated to form the constituencies for the election to the House of the People and the States Legislatures. Because the constituencies were not yet delimited, the aggregated composite lists of voters were divorced, albeit temporarily, of regional identities or partisan dispositions. These lists from across the country represented an assemblage of the smallest jurisdictional units that, put together, composed India. The resulting new democratic cartography represented India as a 'republic of villages', to use M. K. Gandhi's phrase. These voters' lists, which were like the building blocks of the House of the People, produced the unity of India.

In *Producing India*, Manu Goswami astutely analyses the global economic and Indian-local historical processes that drove the emergence of India 'as a spacially bounded and singular national entity'.[128] India came to be imagined as a bounded national space. But the 'autocratic state machinery' of the Raj bounded it as well.[129] In 1949–1950, the printed lists of voters, based on adult franchise, imbued that national entity, while its territory was evolving into a new federal structure, with a democratic imaginary.

Almost all the governments of the provinces and the states agreed in principle to the suggestion that the printed preliminary rolls with any necessary omissions together with the supplementary list of any necessary additions would form the final rolls.[130] Some governments suggested changes in the layout of the printed roll, like reducing the number of columns to simplify it and to cut the costs of printing, or to adjust the form to the administrative unit for which the roll was prepared.[131] The

---

[128] Manu Goswami, *Producing India. From Colonial Economy to National Space*, Chicago: University of Chicago Press, 2004, p. 7. For an important study of the production of national identity and the imagination of nationhood in postcolonial India see Srirupa Roy, *Beyond Belief: India and the Politics of Postcolonial Nationalism*, Durham: Duke University Press, 2007.

[129] See Legg, 'Dyarchy: Democracy, Autocracy, and the Scalar Sovereignty of Interwar India', p. 65.

[130] The Government of Bombay was an exception. It did not agree at that time with the CAS's suggestion because it anticipated 'huge alterations in the rolls', and therefore a need to reprint the draft rolls for final publications after claims and objections have been invited. It was also 'apprehensive that if the omission of names from the draft rolls is done in ink, they are likely to be tempered with at the time of elections...' S. no. 48, 13–21 June 1949, CA/1/FR/49-III, ECIR.

[131] For example, the Government of West Bengal suggested four columns to the rural areas, instead of the seven in the CAS's original form by including the name of elector, age, and father's/husband's/mother's name in one column. Letter from the Deputy Secretary to the Government of West Bengal to CAS, 25 February 1949, CA/18/FR/49, ECIR.

CAS generally agreed to such suggestions.[132] The Government of East Punjab even requested, already in April 1949, to unofficially publish and sell copies of the printed draft electoral rolls in order to enable the large number of displaced persons to acquire the qualification relating to citizenship as soon as the citizenship articles were passed. The same was considered for West Bengal and Assam.[133] Initially the CAS agreed, but then decided to postpone the publications of the preliminary rolls until article 5 on citizenship of the Draft Constitution was agreed.[134]

Moreover, the governments of the provinces and the states were now drawn to think about how many copies they would make of the rolls, how many reams of papers they would require, and the materials and labour involved. The numbers of copies of the preliminary rolls that most of the provinces and the states proposed to print were, in the CAS's view, 'excessive'. This was its repeated reply to nearly all the proposals. The Government of the United State of Saurashtra, for example, initially suggested printing 700 copies.[135] The CAS wrote that 'Complete copies will be required only by the Secretariat [CAS] and the office of the Deputy Commissioner. As far as tehsils are concerned, it will be sufficient if that part of the electoral roll as relates to that tehsil is published in that area. Similarly, no member of the public will be interested in or is likely to purchase the complete copies of the rolls.'[136] The CAS, in turn, suggested

---

[132] B. N. Rau commented on the West Bengal proposal that 'this is a matter of detail. So long as all the information required is contained in the form, it does not matter very much how the information is arranged. Economy to the maximum possible extent is certainly desirable.' S. no. 31, 22 March 1949, CA/17/FR/49, ECIR.

[133] Draft letter from CAS to the Governments of Bombay, Orissa and Madras, 18 December 1949, CA/1/FR/49-IV, ECIR. This was in response to a query from these governments, after they 'compared notes' with, in this case, the government of Assam. In late November 1949 the Government of Madras wrote to CAS enclosing a letter of the Reforms Commissioner of Assam of 14 November 1949, in the matter of the 'Publication of the printed draft electoral rolls "Unofficially"'. They asked for a copy of the CAS's letter in the matter of 19 October 1949, which the Reforms Commissioner of Assam referred to. Similar queries arrived from Bombay and Orissa. Letter from the Additional Secretary Government of Madras to CAS, 25 November 1949, CA/1/FR/49-IV, ECIR.

[134] S. no. 115, 24 August 1949, CA/1/FR/49-III, ECIR.

[135] Letter from the Joint Secretary, Assembly Department, United State of Saurashtra to CAS, 23 March 1949, CA/1/FR/49-II, ECIR. The Saurashtra Government calculated on the basis of the ratio of population to constituency as set in draft Article 67(5)(b) that there will be 50 polling stations per constituency, and that each presiding officer of a polling station needs 'one complete copy of the whole roll'. Ibid.

[136] Letter from CAS to the Deputy Chief Commissioner for Himachal Pradesh, 5 April 1949, CA/1/FR/49-I, ECIR. Also see for similar replies, for example: letter from CAS to the Government of the Central Provinces and Berar, 15 May 1949, CA/1/FR/49-III, ECIR; letter from CAS to the Joint Secretary, Government of Saurashtra, 16 April 1949, CA/1/FR/49-II, ECIR; letter from CAS to the Secretary to the Government of Cochin, 16 April 1949, CA/1/FR/49-II, ECIR; Draft letter from CAS to the Chief Minister, Cooch Behar State, 9 July 1949, CA/1/FR/49-II, ECIR.

what should be the necessary number of copies, which generally ranged between 50 and 300.[137] Almost all governments agreed with the CAS's suggestion.[138]

The dimensions of the electorate that emerged made real the 'colossal' scale of the preparation for the elections on the basis of universal franchise under the new constitution. For example, the Government of Orissa reported that in the Province and the 24 states ceded to it:

There will be about one lakh and 30 thousand pages of printed electoral rolls for about 75 lakhs of voters. 200 copies of each roll are also being prepared. The difficulty for storage accommodation for the huge quantity of printed rolls in the press has been felt. Arrangements for safe storage of loose sheets of printed rolls at places other than press premises where the rolls are being printed, also presents difficulties on account of unavailability of suitable buildings.[139]

The correspondences on the printing of the preliminary electoral rolls were not, however, simply reduced to numbers: voters, reams of papers, and costs. These exchanges were complemented by detailed narrative accounts of the work governments across the country and their administrators had done. Because these bureaucratic accounts described in detail, and in a straightforward manner the process of democratic state building, it is worth quoting at length an extract from one such account, for example, from Madras:

As a first step towards the preparation of the rolls, a permanent scheme of numbering of houses throughout the Province was introduced by this Government... After the numbering of the houses, house to house enumeration was undertaken

---

[137] The CAS calculated the number of the printed rolls that will be required: 2 for publication in each village and ward of town because in big villages and towns the rolls will be published at more than one place in the village or wards; 1 for Polling Station (Thana); 1 for each Registration Officer's office; 1 for the record of the Registration Officer's office; 1 for each Revising Officer's office; 1 for the record of each Revising Officer's office; 1 for each Returning Officer's office; 1 for the record of each Returning Officer's office; 1 for publication in the Election Commissioner's office; 5 for the record of the Election Commissioner's office; 10 for the Secretariat (if they want); 10 for the Central Government (if they want); for the sale to: Candidates (5), their agents (5), Political Parties (5), Independent citizens (5); for the use at the time of polling 1 for presiding officer and 9 for Polling Officers; and another 40 for the State's Assembly Elections. For the purposes of election of Municipalities, District Boards and Gram Panchayats, 5 copies were calculated. Another 40 were estimated for 'future use until new rolls are prepared'. See 'The revised scheme for the distribution of Electoral rolls'), undated, CA/1/FR/49-II, ECIR.

[138] See, for example, letter from the Government of Patiala & East Punjab States Union to CAS, 30 September 1949, CA/1/FR/49-II, ECIR; letter from the Chief Secretary United State of Saurashtra to CAS, 29 June 1949, CA/1/FR/49-II, ECIR.

[139] Letter from the Government of Orissa, Home (Election) Department to CAS, 3 September 1949, CA/1/FR/49-III, ECIR. The Orissa Government requested that the CAS now 'supply copies of electoral laws and rules, if framed'. Ibid.

throughout the Province. After the general and supplemental enumerations, the manuscript electoral rolls of voters were written up from the enumeration forms. The printing of these manuscript draft electoral rolls has just commenced and is expected to take about four to six months for its completion. For all these operations the Provincial Government have been incurring heavy expenditure from September 1948, on the assumption that the Government of India will bear their share of the expenditure. The Government of India will appreciate that the preparation of rolls of adult voters is not an easy task. The electorate under the adult franchise is very large and the enumeration of all qualified adult voters was indeed a colossal task – nearly 26 million voters have been enumerated. The Government have had to detail large staff in all centres in the districts continuously and had to incur considerable expenditure. The cost of preparation of electoral rolls which included the cost of numbering of houses in villages, the enumeration of qualified persons, preparation of manuscript electoral rolls and printing of the rolls is estimated to be about Rs.57/- lakhs. After the publication of the preliminary electoral rolls under the new Electoral Law to be promulgated after the New Constitution is passed a list of additions, alterations and omissions will have to be prepared. The preparation and printing of this list may cost about another Rs.3/- lakhs.[140]

Such bureaucratic accounts from across the country became the institutional story of the construction of India's federal House of the People.

Conclusion

Federation was the big thing before India. Making that federation was contingent to a large extent on the successful amalgamation of the states. The integration of the states, however, posited significant constitutional and administrative challenges to the making of the Indian federation. Moreover, turning the people of the states and the provinces, who held distinct political identities, into Indians was an arduous task. The Chief Minister of Saurashtra between 1948 and 1954, U. N. Dhebar, conveyed the magnitude of these challenges:

The Saurashtra state was formed on 15 February 1948. We had there before us the problems of integration. These problems were at various levels. There had to be, first of all, political integration, that is taking over the State by the new Government. That was completed in two months' time, which was not a very long time, considering that there were 75 administrative units and 202 States.

---

[140] Letter from the Additional Secretary to the Government of Madras to the Secretary to the Government of India, Ministry of Law (Sub: Elections – New Constitution – Electoral rolls Preparation – Expenditure – Apportionment between the Central and Provincial Governments'), 25 May 1949, CA/18/FR/49, ECIR. For other accounts see, for example, letter from the Deputy Secretary to the Government of Central Provinces and Berar to CAS, 21 April 1949, CA/1/FR/49-III, ECIR; letter from the Joint Secretary to the Government of West Bengal to CAS, 26 April 1949, CA/1/FR/49-III, ECIR.

We had then the problem of administrative integration, meaning integration of administrative services. There was nothing like a system of administration in the States defining the qualifications for the posts or even the number of posts... We had, simultaneously, to organise the territory of Saurashtra into districts, tehsils and so on. And this caused so many head-aches, (e.g.) people wanting the identity of their own old State to be preserved, which some times it was possible, whereas on other occasions it was not. We had before us the question of organising the financial structure... This was integration at the level of State. There was another part of the process of integration that was the crux of the integration and that was integration with the country as a whole.[141]

In the face of these challenges, I argue, the preparation of electoral rolls on the basis of universal franchise for the House of the People became a key instrument in driving the 'integration with the country as a whole'. The production of an Indian electorate out of the people of the provinces and the subjects of 552 princely states and their territories created a de facto constitutional and administrative template for the Indian federation. The binding of the territories of the provinces and the states, and the people into a unified democratic order was at the crux of the preparation of the electoral rolls for the first elections under the new constitution.

In managing and overseeing the preparation of rolls from Delhi, the CAS brought together all the units forming the future federation into an all-India project, which demanded a thorough engagement with the entire adult population of the country. The ongoing correspondences on the preparation of rolls between the CAS and the governments of the provinces and the states highlighted constitutional gaps and administrative problems in the throes of mergers. The governments of the provinces and the states worked towards a set deadline for completing the preliminary work, 'so that the draft rolls may be ready by the time the new Constitution and electoral law thereunder are passed'.[142] The CAS resolved to 'keep up to the programme that the draft rolls should be printed ... by the end of 1949', even in the absence of a decision on the costs.[143] The preparation of rolls therefore compelled the CAS and the governments of the forming States of the Union to address in practice and in good time the challenges that the integration wrought, and that surfaced during the work. Consequently, the preparation of rolls

---

[141] Interview with U. N. Dhebar (interviewed by Uma Shankar, 12 August 1970), f. 156b, Audio Archive, Centre of South Asian Studies, University of Cambridge. Available at http://www.s-asian.cam.ac.uk/archive/audio/collection/u-n-dhebar/ (accessed 28 June 2017).

[142] Internal note (undated), CA/1/FR/48-I, ECIR.

[143] S. no. 31, 18 March 1949, CA/17/FR/49, ECIR.

effectively fostered the process of integration. It set in motion and disciplined the federal relations.

The detailed accounts from across the country on the progress of work concretised the way the mergers of states took place. The bureaucratic paper trails of instruction letters, additional circulars and directives, queries, and the string of reports from the provinces and the states connected democratic state building from the centre down to the most local level. These bureaucratic exchanges also indicated where the process failed. Indeed, not all states simply fell in line, and some lagged behind. For example, only after three request letters for a report on their progress did the Chief Secretary of the Government of the United State of Vindhya Pradesh eventually respond to the CAS in October 1949. He wrote that they had not yet started preparing preliminary electoral rolls, 'although steps are now being taken to start the work'.[144] The CAS requested that they take up the work immediately. They asked of the Vindhya Pradesh government to 'appreciate the urgency of the matter' and to 'make every effort to fall in line with the other Provincial and State Governments in this behalf'.[145]

The CAS's periodic review of the 'state of the States', which was informed by the on-going exchanges with administrators and governments across the country, described the actual creation of the new federal entity into the forming democratic order. In early October 1949 the CAS addressed a circular letter to 30 units: 9 provinces, 10 Chief Commissioners' Provinces, 6 Unions, and 5 individual states.[146] In December 1948 the review covered 37 territorial units; and in March–April 1948 more than 229 units.[147] A review prepared at the CAS in late October 1949 stated: 'There now remain the following 3 individual states in Part III of the First Schedule of the Draft Constitution as adopted by the Constituent Assembly: 1. Hyderabad 2. Jammu & Kashmir 3. Mysore.'[148] Upon a consultation with the Ministry of States, the CAS sent a letter to Hyderabad, informing them that the electoral rolls on the

---

[144] Letter from the Chief Secretary of the Government of the United State of Vindhya Pradesh to CAS, 11 October 1949, CA/1/FR/49-VI, ECIR. 35 states covenanted into the United State of Vindhya Pradesh on 2 April 1948. *White Paper on Indian States*, 1948, p. 99. On 1 January 1950 it was taken over by the India Government.

[145] Draft letter from CAS to the Chief Secretary of the Government of the United State of Vindhya Pradesh, 8 November 1949, CA/1/FR/49-VI, ECIR.

[146] Letter from the Joint Secretary CAS 5 October 1949, CA/1/FR/49-III, ECIR. The list included at that point the Chief Secretary to the Government of Kashmir, and the Adviser to His Excellency the Government of Assam for excluded areas and states (Khasi states).

[147] See n. 39 above.

[148] Internal notes, 27 October 1949, 6/50-Elec, ECIR.

basis of adult suffrage that have already been prepared in Hyderabad in connection with the elections to the State Constituent Assembly would require modifications and alterations before they could be used for elections for the House of the People under the new Constitution. They attached a copy of each of the 14 letters that they had sent from time to time with regard to the preparation of electoral rolls, thus bringing Hyderabad very quickly in.[149] As for Jammu & Kashmir, the Ministry of States asked that the CAS should not take up with its government the question of preparation of electoral rolls at present.[150]

The preparation of rolls thus rendered the integration concrete even before mergers were completed. At a time when the territory was in great flux, roll making, in effect, delineated the limits of India. Moreover, the preparation of the list of voters for the future House of the People enabled the transition from state subjects to Indian citizens at a point when the question of 'Who is an Indian' was undecided and contested constitutionally, administratively, and notionally. In the preparation of rolls, 'An Indian is a voter' became the clearest answer to that question.

In the process of the preparation of the electoral rolls all units of the forming federation were brought effectively under the jurisdiction of the future constitution. This work was done, and created the fact of electoral democracy on the ground, in anticipation of the constitution and the electoral law. In doing so, the draft constitution was not only tested, while it was still debated, but it was also, in some ways, shaped from below.

---

[149] Draft letter from CAS to the Chief Secretary to the Government of Hyderabad, 16 December 1949, CA/1/FR/49-VI, ECIR. The Government replied that 'action is being taken in accordance with the instructions' the CAS sent. Letter from the Election Commissioner and Joint Secretary to the Government of Hyderabad to CAS, 26 December 1949, CA/1/FR/49-VI, ECIR. In Mysore 'electoral rolls on adult franchise basis were already prepared for elections to the State Legislature and they are now being revised to suit as the rolls for elections to the House of the People'. Internal notes, 27 October 1949, 6/50-Elec, ECIR.

[150] Note from the Ministry of States, 9 December 1949 and 13 December 1949, CA/1/FR/49-VI, ECIR. The government of Kashmir responded to the CAS's letter of instructions of 15 March 1948, stating that the matter was under their consideration. But no further letters were received from that Government in spite of several reminders.

5 Shaping the Constitution from Below and the Role of the Secretariat

The news that a new constitution was to be implemented had brought him at the doorstep of a new world. He had switched on all the lights in his brain to carefully study the implications of the new law that was going to become operational in India...

(Saadat Hasan Manto, 'The New Constitution')[1]

Mr. Iengar, if one wants to study the making of the Indian Constitution, would one get the real truth by studying the proceeding of the committee?

Iengar: I would say 'No' for the reason I have just explained to you that the committee proceedings recorded what took place in the meeting themselves, but a good part of the work was done in informal discussions outside.

(Interview with H. V. Iengar)[2]

Upon this work [compilation of the rolls] done sincerely and carefully, depends the success of the New Constitution and the Democracy, which *Free India* aspires to establish.

(K. G. Lele, Secretary. East Khandesh District Congress Committee)[3]

But the constitution has not yet been passed and we can still make our ideas clearer while there is time.

(M. M. Basu, ICS)[4]

The preparation of the electoral rolls on the basis of universal franchise was inextricably linked to the process of constitution making. The first stipulation for a place on the electoral roll was Indian citizenship. Roll

---

[1] Saadat Hasan Manto, 'The New Constitution', in Khalid Hasan (ed. and transl.), *Bitter Fruit: The Very Best of Saadat Hasan Manto*, New Delhi: Penguin Books, p. 208.

[2] Interview with H. V. Iengar, *Oral History Transcript*, no. 303, NMML.

[3] Letter from K. G. Lele, Secretary, East Khandesh District Congress Committee to the Secretary of CAS, 21 July 1948, CA/12/FR/48, ECIR.

[4] Letter from M. M. Basu, ICS (Indian Civil Service), West Bengal Secretariat, Home (C&E) Department, to S. N. Mukherjee, Joint Secretary, Constituent Assembly, 29 November 1948, CA/18/FR/48, ECIR.

making was also tied to constitutional provisions for the conduct of elections, and to the structure of representative bodies in the federal and state legislatures.

While the principle of universal adult franchise was agreed at the beginning of the constitutional debates, the key constitutional provisions for franchise and elections were only debated and passed in June 1949.[5] The first debates on citizenship took place on 29 April 1947. But unlike the principle of adult franchise, the draft citizenship clause did not go unchallenged. Because it was controversial it was referred to a small committee of experts for a redraft. The new draft, which was discussed a few days later on 2 May 1947, remained contested, so the Assembly decided that the citizenship clause would be held over for further consideration by an ad hoc committee.[6] A far more detailed draft citizenship article was briefly brought again before the Assembly on 21 July 1947 as part of the presentation of the *Report on the Principles of the Union Constitution*. The report noted that it was subject to a decision of the ad hoc committee on the citizenship clause, and that it was only a basis for discussion. The final draft article on citizenship came before the Constituent Assembly

[5] Both the Fundamental Rights Sub-Committee and the Minorities Sub-Committee agreed that, as a fundamental right, '[e]very citizen not below 21 years of age shall have the right to vote ... subject to such disqualifications ... as may be required, by or under the law'. Interim Report of the Advisory committee on the Subject of Fundamental Rights (presented on 29 April 1947 – date of Report, 23 April 1947), *Constituent Assembly of India, Reports of Committees (First Series) 1947* (From December 1946 to July 1947). New Delhi: The Manager, Government of India Press, 1947, p. 20. Also see *Constituent Assembly Debates* (hereafter *CAD*), 29 April 1947 (available on http://parliamentofindia. nic.in/ls/debates/debates.htm, accessed 28 June 2017). All references to the *CAD* hereunder are taken from this source. The Advisory Committee agreed in principle with the clause, but recommend that 'instead of being included in the list of fundamental rights, it should find a place in some other part of the constitution'. Ibid. Accordingly, the Reports of the Model Provincial Constitution and the Union Constitutions both contained provisions for elections on the basis of adult suffrage (clause 19 (2) and clause 14 (2) respectively). The Constituent Assembly adopted these clauses of the reports on 18 July 1947 and on 31 July 1947 respectively. Also see B. Shiva Rao, *The Framing of India's Constitution: A Study*, Nasik: The Manager, Government of India Press, 1968, p. 471. It is noteworthy that there was no debate about the principle of universal adult franchise when the Assembly discussed the Interim Report. On 2 May 1947, upon a suggestion of Mr B. K. Sidhwa that the opinion of the House should be taken in the matter, the President put paragraph 9 of the Report to vote, and it was adopted with no comments. In the main, members of the Assembly commented and reflected on the introduction of adult franchise in the Constitution only in retrospect, during the discussions of the February 1948 Draft Constitution in November 1948, and during the final constitutional debates in November 1949. On 27 August 1947 the Constituent Assembly adopted the motion that elections to the Central and Provincial legislatures would be held on the basis of joint electorates.

[6] *CAD*, 2 May 1947. On 30 May 1947 B. N. Rau, the Constitutional Advisor, removed the citizenship clause from the list of Fundamental rights and set it as a separate section in the Draft Constitution.

for debate only two years later, in August 1949. And yet, the preparation of the preliminary electoral rolls on the basis of universal franchise under the new constitution was undertaken from March 1948. The sole legal authority under which the work was undertaken was the draft constitution. Almost every letter of the vast correspondence on the preparation of the electoral rolls contained the phrase 'under the new constitution' in the subject line.

The preparation of the rolls was based on the *anticipatory* citizenship and electoral provisions of the February 1948 draft constitution. As already mentioned in Chapter 1, at the time of issuing the instructions for the preparation of the rolls the Secretary of the Constituent Assembly Secretariat (CAS) explained that 'electoral rolls cannot be compiled without statutory authority. All that we can do now is to compile them in anticipation of such statutory authority, so that the draft rolls may be ready by the time the new Constitution and electoral law thereunder are passed.'[7] As for the instructions, 'presumably', the Secretary commented, 'the same provisions would be prescribed by the electoral law when enacted under the new constitution'.[8] The CAS's 15 March 1948 instruction letter stated that: 'Provisions for all these purposes will doubtless be made by an election law after the new Constitution comes into force. But, for the present, it would suffice if draft rolls, prepared under executive instructions … were kept ready to be published and revised under the new electoral law when the law is enacted'.[9] In spite of these instructions, some provincial governments nonetheless asked for the rules for the preparation of rolls for the union parliament and inquired about 'draft model rules' for the preparation of rolls for the provincial legislatures.[10] The CAS explained that 'Electoral Law cannot be drafted until the Constitution is finally adopted', and referred government officials to their 15 March instruction letter.[11] The work on the rolls thus proceeded in anticipation of the Constituent Assembly finalising the constitution, the electoral laws, and on the presumption that the qualifications for enrolment 'will not be materially different from the existing provisions'.[12]

---

[7] Internal note, 11 March 1948, CA/1/FR/48-I, ECIR.

[8] Ibid.

[9] Letter No. CA/64/RR/47, 15 March 1948, CA/1/FR/48-I, ECIR.

[10] See, for example, letter from J. K. Tandon, Legislative Department, Government of the United Provinces, 10 April 1948, CA/I/FR/48-I, ECIR.

[11] Letter from the Under Secretary of CAS to J. K. Tandon, Legislative Department, Government of the United Provinces, 1 May 1948, CA/I/FR/48-I, ECIR. Also see internal note (by the Joint Secretary of CAS, S. N. Mukherjee), CA/1/FR/48-I, 2 July 1948, ECIR.

[12] Note by B. N. Rau, March 16, 1948, CA/1/FR/48-I, ECIR.

The conventional understanding is that the Indian constitution was endowed from above by India's nationalist leaders.[13] The study of the making of the constitution has been dominated, in the main, by a 'high politics' perspective and a legal doctrinaire approach.[14] Scholars have focused on the deliberations of the Constituent Assembly. They have examined the ethical vision and political theory that underlie the constitution, and the process and role of debate in arriving at the final constitutional settlement.[15] Legal and political scholars have argued that the 'people' had little or no impact on the process of constitution making, and that the constitution 'bore little trace of the imaginative concerns of ordinary Indians'.[16] As Rohit De shows, people related to the constitution and used it to find solutions to their problems within months of its enactment.[17] The speed with which this happened calls into question

---

[13] The constitution is described, for example, as 'a gift of a small set of India's elites'. See Sunil Khilnani, 'Arguing Democracy: Intellectuals and Politics in Modern India', Centre of the Advanced Study of India (CASI) Working Paper Series, University of Pennsylvania, 2009, p. 26.

[14] See, for example, Granville Austin, *The Indian Constitution: Cornerstone of a Nation*, New Delhi, Oxford University Press, 2006 (first published 1966); Rao, *The Framing of India's Constitution* (five volumes). For a comprehensive critique of Austin's approach see Upendra Baxi, 'The Little Done, the Vast Undone: Some Reflections on Reading Granville Austin's *The Indian Constitution*', *Journal of the Indian Law Institute* 9, 1967, pp. 323–430.

[15] See, for example, Rajeev Bhargava (ed.), *Politics and Ethics of the Indian Constitution*, Delhi, Oxford University Press, 2008; Rochana Bajpai, 'The Conceptual Vocabularies of Secularism and Minority Rights in India', *Journal of Political Ideologies* 7, no. 2, 2002, pp. 179–97; Aditya Nigam, 'A Text without Author: Locating Constituent Assembly as Event', *Economic and Political Weekly* 39, no. 21, 22 May 2004, pp. 2107–13. For suggested new directions in the study of constitution making see Arvind Elangovan, 'The Making of the Indian Constitution: A Case for a Non-nationalist Approach', *History Compass* 12, no. 1, 2014, pp. 1–10. Also see Pratap Bhanu Mehta, 'What is Constitutional Morality', *Seminar*, no. 615, November 2010; Sandipto Dasgupta, '"A Language Which Is Foreign to Us": Continuities and Anxieties in the Making of the Indian Constitution', *Comparative Studies of South Asia Africa and the Middle East* 34, no. 2, 2014, pp. 228–42; Sujit Choudhry, Madhav Khosla, and Pratap Bhanu Mehta, 'Locating Indian Constitutionalism', in Sujit Choudhry, Madhav Khosla, and Pratap Bhanu Mehta (eds), *The Oxford Handbook of The Indian Constitution*, Oxford: Oxford University Press, 2016, pp. 1–13; Eleanor Newbigin, Ornit Shani, and Stephen Legg, 'Introduction: Constitutionalism and the Evolution of Democracy in India', *Comparative Studies of South Asia, Africa and the Middle East* 36, no. 1, 2016, pp. 42–3.

[16] Khilnani, 'Arguing Democracy', p. 26. On the view of the little impact of people on constitution making also see Sunil Khilnani, *The Idea of India*, London: Hamish Hamilton, 1997 (particularly pp. 34–35); Austin, *The Indian Constitution*; Baxi, 'The Little Done, the Vast Undone'.

[17] Rohit De's groundbreaking work testifies to 'the daily use of constitutional structures and languages made by thousands of people within months of the constitution's commencement', and reveal continuous constitutional conversations between people and the state. Rohit De, 'Rebellion, Dacoity, and Equality: The Emergence of the Constitutional Field in Postcolonial India, *Comparative Studies of South Asia, Africa and the Middle*

the notion that people were bystanders when the constitution was made. Indeed, people already engaged with and demonstrated an understanding of the constitution even before its enactment.

As we have seen in the previous chapters, in the context of the preparation of the preliminary electoral rolls people made claims of the state – their local bureaucrats and the CAS – on the basis of the draft constitution. They deliberated over the draft constitution and frequently made use of its language. They even enacted some draft-constitutional provisions, based on their reading of the text, to assert their democratic citizenship rights. In doing so, people and social groups not only engaged with the constitution, but also entered into dialogues with the CAS and their local governments about the draft citizenship provisions. Moreover, the correspondences between people and the CAS over the preparation of the electoral rolls demonstrated that people imagined their place in the new Indian constitutional order based on adult franchise. They also conceived of their capability to shape their lives within this new realm.[18]

I have argued thus far that as a result of these interactions between people and the CAS the abstract language, forms and principles of the democratic constitution that were produced in the process of constitution making from above, obtained a practical basis and became a convention while the constitution was still in the making. In this chapter I further propose that this process led to the shaping of the constitution from below in three main ways. First, as I already indicated in Chapter 2, in the context of the preparation of rolls some fundamental draft constitutional provisions for the working of universal franchise and electoral democracy became a fact that could not be easily reversed. Second, the preparation of the rolls engendered constitutional debates outside the Constituent Assembly between administrators, people and the CAS on citizenship and election draft constitutional provisions, and on a range of other topics. The Joint Secretary of the CAS, S. N. Mukherjee, who was directly involved in many of these correspondences, was also the chief draughtsman of the Constituent Assembly for Independent India's Constitution. Consequently, the process of constitution making was routinely informed by the way people and administrators received it on the ground. In this process the new constitutional order was tested and became institutionalised. Third, the CAS, as a

---

East 34, no. 2, 2014, p. 263. Also see De, 'Beyond the Social Contract', *Seminar*, 615, November 2010, *The People's Constitution (1947–1964)*, Princeton: Princeton University Press (forthcoming).

[18] See the discussions in Chapters 2 and 3.

result of its experience of the preparation of the preliminary electoral rolls effected changes in the final articles on the conduct of elections, which had significant implications for the successful establishment of electoral democracy in India.

This chapter explores these consequences of roll making on the constitution.[19] The first section examines the Constituent Assembly debates on the motion on the preparation of the electoral rolls, which was brought before the Assembly in January 1949, almost ten months after the work was undertaken and in some places was nearing completion and the rolls were prepared for printing. The second section focuses on discussions of the constitution outside the Constituent Assembly between administrators, people, and the CAS. The final section examines the role of the CAS in the framing of the articles on elections, which the experience of roll making wrought.

Making a Fact of the Universal Franchise

The motion 'that instructions be issued forthwith to the authorities concerned for the preparation of electoral rolls and for taking all necessary steps so that elections to the legislatures under the new Constitution may be held as early as possible in the year 1950' came before the Constituent Assembly for the first time on 8 January 1949.[20] The proposed resolution was presented to the Assembly ten months after the work of the preparation of rolls had started. The House was asked, in effect, to approve ex-post by an official resolution the work already undertaken. Indeed the Chair of the Assembly explained that: 'As a matter of fact, the Constituent Assembly Secretariat has, under the direction of the President, already taken certain steps for the purpose.'[21] This motion thus gave rise to both substantive and legal-technical arguments among members of the Assembly.[22]

---

[19] In doing so, I hope to contribute to understanding the role played by administrators, the Constituent Assembly Secretariat and the people in making the Indian constitution. These are directions of study recently called for. See, for example, Elangovan, 'The Making of the Indian Constitution', p. 9.

[20] 'Motion Re Preparation of Electoral Rolls', *CAD*, 8 January 1949.

[21] Ibid. The Vice President, H. C. Mookerjee, was in the Chair.

[22] Initially, the motion was to be moved from the Chair of the assembly. This procedure meant that no discussion of the motion would be allowed. The Vice President of the assembly explained that: 'This matter was considered at a meeting of the Steering Committee held on 5th January 1949 and that Committee decided that a resolution on the subject should be brought forward before the Assembly and that it would be in

The resolution stated:

Resolved further that the State electoral rolls be prepared on the basis of the provisions of the new Constitution already agreed to by this Assembly and in accordance with the principles hereinafter mentioned, namely:

(1) That no person shall be included in the electoral roll of any constituency
    (a) if he is not a citizen of India; or
    (b) if he is of unsound mind and stands so declared by a competent court.
(2) That 1st January 1949 shall be the date with reference to which the age of the electors is to be determined.
(3) That a person shall not be qualified to be included in the electoral roll for any constituency unless he has resided in that constituency for a period of not less than 180 days in the year ending on the 31st March 1948. For the purposes of this paragraph, a person shall be deemed to be resident in any constituency if he ordinarily resides in that constituency or has a permanent place of residence therein.
(4) That, subject to the law of the appropriate legislature, a person who has migrated into a Province or Acceding State on account of disturbances or fear of disturbances in his former place of residence shall be entitled to be included in the electoral roll of a constituency if he files a declaration of his intention to reside permanently in that constituency.[23]

Nehru tried to pre-empt some of the concerns members of the House raised before he moved the resolution and explained that 'even if this Resolution was not passed, the Government of course can proceed with the preparation of these rolls', which they asked provincial governments to prepare.[24] But a difficulty will arise in case the Assembly at a later stage would change the qualifications on the basis of which the rolls are prepared, because then the rolls 'might become useless'.[25] He claimed that 'in effect there is nothing new in this which the House has not decided. It may be there in some minor variation.'[26]

Assembly members, however, raised several objections and questions for clarification. First, members pointed out that the Assembly had not yet passed the article on citizenship, but the motion stated that 'no

the fitness of things if such a resolution were moved from the Chair.' Ibid. In the face of members' objection to that procedure, the Chair withdrew it and Nehru moved it instead, making it open for debate.
[23] Ibid.
[24] Ibid.
[25] Ibid.
[26] Ibid.

person shall be included in the electoral roll ... if he is not a citizen of India'. Some wondered 'How can there be any electoral roll unless we have decided the fact as to who is a citizen of India and who is not?'[27] Second, members of the House also expressed concerns about the ability of the refugees to be enrolled because filing a declaration before a District Magistrate will be expensive and complicated. They would likely not be able to carry the burden of a stamp (fee) for the declaration.[28] Many refugees were also illiterate. Moreover, since large numbers of the refugees were in camps and due to be transferred to other places, members wondered how could they declare their intention to 'reside permanently' while registering as voters.[29] Third, Assembly members questioned that electoral rolls could be prepared before the delimitation of constituencies. Some suggested that the determination of citizenship and the delimitation of constituencies must be done before electoral rolls could be prepared.[30] Finally, Assembly members noted that according to the proposed resolution elections should be held in 1950. But the date with reference to which the age of electors was to be determined was 1 January 1949. They, therefore, thought that the fixed date should be changed to 1 January 1950 so as not to exclude a large number of people (estimated at 'about a crore'), who would turn 21 by 1 January 1950.[31] Some suggested that in the light of the delay in the passing of the constitution and the holding of elections the date set for the residence qualification should also be changed.

Assembly members also questioned the legal standing of the resolution. The resolution stated that 'electoral rolls be prepared on the basis of the provisions of the new Constitution already agreed to by this Assembly'.[32] The Assembly had neither passed the Citizenship article, nor article 149 (2) on adult suffrage.[33] Mahavir Tyagi claimed

---

[27] Ibid. Algu Rai Shastri. Also see ibid. H. V. Kamath. Thakur Dass Bhargava questioned this in the light of the legality of the process thus far. Ibid.

[28] Ibid. Also see comments by Bhopindar Singh Man, Bikramlal Sondhi, Shibban Lal Saksena, and S. Nagappa, ibid.

[29] Ibid. For example, Rohini Kumar Chaudhari.

[30] Ibid. For example Algu Rai Shastri, S. Nagappa, and Thakur Dass Bhargava.

[31] Ibid. Shibban Lal Saksena. Also see Thakur Dass Bhargava, K. Santhanam, and Mohammed Ismail Sahib.

[32] Ibid.

[33] Article 149 (2) on the Legislative Assemblies set that the 'election shall be on the basis of adult suffrage'. The Drafting Committee, Constituent Assembly of India, *Draft Constitution of India*, New Delhi: The Manager Government of India Press, 1948, p. 66. The Assembly began discussing article 149 on 6 January 1949, but adopted clause (2) on 8 January 1949 after the debate on the motion on the preparation of rolls. The Assembly adopted article 67 (6), which provided that elections to the House of the People shall be on the basis of adult suffrage and principally stipulated the same qualification provided

that 'the Government cannot act without a definite article in the Constitution'.[34]

Nehru tried to assuage the concerns of members of the House:

Whatever the future decision of the Assembly in regard to the citizenship clause might be it will only affect the preparation of those rolls slightly. The citizenship does not affect the vast number of people in this country. It affects only two types of persons ultimately, (1) persons who may be called 'refugees' (2) Indians who reside outside India... So far as the refugees are concerned... we accept as citizens anybody who calls himself a citizen of India.[35]

Questioned about the legal standing of the resolution, Nehru appeared to struggle: this 'is not in any sense an official resolution'; he asked the House 'to consider that this is not part of the Constitution. It is not a statute. The words need not be precisely looked upon from the point of view of a statute. These are general directions given to the Governments which they will transmit to the enumerators.'[36] In his answers to questions regarding the refugees he referred intermittently to past and future actions. He said that 'some special provisions should be made to permit them to vote. For the moment, suddenly, I cannot say what it should be.'[37] And that 'as far as I can say straight off, I do not think any stamp [fee] will be necessary'. But when a member said in turn that provincial governments required declarations to be made on stamp paper, Nehru said that 'No stamps are necessary. To facilitate this, we shall inform the provincial governments that this will be free.'[38] He then added: 'I understand that instructions have been issued that there should be no fees or stamps for this.'[39]

The issues that members of the Assembly raised made it apparent that some of them were unaware that the preparation of the rolls was already well under way. It suggested that members of the Constituent Assembly were at some distance from the preparatory work for elections in their provinces and states.[40] The CAS, as we saw in the previous

in article 149 (2), on 4 January 1949. On 14 October 1949 articles 149(2) and 67(6) were omitted from the constitution, since both were by that point included in the new article 289-B, which was adopted on 16 June 1949.

[34] *CAD*, 8 January 1949. Also see for similar arguments by Shibban Lal Saksena, Thakur Dass Bhargava, and Deshbandhu Gupta, ibid.

[35] Ibid.

[36] Ibid.

[37] Ibid.

[38] Ibid.

[39] Ibid.

[40] Four days earlier, during the discussion of article 67 (6), which stipulated adult suffrage for that elections to the House of the People assembly member Biswanath Das appealed to the Government 'to take immediate action in time to set up the machinery to carry out this stupendous task [elections]'. M. Ananthasayanam Ayyangar said that he

chapters, publicised the work of the preparation of rolls and the press reported on it. People engaged with the constitutional implications of the work. One organisation observed in their letter to the President of the Constituent Assembly in May 1948 that 'though the Draft Constitution has not yet been adopted it is reported that the work of preparing the electoral rolls may be undertaken on the basis of the provisions of this Constitution'.[41]

Remarkably, all the concerns that members of the Constituent Assembly raised in the discussion on the motion on the preparation of electoral rolls were already brought from the bottom by people, social groups and administrators soon after the work of the preparation of rolls was taken up. Some of the amendments that members submitted, in effect represented actions already undertaken by the CAS as it dealt with the various concerns that people and administrators brought up. Although the Constituent Assembly did not yet decide who is a citizen of India and who is not, the registration of voters was done on the basis of the draft citizenship article. Administrators grappled with the problem of enrolling the refugees because their citizenship and residential status, two key qualifying criteria for registration as voters, were at odds with both the draft citizenship provisions and the residential qualifications set in the CAS's instructions. The CAS found a solution. Then, from July 1948, shortly after the work commenced, problems arose, as Constituent Assembly members anticipated on 8 January 1949, over the demand of some governments for a stamp fee on the refugees' declaration for their registration as voters. The CAS instructed forthwith that no fees should be imposed on the refugees' declaration. It clarified that a refugee declaration could be made before any responsible officer, not necessarily before a District Magistrate. In the case of women refugees, the CAS allowed for the declarations on their behalf to be made and signed by their husband or a parent.

In late 1948 administrators in the provinces and the states raised the problem of printing the preliminary rolls in the absence of constituencies. They were concerned, as were subsequently Constituent Assembly members, that the likelihood of holding the elections in late 1950 would require altering the date with reference to the age of voters and that it would result in many changes in the rolls. The CAS asked that the governments not defer the printing until after the delimitation of the

---

'believe that the Central Government will take steps to issue instructions to Provincial Governments to prepare these lists and also delimit constituencies early with a view to have the elections early next year. *CAD*, 4 January 1949.

[41] Letter from the East Bengal Minority Welfare Central Committee, Calcutta, to Rajendra Prasad, 12 May 1948, CA/9/FR/48, ECIR.

constituencies.[42] It instructed to print the rolls by units of villages and town wards, which would be assembled later into constituencies once they were delimited.

The Joint Secretary of the CAS deliberated on the legal-constitutional implications of the CAS's actions. At the time the CAS came up with the solution for the registration of the refugees he noted that: 'Under the Draft Constitution the detailed qualifications for inclusion in the electoral rolls have been left to be prescribed under the electoral law to be passed by the Legislature after the new Constitution comes into operation... Whatever action is being taken in this connection at this stage is of an anticipatory nature. *Steps will have to be taken for relaxation of the residential qualification in the case of refugees when making the electoral law.*'[43] When the question of the prospect of changes of the date of reference to the age of a voter came up in the context of printing, he explained that '[a]ny change with reference to the age of the elector ... will only mean the addition of some new names'.[44] Moreover, the Joint Secretary suggested that:

Whatever may be the time of holding the elections, the residential qualification in respect of persons other than refugees must be determined with reference to the financial year 1947–48. *In view of the huge expenditure already incurred, we think it will not be difficult to persuade the Legislatures, which will have to make the law, agree to this qualification.*[45]

The CAS, thus, foresaw not only the constitutional implications of its actions, but also the prospect of these actions shaping a constitutional reality.

The fact of electoral rolls on the basis of adult franchise was created on the ground. The Chairman of the Constitution Drafting Committee, B. R. Ambedkar, who addressed the amendments that Assembly members proposed during the debate on the motion on the preparation of rolls, revised the resolution to reflect more accurately the constitutional

---

[42] See the discussion in Chapter 4.

[43] Internal discussion, 24 August 1948, CA/9/FR/48, ECIR (emphasis added). Also see discussion of this subject in Chapter 2.

[44] Letter from the CAS (to all provinces and states), 21 December 1948, CA/1/FR/49-II, ECIR. He also noted that the rolls, which were under preparation, could 'still be utilised after suitable revision'. S. no. 1, 3 December 1948, CA/17/FR/49 (note by the Joint Secretary S. N. Mukherjee).

[45] Ibid. (emphasis added). Similarly, as already mentioned in Chapter 4, when addressing the question of the apportionment of the costs of the preparation of the rolls the Joint Secretary wrote to the governments of the provinces and the states that 'We cannot anticipate the decision of the Government of India but it is not difficult to guess how they are likely to view the problem.' Letter from the Joint Secretary of the CAS (to all the provinces and the states), 21 December 1948, CA/1/FR/48-IV, ECIR.

provisions already agreed to by the Constituent Assembly. But at the same time he ensured that the work done so far remained intact. To resolve the problem that arose from the Assembly not yet adopting, for example, article 149 (2) that dealt with adult suffrage, Ambedkar deleted the word 'already' from the 'electoral rolls be prepared on the basis of the provisions of the new Constitution already agreed to by this Assembly'. Similarly, to resolve the difficulty as to who is a citizen, Ambedkar suggested that the explicit mentioning in the first clause of the proposed motion that a voter had to be a citizen of India was not really needed and was redundant because the purpose of that clause was embodied in the following clauses that dealt with residential qualifications.[46] He substituted the word 'constituency', which appeared in the resolution, for the word 'area', thus meeting the criticism that constituencies did not yet exist. In the clause on the refugees' declarations, he added after the word 'files' the words 'or makes', which permitted an oral declaration to be made before an officer who was preparing the electoral rolls, and not necessarily a District Magistrate. It also met the criticism that many refugees were illiterate.

However, in response to Assembly members' suggestions to make changes in the qualifying dates for registration, or the date fixed for determining the age of a voter, Ambedkar stated that 'it is not possible' because of the work that had already been done. He explained that instructions were already issued to prepare the electoral rolls on the basis of adult suffrage. And if changes are made 'we shall have to waste all the work that has already been done by Provincial Governments on that basis'.[47]

The Assembly's resolution essentially confirmed the rules made up so far. The CAS did not issue further instructions regarding the preparation of the rolls following the resolution adopted by the Constituent Assembly.[48] It did, however, subsequently recast its narrative of the issuing of instructions for the preparation of rolls. The CAS wrote, for example, in December 1949 that 'the instructions regarding preparation and printing of the electoral rolls have so far been issued by this Secretariat in pursuance of the resolution adopted by the Constituent

---

[46] Thus, clause (a) from sub-clause (1): 'if he is not a citizen of India' was deleted. *CAD*, 8 January 1949. Also see Ministry of Law, Justice and Company Affairs, f. CA/6/49/1949/ Cons, National Archives of India (hereafter NAI), New Delhi.

[47] *CAD*, 8 January 1949. Nehru made the same point earlier in the discussion stating that the date 'was simply given there because some rolls have already been prepared on that basis and if this is not done they might become useless and one has to start afresh'. Ibid.

[48] See, for example, letter from CAS to the Reforms Commissioner of Assam, and a letter to the Chief Secretary of the Government of Bombay, 2 February 1949, CA/1/FR/ 49-I, ECIR.

Assembly on the 8th January 1949'.[49] It actually issued the instructions for the preparation of rolls ten months earlier.

The preparation of rolls on the basis of draft constitutional provisions, not only turned the idea of the universal franchise into a reality, but also generated debates on the constitution outside the Constituent Assembly. Various civic organisations and administrators engaged with an array of constitutional provisions. In that context, the future constitutional vision as a whole was deliberated, interpreted, tested, and forged.

Debating the Constitution Outside the Constituent Assembly

In late July 1948 the President of Devicolam Taluq Travancore wrote to the CAS:

Travancore, though acceded to Indian Union, have denied the privileges of voting rights, to 120000 Tamilians who are residing in Devicolam and Peermade Taluqs of Travancore State. We emigrated to these Taluqs over 50 years ago, to work in the extensive plantations and to us and our children who are born here, Travancore is our adopted Home. Amongst us there are thousands of land owners and innumerable number of Traders who have invested millions of capital in Travancore State. We have no voting rights in our ancestral Home, as our sojorn there is short as a holiday trip. To-day there is none to represent our cause, either in Travancore Government or Indian Union… When India is fighting for the franchise and other rights of her people in South Africa and Ceylon I am fully confident that your Honour will immediately take up this matter with the present Congress Government now functioning in Travancore and get the most coveted right of voting and other privileges same as that a Travancorian enjoys in the State.[50]

A member of the CAS prepared a note on the letter. He explained that the government of Travancore refused to register these Tamilians in the electoral roll it recently prepared for elections to the State Legislature because they were not naturalised subjects of the State. He noted that 'a similar question arose in the Cochin State where only Cochin State subjects born or naturalised under the Cochin Nationality and Naturalisation Act have been registered as voters for the Cochin State Legislature.'[51] Travancore and Cochin were not the only states that retained notionally

---

[49] Letter from CAS to the Chief Commissioner of Coorg, 6 December 1949, CA/17/FR/49, ECIR.

[50] Letter from the President of Devicolam Taluq Travancore Tamilnad Congress, Munar, to the President of the Constituent Assembly, 28 July 1948, CA/12/FR/48, ECIR.

[51] S. no. 27 (by A.A. Abidi), 17 August 1948, CA/12/FR/48, ECIR. The CAS told the Government of Cochin that there would be only one common law of citizenship throughout the union under the draft constitution, and the Government of Cochin agreed to

and in practice their state's citizenship for its subjects. In July 1947 the Government of Tripura appointed a committee to determine the question of the state citizenship and naturalisation for the purpose of preparing the electoral rolls for the state legislature.[52]

The CAS's Joint Secretary wrote to the Chief Secretary of the government of Travancore stating that 'under the Draft Constitution of India there will be only one common law of citizenship throughout the Union and it is not contemplated that each State should have nationality laws of its own as distinct from the union Nationality law'.[53]

The Chief Secretary to the Travancore Government took three more months before sending to the CAS a substantial response to the matter. His reply contested the CAS's opinion. He explained that according to Rule 7 of the Representative Body Electoral Rules of 18 November 1947, under the Travancore Interim Constitution Act, every person who is a Travancore subject as defined in the Travancore Naturalization Act XIV of 1945 is entitled to have his name registered in the electoral roll. The Tamilians residing in Devicolam and Peermade Taluqs were not qualified to be included in the electoral rolls because they were not Travancore subjects. They came from the adjoining Madras districts as labourers. They did not come to settle in the State.[54] Moreover, in the Chief Secretary's opinion:

The enactment of common law of citizenship throughout the Union of India as indicated in the draft Constitution of India cannot alter the position of those Tamilians in respect of franchise for elections in the State, as neither in law nor in fact is there any necessary connection between citizenship and voting. Voting is a right which a citizen obtains by showing himself possessed of the qualifications which are established by the State in which he resides. Matters pertaining to

revise the rolls and include citizens of the Dominion of India for elections to the Federal Parliament at the time of revision of the rolls. For the question of State nationality, which the Government of Cochin raised see S. no. 112, 27–29 July 1948, CA/1/FR/48-II, ECIR. In the ensuing discussion of the letter from Devicolam, the members of the CAS reviewed the Travancore rules for preparation of rolls and for registration of adults.

52 A similar challenge surfaced in mid-1949 with the Manipur state. Letter from the Dewan of Manipur State to the Joint Secretary of the Constituent Assembly 30 July 1949, CA/1/FR/49-II, ECIR. This illuminates further the discussion on constitutional discrepancies between the integrating states and the new forming Union in Chapter 4.

53 Draft letter from the Joint Secretary of CAS to the Chief Secretary Government of Travancore, 23 August 1948, CA/12/FR/48, ECIR. The CAS also updated the President of the Devicolam Taluq Travancore, saying that 'the matter is receiving attention'. Letter from the Under Secretary, CAS to the President of Devicolam Taluq Travancore Tamilnad Congress, Munnar, 20 August 1948, CA/12/FR/48, ECIR.

54 Letter from the Chief Secretary to the Government of Travancore to the Joint Secretary, CAS, 27 November 1948, CA/12/FR/48, ECIR. Under the Act a Travancore subject was either a natural-born Travancore subject, or a person to whom a certificate of naturalisation was granted.

suffrage will have to be regulated by the State, and it will be for the State to determine who shall vote at elections. The framing of a constitution for Travancore is under the consideration of the Travancore Representative Body.[55]

The Joint Secretary of the CAS responded:

[W]hile it is no doubt open to the State to prescribe qualifications for the purpose of voting, such qualifications must not be inconsistent with the provisions of part III [fundamental rights] of the Draft Constitution. Clause (1) of Article 9 of the Draft Constitution prohibits discrimination against any citizen of India on the ground only of place of birth. If a citizen of India after the commencement of the new Constitution possesses all the qualifications prescribed for voters born in the State, it will not be permissible for the State to disqualify him from voting merely on the ground of place of birth.[56]

The Joint Secretary also pointed out that it has been proposed to insert a new article 289B, which, if adopted, will entitle every citizen of India to be registered as a voter at elections to the legislature of the State. He attached a copy of the proposed new article. Accordingly, he explained, after the commencement of the constitution the current Travancore Representative Body Electoral Rules 'will to the extent of inconsistency be void'.[57] Therefore, he suggested that the Travancore Government should amend the rule in question, 'so as to entitle all persons who satisfy the requirements as to residence and are not otherwise disqualified, to be included in the electoral rolls for elections to the State Legislature'.[58]

The CAS, in its correspondence with the Chief Secretary to the Government of Travancore, provided an interpretation of the workings of specific provisions of the constitution in relation to the larger body of the text, and to its future pending amendments. The CAS did so in the first place because the Tamilians residing in Devicolam and Peermade Taluqs brought the problem to their attention. The matter of their registration on the electoral roll remained unsettled for a while.[59] Only in September 1949 the Government of the United States of Travancore and Cochin published an order, which stipulated the inclusion of 'citizens of

---

[55] Ibid.

[56] Letter from the Joint Secretary, CAS, to the Chief Secretary Government of Travancore, 22 December 1948, CA/12/FR/48, ECIR.

[57] Ibid.

[58] Ibid. The letter was based on the CAS's thorough discussion of the matter. See Internal notes (by the Under Secretary), 'Tamilians residing in Travancore', 14 December 1948, CA/12/FR/48, ECIR.

[59] During the negotiations on the formation of the Union of Travancore and Cochin in March 1949, the premier of Travancore 'pointed out that they were confronted with the problem of reconciling the Tamil section of the population in the Southern districts of Travancore'. Menon, *The Integration of the States*, pp. 264–5. The Union was formed in May 1949. Also see letter from the Joint Secretary, Travancore Tamil Nadu Congress

India who were not included in the original electoral rolls since they were not subjects of Travancore' on the electoral roll.[60]

Social organisations engaged primarily with draft constitutional provisions that related to citizenship and voting rights. But in the context of the preparation of rolls, they also deliberated on broader constitutional subjects. For example, they also examined how some provisions of the constitution would affect the legislative powers and even present actions of their state government. The Assam Citizens' Association Dhubri wrote to the CAS, stating:

That the Association respectfully *urges for the following amendments* in the various Articles of the Draft Constitution of India. (1) In view of the fact that clause (5) [of article 13] will confer unfettered powers on the Provincial Governments to make legislation curtailing fundamental rights given by sub-clauses (d), (e), (f) of clause (1) of Article 13, and also in view of the fact that the Government of Assam has been already making legislations like Assam Land and Revenue (Amendment) Act, 1947, which masquerading as a piece of legislation protecting backward classes really curtails the fundamental rights [of] ordinary citizens, clause (5) of Article 13 be altogether deleted.[61]

Another organisation, the Assam Citizens Association Gauhati Branch wrote to the CAS: 'this Association *respectfully suggest the following amendments in the draft Constitution* (1) Article 13(5) the words 'either ... public or' be either totally omitted, or the wording of the original draft as approved by the Constituent Assembly before sending to the drafting Committee be substituted in its place'.[62]

Article 13 of the draft constitution dealt with the protection of certain rights regarding freedom of speech. Sub-clauses (d), (e), and (f) of clause (1) of article 13, which the Assam Citizens' Association Dhubri referred to, dealt, respectively, with (d) the freedom to move freely throughout the territory of India; (e) the freedom to reside and settle in it; and (f) with the freedom to acquire, hold or dispose of property. Clause (5) of article 13 set that 'Nothing in sub-clauses (d), (e) and (f) ... shall affect the

to the Minister of States, Government of India, 10 November 1949, Ministry of States (MoS), f. 17(25)-P. NAI.

[60] 'Proceedings of the Government of the United States of Travancore and Cochin', Order No. LD4-427/49/Law, Trivandrum, dated 19 September 1949 (in a letter from the Chief Secretary to the Government of the United States of Travancore and Cochin to CAS, 16 November 1949, CA/1/FR/49-VI, ECIR.

[61] Letter from the Assam Citizens' Association Dhubri, to the Joint Secretary, Constituent Assembly, 29 August 1948, CA/9/FR/48, ECIR (emphasis added).

[62] Letter from the Secretary, Assam Citizens Association Gauhati to CAS, 18 August 1948, CA/9/FR/48, ECIR (emphasis added). This amendment proposal represented 'Resolution No. 7' of the proceedings of the association's executive committee meeting held on 7 August 1948.

operation of any existing law, or prevent the State from making any law imposing restrictions on the exercise of any of the rights conferred by the said sub-clauses either in the interests of the general public or for the protection of the interest of any aboriginal tribe'.[63]

The Assam Citizens' Association Dhubri, which struggled for the citizenship and voting rights of the refugees, asked to delete clause (5) of article 13 to specifically prevent their government from restricting their freedom to acquire property in areas designated as tribal land. Indeed, at the time, the Assam Land and Revenue (Amendment) Act, 1947, which intended to protect the tribal land, prohibited the transfer of tribal land (defined as the 'belt and block' area) to a person, even a permanent resident, who did not belong to the tribes notified under the act. The original wording of clause (5), which the Constituent Assembly adopted in April 1947 before the drafting committee considered it for the February 1948 draft constitution, stated: 'either in the interests of the general public or for the protection of the interest of minority groups and tribe'.[64] The Assam Citizens Association Gauhati used this formulation when making a similar proposal in August 1948.[65] In December 1948, during the debate on article 13 in the Constituent Assembly, Mr Mohd. Tahir suggested a similar amendment.[66] He explained that 'the removal of these words would make the clause of a general character, which certainly includes the safeguards of the interests of the aboriginal tribes as well'.[67]

The Assam Citizens' Association Dhubri also proposed a series of amendments to article 23, which dealt with cultural and educational rights, protection of interests of minorities. Article 23(2), stated that: 'No minority whether based on religion, community or language shall be discriminated against in regard to the admission of any person belonging to such minority into any educational institution maintained by the state.'[68] The organisation suggested that in article 23 (2) 'after the word "maintained" the words "or aided" be added'.[69] On 8 December 1948, when

---

[63] The Drafting Committee, Constituent Assembly of India, *Draft Constitution of India*, p. 7. Also see Rao, *The Framing of India's Constitution*, Vol. III, p. 523.

[64] Rao, *The Framing of India's Constitution, A Study*, p. 218.

[65] Letter from the Secretary, Assam Citizens Association Gauhati to CAS, 18 August 1948, CA/9/FR/48, ECIR.

[66] Mohd Tahir suggested 'that in clause (5) of article 13, the word "either" and the words "or for the protection of the interests of any aboriginal tribe" be omitted'. *CAD*, 1 December 1948.

[67] Ibid. The amendment was not accepted. In the final article 'aboriginal' was changed to Scheduled Tribes. *CAD*, 2 December 1948.

[68] Rao, *The Framing of India's Constitution*, Vol. III, p. 525.

[69] Letter from the Assam Citizens' Association Dhubri, to the Joint Secretary, Constituent Assembly, 29 August 1948, CA/9/FR/48, ECIR. The Assam Citizens Association

the Constituent Assembly debated the article, Thakur Das Bhargava moved a similar amendment, which read: 'maintained by the State or receiving aid out of State'.[70] The House adopted the amendment.

Organisations sent their general resolutions to place 'before the concerned so that these may be included in the Constitution of the country'.[71] The Swarajya Sabha, Delhi, asked, for example, that 'while making the constitution of the Indian Union', the Constituent Assembly consider a way of assigning administrative positions to 'men of experience and knowledge and judge the progress of various Departments with occasional scrutiny'.[72] Another organisation, the East Bengal Minority Welfare Central Committee, Calcutta, indicated possible contradictions between articles in the draft constitution. They invited the attention of the President of the Constituent Assembly 'to Clause (d) of Article 167 which has been incorporated by the Drafting Committee. The clause disqualifies a person from being a member of the legislature if he is "entitled to the rights or privileges of a subject or a citizen of a foreign power"... In the opinion of the Committee, this provision does not also exactly fit in with Article 5 (b).'[73] And in a three-page note entitled 'Some Hints to the Constitution Makers', a former member of the Madras Legislative Council, made six suggestions regarding the constitutional provisions for elections based on adult suffrage.[74]

Thus, people and various organisations not only fought for their future constitutional citizenship and voting rights, but also sought in the constitution solutions to their present or anticipated problems. The proposed amendments of the Assam Citizens' Association Dhubri, for example, indicated that they saw the constitution as an instrument of ensuring their access to land and education in the face of recent provincial governments' legislation. People, thus, linked the abstract constitutional text to their everyday lives, and recognised the prospect of using the

Gauhati proposed an identical amendment. See letter from the Secretary, Assam Citizens Association Gauhati to CAS, 18 August 1948, CA/9/FR/48, ECIR.

[70] Rao, *The Framing of India's Constitution, A Study*, pp. 277, 281.

[71] Letter from the President of the Swarajya Sabha Delhi (a non-party body of Indian Nationalist politicians), to the President of the Constituent Assembly, 5 January 1949, CA/12/FR/48, ECIR.

[72] Ibid. The CAS acknowledged the receipt of their letter on 17 January 1949.

[73] Preparation of Electoral rolls and citizenship of the immigrants from Pakistan, letter from the East Bengal Minority Welfare Central Committee, Calcutta, to Rajendra Prasad, 12 May 1948, CA/9/FR/48, ECIR.

[74] K. P. Mallikarjunudu, 'Some Hints to the Constitution Makers', 15 November 1948, 14/50 Elec-I, ECIR. Mallikarjunudu was at the time the President, Town Congress, Masulipatam. He was a member of the Madras Legislative Council between 1937 and 1940.

constitution to resolve their discords with the state.[75] The CAS read and acknowledged the receipt of copies of the resolutions and proposals they received from the public.[76] Its members sometimes marked and placed comments on the proposed amendment.

Interest in the particulars of draft constitutional provisions was not limited to the public. Senior administrators entered into substantial constitutional conversations with the CAS. A 'demi-official' exchange of letters between the Deputy Secretary of the Government of West Bengal, M. M. Basu, and the Joint Secretary of the Constituent Assembly, S. N. Mukherjee, provided a lens to some material debates on the constitution outside the Constituent Assembly and its committees.

My dear Mukherjee,

I daresay you have now heard that it has been recommended that West Bengal should have a bi-cameral legislature. This has made Article 150 of the Draft Constitution relevant for my own purposes, for formerly I have not bothered about it.[77]

Article 150 dealt with the Composition of the Legislative Councils. In a three-page letter, Basu delved into the minutiae of the phrasing of the five clauses of article 150. He questioned the clarity of the article in the light of different possible interpretations of some of its clauses. Basu also discussed the relations between article 150 and articles 151 and 291, which dealt, respectively, with the duration of state legislatures and with elections to the legislatures of states. Basu indicated possible 'gaps of principles which the Constitution may have accidently overlooked', and even went so far as drawing a scenario whereby his arguments on the articles 'were ever taken to a court of law.'[78] He urged that '*the constitution has not yet been passed and we can still make our ideas clearer while there is time*'.[79]

Moreover, Basu argued that 'Article 151(2) contains an inadequate expression, from the drafting point of view...' He noted, for example,

---

[75] Rohit De argues that after the commencement of the constitution, 'constitutional litigation became the way through which people inserted themselves into a conversation with the state'. He shows how through these litigations the constitution entered everyday life. De, 'Beyond the Social Contract', p. 2; *The People's Constitution (1947–1964)*. The way people related to the draft constitution in the context of the preparation of rolls, was to some extent, a prelude to their use of the constitution once it came into force.

[76] See, for example, S. no. 88, draft letter from the Under Secretary of CAS to the President, the Swarajya Sabha, Delhi, 17 January 1949, CA/12/FR/48, ECIR.

[77] Letter (D.O.NO. 1767AR) from M. M. Basu (I.C.S) to S. N. Mukherjee, Joint Secretary of the Constituent Assembly, 29 November 1948, CA/18/FR/49, ECIR. Basu was the Deputy Secretary to the Government of West Bengal, Home (C&E) Department.

[78] Ibid.

[79] Ibid. Emphasis added.

that the article provided for 'how the vacancies in the Council shall occur. It is silent about … how the vacancies shall be filled up'.[80] Basu contrasted this article with the provisions for the composition of the House of Parliament in article 67. He wrote: 'While very clear provision has been made about the nature and composition of the membership of the House of the People as well as the manner of election thereto in terms of constituencies, one is left completely in the dark about the Council of States and feels that a lot is missing.'[81]

To stress his point about the 'obscurity of expression in regard to the constitution of the Council of States', Basu referred to the American Constitution, and suggested to learn one's lesson from it.[82] 'We have', he commented, 'travelled away from the days of Hamilton, Madison and Jay when Constitution-making as a positive art was still in its infancy. I need not remind you about the many absurd results which the judgements of the U.S. Supreme Court have given rise to in interpreting many fundamental provisions of the American Constitution which badly suffered from want of clarity of expression.'[83] Concluding his point, Basu asserted: 'Modern Constitution-making with its knowledge of the texts of so many extant constitutions and the experience of their working naturally takes care to avoid known pitfalls by ensuring clarity of expression as much as foreseeable.'[84] At the same time, Basu applauded the use of the phrase 'established by law' in Article 15, which dealt with the protection of life and personal liberty and equality before law, rather than the 'American expression "without due process of law" '.[85] Notably he added at the end of the letter:

These are entirely my personal observations made for the purpose of my own clarifications as I am anxious to know the exact line of thinking being followed by your Secretariat and would welcome more light to be thrown on the matter. This is why I am writing demi-officially. They should not be understood as suggestions for amendments. I merely want to ascertain the correct position in which the Articles discussed really stand.[86]

In his reply to Basu regarding the second chamber in the states, the Joint Secretary wrote: 'From the general impression of the attitude of the

---

[80] Ibid.
[81] Ibid. Basu also raised questions about article 172 that dealt with joint sitting of both houses in the states in certain cases.
[82] Ibid.
[83] Ibid. Basu exhibited comprehensive knowledge in the American constitution and in its adjudication and amendments.
[84] Ibid.
[85] Ibid.
[86] Ibid.

House to similar provisions, I feel certain that the present Article 150 is bound to be recast completely.'[87] He therefore suggested that Basu should not concern himself with these provisions at present. Basu replied:

I quite appreciate that is not possible to foresee the exact attitude that the Constituent Assembly will take at the time of considering these provisions. Nevertheless, I feel, *the Drafting Committee must be ready with its own amendments in case it is satisfied that Articles 150 and 151 are defective in the light in which they have been presented by me* ... no matter that the Constituent Assembly might actually take a different view so as to completely recast the Articles.[88]

In effect, Basu, a senior ICS officer, saw a scope for influencing the framing of the constitution. He, as well as other bureaucrats, studied the draft constitution and became well versed in its provisions. He examined the workings of different articles of the draft constitution in themselves and in relation to other related articles. He wanted, as he wrote, to avoid pitfalls and ensure clarity. He raised his concerns about possible defects in the constitution. He entered into thick constitutional conversations with the CAS's Joint Secretary, who was one of the most influential bureaucrats who took part in the framing of the constitution. The Joint Secretary, Mukherjee, was, as already mentioned, the Chief Draughtsman. He attended the meetings of the Union Constitution Committee and the Drafting Committee of the Constituent Assembly.[89] He and other members of the CAS were instrumental in the everyday work of the process of constitution making.[90] Mukherjee wrote relevant notes for the

---

[87] Letter from S. N. Mukherjee, Joint Secretary, Constituent Assembly, to M. M. Basu, Deputy Secretary, Government of West Bengal Home (C&E) Department, 20 January 1949, CA/18/FR/49, ECIR. Mukherjee addressed him as 'My dear Basu'. He explained that he did not write earlier because he thought he would be in a better position to give him 'a satisfactory reply' after the adjournment of the session of the Assembly.

[88] Letter from M. M. Basu, Deputy Secretary to the Government of West Bengal, Home (C&E) Department, to S. N. Mukherjee, Joint Secretary of the Constituent Assembly, 26 January 1949, CA/18/FR/49, ECIR. Emphasis added. Article 150 was brought before the constituent assembly on 2 June 1949 and was held over before a discussion. On 30 July 1949 a debate on the article took place, but after three amendments were moved, the House decided to return it to the Drafting Committee for a redraft. During the debate members of the Constituent Assembly expressed arguments similar to the ones that Mr Basu made about the lack of clarity in the article regarding the constitution of the Council of States. See *CAD*, 30 July 1949. The article finally came before the Assembly on 19 August 1949. The final article was very different from its original draft.

[89] See, for example, Draft minutes of the meeting of the Union Constitution Committee held on 24 August 1947 at 10:30 a.m. (No.CA/63/Cons/47 Confidential), 26 August 1949 (written by H. V. R. Iengar, Secretary), CA/3/FR/48, ECIR.

[90] Indeed, sometimes, other members of the CAS, such as the Under Secretaries K. V. Padmanabhan, and after him P. S. Subramanian, also attended the meetings, especially at the early stages of the discussions. See, for example, 'Record proceedings of the Union Constitution Committee held at 3 p.m., on 1st December, 1948, in Room No. 63, Council House (written by S. N. Mukerjee, Joint Secretary), 1 December 1948'.

CAS based on decisions of the Drafting Committee.[91] Decisions of the Committee sometimes required information from the governments of the provinces and the states, which the CAS followed up on.[92] The Joint Secretary, and when necessary the Constitutional Advisor, provided the ultimate interpretation of the Drafting Committee's decisions and draft articles on an everyday basis. He read the notes and draft letters prepared at the CAS and frequently modified or revised them according to his rendition of the draft articles that were relevant for these notes and letters.[93] It was for these reasons that the Chairman of the Drafting Committee, Ambedkar, told the Assembly at the end of the constitutional debates that much greater share of the credit of the drafting of the constitution must go to Mr S. N. Mukherjee.[94]

The Joint Secretary and other members of the CAS, engaged substantially with letters from administrators, addressing their queries and suggestions in great detail. Sometimes the CAS recognised the constitutional shortcomings administrators pointed to. Thus, in another exchange with M. M. Basu on the Fifth Schedule, Mukherjee agreed with Basu's critique that 'The words ... in lines 4 and 5 of paragraph

---

Ibid. The Constitutional Advisor, B. N. Rau attended those meetings too. Also see 'Minutes of the meetings of the Drafting Committee August 1947–February 1948', in Rao, *The Framing of India's Constitution: Vol. III*, pp. 316–503. In an important analysis of the Indian Civil Service in relation to the constitutional reforms and the political developments in India from 1919 until independence, Arudra Burra notes that, based on the role of the Constitutional Advisor, B. N. Rau, and the planned structure of the work of the Constituent Assembly Secretariat, the ICS had a role in the framing of the Constitution from its inception. Burra's analysis, however, focuses on the general attitudes of the Constituent Assembly towards the ICS. Arudra Burra, *The Indian Civil Service and the Raj: 1919–1950* (11 February 2007). Available at SSRN: http://ssrn.com/abstract=2052658 (accessed 29 June 2017), pp. 123–128. For a discussion of the power of the administrator in relation to the operation of the constitutional acts under colonialism see Dasgupta, 'A Language Which Is Foreign to Us', pp. 228–42.

[91] See, for example, S. no. 21 February 1948.

[92] See, for example, note for orders in reference to paragraph 3 of the draft minute of the Union Constitution Committee held on 24 August 1947, 5 September 1947, CA/3/FR/48, ECIR.

[93] For example, an internal memo relating to the 'preparation of electoral rolls under the New Constitution in the Governor's Provinces and the centrally administered areas', noted that the Union Constitution Committee decided in its meeting of 24 August 1947 to allot to the Andaman & Nicobar Islands one seat in the House of the People. For representation in the Council of States they decided to allot one seat to the Andaman & Nicobar Islands, Ajmer-Merwara, Panth Piploda, and Coorg together. The note stated that 'in view, however, of the provisions of Article 215 of the Draft Constitution in respect of the territories specified in part IV of the First Schedule electoral rolls in Andaman & Nicobar Islands need not be prepared'. S. no. 35, 5 May 1949, CA/1/FR/49-III, ECIR. The Joint Secretary commented on the memo and wrote that he agreed. 'But the reason for this is to be found in clause 7 of article 67 and not article 215. I have modified the draft (reply) accordingly.' Note on S. no 35 (undated), CA/1/FR/49-III, ECIR.

[94] *CAD*, 25 November 1949.

9(1) on page 172 [Fifth Schedule] of the Draft are ... to a certain extent misleading'.[95]

The preparation of the electoral rolls, moreover, drove administrators to think ahead of the Constituent Assembly debates about provisions of the draft constitutions that were related to elections. Sometimes they indicated possible required amendments. Thus, the Additional Secretary to the Government of Madras wrote to the CAS with thoughts and queries regarding Article 289 (2) of the Draft Constitution, which provided for the appointment of an Election Commission for the superintendence, direction and control of elections to the legislatures of the State. 'A doubt has arisen', he wrote, as to whether questions relating to the disqualification of elected members should be dealt with by the election commission of the state, or by the Governor of the state in consultation with his ministers, as was the practice under section 69 (1) of Government of India Act, 1935.[96] Article 289 (2) of the draft constitution did not contain reference to the matter of disqualification of elected members. But in the view of the Additional Secretary to the Government of Madras, 'having regard to the intention underlying this Article and the reasons which have been given during the debate in the Constituent Assembly for setting up these Election Commissions, it would seem that such questions should be dealt with by the Provincial Election Commission and not by the Government of the day'.[97]

The Additional Secretary to the Government of Madras pointed to other problems regarding related issues, such as the appointment of election tribunals and the readjustment of representation for the states in the House of the People and the Legislative Assemblies upon each census, which were set in articles 67 (8) and 149 (4).[98] He thought that these

---

[95] Letter from the Joint Secretary, S. N. Mukerjee to M. M. Basu, Deputy Secretary to the Government of West Bengal, Home (C&E) Department, 14 January 1949, CA/18/FR/49, ECIR. This was in response to letter (D.O.NO. 1762-AR) from M. M. Basu (I.C.S) (Deputy Secretary to the Government of West Bengal, Home (C&E) Department) to S. N. Mukherjee, Joint Secretary of the Constituent Assembly, 29 November 1948, CA/18/FR/49, ECIR. In this letter the Joint Secretary's name is spelt Mukerjee. It is also spelt Mukherjee in other letters.

[96] Elections – New Constitution – Provincial Election Commission – Functions of, letter from S. Venkateswaran, the Additional Secretary to the Government of Madras to CAS, 26 May 1949, CA/18/FR/49, ECIR.

[97] Ibid.

[98] The Constituent Assembly debated and adopted article 67, which dealt with the composition of House of Parliament, on 4 January 1949. Clause 8 of article 67 dealt with the readjustment of seats in the legislatures upon the completion of each census. See *CAD*, 4 January 1949. Article 149 (4), passed on 8 January 1949, dealt with the same issue in relation to the composition of the Legislative Assemblies.

subjects were presumably to fall under Article 289, or referred explicitly to Article 289. But, the Additional Secretary wrote, '[t]he intention and effect of the reference to Article 289 of the Constitution in these provisions is not clear... I am to request that clarifications on the above points may be sought during the debates in the Constituent Assembly and the position made clear by amending Article 289 of the Draft Constitution, if necessary.'[99] Notably, at that time, irrespective of the letter from Madras, the CAS, as we will see in the next section, was engaged with the reframing of Article 289.

Indeed, by the time the CAS discussed at length the letter from the Additional Secretary to the Government of Madras, Article 289 was materially changed.[100] The Joint Secretary, therefore, attached to his reply a copy of the new Articles 289–291 as agreed by the Constituent Assembly. The redrafted articles addressed most of the issues that the Additional Secretary raised. Regarding the question of disqualification of elected members, the Joint Secretary referred the Additional Secretary to the new Article 167A, which addressed the points he made in his letter, and which the Assembly adopted on 14 June 1949. The Joint Secretary, however, recognised the lack of clarity over the reference to Article 289 in Articles 67 (8) and 149 (4). He stated that 'in view of the doubts expressed the clauses in question will be scrutinised further before the Constitution is finally adopted'.[101]

Deliberations on the draft Constitution were not confined to the Constituent Assembly and its committees. The constitutional discussions outside the Constituent Assembly indicated that administrators and members of the public recognised the intended authority of the text, and its possible implications. Their engagement with various articles, their sub-clauses, principles, words and phrases suggested that they saw at least some scope for influencing what was to become their frame of reference as citizens and their guarantor of fundamental rights.

---

[99] Elections – New Constitution – Provincial Election Commission – Functions of, letter from S. Venkateswaran, the Additional Secretary to the Government of Madras to CAS, 26 May 1949, CA/18/FR/49, ECIR.

[100] S. no. 4, 30 June 1949–5 July 1949, CA/18/FR/49, ECIR. It is noteworthy that the Additional Secretary to the Government of Madras copied the letter to the Ministry of Home Affairs, which passed it to the Ministry of Law. The latter passed it to the CAS for disposal. See S. no. 4 (an exchange of notes between the Ministry of Law and Ministry of Home Affairs and the CAS), 1–4 June 1949, CA/18/FR/49, ECIR.

[101] Letter from the Joint Secretary, Constituent Assembly, to the Additional Secretary to the Government of Madras, 8 July 1949, CA/18/FR/49, ECIR. In the discussion at the CAS the Under Secretary acknowledged the points made by the Additional Secretary to the government of Madras and noted that 'Articles 67(8) and 149(4) will have to be altered suitably.' S. no 4, 1 July 1949, CA/18/FR/49, ECIR.

Administrators' discussions of the draft constitution appeared to be motivated both by their professionalism as civil servants and their commitment to the new state, more than to the government of the day.[102] But the CAS went beyond conducting constitutional discussions with administrators and future citizens. As far as the final provisions for elections were concerned, there is little doubt, as the next section will show, that the CAS's experience of the preparation of the rolls while the constitution was still in the making played an important role in bringing about some far-reaching changes in the final constitution.

The Secretariat and the Shaping the Constitution

Article 289 of the February 1948 draft constitution dealt with the superintendence, direction, and control of elections. The draft article provided for one election commission for elections to the central legislature and for separate election commission for each of the states. This was in accordance with the decision the Constituent Assembly took on 29 July 1947 when it considered the report of the Union Constitution Committee.[103] Yet the article that came up for discussion in the House on 15 June 1949, was, Ambedkar said, 'a fundamental departure from the existing provisions of the Draft Constitution'.[104] The new article stipulated that the

---

[102] Also see for this point Arudra Burra's discussion of the question of the loyalty of the civil service in the context of the transition to independence. Burra, *The Indian Civil Service and the Raj*, particularly pp. 124–7. The draft constitution was a term of reference for administrators throughout the preparation of rolls. As discussed in Chapter 4, for example, administrators in some of the provinces and the states calculated the number of copies of electoral rolls they proposed to print on the basis of article 67 (5) (b) of the Draft Constitution. Letter from the Joint Secretary, Assembly Department United State of Saurashtra to CAS, 23 March 1949, CA/1/FR/49-II, ECIR.

[103] Clause 24 of the report of the Union Constitution Committee stipulated that 'The superintendence, direction and control of all elections, whether Federal or Provincial, held under this constitution including the appointment of election tribunals for decision of doubts and disputes arising out of or in connection with such elections shall be vested in a Commission to be appointed by the President.' *CAD*, 29 July 1947. It vested the direction and control of all elections, centre or states, in a single central commission. It aimed to ensure the independence of the election machinery from the executive government. During the discussion, H. V. Pataskar moved an amendment suggesting to constitute separate independent commissions for the direction and control of elections to the provincial (state) legislatures, appointed by the Governor of the state. The amendment was adopted. *Ibid.* Also see *CAD*, 15 June 1949; Rao, *The Framing of India's Constitution*, Vol. IV, pp. 538–40. Earlier, both the Fundamental Rights Sub-Committee and the Minorities Sub-Committee agreed that: 'The superintendence direction and control of all elections to the legislature, whether of the Union or of a Unit, including the appointment of Election Tribunals, shall be vested in an Election Commission for the Union or the Unit, as the case may be, appointed, in all cases, in accordance with the law of the Union.' *CAD*, 29 April 1947.

[104] *CAD*, 15 June 1949.

election machinery for all elections to parliament and to the legislatures of every state would be vested in a single central Election Commission at the centre.[105] Moreover, on the next day, two new articles 289-A and 289-B, and an amended version of articles 290 and 291 – all dealing with elections – were adopted by the Constituent Assembly.[106] The revised constitutional election provisions aimed to ensure and fortify the autonomy and integrity of the election machinery, and to safeguard and give an explicit expression to the notion of universal franchise on the basis of a single joint electoral roll.[107]

I argue that the 'radical change' of article 289, as well as the amendments of other provisions for elections and the introduction of new ones, was largely driven by the experience of the preparation of electoral rolls from March 1948.[108] The CAS, informed by its experience of the preparation of rolls on the ground, motivated, and in the case of article 289 initiated, the reframing of the future constitutional election provisions.

As we saw in Chapter 2, once the registration of voters began numerous citizens, refugees, and other social organisations informed the CAS about attempts of disenfranchisement, and about breaches of the Secretariat's instructions by provincial governments. Various organisations also reported on infringements in the registration process by Deputy Commissioners and Sub Divisional Commissioners at the districts level. Thus, during the preparation of the draft electoral rolls for the first elections, the CAS witnessed problems in implementing the universal franchise at the provincial and state level. Moreover, some state governments, for example Travancore, did not register some of its population because they did not consider them to be citizens of the state, and because the draft constitution gave them, in principle, the discretion to do so. The field-testing of some draft constitutional articles relating to the conduct of elections, and the problems that surfaced as the work progressed, impelled the CAS to review these provisions.

As mentioned above, in December 1948 the Joint Secretary sent to the Chief Secretary to the Government of Travancore a copy of the proposed

---

[105] The commission was to be appointed by the President. It was also vested with the responsibility to direct and control elections to the offices of President, Vice-President and the appointment of election tribunals for the decision of doubts and disputes arising in connection with elections to all legislatures.

[106] *CAD*, 16 June 1949. At the revision stage these articles were enumerated in the final constitution as 324 (289), 325 (289-A), 326 (289-B), 327 (290), and 328 (291). Another new article related to elections, 291-A, which became 328, was also adopted on 16 June 1949.

[107] Article 289-B ensured the registration of all adult citizens as voters, and Article 289-A stated in 'express terms' the notion of a joint electorate.

[108] Ambedkar referred to the revised article 289 as a 'radical change'. *CAD*, 15 June 1949.

new article 289-B, providing constitutional grounds to his request that the government register the Tamilians who resided in the state but who were not Travancore subjects.[109] The new article entitled in principle every adult citizen of India to be registered as a voter. At the time the CAS also reviewed article 289 on the superintendence, direction, and control of elections. It did so in the context of its on-going correspondence with administrators and provincial governments on their breaches in the enrolment procedures and incidents of exclusion from registration on the electoral roll.

It was also at that time, in December 1948, the CAS initiated the query with Nehru about the apportionment of the expenditures of the preparation of rolls between the centre and the states. This query led, for the first time, to a contested discussion between the Prime Ministers' office, the Law Ministry and Rajendra Prasad on the role of the CAS in managing the preparation of the electoral rolls.[110] Nehru asked the Ministry of Law for their view on who should incur the expenses connected with the preparation of rolls.[111] The Secretary of the Law Ministry wrote that 'it is desirable to set up a Constitution Branch in this Ministry and make it responsible for dealing with all questions of this type', and that the Ministry of Law was 'in a position to take over this work forthwith if so directed by the H.P.M. [Prime Minister]'.[112] The Prime Minister's office passed the note for comments to the Ministry of Home Affairs. The Secretary to the Ministry, H. V. R. Iengar, wrote that he discussed the matter with B. N. Rau and the Secretary of the Law Ministry. He stated: 'We are all three agreed that a Constitution Branch should be

---

[109] Letter from the Joint Secretary, CAS, to the Chief Secretary Government of Travancore, 22 December 1948, CA/12/FR/48, ECIR. From later documents of the CAS it can be inferred that originally the plan was to bring these articles before the Constituent Assembly at the sessions it held between November 1948 and January 1949. The articles ultimately came before the Assembly on 15 June 1949.

[110] As mentioned in Chapter 4 this was the first time the CAS addressed the government of India since it undertook the preparation of electoral rolls. Prasad wrote to Nehru on the question of costs on 13 December 1948. See S. no. 4, copy of letter from Rajendra Prasad to the Prime Minister, 13 December 1948, CA/18/FR/49, ECIR. Nehru wrote a month later saying: 'I am having this matter enquired into.' Letter from Jawaharlal Nehru to Rajendra Prasad, 16 January 1949, CA/1/FR/49-I, ECIR.

[111] Letter from Nehru to the Ministry of Law, 16 January 1949. See Valmiki Choudhry (ed.), *Dr Rajendra Prasad: Correspondence and Selected Documents*, Vol. 11, New Delhi: Allied Publishers, 1988, p. 339.

[112] Letter from K. V. K. Sundaram, Secretary, Ministry of Law, to Prime Minister's Secretariat, 19 January 1949. Ibid., p. 341. Sundaram wrote that the institution of a constitution branch in the ministry 'was in fact anticipated in another connection (vide correspondence resting with Nehru's secretary, Mr. A. V. Pai's letter No. 32/48/48-P.M.S., dated 28th September 1948 to the President) and financial sanction was obtained to the erection of a nucleus branch in the Ministry with effect from 1st March 1949.' Ibid.

set up in the Ministry of Law with effect from the 1st March 1949...
There is a great deal of work to be done... It is appropriate that these
questions should be taken up by a Ministry of government and not by
the Constituent Assembly Secretariat.'[113] He added that 'the President
of the Assembly has, in the absence of a specific understanding with
Government, dealt hitherto with the question of the preparation of electoral rolls. This is a matter which we think should appropriately fall on the
Law Ministry...'[114] Nehru answered: 'I agree'.[115]

In mid-February 1949 Nehru's Secretary wrote to Prasad that it was
agreed that the Law Ministry should deal with the provinces in the
matter of costs of printing. He noted that the 'Law Ministry and the
Secretariat of the Constituent Assembly will, no doubt, be going ahead
with the establishment of a Constitution Branch in that Ministry and
with the transfer of suitable personnel from your Secretariat, as originally
contemplated.'[116]

Prasad, however, challenged these suggestions. In a long letter he wrote
to Nehru: 'At its last meeting the Constituent Assembly passed a resolution giving certain directions upon the electoral work to be done under
the new Constitution.'[117] He gave a summary overview of the actions
undertaken by the CAS for the preparation of rolls even before that resolution, and suggested that a 'further question which naturally arises at
the present stage is what machinery should be employed to implement
the directions of the Constituent Assembly'.[118] Prasad stated:

This is a matter which requires careful consideration. There has been an idea
that the work connected with the new elections should be entrusted to one of

[113] Letter from H. V. R. Iengar, Secretary, Ministry of Home Affairs, to Prime Minister's
Secretariat, 2 February 1949, ibid, pp. 341–2. Iengar noted, like the Secretary of the
Law Ministry, that 'Orders to this effect are already in existence. It is true that when
these orders were issued it was assumed that the new Constitution would have been
passed by the end of 1948 and that the Constituent Assembly Secretariat would have
been virtually wound up by that time. But although this assumption has not proved
correct we are now agreed as to the necessity of a Constitution Branch.' Ibid.
[114] Ibid., p. 342. Iengar also wrote that 'the Constitutional Adviser has promised to put
this point to Dr. Rajendra Prasad. I do not think there will be any serious difficulty in
getting his approval.' Ibid.
[115] Nehru note, 4 February 1949, Ibid. Rajendra Prasad was at that time away from Delhi.
The Constitutional Advisor therefore did not immediately write to him and these
papers for his consideration were submitted upon his return on 15 February 1949,
ibid., p. 343.
[116] Letter from A. V. Pai to Rajendra Prasad, 14 February 1949, CA/18/FR/49, ECIR. Pai
referred to Prasad's letter of 13 December 1948 regarding the costs of the preparation
of rolls.
[117] Letter from Rajendra Prasad to Nehru, 19 February 1949, in Choudhry (ed.), *Dr
Rajendra Prasad: Correspondence and Selected Documents*, p. 37.
[118] Ibid.

the Ministries of the Government of India, preferably the Law Ministry, in view of the financial commitments involved. But other aspects of the case have to be considered. It has been hinted in a section of the Press that in some Provinces, Government is attempting to register its own supporters in the electoral rolls... To avoid giving ground for any such suspicion, it seems important that the machinery to be set up to direct and control elections ... be an impartial and independent body, above party politics... In the Draft as it stands at present, separate Election Commissions for the Centre and for the Provinces are contemplated [in Article 289]. There is, however, a feeling among members that the interests of the country would be better served if there were only one all-India Commission controlling all the elections, Central, as well as Provincial... It is highly desirable that everything connected with the elections including preparation of electoral rolls, delimitation of constituencies, and conduct of elections, should be done by an independent body.[119]

A few days later Prasad sent a note to the CAS, asking 'what authority controls elections in other countries and through what agencies. Here we have got no agency except the Provincial Governments. What are the agencies in other countries and who is ultimately responsible for the conduct of elections?'[120] The Research Officer of the CAS, Brij Bhushan, prepared a note with information about the authorities who conduct elections, the means of appointment and removal from office of their personal, and the level of independence of the election management bodies in the UK, USA, the Dominions of South Africa, Australia, and Canada, as well as in the South American countries of Brazil, Chile, Cuba, the Dominion Republic, Ecuador, Nicaragua, Panama, and Uruguay.[121] He described in detail the superintendence of elections in the UK and the USA and concluded that: 'It is clear that no independent organization exists to secure the impartiality and fairness in elections in these countries... the political gangsterism is far from eradicated from the latter [USA], while in the former [UK], the din of election brawls so aptly described by Charles Dickens are not yet extinct'.[122] The

---

[119] Ibid., p. 38. To strengthen his point, Prasad noted that the preliminary work in connection with the enforcement of the 1935 Act as also of 1920 was not done by the Government of India, but by a Reforms Department under the Governor-General.

[120] Internal note, 23 February 1949, CA/20/FR/49, ECIR.

[121] Internal note, 5 March 1949, CA/20/FR/49, ECIR. The note was prepared on the basis of acts or constitutional provisions relating to elections in the various countries. Over the following two months, the Research Officer gathered additional information on the subject from the Indian Council of World Affairs. See letters from the Administrative Secretary of the Indian Council of World Affairs (M. S. Rajan) to Brij Bhushan, CAS, 16 May 1949 and 28 May 1949, CA/18/FR/49, ECIR. These letters referred to Bhushan's letter of 11 March 1949. Also see S. no. 3, draft letter from Brij Bhushan, Research Officer, CAS, to the Administrative Officer, Indian Council of World Affairs, 31 May 1949, CA/18/FR/49, ECIR.

[122] Internal note, 5 March 1949, CA/20/FR/49, ECIR.

Research Officer commended Australia, and particularly Canada, where 'the Electoral Officials are completely out of party control'.[123] The Joint Secretary reviewed the note on 11 April 1949, and it was passed on to Prasad.

In May 1949 the CAS submitted to the Drafting Committee a 'note on election commission'.[124] The first part of the note reiterated much of Prasad's letter of 19 February 1949 to Nehru.[125] It recapped the actions already undertaken by the Constituent Assembly Secretariat, and reiterated from Prasad's letter that the 'question which naturally arises at the present stage is what machinery should be employed to implement the directions of the Constituent Assembly'.[126] The CAS then argued at length the importance of setting up an impartial and independent body to direct and control the elections. It mentioned the recognition given to that principle by the Fundamental Right Sub-Committee and the Minorities Sub-Committee, the Advisory Committee, and the Union Constitution Committee. It then presented an overview of the Constituent Assembly discussions of the clause on the superintendence, direction and control of elections in July 1947, when the House considered the Report of the Union Constitution Committee, and which was adopted and set in article 289.

The CAS wrote that the provision in article 289 'as it stands now, contemplates separate Election Commissions for the Centre and for each of the Provinces'.[127] It then stated:

There is, however, evident in recent months in certain parts of the country a growing feeling that the interests of the country would be best served if there were to be only one all-India Commission controlling all the elections, Central as well as Provincial. If the Constitution for the Indian States is also to form an

---

[123] Ibid. Moreover, the note suggested that Provisions for a comparatively independent election machinery existed in the Dominions. The South American countries provided in their constitutions for independent election machinery, and in most cases also for how this machinery shall be constituted. In these countries, 'party conflicts invariably give rise to political gangsterism, "boot-legging", "gerry-mandering" etc., and recently the South American countries, with not very deep-rooted democratic habits, have tried to set up an independent machinery to look after the important fundamentals of a democracy'. Ibid.

[124] 'Note on election commission by the Secretariat of the Constituent Assembly May 14, 1949', in Rao, *The Framing of India's Constitution, Vol. IV,* pp. 537–43.

[125] It is noteworthy that Prasad's letters in the matter of the preparation of rolls, for example, his letter to Nehru of 13 December 1948 on the question of costs, were based, often verbatim, on drafts prepared by the CAS. The CAS's 'note on election commission' contained, particularly in its beginning, passages which were identical to passages in Prasad's letter of 19 February 1949 to Nehru. This suggests that the CAS was involved in drafting his letter to Nehru.

[126] Rao, *The Framing of India's Constitution, Vol. IV*, p. 537.

[127] Ibid., p. 540.

integral part of the Draft Constitution for the Centre and the Provinces – as has been suggested in responsible quarters – the elections to the Legislatures of these States can also be brought within the purview of this Central Commission. It has also been suggested that a single electoral authority controlling all elections in India will have the advantage that the electoral procedure and practice adopted will be uniform for all units of the Union.[128]

The CAS suggested that the revised clause on a centralised Election Commission in articles 289–291 should be brought for the approval of the Constituent Assembly once it reassembled on 16 May 1949. After adoption, immediate steps should then be taken to appoint an interim Election Commission, 'pending the coming into operation of the new Constitution'.[129] The CAS even included in its note a proposed draft of a resolution for that purpose, and explained the procedure it envisaged once the resolution was passed: 'the President will request the Government to make ... a lump sum grant for the Commission's support so that its independent status may be maintained. In all matters where the Government's sanction is required or when further expenditure on behalf of the Government has to be incurred, this body will consult the appropriate Ministry of the Government.'[130]

With a single proposed constitutional change, which it ultimately brought about, the CAS was able to redress three key problems that it encountered in the process of the preparation of the draft electoral rolls under universal franchise: first, provincial governments sometimes issued their own procedures, in contravention of the CAS's instructions, as they used to do under the colonial legal framework of elections. Moreover, there were attempts at disenfranchisement of some groups of people at the provincial level.[131] Second, the proposal to centralise the management of all elections for all units would overcome many of the constitutional discrepancies between the Indian draft constitution and the constitutional status of the merging states, which arose in the context

---

[128] Ibid.
[129] Ibid., p. 541.
[130] Ibid. The CAS suggested that the provisions relating to the election commission might be compared with the provisions of the Canadian Dominion Elections Act of 1920, which secured the independence of the Chief Electoral Officer in conducting the elections. He had similar employment conditions and could only be removed from office like a judge of a Supreme Court. The new draft article 289 provided that 'the Chief Election Commissioner shall not be removed from the office except in like manner and on the like grounds as a judge of the Supreme Court and the conditions of the service of the Chief Election Commissioner shall not be varied to his disadvantage after his appointment'. *CAD*, 15 June 1949. During the Constituent Assembly debate on the new draft article, K. N. Munshi noted the difference with the Canadian Act, which provides for a Chief Election Officer and not a Commission.
[131] See discussion in Chapter 2.

of the preparation of rolls.[132] The centralisation of the direction and control of elections would foster not only the welding of the federation, but also its democratisation. Third, the suggested amendments and action plan would ensure that the election management body would be independent of the government of the day.[133]

When Ambedkar moved the new article 289 on 15 June 1949 he said to the House that 'this is undoubtedly a radical change',[134] and explained:

But, this change has become necessary because today we find that in some provinces of India, the population is a mixture. There are what may be called original inhabitant, so to say, the native people of a particular province. Along with them, there are other people residing there, who are either racially, linguistically or culturally different from the dominant people who are the occupant of that particular Province. It has been brought to the notice both of the Drafting Committee, as well as the Central Government that in these provinces the executive Government is instructing or managing things in such a manner that those people who do not belong to them either racially, culturally or linguistically, are being excluded from being brought on the electoral rolls. The House will realise that franchise is a most fundamental things in a democracy. No person who is entitled to be brought into the electoral rolls ... should be excluded merely as a result of the prejudice of a local Government, or the whim of an officer. That would cut at the every root of democratic Government. In order, therefore, to prevent injustice being done by provincial Governments to people other than those who belong to the province ... it is felt desirable to depart from the original proposal...[135]

Ambedkar's reasoning for the departure from the original draft article echoed letters that citizens' organisations sent to the CAS, as they struggled for a place in the roll. For example, in response to the instructions of the Reforms Commissioner of Assam to avoid registering 'the floating

[132] See discussion in Chapter 4.
[133] The CAS continued to manage the work on the electoral rolls and the preliminary action for the preparation of the first elections. Between April and September 1949 it sent a few queries to the Ministry of Law asking whether a decision on the costs was taken and requesting an early decision on the matter. It could be inferred from the archival files that a Constitutional Branch was established at the Ministry of Law by November 1949. But the CAS, through its Franchise Section, continued overseeing the preparation for the elections. An office of the Election Commission of India, Ministry of Law began operating from February 1950. S no. 28, 3 February 1950, 2/50, ECIR. P. S. Subramanian, who was the Under Secretary and then the Special Officer on Duty at the CAS was signed on the note. He became the Secretary of the Election Commission. On that date the title of the archival files changes from 'Franchise Section, Constituent Assembly of India Secretariat', to 'Office of the Election Commission, Ministry of Law'. In effect the Ministry of Law is the 'appropriate Ministry of the Government', which the Election Commission consults in matters where the government's sanction is required, as envisaged by the CAS.
[134] *CAD*, 15 June 1949.
[135] Ibid.

and "non-resident" population of the District',[136] citizens' organisations complained 'that attempts are being made to exclude all persons who were not born in Assam as constituted now';[137] and that persons who are 'not regarded as "children of the soil" by the administration' are not registered.[138] They called upon the Constituent Assembly 'to realise how simple provisions under the constitution could be misconstrued and how persons holding responsible positions may fail to implement the provisions of the constitution in accordance to its spirit and may even defeat its purpose by issuing directions that will lead to a negation of the fundamental conception of adult suffrage'.[139]

During the Assembly debate on the new draft article, K. M. Munshi, a member of the Drafting Committee, made explicit reference to such peoples' grievances and the revised article. When addressing criticism that the new article exhibits mistrust in provincial governments he said: 'My friend coming from Assam ought to know that complaints after complaints have been received from Assam that ingenious devices are found to shut out people who have settled in Assam from the electoral rolls. The fact that such complaints come *is the reason why provincial Governments cannot be trusted*, in the condition in which we are, to be as impartial in the elections as they should be.'[140]

The constitutional changes in the articles on the conduct of elections in June 1949, which safeguarded the independence and integrity of the election machinery, likely reshaped the course of India's democratic trajectory. These changes were not predestined. It was to a great extent the CAS's actions, on the basis of its on-going experience with the work of the preparation of rolls that brought about these significant changes. The CAS's fundamental premise in recommending a centralised electoral machinery was that this would be the best way of serving the 'interests of the country', and of ensuring the independence and integrity of elections for the edifice of India's future democracy.[141] The respect that the

---

[136] Letter from the Reforms Commissioner of Assam to all District Officers, 28 May 1948 (circular No. L.801/47), CA/1/FR/48-II, ECIR. Also see discussion in Chapter 2.

[137] Letter from the Secretary of the Surma Sammilani, Assam, to CAS, 14 July 1948, CA/12/FR/48.

[138] Letter from the Assam Citizens' Association, Goalpara, to Rajendra Prasad, 2 September 1948, CA/9/FR/48, ECIR.

[139] Letter from the Chair of Cachar District Congress Committee to the Chairman of the Advisory Committee on Fundamental rights, 18 June 1948 CA/1/FR/48-II, ECIR.

[140] K. M. Munshi, *CAD*, 16 June 1949. Emphasis added. Munshi referred specifically to the critique of Kulandhar Chaliha from Assam. He and other members of the Assembly objected to the article mainly on the grounds that it took away provincial autonomy, and displayed distrust in the people of the provinces. See H. V. Pataskar, ibid., and Kuladhar Chaliha. Ibid.

[141] 'Note on election commission by the Secretariat of the Constituent Assembly May 14, 1949', Rao, *The Framing of India's Constitution, Vol. IV*, p. 538. This may indicate the

individuals who conducted much of the work on the preparation of rolls at the CAS elicited, through their hard work, competence, and dedication, made them persuasive.[142] Indeed, the proposition at the time that the Law Ministry should assume responsibility for the preparatory work of the elections, would have been detrimental to the effective autonomy that the CAS had established in conducting the preparation of the draft rolls until that point. In bringing about the constitutional changes in the articles on elections, the CAS, as well as people and administrators who informed them about the implementation of the preparation of rolls from the bottom, became real agents of constitution making.

Some members of the Drafting Committee gave, at the end of the constitutional debates, recognition to the role of the CAS in the process of constitution making. T. T. Krishnamachari stated that he would be 'failing in my duty if I do not mention ... the fact that we were able to find a Joint Secretary and Draftsman of the calibre of Shri S. N. Mukherjee. It is no exaggeration to say that he was a real find. Not only is his ability as a draftsman so profound, but more than that, his willingness to work was even greater... practically everybody from Mr. Khanna [deputy secretary] downwards, to the clerks superintendents and the reporters, have had to work very hard... I do hope that the House will recognise the work done by them in framing this Constitution which is of a very vital and important nature.'[143] Ambedkar told the House that Mukherjee's 'ability to put the most intricate proposals in the simplest and clearest legal form can rarely be equalled, nor his capacity for hard work. He has been an acquisition to the Assembly. Without his help, this Assembly would have taken many more years to finalise the Constitution. I must not omit to mention the members of the staff working under Mr. Mukherjee. For, I know how hard they have worked and how long they have toiled sometimes even beyond midnight. I want to thank them all for their effort and their co-operation.'[144] The members of the Assembly, according to the transcripts of the constitutional debates, cheered. Except for these few

---

source of some of the innovative features of the Indian constitution. As Bruce Ackerman argues in his discussion of 'the new separation of powers', and Madhav Khosla's analyses, the Indian Constitution moves beyond the classic separation of powers in its creation of an independent Election Commission. See Bruce Ackerman, 'The New Separation of Powers', *Harvard Law Review* 113, no. 3, 2000, pp. 715–16; Madhav Khosla, *The Indian Constitution*, New Delhi: Oxford University Press, 2012, pp. 38–43.

[142] The individuals who were directly and continuously involved in the work of the preparation of rolls at the CAS's Franchise Section were the Joint Secretary, S. N. Mukherjee, the Under Secretary K. V. Padmanabhan, an additional Under Secretary who joined later, P. S. Subramanian, the Constitutional Advisor, B. N. Rau, and the research officers, A. A. Abidi and Brij Bhushan.

[143] *CAD*, 25 November 1949.

[144] Ibid.

comments, however, the remarkable achievements and contributions of these men at the Secretariat and their work on the making of the universal franchise was obscured from the records of the history of India's democracy.[145]

Conclusion

Members of the CAS were involved in the day-to-day work of constitution making. The preparation of the electoral rolls, however, entailed a completely different engagement with the process of constitution making. The CAS initiated the preparation of the electoral rolls. It conducted correspondences and consultations with administrators in the provinces and the states as part of the process of designing the instructions. The CAS based the instructions for the preparation of rolls on provisions of the February 1948 draft constitution. The CAS thus began implementing core provisions of the future constitution in anticipation of its adoption. The enrolment of voters, created facts on the ground and constrained, as we saw, the extent to which the Constituent Assembly could change or reverse the work that was done over the ten months before it considered the motion that instructions for the preparation of rolls would be issued. During the debate on the motion on the preparation of rolls in January 1949 some members suggested to wait with this undertaking until the citizenship article was settled and the constituencies delimited. If this suggestion, as well as the concerns members of the House raised during the debate, would have been made ahead of the preparation of rolls, rather than, as it happened, subsequent to much of the work already having been completed, the universal franchise would have remained an abstract principle and an unfulfilled promise far longer. It is likely that such a delay would have been to the detriment of India's electoral democracy.

Moreover, in the process of making a fact of the universal franchise ahead of the final constitutional deliberations on the articles on elections and citizenship, these constitutional provisions turned into a set of living practices, which were contested and tested. The preparation of rolls, therefore, provided a concrete opportunity for people and administrators across the country to use the constitution. As the chapter demonstrated, people discussed the constitution and suggested amendments because they saw the constitution as a means of resolving their disputes with the state and of securing their fundamental rights. Likewise, administrators

---

[145] See Chapter 5, Appendix 5.1, 'Unsung Heroes of India's Democracy: The Members of the Constituent Assembly Franchise Branch'.

engaged substantially with the minutiae of constitutional provisions, and with constitutionalism more broadly. They saw the constitution as a practical instrument of their work for the state. They discussed it with the CAS as a matter of professional pride.[146] Thus, in the context of the preparation of rolls, both people and administrators began using the form of the constitution as a common language for addressing the new state and their governments. They acted in accordance with the form and practices of the constitution.

Subsequently, in the process of the preparation of the electoral rolls, the CAS received from people and administrators on-going reporting on the working of draft constitutional provisions that related to elections. These provisions were implemented across the country. On the basis of this feedback, the CAS initiated revisions in the draft constitution. The CAS's contributions to the framing of the election provisions emanated from insights that were evidence-based, rather than deriving from the conventions of constitutional theories.

When in November 1948 Ambedkar moved the motion that the Draft Constitution 'be taken into consideration', he expressed his concern about the absence of constitutional morality among the people of India. 'We must realize', he said, 'that our people have yet to learn it [constitutional morality]. Democracy in India is only a top-dressing on an Indian soil, which is essentially undemocratic.'[147] Ambedkar cited the classicist George Grote, explaining that constitutional morality meant 'a paramount reverence for the form of the Constitution, enforcing obedience to authority acting under and within these forms, yet combined with the habit of open speech, of action subject only to definite legal control ... with a perfect confidence in the bosom of every citizen amidst the bitterness of party contest that the forms of the Constitution will not be less sacred in the eyes of his opponents than in his own'.[148] For Ambedkar, as

---

[146] After the adoption of the new article 289 some administrators in the provinces wrote to the CAS in the matter, enquiring whether the preparation of rolls became a responsibility of the centre. Letter from Deputy Secretary Government of West Bengal to the Joint Secretary, CAS, 29 June 1949, CA/1/FR/49-III, ECIR; Fortnightly Report, Government of Assam, 5 September 1949; and letter from the Joint Secretary, CAS, to the Reforms Commissioner of Assam, 21 September 1949, CA/1/FR/49-III, ECIR. The Joint Secretary explained that none of the new provisions 'affect in any way the responsibility of the Provincial Government for the preparation of the electoral rolls'. Letter from the Joint Secretary, CAS, to the Deputy Secretary Government of West Bengal, 6 July 1949, CA/1/FR/49-III, ECIR.

[147] *CAD*, 4 November, 1948. Ambedkar expressed this concern in the context of justifying the inclusion of the details of the administrative machinery in the constitution, which was subject to criticism.

[148] Ibid.

Pratap Bhanu Mehta has argued, achieving constitutional morality was a key for ensuring an adherence to the constitutional method.[149]

This chapter showed that the experience of the preparation of the rolls fostered the cultivation of constitutional morality among people and administrators. When Ambedkar expressed his concerns in November 1948 about the lack of constitutional morality, which was indispensible for the workings of the constitution, he could not yet appreciate the extent to which the preparation of the electoral rolls would fill that gap.

The preparation of the electoral rolls informed and affected constitution making. At the same time, the progress in the making of the constitution also influenced roll making. In this process, as the next chapter explores, there were sometimes limits to inclusion.

Appendix 5.I

Unsung Heroes of India's Democracy: The Members of the Constituent Assembly Secretariat Franchise Branch

Remembrance of you [B.N. Rau] will, I am confident, be among the very last to fade. My talks with you (in October 1947) were among the pleasantest and most satisfying of all my experiences in Washington. On more than one occasion I said behind your back – and so I shall dare offend your modesty and say it to your face – that you are one of the few people I ever encountered who had a deep, instinctive sense of justice.

(US Supreme Court Justice Felix Frankfurter)[150]

Sir Benegal Rau, who had been taking notes, started to speak; and with very clear voice and melodious accent he read what he had written from the notes he had taken. His language was almost precious due to its perfection. The way of talking was elegant and somewhat remote – as if the speaker were not there... But he was there... And the solution he proposed was practical and under the circumstances the only one capable of satisfying everybody.

(Gilberto Amado (Brazil), Member of the
UN International Law Commission)[151]

---

[149] For an analysis of Ambedkar's invocation of the concept of constitutional morality see Bhanu Mehta, 'What is Constitutional Morality'; Choudhry, Khosla, and Bhanu Mehta, 'Locating Indian Constitutionalism', pp. 2–4; Dasgupta, "A Language Which Is Foreign to Us'. Also see Ambedkar's speech, *CAD*, 25 November 1949.

[150] A quote from a letter from Justice Frankfurter to B. N. Rau, 1952. Quoted in B. N. Rau, *India's Constitution in the Making*, ed. B. Shiva Rao, Madras: Orient Longmans, 1960, p. xxx.

[151] The quote is related by 'A Brazilian colleague' of Rau at the first session of the UN International Law Commission in 1949. Quoted in Rau, *India's Constitution in the*

Mr S. N. Mukerjee, Joint Secretary and Draftsman, Constituent Assembly of India, who has borne, along with Mr B. N. Rau, Constitutional Adviser, the main brunt of drafting the articles of the Constitution.

(*The Hindustan Times*, 26 January 1950)[152]

He [K. V. Padmanabhan] had great pose, ran the office admirably and had considerable knowledge of the constitution, but his main contribution was to assist me in the administrative work... in fact the credit should go to him.

(Interview with H. V. Iengar)[153]

The Constituent Assembly Secretariat (CAS) was established in May 1946 to assist with the drafting of the new Union Constitution. It was an interim bureaucratic body. The CAS was led by B. N. Rau, the Constitutional Adviser (CA). The other key staff members who were directly and continuously involved in the work of the preparation of the electoral rolls, what became to be known as the Franchise Section, were the Joint Secretary, S. N. Mukerjee, the Under Secretaries, K. V. Padmanabhan, and P. S. Subramanian, who joined in late 1948 and then took over from him, and A. A. Abidi and Brij Bhushan, who served, in the main, as research officers at the CAS. I did not come across any women among the staff of the CAS.

The archival records of the colossal undertaking of the making of the universal franchise that I researched, suggests that these were extraordinary people. There were, of course, others, both within the CAS and in the states and provinces who contributed to this achievement.[154] These men have largely remained unknown heroes of India's democracy.[155] Indeed,

---

Making, p. xxv. It therefore must have been Mr Gilberto Amado. See http://legal.un.org/ilc/sessions/1/members.shtml (accessed 29 June 2017); http://iconografiaamado.blogspot.co.uk/2009/01/gilberto-amado.html (accessed 29 June 2017).

[152] S. N. Mukerjee, 'The Constitution of India – an Analysis', *The Hindustan Times (HT)*, 26 January 1950, p. II.

[153] Interview with H. V. Iengar, *Oral History Transcript*, no. 303, p. 129, NMML.

[154] The Secretary of the Constituent Assembly, H. V. R Iengar was involved in the work relating to the preparation of the roll and constitution making only at the very beginning. Indeed, he recalled in an interview years later that he 'played no part whatsoever in the actual framing of the constitution. The principal man concerned with this was Sir B. N Rau... the only time I was in real touch with what was happening in the Constituent Assembly was between the day it started its work and the end of August, 1947... anything that happened in the Constituent Assembly after 1947, is, to me a matter outside the range of my personal knowledge'. Interview with H. V. Iengar, *Oral History Transcript*, no. 303, p. 154, NMML. There were other staff members, among them, P. N. Krishna Mani who was Rau's assistant on the legal side at the Constitutional adviser office. R. K. Ramadhyani was Under Secretary in the early months of 1947. Badruddin Tyabji was a Deputy Secretary of the Constituent Assembly, but was not involved in the preparation of the electoral rolls.

[155] For new research on B. N. Rau see Arvind Elangovan, *A Constitutional Imagination of India: Sir Benegal Narsing Rau amidst the Retreat of liberal Idealism (1910–1950)*,

their personal contributions to the critical operation merits a much more detailed account, beyond what this book is able to offer.

In the following pages I attempt, nonetheless, to provide a sketch of the main persons involved with the preparation of the electoral rolls beyond the dusty archival records. During the long process of reading the archival records, I felt as if I got to know these people a little. I became familiar with their handwriting, their tone and style, and even their way of thinking about problems that arose. I had so many questions for them and I wished to hear much more beyond what the records could tell me. I regretted finding so little had been written about them. I hope the outline I was able to assemble below can form a beginning of a recovery, through other sources, of the life and work of these remarkable men.

Sir Benegal Narsinga Rau (1887–1953) (see Figure 2), the Constitutional Adviser of the Constituent Assembly oversaw the preparation of the draft electoral roll on the basis of universal adult franchise. Rau assumed charge of the office of the Secretariat of the Constituent Assembly in July 1946, preparing for the beginning of the discussions of the Constituent Assembly from December 1946. Over the previous two decades he served as a member of the Indian Civil Service in prominent positions in the legal and judicial fields. He was the Legal Remembrancer and Secretary to the Government of Assam, and was invited by the Government of India to take charge of the adaptation of all central and provincial statutes in accordance with the Government of India Act, 1935.[156]

Rau prepared all the background materials for the members of the Assembly. He wrote, ahead of preparing the first draft constitution of October 1947, *Constitutional Precedents*, discussing, analysing, and comparing the basic elements of the constitutions of the principal federations and unions in the world; he also took part, at the time, in the drafting of

Unpublished PhD Thesis, University of Chicago, 2012. Also see Uma Narayan, 'The Constituent Assembly of India: Recollecting Contributions of Sir Benegal Narsing Rau, the Constitutional Adviser', *International Journal of Legal Information*, 44, no. 3, 2016, pp. 225-34.

[156] For the most detailed accounts thus far of the life and extraordinary work and contribution of Rau to India's constitutional and administrative development see the posthumous collection of notes and memoranda that he prepared over the years and that his brother, B. Shiva Rao, edited in Rau, *India's Constitution in the Making*; Arvind Elangovan, 'Provincial Autonomy, Sir Benegal Narsing Rau, and an Improbable Imagination of Constitutionalism in India, 1935–38', *Comparative Studies of South Asia, Africa and the Middle East* 36, no. 1, 2016, pp. 66–82; Elangovan, 'The Road Not Taken'. Sir Benegal Narsing Rau and the Indian Constitution', in Sekhar Bandopadhyay (ed.), *Decolonization and the Politics of Transition in South Asia*, New Delhi: Orient Blackswan, 2016, pp. 141–59.

Figure 2 B. N. Rau, the Constitutional Advisor of the Constituent Assembly of India

the new constitution for the Union of Burma.[157] Rau, as the President of the Constituent Assembly, Rajendra Prasad, wrote about him in hindsight, 'was the person who visualised the plan and laid the foundation' of the Indian constitution.[158] The Secretary of the Constituent Assembly, H. V. R Iengar, stated in his recollections that 'the principle man concerned with the framing of the constitution was B.N. Rau'.[159]

As for the preparation of the electoral rolls, Rau guided and oversaw closely the undertaking from its inception until the end of 1948. He continued being involved later on when it was necessary. Rau envisioned the 'plan for India as a whole nation' for making the universal franchise, and wrote a summary note on 'preparation of electoral rolls under the new constitution', which set the undertaking as a new bureaucratic precedent for the

[157] B. N. Rau, 'The Constitution of the Union of Burma', *23 Wash. L. Rev. & St. B. J.*, 288, 1948, pp. 188–300; *Constitutional Precedents*, New Delhi: The Government of India Press, 1947.
[158] Rajendra Prasad, 'Forward', in Rau, *India's Constitution in the Making*, p. vi.
[159] Interview with H. V. Iengar, *Oral History Transcript*, no. 303, NMML, p. 154.

republic.[160] Rau was the leading authority in guiding the process of making the universal franchise from a constitutional perspective. While he did not directly respond to queries and grievances from various organisations and individuals, he read them or the summary notes on these letters that the members of the CAS prepared, and engaged with them in the decision-making process. Rau's sense of justice and pursuit of pragmatic satisfying solutions under very difficult circumstances – the qualities that made profound impressions on renowned Justices, such as Felix Frankfurter and other international legal minds who encountered him – were the same qualities that he demonstrated when he found solutions to the problems of implementing the franchise. This, for example, was the case with the formula that was ultimately devised for the registration of partition refugees on the electoral rolls.[161]

Rau took the job of Constitutional Adviser and of setting up the CAS on the condition that 'The whole organisation is non-political and non-party in character and its services are equally available to every member, irrespective of party or creed.'[162] The records of the preparation of the rolls, especially the CAS's responses to administrators, organisations and people throughout the country, as well as to political leaders, among them the President of the Assembly, attested to them being solely guided by the emerging constitutional vision for independent India. Rau played a significant role in making this vision a reality.

Two years into his job he wrote to Rajendra Prasad: 'when I took it [the position of a Constitutional Adviser], I made it a condition that it should be on an honorary basis. It has largely been a labour of love all through, and I have been doing it in spite of various difficulties... We are now nearing the end of our labours ... and I hope you will be able to spare me as soon as any work which is congenial to me offers itself'.[163] In a way, Rau fulfilled by that time his own wish. Three years earlier, in June 1945, Rau expressed to the Private Secretary of the Viceroy, Lord Wavell, his wish to see the accomplishment of a federal scheme for India.[164]

From late 1948 onwards, Rau represented the Government of India in various capacities at the United Nations. In October 1948 he was elected

---

[160] See discussion in Chapter 1.
[161] See discussion in Chapter 2.
[162] B. Shiva Rao, *The Framing of India's Constitution, Vol. I*; Nashik: The Manager, Government of India Press, 1968, p. 371.
[163] Rau, *India's Constitution in the Making* ('A Biographical Sketch'), p. xxiii. At the time it was expected that the draft constitution would be adopted in January 1949.
[164] Letter from B. N. Rau to the Private Secretary of the Viceroy, Lord Wavell ca. June 1945, in ibid., p. xix. Also see Chapter 4.

Figure 3 S. N. Mukherjee, Joint Secretary Constituent Assembly Secretariat

to the International Law Commission.[165] Between 1950 and 1952 he was India's representative in the United Nations Security Council.[166] At the end of 1951 he was elected to the International Court of Justice, in The Hague, where he served just over a year. He died in November 1953 in a hospital in Zurich.

Shri Surendra Nath Mukerjee (S. N. Mukerjee) (1898–1963) (see Figure 3), the Joint Secretary of the Constituent Assembly Secretariat. He was the Principal Draftsman, Government of India, and then the Chief Draftsman of the Constituent Assembly of India for drafting Independent India's Constitution. From 1952 onwards he was the

---

[165] Ibid., p. xxv.
[166] Ibid. Also see https://www.britannica.com/biography/Benegal-Narsing-Rau (accessed 29 June 2017).

Secretary of the Rajya Sabha. In 1962 he received the Padma Bhushan, one of India's highest civilian awards.[167]

Mukerjee was the most senior person directly involved in the everyday work relating to the preparation of the electoral rolls. B. N. Rau frequently sought his opinion before making his final suggestions on matters that came up for decisions. As already mentioned in Chapter 5, Mukerjee read the notes and draft letters prepared at the Secretariat and frequently modified or revised them according to his interpretation of the draft constitutional articles that were relevant for these notes and letters. In that way, Mukerjee ensured that the actions undertaken in the preparation of rolls were aligned with the constitution in the making. He made sure that every decision took place within the framework of the constitution.

There is no doubt, I suggest, that Mukerjee's deep engagement with the public and administrators throughout the country, and the seriousness with which he took into account and addressed their disparate concerns, played a critical role in the successful institutionalisation of the universal franchise. He was the main person who corresponded directly with administrators and the public about constitutional and franchise matters. In doing so he became a role model for the process of mentoring bureaucrats and the public in the institutional and procedural principles of an electoral democracy, discussed in Chapter 2.

On 26 January 1950, the day of inauguration of the Indian republic, Mukerjee published a detailed analysis of the Indian Constitution for the layperson in both *The Hindustan Times* and in the *Times of India*.[168] 'On January 26', he wrote, 'the world will witness the birth of a new Republic – the Republic of India.' He explained to the readers that 'The Constitution proclaims India to be a sovereign Democratic Republic', and that the 'Preamble to the Constitution makes it clear that the sovereign authority emanates from the people of India.'[169] Mukerjee addressed the fact that the Constitution was very long and elaborated: 'It is true', he stated, 'that many of the provisions in the Indian Constitution are in other Constitutions left to be dealt with by common law, but the reasons for such detailed provisions will be apparent if one only remembers the vastness of the country, the diversities of its population and the varieties of interest therein requiring safeguards.'[170]

---

[167] 'Biographical Sketches of Secretaries – General, Rajya Sabha', available at: http://rajyas-abha.nic.in/rsnew/pre_member/1952_2003/sec_general.pdf (accessed 29 June 2017).

[168] S. N. Mukerjee, 'The Constitution of India – an Analysis', *HT*, 26 January 1950, p. II, X; Mukerjee, 'Constitution of Indian Republic Analysed', *The Times of India* (*TOI*), 26 January 1950, pp. 8–12.

[169] Ibid., p. 8.

[170] Ibid.

Figure 4 K. V. Padmanabhan, Under Secretary, Constituent Assembly
Secretariat

The Hindustan Times explained to the readers: 'This article which
provides an analysis of the salient features of the Constitution of India
is written by Mr S. N. Mukerjee, Joint Secretary and Draftsman,
Constituent Assembly of India, who has borne, along with Mr B. N.
Rau, Constitutional Adviser, the main brunt of drafting the articles of
the Constitution'.[171] This was, to my knowledge, the only time, until he
received the Padma Bhushan, that Mukerjee received public recognition
for his pivotal role in the making of the constitution and the universal
franchise.

K. V. Padmanabhan (1911–1994) (see Figure 4), Under Secretary of
the Constituent Assembly Secretariat. Initially, he served as an Assistant
Secretary to the Constituent Assembly. The high quality of his work led to
a rapid promotion by the Secretary of the Constituent Assembly, H. V. R
Iengar and the Constitutional Adviser (CA), B. N. Rau.[172] In January 1947

---

[171] Mukerjee, 'The Constitution of India – an Analysis', p. II.
[172] Note by the Secretary of the Constituent Assembly, H. V. R Iengar, regarding a request
to raise the status of K. V. Padmanabhan to that of an Under Secretary, 8 January 1947,

Iengar wrote to the Staff and Finance Committee: 'From the very inception of the office of the Constitutional Adviser last July [1946], Mr. K.V. Padmanabhan, Assistant Secretary, has been doing work of a most arduous nature... He has performed these duties with an ability and thoroughness which have won the high approval both of the CA and the Secretary, and in fact of all those who came to contact with him or had an occasion to use his services. In view of the onerous and responsible duties which Mr. Padmanabhan is call upon to perform, the President recommends that Mr. Padmanabhan should have his status raised to that of an under secretary.'[173]

Between October and December 1947 Padmanabhan joined B. N. Rau on a study tour of constitutions in Great Britain, Ireland, the United States, and Canada, meeting leading constitutional authorities in these countries. In September 1948 Padmanabhan was selected to the Indian Foreign Service. He left the Constituent Assembly Secretariat in April 1949 to take the post of First Secretary at the Indian Embassy in Paris.[174] This would be the first posting in an illustrious career in the Indian Foreign Service.

Padmanabhan was the main person who produced the summary notes on various issues that arose, both from administrators and the public, in the matter of the preparation of the rolls. His notes formed the basis for the discussions that the members of the CAS held and informed their decision making. Padmanabhan did not simply produce synopses of the matters at hand. He almost always proposed an analysis of the problem, a well-reasoned solution, and/or a draft reply. On many important matters he went beyond bringing notes for discussion, to suggesting a course of action. For example, when he concluded upon his reading of the expert report on the question of the preparation of rolls versus a census he suggested that 'we should initiate the preparations of Electoral rolls as a separate operation and address the provincial governments in the matter'.[175] And when Rau asked Padmanabhan 'to prepare a plan [for the preparation of rolls] for India as a whole nation on the lines of the Travancore plan and bring up for discussion',[176] he not only prepared the note but

Ministry of Law, Justice and Company Affairs, f. CA/180/est. 1947 (Subject: K. V. Padmanabhan, Assistant Secretary), National Archives of India (NAI), New Delhi.

[173] Copy of a note from H. V. R Iengar to the Staff Finance Committee (Subject: Creation of a post of Under Secretary), January 1947, ibid. The Committee decided at that point that Mr Padmanabhan should continue to be an Assistant Secretary, but that his pay should be increased. See 'Extract from the minutes of the staff and finance committee held on 18 January 1947', ibid. Padmanabhan was ultimately promoted to the position of Under Secretary with effect from 5 June 1947.

[174] S. no. 16, Ministry of Law, Justice and Company Affairs, f. CA/180/est. 1947, NAI.

[175] Note by Under Secretary, K. V. Padmanabhan, 18 October 1947, CA/I/FR/48-I, ECIR.

[176] Internal note, 16 February 1948, CA/1/FR/48-I, ECIR. Also see discussion in Chapter 1.

also, as he wrote, 'drafted it in the form of a memorandum which can be sent to the States and Provinces'.[177]

Padnamabhan comments in the notes he prepared demonstrated his ability to identify with the 'weak'. It was he who first noted on the question of the registration of the refugees that they 'are always on the move, and, therefore, no residential qualification can be prescribed for them, if they are to be given the right of vote in the next elections'.[178] The Joint Secretary, Mukerjee, rarely made significant revisions to Padmanabhan suggestions. In effect, many of his draft notes, with minor revisions, became the final draft letters.

Padnamabhan's contributed to the documentation of the making of the Indian constitution beyond his work as the Under Secretary of the CAS, as a contributor author to the five volumes on *The Framing of India's Constitution*, edited by B. Shiva Rao, B. N. Rau's brother.[179] Padmanabhan provided many of the original documents that appear in these volumes.

I am grateful to Padmanabhan's daughters, Manjula Padmanabhan, Geeta Doctor and Surya Naranayan, and to his grandson, Vikram Doctor, for glimpses into the personality of this extraordinary man, during my short communication with them.[180]

P. S. Subramanian (see Figure 5) joined the CAS's Franchise Branch as an Under Secretary from late 1948.[181] In the final stages of the preparation of the draft electoral rolls, and as the process of constitution making neared its completion, his designation changed to Special Officer on Duty.[182] It appears from the archival documents that Subramanian caught up with the work that was done until he joined very quickly. Subramanian became the Secretary of the Election Commission of India from its establishment. He was key to ensuring the bureaucratic continuity between the CAS and the Election Commission of India, which started functioning in March 1950.[183]

---

[177] Internal note, 20 February 1948, CA/1/FR/48-I, ECIR.
[178] Internal note, 8 June 1948, CA/9/FR/48, ECIR. Also see discussion in Chapter 2
[179] Rao, *The Framing of India's Constitution*.
[180] Padmanabhan unpublished memoirs are held with the family. Also see Geeta Doctor, 'A Toast to Another Age', *The Hindu*, 28 June 2014; Vikram Doctor, 'A Witness to the Birth of a Nation', *The Economic Times*, 16 August 2011; Magnolia Lotus (Manjula Padmanabhan) 'My Dad's Birth Centenary', http://marginalien.blogspot.co.uk/2011/02/my-dads-birth-centenary.html (accessed 29 June 2017).
[181] His name appears in the CAS's archival notes from late September 1948.
[182] Sometimes it appeared as OSD – Officer on Special Duty. This was his designation from at least October 1949.
[183] As already mentioned in Chapter 5, on 3 February 1950 the files shift from 'Franchise Section, Constituent Assembly of India Secretariat', to 'Office of the Election Commission, Ministry of Law.' S. no. 28, 3 February 1950, 2/50, ECIR.

Figure 5 P. S. Subramanian, Secretary to the Election Commission of India (right), and Sukumar Sen, first Chief Election Commissioner (left). Previously Subramanian was Under Secretary, Constituent Assembly Secretariat

Indeed, Subramanian worked very closely with the first Chief Election Commissioner, Sukumar Sen (see Figure 5), who assumed his position on 21 March 1950. Sen was not involved in the preparation of the draft rolls for the first elections in the preceding two years. During the work of the preparation for the first elections from March 1950 until October 1951, Subramanian made sure that the Commission's work was based on the work done until that point by the CAS.

By the 1967 elections Subramanian was a Deputy Election Commissioner in the Election Commission of India, and a Secretary of the Delimitation Commission.

A. Abidi and Brij Bhushan, served, in the main, as research officers at the CAS. It appears that Abidi was at the CAS from the start of the work of the preparation of the rolls and that Bhusan joined some time later. They worked closely with and under the instructions of Padmanabhan. They were instrumental, in particular, in preparing summary analyses and reviews of the replies received from the governments of the provinces and the states to the CAS's main circular letters. They were also tasked with finding precedents from other countries at various points when problem arose. Thus, Abidi prepared the first summary note on suggestions from the provinces and the states on the preparation of rolls ahead of the designing of the instructions.[184] Bhushan prepared the note with information about the authorities who conducted elections, the means of appointment and removal from office of their personnel, and the level of independence of the election management bodies in a host of countries around the world.[185] I was not able to find out more about their careers after the CAS.

---

[184] See discussion in Chapter 1.
[185] See discussion in Chapter 5.

> With regard to the qualification as to residence orders are requested
> whether the following categories of persons should be considered to be
> satisfying the qualification as to residence [for enrolment]: … a vagrant
> lives in a hut erected on Municipal land without permission, pays no
> rent but lives with his family in the hut.
>
> (Collector of Bombay, 20 November 1948)[1]

On 20 November 1948, as the Bombay administration worked on the
preparation of the electoral rolls, the collector of Bombay wrote to the
Chief Secretary to the Government of Bombay:

With regard to the qualification as to residence, orders are requested whether
the following categories of persons should be considered to be satisfying the
qualification as to residence: (A) a domestic servant works in a household clean-
ing utensils on a piece work basis, during specified hours and goes to another
household and works there. He thus works in more than half a dozen households
every day but sleeps in the general passage or balcony or the staircase of same
building. (B) a hotel servant works for the day in the hotel, takes his food there
and sleeps inside the hotel on the left or outside the hotel in the rare passage.
(C) [a person] who works in the mill, takes his food in Khanawal or eating house
and sleeps on the foot path. At present there is an appreciable number of such
persons in Bombay. (iv) [a person who] works in Pedhi or shop, prepares his food
somewhere in the pedhi or shop and sleeps therein at night. (v) a vagrant lives in
a hut erected on Municipal land without permission, pays no rent but lives with
his family in the hut.[2]

The Chief Secretary to the Government of Bombay sought the opinion of the Remembrancer of Legal Affairs on these questions. On the
basis of various English legal precedents the Remembrancer suggested
that: 'Persons sleeping in a *pedhi* or shop or servants sleeping in the loft
of a hotel can be considered as residing therein. Vagrants living in huts
erected on Municipal land will also have to be considered as residing

---

[1] Copy of the letter from the Collector of Bombay (subject: Qualification as to residence of
voters), No. ADM.236, 20 November 1948, CA/1/FR/49-I, ECIR.
[2] Ibid. Pedhi is a low line table (raised above the floor). Khanawal is a restaurant.

therein... The position of domestic servants who sleep in general or rear passages, balconies or staircases of buildings as also of persons who sleep on footpaths is rather doubtful.'[3] However, he explained that while dealing with a franchise based on adult suffrage, 'residence is intended merely for the purpose of allotting the voter to a particular territorial unit, provided he is otherwise not disqualified. It is a well-known fact that, for lack of housing accommodation in Bombay, a number of persons, who work, earn their living and live in Bombay, are perforce obliged to sleep on pavements and on footpaths and similarly for lack of arrangements made for domestic servants, they have to sleep at all sorts of odd places such as passages, below the staircases, etc.'[4] He, therefore, concluded that 'if it be proved that such persons have uninterruptedly lived in Bombay for over six months in the sense of having worked and having taken the meals in Bombay, it would be unjust that they should be deprived of the valuable right of franchise merely on the ground that they have the misfortune of not having some assignable niche for themselves in the city to which they can return for sleeping'.[5]

The Chief Secretary to the Government of Bombay sent both the legal opinion and the Bombay Collector's letter to the CAS for their view.[6] The matter also received some public attention. The *Times of India* reported on the Collector of Bombay's query, and stated that there is an estimate of 100,000 adults of Bombay city who are eligible to vote, 'but cannot do so because they have no fixed "sleeping place"'.[7]

The CAS agreed in general with the opinion of the Remembrancer of Legal Affairs of the Bombay Government. The note prepared on the question stated: 'As the fresh elections are to be conducted on adult franchise basis such persons cannot be deprived of their franchise.'[8] It was commented that although none of the other provinces addressed the

---

[3] Remembrancer of Legal Affairs, U.R. to P & S.D. No. 1715, 14 February 1949, CA/1/FR/49-I, ECIR. He based his legal opinion by applying the test of the Halsbury's Law of England, Hailshan Edition, Vol. 12, p. 179, according to which 'A person may reside on the premises as a guest or even as a trespasser', and on (cf. Beal V. Ford, 1877 8 C.P.D., 73), for the case of vagrants.

[4] Ibid.

[5] Ibid.

[6] Letter from the Chief Secretary to the Government of Bombay, Political and Services Department to the Secretary to the Constituent Assembly, 18 March 1949, CA/1/FR/49-I, ECIR; letter from the Chief Secretary to the Government of Bombay, Political and Services Department to the Secretary to the Constituent Assembly, 2 April 1949, CA/1/FR/49-I, ECIR.

[7] *Times of India (TOI)*, 8 April 1949, p. 5.

[8] S. no. 88, 26 March–9 April 1949, CA/1/FR/49-I, ECIR.

CAS with this question thus far, 'such cases are not likely to be few in almost all big cities'.[9] The CAS ultimately decided that:

Persons sleeping in a *pedhi* or shop or servants sleeping in the loft of a hotel will be entitled to be included in the electoral roll for the areas in which the *pedhi* or the shop or the hotel as the case may be is situated. Similarly vagrants living in huts erected on municipal land will also be entitled to be registered as voters. Domestic servants who sleep in general or rear passages, balconies or staircases are also eligible for inclusion. But persons who sleep on foot paths cannot be included in the rolls since it is difficult to ascertain with any amount of accuracy whether such persons have actually reside in the area for the prescribed period.[10]

The proactive steps of the collector of Bombay, and his concern over the voting rights of those at the very margins of the society – the vagrants, servants and footpath dwellers – expressed a commitment to procedural equality that was cultivated in the process of the preparation of the draft electoral roll on the basis of universal franchise. However, as in the case of those who slept on footpaths, there were also limits to inclusion. By extension, excluding someone from the franchise was also a way to define who was not a full democratic citizen of the state. Although the constitutional provisions for eligibility to be a voter were universal, and stipulated very few limits, there were some notable exceptions.[11]

The preparation of the electoral rolls was largely done in anticipation of the constitution, thus creating facts on the ground. At the same

---

[9] Ibid.

[10] Letter from the Under Secretary of CAS to the Chief Secretary to the Government of Bombay, 9 April 1949, CA/1/FR/49-I, ECIR. The CAS also referred to the case of labour. They were entitled to be registered in the particular area where they resided for 180 days. The inclusive and enabling registration practice of homeless persons in India today may have its origins in the new attitudes towards enfranchisement that emerged among some administrators during the time of the making of the universal franchise. Nowadays for a homeless person to fulfil the requirement of a place of residence, 'The BLO [Booth Level Officer] will visit the address given ... at night to ascertain that the homeless person actually sleeps at the place which is given as his address... If the BLO is able to verify that the homeless person actually sleeps at that place, no documentary proof of place of residence shall be necessary.' *Hand Book for Booth Level Officers*, Election Commission of India 2011, New Delhi, 41. Also see V. S. Devi and S. K. Mendiratta, *How India Votes: Election Laws, Practice and Procedure* (Second Edition, S. K. Mendiratta), New Delhi: LexisNexis, 2017, p. 295; 'The Homeless Heroes', in Election Commission of India, *Belief in the Ballot: 101 Human Stories from India Elections*, Publication Division Ministry of Broadcasting and Information, Government of India, 2016, pp. 40–1.

[11] The provisions delimited inclusion on the roll to persons who were below the age of 21, which was common at that time, and to persons who were of unsound mind and stands so declared by a competent court. It is noteworthy, from a global perspective, that among the first modern states to call themselves democratic, in France women got the right to vote only in 1946, just a year before all adult Indians; and in the US, only the Voting Rights Act of 1965 ended the legally sanctioned barriers for all adult citizens.

time some draft constitutional provisions, and the implications of constitution making delimited the universality of the franchise. Incidents of
exclusions from the electoral roll, as previous chapters showed, sometimes derived from administrative malpractices, local incompetence or
from inadvertent omissions. But constitution makers also set some limits
on the franchise. Moreover, the enrolment of a large number of people,
in particular the refugees, was pending on the Constituent Assembly's
decision over the citizenship articles which would determine their citizenship status. Citizenship, furthermore, was not the only matter that
awaited a final constitutional resolution that would effect changes in the
electoral roll. The Constituent Assembly settled the question of reservation safeguards for caste and religious minorities only in May 1949. By
then the electoral rolls were prepared for printing in many places. The
Assembly's decision on reservation of seats for minorities in the legislatures would be consequential to the future nature of electoral politics.
Indeed, some breaches in the registration of voters emanated from the
anticipation of electoral politics, resulting particularly from the political
possibilities, which the new regime of the universal franchise opened
up. The institutionalisation of the universal franchise, as revolutionary
and transformative as it was, could not necessarily subvert or replace
the particularisms of society, locality or region. In some cases it even
enabled these to take new forms and to gain in strength within a new
broader framework.

This chapter explores the limits of inclusion in the making of the
universal franchise that emanated from the long process of constitution making. In doing so, it also brings to closure some of the still open
questions in the story of the making of the universal franchise. What,
for example, happened with partition refugees who were registered
provisionally on the electoral roll? What happened with the column
for caste and religion in the form of electoral roll once the question of
reservation for minorities was decided in May 1949? The first section
examines the constitutional exclusion of some territories and groups
of people from the franchise. The second section assesses the implications of the constitution of citizenship on the electoral roll. The third
section looks at the relations between religion, caste, and the preparation of the electoral rolls. Each of the sections indicates the roots of
some future challenges to India's democracy. The origins of community and caste politics that evolved in India's electoral politics after
independence, I suggest, was inherent to the making of the universal
franchise and to the historical moment in which this endeavour was
undertaken.

Beyond the Pale of the Franchise

The Sixth Schedule of the Draft Constitution of February 1948 stipulated provisions for the administration of tribal areas in Assam. It excluded from the purview of the franchise the Sadiya and Balipara Frontier Tracts, the Tirap Frontier Tract (excluding the Lakhimpur Frontier Tract), and the Naga Tribal Area. These areas specified in Part II of the table appended to paragraph 19 of the draft Sixth Schedule were to be administered 'by the President through the Governor of Assam as his agent'.[12]

Historically, the Government of India Act, 1919 made provision for the notification of areas that were excluded from the authority of the reformed provincial governments on the grounds that in these 'backward areas' the people were 'primitive and there is as yet no material on which to found political institutions'.[13] The ensuing Government of India Act, 1935, defined excluded and partially excluded areas, for which no act of the federal or provincial legislatures applied, unless the Governor so directed. Again, the exclusion of these areas from the democratic reforms was based on the view that the state of development of the inhabitants of these areas 'prevents the possibility of applying to them methods of representation adopted elsewhere'.[14] Colonial administration was

---

[12] The Drafting Committee, Constituent Assembly of India, *Draft Constitution of India*, New Delhi: The Manager Government of India Press, 1948, p. 187. In May 1948 the Sadiya Frontier Tract was divided into two separate units of administration: the Abor Hills District and the Mishmi Hills District. See The North-East Frontier Tract (Internal Administration), Regulation, 1948, in P. N. Luthra, *Constitutional and Administrative Growth of the North-East Frontier Agency*, Director of Information and Public Relations, NEFA (North-East Frontier Agency Administration), 1971, pp. 105–9. In the final constitution of January 1950 these areas were specified in Part B of the table appended to paragraph 20 of the Sixth Schedule, and were defined as the North-East Frontier Tract and the Naga Tribal Area. The former included the Balipara Frontier Tract, Tirap Frontier, Abor Hills District, and the Mishmi Hills District. The population of these areas, thus, was 'to be governed not by other relevant provisions of the Constitution which apply to the other constituent States of the Union of India, but by the provisions contained in the Sixth Schedule'. 1966 AIR 1220, 1966 SCR (2) 770.

[13] Constituent Assembly of India Advisory Committee Tribal and Excluded Areas, *Pamphlet: 'Excluded and Partially Excluded Areas'*, Parts I & II (General Note and Appendices, Statements and Factual Memoranda of Provinces), Constituent Assembly, 26 February 1947, p. 2 (quoted from the Report on Indian Constitutional Reforms of 1918). For an analysis of excluded areas under the Government of India Act, 1919 also see Stephen Legg, 'Dyarchy: Democracy, Autocracy, and the Scalar Sovereignty of Interwar India', *Comparative Studies of South Asia, Africa and the Middle East* 36, no. 1, 2016, pp. 44–65.

[14] Constituent Assembly of India Advisory Committee Tribal and Excluded Areas, *Pamphlet*, p. 3 (quoted from the Indian Statutory Commission). Also see Report of the North-East Frontier (Assam) Tribal and Excluded Areas Sub-Committee, 28 July 1947, in B. Shiva Rao, *The Framing of India's Constitution*, vol. III, Nasik: The Manager, Government of India Press, 1968, p. 693. For a comprehensive explanation of the

scarcely established in these areas. The partially excluded areas, however, were generally included in the electoral constituencies, and by independence had representation in the provincial legislatures.[15] The Cabinet
Mission's Statement of May 1946 prescribed for an Advisory Committee
(on the rights of citizens, minorities and tribal and excluded areas) to
report to the Constituent Assembly, among other things, on a scheme for
the administration of the tribal and excluded areas.[16]

On 27 February 1947 the Constituent Assembly Advisory Committee
on Fundamental Rights and Minorities set up three sub-committees for
that purpose. One of the Sub-Committees was assigned to report on the
North-East Frontier (Assam) tribal and excluded areas.[17] The Advisory
Committee directed the Sub-Committee to look into how the excluded
areas should be treated and whether they should have any representation
in the legislature or the executive. The general note that was prepared for
the meeting at that early stage of appointing the Sub-Committee already
presumed the exclusion of some of these areas from the franchise. It
stated:

In some of the backward areas the difficulty is said to be that of finding a person
capable of representing the community ... or even of understanding the significance of the vote... Areas where no system of representation is practicable must
remain unenfranchised and the question arises as to the best way of administering the area.[18]

---

legal position of these territories, especially as defined in the order in Council, the
Government (Excluded and Partially Excluded Areas) Order, 1936, see A Note (10
pages) by R. A. Gopalaswami, Registrar General, Ministry of Home Affairs, 'Seats for
Assam in the House of the People', 6 July 1950, Ministry of Law, Justice and Company
Affairs, f. 125/1950/C, National Archives of India (NAI), New Delhi.

[15] Constituent Assembly of India Advisory Committee Tribal and Excluded Areas,
Pamphlet, p. 1.

[16] India: Statement by the Cabinet Mission, HL Deb 16 May 1946, vol. 141, cc 271–87.
Available at: http://hansard.millbanksystems.com/lords/1946/may/16/india-statement-
by-the-cabinet-mission (accessed 29 June 2017).

[17] The Advisory Committee appointed two additional Sub-Committees: for the excluded
and partially excluded areas (other than Assam), and for the North West Frontier
Province and Baluchistan, which ultimately did not function, as these areas became
part of Pakistan. Large portion of the tribal population lived outside the excluded and
partially excluded areas (in Assam an estimate of 64%), and thus consequently the Sub-
Committee 'did not adequately cover the backwardness of tribal people' as a whole. See
Rao, *The Framing of India's Constitution: A Study*, p. 761.

[18] Constituent Assembly of India Advisory Committee Tribal and Excluded Areas,
Pamphlet, p. 9. The 'Excluded Areas' of Assam under the Government of India Act,
1935, included the North-East Frontier (Sadiya, Balipara and Lakhimpur) Tracts; the
Naga Hills District; the Lushai Hills District; and the North Cachar Hills Sub-Division
of the Cachar District. The *Pamphlet* on the 'Excluded and Partially Excluded Areas',
containing a General Note and Factual Memoranda from the provinces on their partially excluded and excluded areas were prepared for that meeting.

The Factual Memorandum from Assam also advised against the possibility of enfranchisement in the excluded areas. It stated that it was 'too premature' to think of a system of representative Government for some of the tribes of the excluded areas.[19] The Memorandum, notwithstanding, recognised that 'a new wave of political consciousness of unprecedented intensity has spread over the whole of excluded and partially excluded areas. Everywhere one finds in these people a strong desire to govern themselves, form themselves into larger units and to establish some kind of political machinery through which they could not only express themselves but also relate themselves to provincial Government or the Central Government.'[20] Yet it cautioned that: 'certain facts which are always lost sight of by every enthusiastic advocate of freedom deserve to be stated in order that an appropriate view can be taken on this very important question ... it would give us a better analysis of the political conditions of these tribes if we treated them separately according to the geographical position they occupy and the various degrees and stages of civilization in which these tribes are found'.[21]

The Sub-Committee on the North-East Frontier (Assam) Tribal and Excluded Areas toured the hill districts and divisions between April and June 1947, but not the places in the interior. It examined witnesses and heard the views of representatives of many of the tribes, some of whom also submitted written memorandums. The Sub-Committee coopted 12 members from the tribes, except from the tribes of the Frontier Tracts and Tribal Areas.[22] In the report it submitted on 28 July 1947, the Sub-Committee recommended to enfranchise and thereby de-exclude the Lakhimpur Frontier Tracts, the Naga Hills District, the Lushai Hills District, and the North Cachar Sub-Division of the Cachar District, which were defined as excluded areas under the 1935 Act.[23] It argued

---

[19] Ibid. 'Memorandum by the Hon'ble Srijut Gopinath Bardoloi, Premier of Assam', p. 69.

[20] Ibid.

[21] Ibid. The estimated population of Assam's excluded areas was 450,756, but this represented the 1931 figures for Lakhimpur Hill Tract. Ibid., Statement V, p. 10.

[22] The Chairman of the Committee was the Premier of Assam, Gopinath Bardoloi. The other members were Rev J. J. Nichols-Ray, Rup Nath Brahma, A.V. Thakkar, Aliba Imti, and its Secretary was R. K. Ramadhiyani (I.C.S). The latter wrote the general note of the *pamphlet* prepared for the Constituent Assembly Advisory Committee meeting of 27 February 1947. See Report of the North-East Frontier (Assam) Tribal and Excluded Areas Sub-Committee, 28 July 1947, in Rao, *The Framing of India's Constitution*, vol. III, pp. 683–732. The Sub-Committee examined a broad range of issues regarding an administrative and development scheme for these areas. I focus my discussion on the question of franchise and representation.

[23] These areas were to be administered as autonomous districts and governed by largely elected district councils. The constituencies were to be confined to the autonomous districts to be established in the areas where tribes predominated. Rao, *The Framing of India's Constitution*, A Study, p. 761. Henceforth, I focus my discussion on the areas

that there was no longer justification for the exclusion of these areas from the franchise, and that 'if there is universal adult franchise elsewhere, that system should be applied to all these hills'.[24] In view of the Sub-Committee, these areas 'reached the stage of development when they can exercise their votes as intelligently as the people of the plains'.[25] However, the other Frontier Tracts (Sadiya, Balipara, and Tirap), and the Naga Tribal Area did not, in its view, reach that stage and remained outside the purview of adult franchise.[26] It recommended that the Union Government through the Government of Assam as its agent administer the Frontier Tracts and the Naga Tribal Area.[27]

Although they would recommend not to enfranchise these tribal areas, the Sub-Committee stated that they 'were much impressed' by the demand of the various tribes in the Sadiya Frontier Tract for representation in the provincial legislature, and by their intelligence.[28] It also recognised that '[t]he idea of Government by the people through their chosen representatives is not a totally new conception to most of the hill people whose ways of life centre around the tribal and village councils'.[29] And yet, the Sub-Committee explained that in the Frontier Tracts 'circumstances are such that until it is declared that an area is or can be brought under regular administration, representation cannot be provided'.[30] It generally maintained that the tribes in these areas have yet to be 'freed from feuds or raids among themselves' and that 'the country is in many ways unripe for regular administration'.[31] The report also stated the need to demarcate the unclear borders at the MacMahon Line, and

that remained excluded from the franchise. For discussion of the areas that were enfranchised and administered as autonomous districts see, for example, Nandini Sundar, *Subalterns and Sovereigns: An Anthropological History of Bastar (1854–2006)*, New Delhi: Oxford University Press, 2008, pp. 183–90; Sanjib Baruah, 'Citizens and Denizens: Ethnicity, Homelands, and the Crisis of Displacement in North East India', *Journal of Refugee Studies* 16, no. 1, 2003, pp. 44–66; *Report of the State Reorganisation Commission*, Delhi: Manager of Publications, 1955, pp. 183–92.

[24] Report of the North-East Frontier (Assam) Tribal and Excluded Areas Sub-Committee, p. 705.

[25] Ibid., p. 690. In the Sub-Committee's general view, which conformed with colonial opinion, the plains people were far more advanced than the inhabitants of the hills.

[26] Ibid., Appendix A Clause P, p. 712. Appendix A contained the recommendation of the Committee in the form of a draft of provisions for the constitution.

[27] Ibid., p. 731.

[28] Ibid., p. 690. Also see pp. 689, 705, 717–18.

[29] Ibid., p. 690.

[30] Ibid., pp. 704–5.

[31] Ibid., p. 690. Regarding the future policy, the Sub-Committee's view was that: 'Until there is a change in the way of life brought about by the hill people themselves, it would not be desirable to permit any different system to be imposed from outside.' Ibid., p. 694. In that context it referred to debates among colonial policy-makers and anthropologist about isolation and assimilation of the excluded areas.

to delineate the frontier with Burma at the Tirap Frontier, which was yet to be drawn.[32]

Considered evidence submitted to the Sub-Committee was incompatible with its conclusions.[33] Preconceived opinions and national security considerations may ultimately have played a decisive role in shaping the final recommendations. Some political officers recommended to the Sub-Committee that the Frontier Tracts should only come under the jurisdiction of the provincial legislature when administration was better established the area. They also described administrative difficulties, such as an absence of surveys of the areas. The Political Officer of the Sadiya Frontier Tract stated that in the North Western area of the Abor Hills, for example, 'all figures about that area are guess-work'.[34] The inhabitants of the area were routinely characterised as 'uncivilised', yet in their submissions to the Sub-Committee, both representatives of the tribes and some political officers challenged common beliefs about the people in these areas: according to the evidence, the tribes were interested in access to education, health, and political representation.

During the examination of the Political Officer of the Tirap Frontier Tract, G. E. D. Walker, about the Kachins tribe, the Chairman of the Sub-Committee, Bardoloi, asked: 'Do they live on friendly terms with the other tribes?' Walker answered: 'Yes, they do.' The Chairman inquired: 'What about the more heinous offences? for example a murder?' Walker replied, 'In practice, of course, they never commit murder. I have never known one among the Kachins.'[35] The Political Officer of the Sadiya Frontier Tract, J. H. F. Williams, testified that Western medicine

---

[32] See for example ibid., pp. 703, 715–16. Indeed, the Sub-Committee mentioned the tribes' need to be freed from 'encroachment and oppression of Tibetan tax collectors' and that the trade blocks Tibetans set up on the Indian side of the MacMahon line 'sometimes create delicate situations'. Ibid., p. 690.

[33] Volume II of the Sub-Committee's Report contained the evidence. It was composed of two separate parts. Part I: Constituent Assembly of India, *North-East Frontier (Assam) Tribal and Excluded Areas Sub-Committee*, Vol. II (Evidence) Part I (Lushai, North-Cachar, Garo, Mikir And Naga Hills), 19 December 1947. Part II related to the areas that were ultimately specified in Part B of the Sixth Schedule, which remained disenfranchised. It contained 285 pages of evidence and the Minutes of the Sub-Committee's final meetings at Shillong in early July 1947. See Constituent Assembly of India, *North-East Frontier (Assam) Tribal and Excluded Areas Sub-Committee*, Vol. II (Evidence) Part II (Margherita, Sadiya Frontier Tract, Balipara Frontier Tract, Khasi and Jaintia Hills and General), 16 February 1948.

[34] Ibid., p. 24.

[35] Ibid., pp. 5–6. Walker also pressed for investing in education facilities for the people in the area. He recommended doing so and drew a plan for that purpose already in 1943. See Bérénice Guyot-Réchard, *Shadow States: India, China and the Himalayas, 1910–1962*, Cambridge: Cambridge University Press, 2017, p. 77.

was 'extremely popular' with the Abors.[36] The Chairman was confused: 'It is very surprising that people who believe in spirits and things like that should believe in Western medicine.'[37] Williams replied: 'They have realised the value of Western medicine. There is a terrific demand for it.'[38]

Representatives of the various tribes from the areas that remained excluded from representation came in large numbers before the Sub-Committee to make their case. Some had marched five days to testify.[39] They expressed a clear wish of advances in health and education. The seven representatives of the Kachins told the Chairman of the Sub-Committee, when he asked 'What do you people want?' 'Sir, we want to live where we are, but must get proper education and we must all make advancement. We must have schools, we must have roads, we must have hospitals and all that.'[40] The Abors (Minyong and Padam), who came in large numbers before the Sub-Committee, also stressed their wish for education and hospital facilities, as did the representatives of the tribes in the Balipara Frontier Tract.[41]

Further undermining the notion that these people were unprepared for enfranchisement, the Political Officer of the Sadiya Frontier Tract testified about the Abor that:

You cannot specifically described it as such but they have an elective system in that a man reaches his position of authority in the tribe or in his own village as the case may be by the general will of the people. It is not done by vote... He will gain his position as a leader in the village council by force of character... There is a council in each village which will meet in the meeting house of the village whenever there is any village subject for discussion.[42]

The representatives of the tribes in the Sadiya Frontier Tract asked for representation. The four witnesses of the Koibartas, who also presented a written memorandum to the Sub-Committee, stated:

We want to come under the sphere of ministerial responsibility and not remain under the Political Officer. We wish that the excluded area of the Sadiya Frontier Tract should be abolished and should be included in the non-excluded areas. We

---

[36] Constituent Assembly of India, *North-East Frontier (Assam) Tribal and Excluded Areas Sub-Committee*, Vol. II (Evidence) Part II, p. 29.

[37] Ibid., p. 30.

[38] Ibid., p. 30. The Political Officer of the Balipara Frontier Tract gave a similar statement on the tribal people appreciation of medicine. Ibid., p. 66.

[39] The representatives of the Bhutias aud Buguns from the Balipara Frontier Tract marched five days to reach the Sub-Committee and testify before it. Ibid, p. 67.

[40] Ibid., p. 12.

[41] Ibid., pp. 47, 68–71.

[42] Ibid., p. 28.

have been deprived of the advantages which our people are getting in the non-excluded areas. We want that those privileges and advantages should be given to us.[43]

The representatives of the Miris and the Mishmis stated the same thing in their oral testimony. In their written memorandum the Miris stated: 'We want to be in intimate relation with Assam or the Central Union according to the advice of our Council in respect of, general schemes for our advancement, communication and higher education.'[44] Most clearly, the Hkamtis stated in their memorandum that: '*In the provincial legislature we should be given representation on the basis of the same franchise as is given to others.* We believe that we will be able to make full use of the opportunities that may be given to us in the matters submitted. We should be assigned one seat in the provincial legislature.'[45] Representatives of various organisations also advocated for representation of the people of the excluded areas under the jurisdiction of the provincial legislature.[46]

A national security case for the Frontier Tract was made by the Political Officer of the Sadiya Frontier Tract in his submission to the Sub-Committee. He suggested that the tribes in the Frontier Tract 'are the natural guardians of India's frontier, and if they are treated well, they will be of immense value, but if, on the other hand, they are not given all facilities for general advancement, they will continue to be more interested in Tibet'.[47] If this point was meant to sway the Committee in

---

[43] Ibid., p. 35. Generally, the testimonies of the representatives of the tribes also contained detailed descriptions of their way of life (social and political) and their produce.

[44] Ibid., p. 39.

[45] Ibid., p. 43. In their oral testimony, the Hkamtis' representatives stated: 'We want to come under ministerial administration. If the safeguards which are being given to the other minorities of the province are given to us, we will be satisfied.' They also stated in their written memorandum a wish to 'create a small state for the Hkamtis' within the boundaries the British assigned to them. Ibid. Notably, representatives of tribes who did not understand the ensuing political changes asked the Sub-Committee to explain it to them. Thus, in examining witnesses from the Balipara Frontier Tract the Chairman of the Sub-Committee told the representatives of the Bhutias and Buguns: 'Hereafter, all the British will go away from our country and the natives, we the black-men will have to take up the rule in all these wide areas. Whom would you like to rule you? Would you like to rule yourselves?' They answered: 'We are not literate and we know very little of what sort of change is coming. We think the existing state of affairs will continue and so we want to continue as we are. Please explain to us the nature of the coming change?' The report then only mentions: 'Chairman explains'. Ibid. pp. 68–9.

[46] See the testimonies of the General Secretary of the Assam Jatiya Mahasabha, Mr A. G. Roy Chowdhury; the General Secretary of the Plains Tribal League, Mr S. C. Basumatury; Mr C. Goldsmith, The Civic Rights Committee of the Assam Christian Association, ibid., pp. (respectively) 241, 244, 250.

[47] Ibid., p. 31. On the unclear territorial boundaries of the Frontier Tracts and Tribal Areas under the British, and political officers' attitudes towards the tribes at the frontier as guardians during the early 1940s see Guyot-Réchard, *Shadow States*, chapter 2.

favour of enfranchisement of the population, it was unsuccessful. The Chairman of the Sub-Committee in his conclusion stated that: 'Those areas could not be administered directly by the Provincial Government, in view of the fact that they are areas which will be more or less necessary from the Defence [sic] and External Affairs Department's point of view and in which the Provincial Government will be acting as agents of the Government of India. The frontier will be under the administration of the Central Government.'[48]

The Sub-Committee excluded the Frontier Tracts and the Tribal Area from democratic political representation, and concluded that 'until administration has been satisfactorily established over a sufficiently wide area' they should be centrally administered.[49] The Sub-Committee's recommendations were incorporated into the Draft Constitution of February 1948. The recommendations were not discussed by the Constituent Assembly prior to that.[50] Thus, the people of the Frontier Tracts and the Tribal Area remained outside the remit of the instructions for the preparation of electoral rolls on the basis of universal franchise. The Constituent Assembly discussed the Sixth Schedule for the first time in September 1949. The Assembly's discussion was predominated by prejudice and hearsay. It resolved that the people of the Frontier Tracts and Naga Tribal Areas were not ready to be enfranchised.[51] The House adopted an amendment that provided for the exclusion of the plains portion of the frontier tracts that were specified in Part II of the Sixth Schedule.[52]

---

[48] Ibid., p. 242. The Chairman responded in this case to the General Secretary of the Assam Jatiya Mahasabha.

[49] Ibid., p. 731. Also see p. 715.

[50] The reason was that when the reports of the two Sub-Committees for the excluded and partially excluded areas of Assam and in areas other than Assam were received the constitution was already drafted. The reports were formally submitted to the Constituent Assembly on 4 November 1948. See Rao, *The Framing of India's Constitution, A Study*, p. 763. A draft already appeared in the Eighth Schedule of the first draft Constitution of October 1947.

[51] For the racist nature of the Assembly debate of the Sixth Schedule see Sundar, *Subalterns and Sovereigns*, pp. 186–7.

[52] The Chairman of the Sub-Committee, Bardoloi, proposed this amendment at the meeting of the Advisory Committee on 24 February 1948, just after the publication of the Draft Constitution on 21 February 1948. The Advisory Committee decided to amend the schedule accordingly. See Rao, *The Framing of India's Constitution, A Study*, pp. 781–2. The amendment the Constituent Assembly adopted in September 1949 stated: 'Provided that the tribal areas specified in Part II of the Table below shall not include any such areas in the plains as may, with the previous approval of the President, be notified by the Governor of Assam in this behalf.' *Constituent Assembly Debates (CAD)*, 7 September 1949 (available on http://parliamentofindia.nic.in/ls/debates/debates. htm, accessed 29 June 2017). All references to the *CAD* hereunder are taken from this source. Notification No. TAD R/35/50/109, 23 February 1951, carved out of the areas

When it became clear that tribal areas defined in Part B of the table appended to paragraph 20 of the Sixth Schedule were going to be excluded from the franchise, the Chief Electoral Officer of Assam made a case in July 1950 to the Election Commission of India that this should not rob Assam of a seat in the National Assembly.[53] He wrote that the population of these areas 'is in the neighborhood of 6,00,000 [600,000]'.[54] With this additional population, he explained, the total population of Assam would be 9.11 million, and as such would become entitled to 13 seats in the House of the People, rather than the 12 that were allotted to it.

The Chief Electoral Officer of Assam wrote to the Election Commission that the 'question of providing representation for this extra population is under the consideration of the State Government ... with the view to allow them the right of franchise by allotting an extra seat in the House of the People'.[55] His rationale for the proposal was symptomatic of the ambivalence displayed in the Sub-Committee's reports to justify the disenfranchisement of these tribes. On the one hand, he suggested that 'Most of this area is marked by continued prevalence of head-hunting, slavery and tribal feuds, and the difficulties in survey, delimitation of boundaries and preparation of electoral rolls ... still continue'.[56] He wrote this despite evidence submitted before the Sub-Committee suggesting that, for example, head hunting was infrequent.[57] On the other hand, he explained that

specified in Part B the plains portion of the Balipara, Sadiya, and Tirap Frontier Tracts. See Luthra, *Constitutional and Administrative Growth of the North-East Frontier Agency*, pp. 111–12. Voters from these plains portion were enrolled for the first elections.

[53] 'Note on the tribal areas specified in Part B of the table appended to paragraph 20 of the sixth schedule', in letter No. LRE.153/48/133 from the Chief Electoral Officer of Assam, R. R. Khaund to the Secretary, Election Commission of India, 16 July 1950, 33/1/50 E-lec, ECIR. Also see letter No. LRE.2400/50/21 From the Chief Electoral Officer of Assam, R. R. Khaund to the Secretary to the Government of India, Ministry of Law ('Representation of the Scheduled Tribes of the Tribal Areas specified in the Sixth Schedule in the House of the People), 22 July 1950, 33/1/50 Elec, ECIR. Also see Ministry of Law, Justice and Company Affairs, f. 125/1950/C, NAI.

[54] Letter No. LRE.153/48/133 From the Chief Electoral Officer of Assam, R. R. Khaund to the Secretary, Election Commission of India, 16 July 1950, 33/1/50 Elec, ECIR. He based his estimation on the population figure estimated by Sir Andrew Clow the Governor of Assam in 1945 and on more recent estimation of the Political Officers.

[55] Ibid. The Chief Electoral Officer of Assam noted, however, that 'it is apprehended that most of these areas will not be accessible at this season of the year'. Ibid.

[56] Letter No. LRE.2400/50/21 from the Chief Electoral Officer of Assam, R.R. Khaund to the Secretary to the Government of India, Ministry of Law, 22 July 1950, 33/1/50 Elec, ECIR.

[57] Political officers did not report on the phenomenon in their examination. The Sub-Committee discussed it at some length with Dr Guha, who gave an anthropologist expert opinion. It was mainly in reference to the Naga areas. Dr Guha stated that not all practice it and that the Abors do not partake in head hunting. Constituent Assembly of India, *North-East Frontier (Assam) Tribal and Excluded Areas Sub-Committee*, Vol. II

The inhabitants of these Part B Tribal Areas are Indian citizens, and, therefore, are entitled to franchise for the purpose of elections to both the House of the People and the State Legislative Assembly. The mere fact that it is not possible to prepare an Electoral Roll for these areas and to apply the General Election machinery therein cannot deprive them of the right of franchise conferred under the Constitution.[58]

The Chief Electoral Officer suggested grouping the Autonomous Districts specified in Part A of the Sixth Schedule with the Part B Tribal Areas for the purpose of elections. He explained that despite the fact that they are 'in the different stages of the so-called stages of civilization', the people of Part A and Part B Tribal Areas 'are of the same stock', and 'share many interests and problems in common'.[59] The interests of the people of Part B Tribal Area, therefore, could be represented adequately and safeguarded by two candidates from the more advanced Part A Tribal Area, instead of the one seat that was allotted to them.

Part B Tribal Areas were ultimately allotted one seat in the House of the People, 'to be filled by a person nominated by the President' and not through elections.[60] From 1954 onwards there was a series of reorganisations of the North-East Frontier Tracts specified in Part B of the Sixth Schedule. These Frontier Tracts continued to be represented in the House of the People by a member nominated by the President until India's sixth general elections in 1977, when the area became the Union Territory of Arunachal Pradesh and its people participated for the first time in Parliamentary elections.[61]

(Evidence) Part II, pp. 276–7. Misconceptions about the practice of head hunting also manifested in the Constituent Assembly debate on the Sixth Schedule, and were based on hearsay. See comments by Rohini Kumar Chaudhuri, *CAD*, 6 September 1949.

[58] Letter No. LRE.2400/50/21 from the Chief Electoral Officer of Assam, R.R. Khaund to the Secretary to the Government of India, Ministry of Law, 22 July 1950, 33/1/50 Elec, ECIR. Also see. 'Note on the tribal areas specified in Part B of the table appended to paragraph 20 of the sixth schedule', in letter No. LRE.153/48/133 from the Chief Electoral Officer of Assam, R. R. Khaund to the Secretary, Election Commission of India, 16 July 1950, 33/1/50 Elec, ECIR.

[59] Letter No. LRE.2400/50/21 from the Chief Electoral Officer of Assam, R. R. Khaund to the Secretary to the Government of India, Ministry of Law, 22 July 1950, 33/1/50 Elec, ECIR.

[60] *Representation of the People Act, 1950*, Part II, Clause 4.

[61] The first readjustment of the North-East Frontier Tracts took place with its reorganisation into the North-East Frontier Agency (NEFA) under the North-East Frontier Areas (Administration) Regulation, 1954 in January 1954. One member nominated by the President of India represented the NEFA in the parliament. At the end of 1957 the reorganisation of NEFA resulted in the creation of the North-East Frontier Tract and Naga Hills-Tuensang Area of Assam (The Naga Hills-Tuensang Area Act, 1957). Both these areas were given separate representation in the House of the People, nominated by the President during the third general elections in 1962. On that year, Nagaland was created as a separate state. It was allotted one seat in the House of the People, and the one allotted earlier to the Naga Hills-Tuensang Area was abolished. One seat

Another territory that was excluded from direct democratic representation were the Andaman and Nicobar Islands. The Islands' indigenous people were described as 'more backward than many tribes in India'.[62] In this case, the Union Constitution Committee made its decision already in August 1947, and it was already incorporated into the Draft Constitution of 7 October 1947.[63] In October 1949 the Chief Commissioner of Andaman and Nicobar Islands wrote to the Joint Secretary of the Constituent Assembly Secretariat (CAS), asking to know what will be the position of the Islands under the new constitution.[64] The total population of the Islands was about 26,000 (16,000 in Andaman and 10,000 in Nicobar). The Chief Commissioner asked: 'Shall we be included as

continued to stand for the North-East Frontier Tract, the only one that was nominated by the president in the fourth general elections in 1967. Thus from the fourth general elections in 1967 all members of the House of the People were elected by direct elections, except the member nominated by the President to represent the North-East Frontier Tract. This continued in the fifth general elections in 1971. In pursuance of the North-Eastern Areas (Reorganisation) Act 1971, NEFA became a Union Territory named Arunachal Pradesh. See Devi and Mendiratta, *How India Votes*: pp. 59–62; Luthra, *Constitutional and Administrative Growth of the North-East Frontier Agency*, pp. 113–19; and Chandra Bhushan Kumar, *Imaging Arunachal Pradesh: The Indelible Ink of Democracy*, Itangar: Chief Electoral Officer, Arunachal Pradesh, 2016, pp. 7–8.

[62] Rao, *The Framing of India's Constitution: A Study*, p. 558.

[63] Rao, *The Framing of India's Constitution*, Vol. III, p. 23. The relevant article was 60(5). At that point it was the only territory for which such a provision was made. On 30 July 1947 the Constituent Assembly decided to appoint a committee to recommend constitutional changes in the administrative system of the Chief Commissioner's Provinces, among them Andaman and Nicobar Islands with a view to 'give them due place in the democratic constitution of free India'. The Committee submitted its report on 21 October 1947. It recommended that the Islands were to be governed through a Chief Commissioner without any representative institutions. Articles 67(7) and 215 gave effect to that in the draft constitution of February 1948. The Constituent Assembly considered the provisions relevant for Andaman and Nicobar on 16 September 1949 and passed them without discussion. Rao, *The Framing of India's Constitution: A Study*, pp. 426, 560, 563, 568. Also see Virendra Kumar, *Committees and Commissions in India: 1947–1973*, Vol. 1: 1947–54, New Delhi: Concept Publishing Company, 2004, p. 31; Discussion at the CAS: S. no. 35, and a note on S. no. 35, 5 May 1949, CA/1/FR/49-III, ECIR. For a new discussion of the governance of the Islands in the transition to independence and the postcolonial period see: Uditi Sen, 'Developing Terra Nullius: Colonialism, Nationalism and Indigeneity in the Andaman Islands', *Comparative Studies in Society and History*, 50, no. 4, 2017.

[64] Letter from the Chief Commissioner Andaman & Nicobar Islands to CAS, 31 October 1949, CA/1/FR/49-V, ECIR. The background to the letter was that in June 1949 there was a proposal to transfer the Andaman and Nicobar Islands from Part IV of the First Schedule to the Draft Constitution to Part II of that Schedule, and in that case it would have been necessary to prepare electoral rolls for the Islands. Note on S. no. 83, 27 June 1949, CA/1/FR/49-III, ECIR. The CAS then wrote to the Chief Commissioner of Andaman and Nicobar asking that he should take no action in the matter of preparation of electoral rolls under the new Constitution until he received further instructions from them. Letter from CAS to the Chief Commissioner Andaman & Nicobar Islands, 23 June 1949, CA/1/FR/49-III, ECIR.

part of another constituency, or shall we be deprived entirely of our rights to elect representatives to the Indian Parliament.'[65] The Joint Secretary of the CAS explained in his reply that the 'territory of the Andaman and Nicobar Islands will have no representation in the Council of States. It will, however, have representation in the House of the People and under clause (2) of article 81 of the Constitution the quantum of this representation shall be such as Parliament may by law provide.'[66] The Islands were also allotted one seat in the House of the People to be nominated by the President.[67]

Finally, the entire state of Jammu and Kashmir was excluded from the franchise for the first three general elections. It was allotted six seats for the Union House of the People that were nominated by the President. While all the other merging states ultimately accepted the constitution of India, it was suggested in October 1949 that 'the conditions in the state are still unusual and abnormal', that parts of the state were 'still in the hands of rebels and enemies', and moreover, India was 'entangled with the United Nations' in regard to the state.[68] For these reasons, an article, 306-A (later enumerated as 370) introduced special provisions for the regulation of the relations of the state with the Union of India. The nomination of six representatives from the state to the House of the People by the president until the 1967 elections was under the Constitution (Application to Jammu and Kashmir) Order 1950, and its pursuant amendments, which made provisions for elections to the Union Parliament from the state.[69]

There were ultimately three territorial Constitutional limits of inclusion to the universal franchise: the Andaman and Nicobar Islands, the 'Part B Tribal Areas' of Assam, and Jammu and Kashmir. The exclusion

---

[65] Letter from the Chief Commissioner Andaman & Nicobar Islands to CAS, 31 October 1949, CA/1/FR/49-V, ECIR. He referred to article 67, according to which there shall be not less than one representative of the House of the People for every 750,000 of the population, and not more than one representative for every 500,000.

[66] Draft letter from Joint Secretary of CAS to the Chief Commissioner Andaman & Nicobar Islands, 1 December 1949, CA/1/FR/49-V, ECIR.

[67] By the fourth general elections in 1967 the people of the Islands participated in the elections. The electorate was 47,064 and the turnout 78.45%. Election Commission of India, *Statistical Report on Genertal Elections, 1967 to the Fourth Lok Sabha*, Vol. I, New Delhi: Election Commission of India, 1968, p. 4.

[68] Rao, *The Framing of India's Constitution: A Study*, p. 552.

[69] See Devi and Mendiratta, *How India Votes*: p. 18; James Michael Lyngdoh, *Chronicle of an Impossible Election: The Election Commission and the 2002 Jammu & Kashmir Assembly Elections*, New Delhi: Penguin Viking, 2004, pp. 22–30; Sten Widmalm, 'The Rise and Fall of Democracy in Jammu and Kashmir, 1975–1989, in Amrita Basu and Atul Kohli (eds), *Community Conflicts and the State in India*, Delhi: Oxford University Press, pp. 149–82. The state held its first assembly elections in 1962.

of these territories, with an estimated 2.5 million voters out of an elect-orate of more than 17.3 Crores (173 million) were exceptions that underscore the underlying thrust of the enterprise.[70] The exclusions in the North-East, though limited, were consequential for the travails that beset this region from independence.[71] This supports Nandini Sundar's argument that in the North-East 'the roots of many of today's problems may be traced back to the anti-democratic and authoritarian impulses of some of the Constitution's makers'.[72]

Establishing the right to vote in anticipation of the constitution was, as I explained in previous chapters, inherently tied to making Indians citizens and to defining India's territory. Indeed, as Chapter 4 showed, the preparation of rolls became a key mechanism of integration, and of binding the territories and the people into a unified democratic order. It also helped forging a common citizenship and nationality. Exclusion from this process produced an ill-defined predicament for the pro-spect of the people of the North-East and these territories to become Indians and part of India. The States Reorganisation Commission's assessment in 1955 of the generally unsatisfactory workings of the Sixth Schedule eight years after the Sub-Committee reported on the North-East Frontier attested to that.[73] Since the electoral roll based on adult franchise would mark the extent to which India would exercise its authority territorially, enfranchisement, despite all difficulties, may have helped mitigate some of the constitution makers' concerns about unity and safety.

---

[70] The estimated population for the Andaman and Nicobar Islands and the Part B Tribal areas was about 600,000. The population of Jammu and Kashmir was estimated to be 4.4 million in 1955. Based on the national averages approximately half of the population would be eligible to vote, i.e. 2.5 million people. In other words, ca. 1.4% of India's eli-gible voters were territorially disenfranchised. For the population of Jammu and Kashmir see *Report of the State Reorganisation Commission*, Delhi: Manager of Publications, 1955, p. 204.

[71] For the tribulations of administering and making the North-East part of India in the first decades after independence see Ramachandra Guha, *Savaging the Civilized: Verrier Elwin, His Tribals, and India*, in *The Ramachandra Guha Omnibus*, New Delhi: Oxford University Press, 2005; *Report of the State Reorganisation Commission*, pp. 183–95. For the challenges to India's border, particularly the 1962 war with China see Srinath Raghavan, *War and Peace in Modern India*, Basingstoke: Palgrave Macmillan, 2010, pp. 227–308; Ramachandra Guha, *India after Gandhi: The History of the World's Largest Democracy*, London: Pan Macmillan, 2008, pp. 331–7. For a recent assessment of the failure's of India's democracy towards its tribal people and areas beyond the North-East see, for example, Nandini Sundar, *The Burning Forest: India's War in Bastar*, New Delhi: Juggernaut, 2016; Ramachandra Guha, *Democrats and Dissenters*, New Delhi: Penguin Random House India, 2016, pp. 105–28.

[72] Sundar, *Subalterns and Sovereigns*, p. 188.

[73] *Report of the State Reorganisation Commission*, pp. 183–95.

While the preparation of the electoral rolls helped forging in practice a common Indian citizenship, the constitutional provisions for citizenship were undecided until August 1949. Since citizenship was a precondition for being a voter, the final citizenship provisions would be critical for the universality of the franchise. This was particularly consequential for partition refugees, whose registration, as discussed in Chapter 2, was pending both on the establishment of their citizenship before the commencement of the constitution, and on the relaxation of the residence qualification for them in the electoral law.[74]

Constituting Citizenship

The citizenship article finally came before the Constituent Assembly on 10 August 1949. The status of refugees lay at the heart of the debate over membership in the nation at the commencement of the constitution.[75] The consolidated amendment of the citizenship article, moved by the Chairman of the Drafting Committee, Ambedkar, was on its face a significant departure from the original draft.[76] The Article was clearly marked by the immediate consequences of partition.

Article 5 gave the qualifications of a person who at the commencement of the Constitution was to be called a citizen of India. The qualifications were domicile or birth in the territory, or being born to one Indian parent, or ordinary residence in the territory of India for no less than

[74] As discussed in Chapter 2, the draft citizenship article provided for partition refugees an easy mode of acquiring domicile, and thereby citizenship. However, the declaration that was required for that under clause (ii) of the explanation to article 5 (citizenship) could not be made 'until auxiliary action whether by legislation or otherwise' had been taken before the commencement of the constitution. See The Drafting Committee, *Draft Constitution of India*, p. 4; letter from CAS to All Provincial Governments, All Chief Commissioners Provinces and All Indian States and Unions, 26 July 1948, CA/9/FR/48, ECIR. As for the residence qualifications, partition refugees registered on the electoral roll on a mere declaration by them of their intention to reside permanently in the town or village concerned irrespective of the actual period of residence, and their enrolment was subject to revision in due time in accordance with the electoral law.

[75] The Chairman of the Drafting Committee explained that the article provided for a situation at the date of the commencement of the Constitution and its continuance until the intervention by the Parliamentary legislation. 'It is not the object of this particular article to lay down a permanent law of citizenship for this country.' *CAD*, 10 August 1949. Also see AIR 1961 MP 110, 1961 CriLJ 516.

[76] Four new articles (5A, 5AA, 5B, 5C), among them one that was brought before the members of the Assembly for the first time on the morning of the discussion (5AA; amendments 130, 131), occupied the Assembly in intense debates over three days before the part on citizenship in the Draft Constitution was eventually adopted. A member of the Assembly, Mr Naziruddin Ahmad, commented on the amended draft article, suggesting that 'such a departure that amounts largely to an amendment in the constitution itself.' Ibid.

five years. Article 5A broadened the category of citizens to include persons who have migrated to the territory of India from Pakistan and laid down the conditions for it. Those who came and were resident in India before 19 July 1948 were automatically deemed to be citizens, whereas those who migrated afterwards had to register as such.[77] Article 5AA, which became the main subject of contention in the Assembly, dealt with people who left India for Pakistan as partition was looming, but then returned to India. The article determined that people who migrated from India to Pakistan after 1 March 1947 lost the right to be citizens of India.[78] An exception was made for persons who returned to India in possession of a permit for resettlement or permanent return issued by government authorities. The vast majority of people in this special category were Muslims.

This Article that dealt with returnees from Pakistan caused fierce debates in the House over whether India should be the state of all its citizens, on the basis of a liberal conception of citizenship, or principally the state of the Hindus, on the basis of an ethno-nationalist notion.[79] That both conceptions co-existed within the evolving citizenship article was acknowledged by Ambedkar, who in the final defence of the contested clause made at once a liberal and an ethno-national claim to ground it. He explained to the Assembly that it is precisely to provide as 'a rule of law' that 'anyone who has gone to Pakistan after 1st March [1947] shall not be entitled to say that he still has a domicile in India', and thus prevent from such persons to claim rights of citizenship, that the contested clause was added.[80] On the one hand, within a liberal constitutional framework, the clause by and large delimited the scope and prospect for Muslims for citizenship in the new state – their original homeland. The exception the Article laid to that general rule marked the restriction it imposed on the eligibility for citizenship to persons who migrated to Pakistan from India. On the other hand, the clause was added to avoid breaching the

---

[77] 19 July 1948 was the date from which the Permit System, which stipulated five different categories for travelling, or transition between India and Pakistan, came into effect. See Vazira Fazila-Yacoobali Zamindar, *The Long Partition and the Making of Modern South Asia: Refugees, Boundaries, Histories*, New York: Columbia University Press, 2007, pp. 126–40; Joya Chatterji, 'South Asian Histories of Citizenship, 1946–1970', *The Historical Journal* 55, no. 4, 2012, pp. 1049–71. Also see AIR 1961 MP 110, 1961 CriLJ 516.

[78] In spite of their fulfilling qualifications for their inclusion in the categories mentioned in either of the two articles 5 and 5A.

[79] For an important discussion of this debate see Niraja Gopal Jayal, *Citizenship and Its Discontents: An India History*, Cambridge, MA: Harvard University Press, 2013, pp. 56–63.

[80] *CAD*, 12 August 1949.

legality of the independent Indian government that allowed, 'whether rightly or wrongly', in Ambedkar's words, to some of those who left India for Pakistan to come back permanently by issuing permits to them.[81] The Clause was moved. The citizenship provisions were re-enumerated as articles 5–11.[82]

The final citizenship articles thus inscribed the dividing lines of the partition in the constitution.[83] They maintained, at the commencement of the Constitution, the distinctions between 'bad' and 'good' refugees, or between refugees and migrants, which characterised the exclusionary ordinances for the control of population movement in the wake of the partition.[84] But the final citizenship provisions did not alter the inclusive principles under which the preliminary electoral roll on the basis of universal franchise was prepared. The adoption of citizenship, however, had implications for the electoral roll. Many people, like refugees, were provisionally enrolled because of their unclear citizenship and residency status, and their registration had to be confirmed.[85]

The draft citizenship article, which formed the basis for the preparation of the rolls, stipulated for partition refugees an easy mode of acquiring domicile, and thereby citizenship. But the declaration it prescribed for that end under article (ii) of the explanation to Article 5 of the draft constitution could not be made 'until auxiliary action whether by legislation or otherwise' had been taken before the commencement of the constitution.[86] The effect of the final citizenship provisions was that those who came to India before 19 July 1948 automatically became

---

[81] Ibid. Nehru was entangled in the same position when he explained to the Assembly: 'Our general rule ... is that we accept practically without demur or enquiry that great wave of migration which came from Pakistan to India... Now, all these rules naturally apply to Hindus, Muslims and Sikhs or Christians or anybody else. You cannot have rules for Hindus, for Muslims or for Christians only. It is absurd on the face of it; but in effect we say that we allow the first year's migration and obviously that huge migration was as a migration of Hindus and Sikhs from Pakistan.' Ibid.

[82] Article 5A became 6, and article 5AA became 7. See Appendix 6.1, Chapter 6 for the final citizenship provisions, as they were re-enumerated with their adoption.

[83] For important analyses of the imprints of the partition on Indian citizenship see Zamindar, The Long Partition and The Making of Modern South Asia; Anupama Roy, Mapping Citizenship in India, New Delhi: Oxford University Press, 2010; Gopal Jayal. Citizenship and Its Discontents; Chatterji, 'South Asian Histories of Citizenship'; Haimanti Roy, Partitioned Lives: Migrants, Refugees, Citizens in India and Pakistan, New Delhi: Oxford University Press, 2012.

[84] See discussion, Chapter 2.

[85] Ibid.

[86] Letter from CAS to All Provincial Governments, All Chief Commissioners' Provinces and All Indian States and Unions, 26 July 1948, CA/9/FR/48, ECIR. At the time, the CAS, as discussed in Chapter 2, wrote to many citizens' organisations that all persons who want to benefit from such declarations would get an opportunity to do so before the commencement of the Constitution and the revisions of the rolls.

citizens under Article 6 (b) (i). Those who came on or after that date had, under Article 6 (b) (ii), to register as citizens before the commencement of the Constitution, provided that they resided in the territory of India at least six months preceding the date of their application. Thus, the last date of migration from Pakistan (or return to India) that would qualify a person for such a declaration was 25 July 1949. Thus, this date marked the limit of inclusion. Those who came to India from Pakistan after that date, and did not have a permit for resettlement or permanent return could not obtain Indian citizenship. Article 5 (c) addressed the citizenship status of those whose original home was what became Pakistan, but ordinarily resided in what became India for carrying on their business or profession. They would become citizens if they ordinarily resided in India for at least five years preceding the commencement of the constitution.[87]

The Reforms Commissioner of Assam expected that in view of the adopted citizenship provisions a 'large number of persons, whose citizenship was previously in doubt' would now 'automatically acquire the rights of a citizen'.[88] As a result, the revisions of the rolls would involve 'a huge volume of work.'[89] He wrote in the immediate that, therefore, three more months would be needed to revise the rolls before printing.[90] The CAS asked that he should proceed with the printing, and explained that revisions in accordance with the adopted citizenship provisions would be made when the rolls would be published for the purpose of inviting claims and objections.[91]

Moreover, the Joint Secretary to the Government of West Bengal noted that according to the adopted citizenship provisions,

[D]isplaced persons who migrated to India on or after the 19th July, 1948 ... must have been registered as Indian citizens before the commencement of the Constitution... As the date of commencement of the Constitution is understood to be the 26th January, 1950, *it is high time that the Government of India now prescribe the necessary form and appoint the necessary officers for the purpose of registering*

[87] The final registration of many people in Assam, for example, was pending on that provision. See discussion, Chapter 2.

[88] Letter No. LRE 253/50/5 from the Reforms Commissioner of Assam to the Joint Secretary of CAS, 20 January 1950, CA/1/FR/49-IV, ECIR. The Reforms Commissioner wrote in the matter already in September: Fortnightly Report, Government of Assam, 5 September 1949, CA/1/FR/49-III, ECIR.

[89] Letter No. LRE 253/50/5 from the Reforms Commissioner of Assam to the Joint Secretary of CAS, 20 January 1950, CA/1/FR/49-IV, ECIR.

[90] Fortnightly Report, Government of Assam, 5 September 1949, CA/1/FR/49-III, ECIR.

[91] Letter from the Joint Secretary of CAS to the Reforms Commissioner of Assam, 21 September 1949, CA/1/FR/49-III, ECIR.

this class of displaced persons as citizens so as to avoid the rush of applications and consequential congestion of work at the eleventh hour.[92]

The CAS stated in its reply, a month later, that 'the Ministry of Home Affairs have already addressed the Provincial Governments in the matter'.[93]

Indeed, the Ministry of Home affairs took over the registration of citizenship from early November 1949. A confidential letter of the Reforms Commissioner of Assam on the 'Registration of persons as citizens of India under the New Constitution' stated that:

it is the desire of Government to finish registration of *a certain class of displaced persons* as citizens of India, under the provisions of clause (b) (ii) of Article 6 read with Article 7 of the Constitution, *positively* before the commencement of the Constitution. There is no time to lose now as every day counts for the displaced persons anxious to register themselves.[94]

He referred to the Ministry of Home Affairs' letter of 8 November 1949, on the registration as citizens under these articles, which instructed that 'the work could begin only after the Constitution is adopted by the Constituent Assembly of India'.[95] He explained that since the Constitution was adopted and authenticated on 26 November 1949 'the

---

[92] Letter No. 1495 AR/RIR.22/47 from the Joint Secretary to the Government of West Bengal to the Joint Secretary, Constituent Assembly, 31 October 1949, CA/1/FR/49-IV, ECIR. Emphasis added.

[93] Draft letter from the Officer on Special Duty (hereafter OSD), CAS to the Joint Secretary, Government of West Bengal, 1 December 1949, CA/1/FR/49-IV, ECIR.

[94] Confidential letter No. LRE.824/48/55 from the Reforms Commissioner of Assam to All Deputy Commissioner, Superintendent, Lushai Hills, Political Officers of Frontier Tract and Subdivisional Officers of Karimganj, Hailakandi, and North Cachar Hills, 7 December 1949, CA/1/FR/49-IV, ECIR. Article 6 (b) (ii) referred to people who came to India on or after 19 July 1948. Article 7 referred to people who left from India to Pakistan after 1 March 1947, but returned to India under a permit for resettlement or permanent return.

[95] Ibid. The Reforms Commissioner referred to letter No. 140/49-F.II, 8 November 1949, which included 'Instructions to Registering Officers'. The letter from the Ministry of Home Affairs noted that 'It is impossible to give even a rough estimate of the number of people who will avail themselves of this provision and register as citizens of India.' The letter laid out a suggestion for how the registration should take place. The Ministry asked to furnish to the Government of India any alternative suggestions by 15 November 1949 at the latest, so that if necessary instructions would be modified by 20 November 1949. A copy of the form of the application was attached and governments were asked to translate it to regional languages. See draft letter, Ministry of Home Affairs to All Provincial Governments, Chief Commissioners, and Governments of the Union of States and Governments of Hyderabad, Jammu, and Kashmir and Mysore, Ministry of Law, Justice and Company Affairs, f. 16/49/1949/C, NAI. Also see Government of Bombay, Central Department, 'Action necessary to be taken in connection with the New Constitution', File 65/6/33-I of 1950, Maharashtra State Archives, Mumbai.

work should be started at once'.[96] In order to expedite the registration as citizens of persons who have migrated from Pakistan to India the Deputy Commissioners in Assam were instructed 'to print locally the Form of Application for Registration as citizen of India under Article 6 of the Constitution. The Reforms Commissioner also printed and sent additional copies of the forms. The forms were to be given free of charge to intending applicants.'[97]

At the beginning of the preparation of the electoral rolls a confusion arose between refugees' declaration for registration as voters for the purpose of relaxing the 180-day residency requirement and the declaration for registration as citizens stipulated in the draft citizenship article. Despite the adoption of the citizenship provisions, similar uncertainties about citizenship prevailed. The Chief Secretary to the Government of Bombay wrote to the CAS that there were 'several thousand displaced persons – in Bombay City alone there are 28,465 of them', who have not filed the declarations regarding their intention to reside permanently in the town or village concerned.[98] He asked whether in view of the citizenship provisions, 6 (b) (i) and (ii) in particular, and despite not making their declarations they should be enrolled, and whether the necessary relaxation regarding the condition of residence will be made in the Electoral Law. The Officer on Special Duty at the CAS explained: 'displaced persons who may not satisfy condition of 180 days residence ... but are citizens under Article 6(b) (i) or 6(b) (ii) are eligible to be included in electoral rolls. Provision for relaxation of qualification as to residence in relation to displaced persons will be made in electoral law.'[99]

---

[96] Confidential letter No. LRE.824/48/55 from the Reforms Commissioner of Assam to All Deputy Commissioner, Superintendent, Lushai Hills, Political Officers of Frontier Tract and Subdivisional Officers of Karimganj, Hailakandi, and North Cachar Hills, 7 December 1949, CA/1/FR/49-IV, ECIR. The letter included additional detailed directions for the registration process. The Reforms Commissioner also noted that 'it is expected that the number of applications will not be large enough as to justify any special temporary staff in your office for this purpose'. Ibid.

[97] Ibid.

[98] Letter from M. D. Bhat, Chief Secretary Government of Bombay to the Secretary of the Constituent Assembly, 27 December 1949, CA/1/FR/49-IV, ECIR.

[99] S. no. 59, copy of expressed telegram from OSD, S. Subramanian, to Chief Secretary Government of Bombay, 4 January 1950, CA/1/FR/49-IV, ECIR. Indeed, the Representation of the People Bill (Part I) adopted by the Indian parliament in April 1950 stipulated as an exceptional provision in sub-clause 7 of Clause 20 that: 'For the purpose of the electoral rolls first prepared under this Act, a person who is a citizen of India and has migrated from any territory of Pakistan into the territory of India before the 25th day of July, 1949, on account of disturbances or fear of disturbances in his former place of residence shall be deemed to have been ordinarily resident during any period or on any date in the constituency in which he was resident on the said day, or if any other constituency is specified by him in this behalf in the prescribed form and manner, in that other constituency.' Letter No. 34/50-Elec, from P. S. Subramanian,

The public also expressed uncertainties about the final citizenship provisions. Citizens' organisations wrote to the Election Commission of India (ECI) soon after its establishment in March 1950 asking for clarification about the mode of acquiring citizenship. For example, the 'Association for the protection of the rights & privileges of residents in Indian Union from before partition whose ancestral homes or birth places are in Pakistan and who desire to acquire Indian citizenship and to live permanently in India' stated:

[I]t is most deplorable that the Constitution is silent with respect to the mode of acquisition of such rights [citizenship] by a vast number of people who are neither migrants refugees nor displaced persons but who are or whose ancestors came from various places of the Indian Union on various professions business or other callings and settled their and who have not acquired citizenship of any foreign State and who are eagerly wiling to acquire the rights of Indian citizenship and to live there as Indian citizens.[100]

The Secretary of the ECI replied: 'Acquisition and termination of citizenship is not a matter which concerns the Election Commission.'[101] He suggested that the Association make a representation to the Ministry of Home Affairs, and drew their attention to Article 5 (c), which stipulated that a person who has been ordinarily resident in the territory of India for not less than five years preceding the commencement of the constitution shall be a citizen of India.[102]

At the beginning of the work on the electoral rolls, citizens' associations demanded citizenship and even enacted draft citizenship provisions in their struggle to secure a place on the roll. After the adoption of the citizenship article, a place on the electoral roll was sometimes

Secretary ECI to All states (except Jammu and Kashmir and Andaman and Nicobar Islands) (Subject: Preparation of Electoral Rolls under the Representation of the People Bill, 1950, as passed by Parliament), 22 April 1950, 2/50-Elec, ECIR. The date, 25 July 1949, was set to align with the requisite stipulated in article 6(b) (ii) on citizenship, of residency in the territory of India for at least six month prior to filing application under that provision. Clause 20 (1) provided a broader meaning for 'ordinarily resident': 'a person shall be deemed to be ordinarily resident in a constituency if he ordinarily resides in that constituency, or owns, or is in possession of, a dwelling house therein.' Ibid. Clause 21 (a) fixed 'the qualifying date in the case of electoral rolls first prepared under the Act as the first day of March, 1950 [instead of 1 January 1949], and the qualifying period for the said rolls as the period beginning on the first day of April, 1947, and ending on the thirty-first day of December, 1949 [instead of 31 March 1948].' Ibid.

[100] S. no. 1, Resolutions of the Association for the protection of the rights and privileges for long termed India Residents etc., Karimganj, Cachar, 15 May 1950, 28/A/50-Elec (in File CA/1/FR/49-VI), ECIR.

[101] Letter from the Secretary ECI to the Association for the protection of the rights and privileges for long termed India Residents etc., Karimganj (Cachar), 20 June 1950, 28/A/50-Elec (in CA/1/FR/49-VI), ECIR.

[102] Ibid.

used to make a case for citizenship, although inclusion on the roll was not evidence of citizenship.[103] Even a starred question in the parliament, which the Ministry of Law referred to the ECI for a reply, confused the National Register of Citizens with the electoral rolls.[104]

Attempts to make claims for citizenship on the basis of having a place on the electoral roll, and the persisting uncertainties about the relations between being a citizen and a voter were not surprising: The citizenship articles did not define a basic principle for citizenship. They were very detailed and attempted to legislate for every conceivable instance wrought by the vexed movement of people as a result of partition. Thus, while appearing to be comprehensive, the provisions' complex clauses were bound to lead to disputes and challenges of interpretation. Furthermore, faced with continued migration from East Pakistan, the citizenship provisions left open-ended the question of determining citizenship from the day after the Constitution came into force.

The final citizenship articles at the commencement of the constitution did not alter the fundamental principles that underlay the preparation of the first draft electoral rolls. They set 25 July 1949 as the limit of inclusion for citizenship at the commencement of the Constitution, and therefore also for a place on the roll. As for partition refugees, according to the ECI, 8,051 certificates of citizenship were issued to refugees who entered India from West Pakistan.[105] A majority of the refugees in Punjab, however, entered India before 19 July 1948 and automatically became citizens under Article 6. They represented 'the first year's migration and obviously', as Nehru assured the Assembly during the debate on citizenship, 'that huge migration was as a migration of Hindus and Sikhs from Pakistan'.[106] The number of Muslim refugees who left for Pakistan and returned on or after 19 July 1948 on the basis of a permit for resettlement or permanent return is not clear. During the fierce Assembly debate on that provision in August 1949, Nehru said he was told that 'very roughly it may be 2,000 or 3,000' persons.[107]

---

[103] For this dynamics after the enactment of the Citizenship Act (1955) See Roy, *Mapping Citizenship*, p. 75, 'Identifying Citizens: Electoral Rolls, the Right to Vote, and the Election Commission of India', *Election Law Journal*, Vol. 11, No. 2, 2012, pp. 170–86, where she argues that the preparation of rolls 'often become imbricated in contests around citizenship'. Ibid., pp. 170, 177. Also see Roy, *Partitioned Lives*, pp. 15, 130–3.

[104] Starred question for Parliament (Ministry of Law), No. 4311, Shri Jangde, 22 January 1951, 5/7/51-Elec, ECIR.

[105] *Report on the First General Elections in India 1951–52*, Vol. I, New Delhi: Election Commission, 1955, p. 71.

[106] *CAD*, 12 August 1949.

[107] Ibid. On the difficulty of administrating the permit system see Chatterji, 'South Asian Histories of Citizenship'. For the detrimental effect of the permit system on Muslims' citizenship, both purposeful and inadvertent, and its protracted life after the constitution

The limit of inclusion for the first elections set by the deadline of 25 July 1949 also affected the citizenship and voting rights of Bengali refugees who came from Eastern Pakistan after that date. In response to a question in parliament about their franchise rights in February 1951, Ambedkar stated that the government had received representations from Bengali refugees. He explained that enfranchising them would entail 'passing a special law conferring citizenship on them ... and by making special provisions in the Representation of the People Act enabling them to register themselves as voters'. Doing so would mean further delays in the completion and final publication of the electoral rolls, and upset the programme of holding the elections. Ambedkar suggested that 'the number of migrants who would become eligible for voting, in any event, be relatively small'.[108]

Muslims who fled to Pakistan in the wake of partition violence and did not return to India before 19 July 1948 marked another important limit of inclusion. This was reinforced in the future legislation of citizenship by parliament and in amendments to the law.[109] Religion, community, and caste were otherwise divorced from the question of the franchise, which was adopted as universal. But in the context of the undetermined constitutional position, especially on the question of reservations and

---

came into force see Zamindar, *The Long Partition*; Chatterji, 'South Asian Histories of Citizenship', pp. 1062–5.

[108] A reply to a Starred question D No.2290 by Prof. S. N. Misra regarding citizenship and voting rights to (Bengali) migrants from Eastern Pakistan after 25 July 1949 (submitted on 30.12.50), 5 February 1951 (reply), Ministry of Law, Justice and Company Affairs, f. 42(1)/1951/C, NAI. Despite requests from members of the House to give a figure of how many people were in that position, Ambedkar claimed that he did not have an exact figure, but reiterated that their number was relatively small. Irene Tinker, who was in India to research the first election at the time it took place, suggested that generally about two million refugees failed to register for citizenship and were not eligible for the vote, 'though some in fact managed to get themselves registered'. Irene Celeste Tinker, *Representation and Representative Government in the Indian Republic*, PhD thesis, University of London, June 1954, p. 269.

[109] The Citizenship Act of 1955 was enacted by the Indian parliament under article 11 of the constitution. For analyses of the development of legal citizenship immediately after the enactment of the constitution and the imprints of the enduring life of the partition on the legislation and the adjudication of citizenship, and forms of exclusions see Roy, *Mapping Citizenship*, particularly chapter 1, 'Identifying Citizens'; Jayal Gopal, *Citizenship and its Discontents*, particularly pp. 52–81, 295 fn. 28; Also see Zamindar, *The Long Partition*; Chatterji, 'South Asian Histories of Citizenship'; and Roy, *Partitioned Lives*. For the trajectory of Muslims' citizenship after independence see, for example, Ornit Shani, 'Conceptions of Citizenship in India and the "Muslim Question"', *Modern Asian Studies* 44, no. 1, 2010, pp. 145–73; Taylor C. Sherman, *Muslim Belonging In Secular India: Negotiating Citizenship in Postcolonial Hyderabad*, Cambridge: Cambridge University Press, 2015; P. Williams, *Everyday Peace? Politics, Citizenship and Muslim Lives in India*, Chichester, UK: Wiley-Blackwell, 2015.

protective measures for minorities at the time of undertaking the preparation of rolls, these categories became entangled with the electoral roll for the first elections.

Caste, Religion, and the Electoral Roll

Column six in the form of the electoral roll, which the CAS prescribed in its instructions for the preparation of the rolls in March 1948, intended for information on whether the elector was 'Muslim, or Scheduled Caste or Scheduled Tribe or (in Madras and Bombay) Indian Christian'.[110] At the time of issuing the instructions the CAS explained that:

Under the new Constitution, there will be no separate electorates for the different communities; but seats will be reserved in certain constituencies for Muslims, the Scheduled Castes, most of the Scheduled Tribes, and in Madras and Bombay for Indian Christians as well. It will thus be seen that one composite roll for all communities will suffice. As, however, it will be necessary to determine whether a candidate for a reserved seat is a voter belonging to the particular community for which the seat is reserved, a column has been inserted in the form of the electoral roll for recording this information.[111]

The inclusion of a column on caste and religion in the form of the electoral roll for the purpose of reserved seats raised public concerns. As already discussed in Chapter 3, some people and organisations wrote to the CAS, suggesting that the column should be deleted otherwise it 'will not only impede the progress of the nation but will possibly hamper it'.[112] The Jat-Pat Torak Mandal, the society for the breaking of caste among Hindus, wrote to the Home Minister complaining that:

Column of caste and sect are present even in the registers given to Patwaris and other enumerators for this purpose [list of voters]. It is absolutely necessary that these columns must be removed at once if the Government do not wish to face a further dissension of Jat and non Jat or Sikh and Hindu, which can prove more disastrous even than that of Hindus and Muslims.[113]

---

[110] Letter No. CA/64/RR/47, 15 March 1948, CA/1/FR/48-I, ECIR. Also see Press Note, 'Electoral Rolls Under the New Constitution', 15 July 1948, CA/1/FR/48-V. Also see discussion in Chapter 1.

[111] Press Note, 'Electoral Rolls Under the New Constitution', 15 July 1948, CA/1/FR/48-V.

[112] Letter from Gagan Dev Bhandari, Ludhiana, to the President of the Constitution Committee, 4 September 1948, CA/12/FR/48, ECIR. Also see, for example, 'Electoral Rolls', letter from Mr Jagan Nath, Member of the Communal Harmony Board, Ambala District East Punjab to CAS, 20 July 1948, CA/12/FR/48, ECIR.

[113] Letter from the President, Jat Pat Torak Mandal to the Minister of Home Affairs, 14 June 1948, CA/12/FR/48, ECIR.

In a follow-up letter, the organisation urged 'to issue instructions to all the Provincial Governments to omit or delete the column of caste from the electoral rolls and not to compel voters to have their castes registered in the rolls.'[114]

The CAS wrote to the Jat Pat Torak Mandal, iterating its explanation in its instructions letter.[115] The Jat Pat Torak Mandal, nonetheless, persisted and asked of the CAS to clarify 'for the guidance of the public' whether it is 'an offence punishable under law for a Hindu not to believe in caste system and refuse to state it for registration in Electoral rolls'.[116] Their letter pointed out that during the 1931 census, following their requests, enumerators were instructed 'not to record the caste of those Hindus who did not believe in it'.[117] They requested to know 'what is the attitude of the National Government in this connection?'[118] The CAS wrote back clarifying that: 'information regarding "communities", "caste", and "religion" is not to be included in the electoral rolls now under preparation except in the case of a person who is a Muslim, a member of a Scheduled Caste or of a Scheduled tribe, or is in the Province of Madras or the Province of Bombay and is Christian, and for whom seats are reserved'.[119]

The undecided constitutional future of reservations for minorities meant that for the time being some community categories were included in the form of the electoral roll. Sometimes this led to obstructions in the registration of voters. For example, the CAS received letters from various Gurdwaras (Sikh Temples) committees, complaining that in Delhi 'the Municipal Staff deputed to prepare lists of voters for the next elections are refusing to enter Sikhs as such in the column

---

[114] Letter from the President, Jat Pat Torak Mandal to the Minister of Home Affairs, 28 July 1948, CA/12/FR/48, ECIR.

[115] Letter from CAS to the President, Jat Pat Torak Mandal, 31 August 1948, CA/12/FR/48, ECIR. In mid-August, the Election Commissioner East Punjab addressed the issue with the CAS.

[116] Letter from the President, Jat Pat Torak Mandal to the CAS, 6 September 1948, CA/12/FR/48, ECIR.

[117] Ibid. The Jat Pat Torak Mandal was a wing of the Arya Samaj. On the Jat Pat Torak Mandal campaign against the inclusion of the caste column already a head of the 1931 Census see U. Kalpagam, *Rule by Numbers: Governmentality in Colonial India*, London: Lexington Books p. 222 fn. 151. Also see R. S. Maheshwari, *The Census Administration under the Raj and After*, New Delhi: Concept Publishing Company, 1996, pp. 106–10. It was the Jat Pat Torak Mandal that cancelled their invitation to B. R. Ambedkar in 1936 when he sent them in advance the text of his planned lecture, 'The Annihilation of Caste'.

[118] Letter from the President, Jat Pat Torak Mandal to the CAS, 6 September 1948, CA/12/FR/48, ECIR.

[119] Draft letter from the CAS to the President, Jat Pat Torak Mandal, 13 September 1948, CA/12/FR/48, ECIR.

provided for religion ... [and] that all Sikhs are being forcibly entered as Hindus'.[120] This letter, from the Secretary Gurdwara Parbandhak Committee Delhi Province, claimed that officials (enumerators) told Sikh voters that 'they have been instructed by the higher authorities to enter all Sikhs as Hindus'.[121] He wrote that 'much resentment now prevails among the Sikh public on account of this highhanded injustice', and demanded that 'all lists prepared upto [sic] now should be cancelled forthwith. Fresh lists should be ordered, and for this purpose Sikh clerks, or Sikh volunteers from the public should accompany those entrusted with the task of preparing the lists of voters.'[122] The Secretary warned that '[i]f no action is taken, the responsibility for the agitation that may follow will rest entirely on the authorities concerned'.[123] The President of the Shironani Gurdwara Parbandhak Committee, Amritsar, sent a similar complaint, stating that 'we feel that it is a deliberate attempt of the Congress Government to finish up Sikhs as a political force'.[124]

In its discussion of the matter the CAS decided that since it was not yet known whether there would be also reserved seats for Sikhs, the column relating to religion in the electoral rolls under preparation for Delhi Province had to be retained.[125] The CAS issued instructions to the Chief Commissioner of Delhi 'that Sikhs should be described as Sikhs and should not be registered as "Hindus" in the Electoral Rolls now under

---

[120] Letter from the Secretary Gurdwara Parbandhak Committee Delhi Province to Dr Yudh Vir Singh, President of Delhi Municipality, 22 September 1948, CA/12/FR/48, ECIR. Also see CA/29/Const/48, ECIR. The letter was passed on to the CAS.

[121] Ibid.

[122] Ibid.

[123] Ibid. The Committee sent a similar letter to the Home Minister on 29 September 1948.

[124] Letter from the Presidents of the Shironani Gurdwara Parbandhak Committee Amritsar to the Home Minister, 8 October 1948, CA/12/FR/48, ECIR. Also see letter from the Secretary of the Sikh Sangat Minto Road, Sat Sang Committee, Gurdwara Mata Sundari Jee, New Delhi, 7 October 1948, CA/12/FR/48, ECIR. The Managing Editor of *The Panth Weekly* also sent a letter and a newspaper report in the matter to the Secretary of the Home Department. Letter from the Managing Editor *Panth Weekly* to the Secretary of the Home Department, 9 October 1948. The attached newspaper report was from 6 October 1948. A reply from the Ministry of Law informed the *Panth* editor that his letter was passed to the Secretariat of the Constituent Assembly for disposal. Letter from the Law Ministry to the Managing Editor *Panth Weekly*, 2 November 1948, CA/12/FR/48, ECIR.

[125] Internal notes, 1 October 1948, CA/12/FR/48, ECIR. The Under Secretary noted that they do not know as yet what would be the future constitution of the Delhi Province. 'If the recommendation of the Ad hoc Committee on Chief Commissioners' Provinces be adopted by the Constituent Assembly then there may be a Provincial Legislature for Delhi Province and provisions relating to reservation of seats for Muslims and Scheduled Castes will also apply to such Legislature.'

preparation and that immediate steps should be taken to correct the rolls already prepared accordingly'.[126]

While in Delhi Sikhs were registered as Hindus, in East Punjab, the Election Commissioner reported that he received complaints from many districts that 'Harijans [Scheduled Castes] were being coerced into getting themselves registered in electoral rolls as Sikhs.'[127] He asked the Deputy Commissioners to 'examine all such complaints and take strong action when the complaints were found to be true. A press note was also issued asking the public to bring all such cases to the notice of Government to enable it to take suitable action.'[128]

Difficulties, moreover, arose because administrators could not always determine who belonged to the Scheduled Castes (SCs) or the Scheduled Tribes (STs). This was particularly the case for the areas comprising the integrated states. This problem coincided in January 1949 with the Ministry of Home Affairs request of the various governments to draw up and publish in the local gazette before the end of 1949 lists of Scheduled Castes (SCs), Scheduled Tribes (STs), and of Other Backward Classes who are nevertheless educationally and economically backward.[129] Thus, the Government of the Central Provinces and Berar reported to the CAS that:

Some difficulty was experienced at the start [of preparation of rolls] as to the Scheduled Castes and Scheduled Tribes to be adopted for the areas transferred to this province on the abolition of Chhattisgarh States. The question has been referred to the Government of India, Ministry of States (copy enclosed) separately. Till final orders are passed the Deputy Commissioner of those districts has been instructed to adopt the list obtaining in the adjoining districts area comprised in the integrated States.[130]

---

[126] Internal notes, 3 December 1948, CA/12/FR/48, ECIR. Initially the CAS asked the Delhi Chief Commissioner for clarifications. It sent him four reminder letters in the matter to no avail (letters of 4 October 1948, 26 October 1948, 19 November 1948, and on 8 January 1949). It ultimately issued the instructions after speaking by phone with his office.

[127] 'Fortnightly Report on the progress made and difficulties encountered in the preparation of electoral rolls, for the 2nd fortnight of September, 1948', from M. R. Bhide, Election Commissioner, East Punjab to the Joint Secretary, CAS, 16 October 1948, CA/1/FR/48-III, ECIR.

[128] Ibid.

[129] See reference to the Ministry of Home Affairs letter (No. 51/1/49-Public) of 6 January 1949 in: letter from the Chief Commissioner of Coorg to the Deputy Secretary to the Government of India, Ministry of Home Affairs, 14 February 1950, 2/50 Elec, ECIR. This was as part of the preparation for the future census.

[130] Letter from the Deputy Secretary to the Government of the Central Provinces and Berar to the Secretary of the Constituent Assembly, 21 April 1949, CA/1/FR/49-III, ECIR.

The Deputy Secretary to the Central Provinces and Berar government explained that the problem has arisen because the relevant constitutional provisions 'as they stand, as present, in the Draft Constitution, are not applicable to the areas of the integrated States'.[131] Similarly, the Government of Rajasthan asked to know the criteria 'for treating a class as a depressed class'.[132] Members of the CAS indeed noted in their discussion of the question that 'the Draft Constitution does not seem to lay down the names of Scheduled Tribes and Scheduled Castes in respect of the States specified in Part III of the First Schedule and as such it is for the Government of Rajasthan to take a decision in this matter'.[133]

The Constituent Assembly settled the question of reservations for minorities only on 26 May 1949, more than a year after the CAS issued the instructions for the preparation of the electoral rolls. The Assembly decided to abolish the reservations of seats for religious minorities. The decision was taken on the basis of the Advisory Committee report on the subject of certain political safeguards for minorities. Reservations for the SCs and the STs were retained, and the Assembly accepted the Committee's recommendation to include, as an exception, in the list of the SCs for East Punjab four groups among the Sikhs.[134]

But adopting that constitutional decision, and dealing with its effects on the preliminary electoral rolls at that advanced stage of their preparation was not straightforward. Moreover, the matter lingered. In discussing a query from the Government of West Bengal about the implications of the decision to abolish reservations for minorities, the CAS's Under Secretary commented:

---

[131] Letter from the Government of the Central Provinces and Berar to the Ministry of States, 8 February 1949, CA/1/FR/49-III, ECIR. The letter referred to the tribes specified in part VII of the Eighth Schedule for the purpose of article 392, and to the castes in Part VII of the Schedule to the Government of India (Scheduled Castes) Order, 1936, for the purpose of article 242. Two lists showing the tribes and castes recommended by the Deputy Commissioners concerned to be specified as SCs and STs in relation to the integrated states in the Central Provinces and Berar were attached to the letter.

[132] S. no 131, 31 January 1949–4 February 1949, CA/1/FR/49-II, ECIR.

[133] Ibid. It was also pointed out that SCs were not enumerated in the 1941 census in Rajputana states while the Tribes, namely Bhils, Girrasias, Merats, Minas, and Rewats, which form the tribal population of Rajasthan, were enumerated.

[134] 'Motion passed by the Constituent Assembly on the 26th May, 1949 on the Report submitted by the Advisory Committee on the subject of certain political safeguards for minorities', CA/1/FR/49-III, ECIR. The four Sikh groups were the Mazhabis, Ramdasis, Kabirpanthis and Sikligars. For an analysis of the debate see, for example, Rochana Bajpai, *Debating Difference: Group Rights and Liberal Democracy in India*, New Delhi: Oxford University Press, 2011, pp. 31–170; Shabnum Tejani, *Indian Secularism: A Social and Intellectual History, 1890–1950*, Bloomington & Indianapolis: Indiana University Press, 2008, pp. 244–65.

I do not see any purpose in including in the electoral rolls information relating to castes. This information is required only in relation to candidates who contest the seats reserved for the Scheduled castes or the Scheduled Tribes... Since the inclusion in the electoral rolls of information about castes serves no other purpose and since the policy of the Government is to omit all references to caste in all government records except where such inclusion is absolutely necessary, we may inform the Government of West Bengal that there it is no longer necessary to include in the electoral rolls now under preparation any information relating to castes.[135]

In early August, following the CAS's consultation with the Constitutional Adviser and with the Minister of Law it was decided that 'the column in the electoral rolls giving information about the Scheduled Caste and Scheduled Tribes need not be included in the copies to be printed for publication'.[136] This was indeed in accordance with the recommendation of the Sub-Committee of the Diwakar Committee at the time to discontinue the mentioning of caste 'with respect to recruitment to services, admission to educational institutions, hospitals, courts, electoral rolls etc.'.[137] Yet, no action was taken in the immediate.

Only on 5 October 1949, however, did the CAS's Joint Secretary send a circular letter to the governments of provinces, states, and union of states, stating in reference to their instruction letter of 15 March 1948 that: 'it has since been decided that column 5 [6] containing information about the religion, caste and tribe need not be included in the copies of the electoral rolls to be printed'.[138] He asked that 'if there is still time to do so this column may be wholly omitted from the

---

[135] S. no. 84, 2–5 July 1949, CA/1/FR/49-III, ECIR. The Under Secretary referred to a letter from the Deputy Secretary to the Government of West Bengal to the Joint Secretary of CAS, 29 June 1949, CA/1/FR/49-III, ECIR. The Joint Secretary suggested on the basis of this reasoning that 'the column relating to religion, caste, or tribe may be wholly omitted from the copies of the electoral rolls to be sent to the presses for the purpose of printing'. Letter from the Joint Secretary of CAS to Deputy Secretary Government of West Bengal, 6 July 1949, CA/1/FR/49-III, ECIR. Thereafter, however, he sent a telegram asking the Deputy Secretary to the Government of West Bengal to postpone action until hearing from the CAS again.

[136] S. no. 97–98, 5 August 1949, CA/1/FR/49-III, ECIR. A note for order was later put forward asking 'whether we should inform the various Provincial and State Govts. to drop the Scheduled Caste column from the electoral roll prescribed by us, in the copies of the electoral rolls to be printed for publication'. S. no. 99–100, 29 August 1949, CA/1/FR/49-III, ECIR.

[137] 'Mention of Caste Not Favoured: Sub-Committee's Views', TOI, 24 September 1949, p. 12. The Sub-Committee was appointed to examine the various forms the central and provincial governments use for official purposes.

[138] Letter from Joint Secretary of CAS to the governments of provinces, states and Union of States, 5 October 1949, CA/1/FR/49-III, ECIR. The relevant column was column 6. A week later the CAS sent a circular correction letter. See letter from CAS, 12 October 1949, CA/1/FR/49-III, ECIR.

copies of the electoral rolls to be sent to the press for the printing and publication'.[139] Yet at the same time, the CAS asked that information regarding the number of SCs and STs voters should be preserved. It may be required, the Joint Secretary explained, 'if it is decided to have the allocation [of seats in parliament] on the basis of the number of voters instead of population'.[140] A month later the CAS asked of all the provincial and state governments for a statement showing the total number of the SCs and STs brought on the draft electoral rolls once the preliminary electoral rolls are completed[141] This was for the purpose of the impending work on the allocation of seats in the House of the People under the new Constitution.

The directions to omit column six from the form of electoral roll did not of course make caste and religion less relevant in India's ensuing electoral politics. In the immediate, too, caste and religion did not just vanish from the electoral rolls. This became clear once the CAS examined the sample forms of electoral rolls and reports provincial and state governments sent.

East Punjab already had printed rolls. The Chief Secretary to the Government of Bihar reported that they used 'M' to indicate Muslim, 'Ha' for Harijan (SCs), 'A' for Anusuchita banjati (STs), 'Hi' for Hindu, 'I' for Isai (Christian) and the mark of a dagger for a female elector. He explained that this was done on the basis of Rules 6 and 7 of the Bihar Legislative Assembly Electoral (Preparation, Revision and Publication of Electoral Rolls) Rules, 1936; and that these symbols and

---

[139] Letter from Joint Secretary of CAS to the governments of provinces, states and Union of States, 5 October 1949, CA/1/FR/49-III, ECIR. It was explained that this information would be required only for determining the eligibility of candidates contesting reserved seats for the SCs and STs.

[140] Ibid. At that time it was thought that the representation of the SCs and STs in the first elections could not be determined on the basis of the ensuing census. The reason was that the reference date for the census was set for 1 March 1951, and the plan at that point was to hold the general elections in the winter of 1950–51. S. no. 4, 9 November 1949, CA/17/FR/49, ECIR. Ultimately, the reservation of seats was decided on the basis of the population of the SCs and the STs as determined by the Census Commissioner to the Government of India, under sub-rule (2) of rule 5 of the Constitution (Determination of Population) Order, 1950, and not on the basis of their numbers on the electoral roll, as the CAS initially contemplated. The information about the voters belonging to the SCs and STs, however, was still necessary to know the concentration of those castes and tribes to reserve seats for them where they mostly concentrated. S. no. 23–27, 23 November 1950, 14/50-Elec I, ECIR.

[141] Letter No. CA/2/FR/49 from Joint Secretary of CAS to All provincial and state governments (Subject: Allocation of seats in the House of the People under the new Constitution), 9 November 1949, 2/50-Elec, ECIR. The CAS sent another request for this information on 21 December 1949. Letter No. CA 2/49-Elec, 21 December 1949, 2/50-Elec, ECIR.

abbreviations used to indicate franchise qualifications.[142] He also commented that 'similar provisions of law will presumably be enacted under the Constitution of India'.[143] Because half of the Bihar rolls were already printed, the CAS decided that 'in the circumstances explained, we have no objection to the electoral rolls for the first elections being printed with symbols and abbreviations to indicate the religion or caste of voters'.[144] The CAS explained, however, that it was not necessary to include provisions for the use of symbol and abbreviations in the new electoral law since elections under the new Constitution would be held on the basis of a joint electorate. The Government of Madras, as another example, asked to retain the column relating to communities 'as it will facilitate identification and effective check'.[145] The CAS agreed to that, and to the Government of Orissa's marking the SC and ST voters by the symbols 'Sh' and 'B' respectively.[146]

The CAS explained from the outset that under the new Constitution there will be no separate electorates, and that therefore one composite roll for all communities will suffice. At the same time, because of the unsettled constitutional position on reservations and safeguards for minorities, a column for the designation of caste, religion, and tribe was included in the form of electoral roll. Then, at a very late stage of the work, when some governments embarked on the printing of the electoral rolls, the CAS directed to delete this column. Nonetheless, it asked the governments of the provinces and the states to continue collecting and preserving the information about the number of SCs and STs voters. All that, and the absence of an electoral law, which stipulated detailed procedures and blueprint forms based on universal franchise, made the task of removing the mark of caste and religion from the draft electoral rolls difficult to achieve. Column six that included this information, though, was omitted from the preliminary rolls that were published for the public to file claims and objections.

Besides, attempts to keep caste on the roll were made by SC organisations, demanding that 'clear designation about them should be given in

---

[142] Letter from the Chief Secretary Government of Bihar to CAS, 6 January 1950, CA/1/FR/49-IV, ECIR. The Chief Secretary claimed that this form and content of the electoral rolls that were printed or in Press were approved by the CAS.

[143] Ibid.

[144] Letter from OSD, P. S. Subramanian, CAS, to the Chief Secretary Government of Bihar ('Deletion of the column relating to religion or caste in electoral rolls under the New Constitution'), 19 January 1950, CA/1/FR/49-IV, ECIR. Also see the CAS's discussion: S. no 61, 14 January 1950, CA/1/FR/49-IV, ECIR.

[145] S. no. 10, 29 October – 8 November 1949, CA/1/FR/49-IV, ECIR.

[146] S. no. 3, 4, 6, 20 January 1950, CA/17/FR/49 ECIR.

the electoral rolls'.[147] In 1950, in the context of the work on the delimitation of constituencies and the allocation of reserved seats for the SCs and
the STs ahead of the first elections, SC organisations requested to ratify
the omission of a distinguishing mark for the SC voters. The President
of the District Valmiki Subha, Kapurthala in PEPSU (Patiala and East
Punjab Union States), for example, sent a petition on behalf of the SCs
voters stating that the omission of a distinguishing mark:

[M]ade it impossible for us to find out the number of such voters and confirm
their ration with others. This omission ... will certainly adversely affect the
decision of the Delimitation Committee... The Scheduled Caste community
is at a loss to understand as to on what data the Delimitation Committee has
been asked to work and if any secret instructions have been issued to them...
Is it to convert the majority into minority, where the Scheduled Castes are in
a majority?[148]

Allegations were also made at the time that 'certain clever "devices" have
been adopted for decreasing the number of Scheduled Tribes and their
representation in the various legislatures'.[149]

The Chief Election Commissioner's reply to such complaints leaned
on the CAS's original directions from a year earlier. He clarified:

It was in October, 1949, that the Constituent Assembly Secretariat directed the
State Governments that information about religion or tribe should be deleted
from the printed copies of the electoral rolls, but should be included in the
manuscript copy of the rolls so that the total number of such persons may be
ascertained for reserving seats for them. The Commission also agreed with the
view of the Constituent Assembly Secretariat that information about religion
or caste of a voter was not required, as under the new Constitution, every voter
irrespective of his religion, caste or creed is eligible to exercise his vote for the
election to a general as well as a reserved seat. There appears to be insufficient
appreciation of the constitutional position in this respect.[150]

---

[147] 'Scheduled Castes in India Demand For Ministry', *TOI*, 5 August 1949, p. 5. This was
in the context of a demand for a separate Ministry in the Central Government for SCs
and STs as part of a resolution of members of the Constituent Assembly representing
the SCs and the STs.

[148] Letter from Jagjit Singh Bhandari, President, District Valmiki Subha, Kapurthala, to
The Honourable Shri Jagjivan Ram, Labour Minister, Government of India. The let-
ter was passed on to the Chief Election Commissioner. See letter from Jagjivan Ram,
Minister for Labour, Government of India, 18 December 1950, 14/50-Elec I, ECIR.

[149] Letter from Sukumar Sen, Chief Election Commissioner to Dharma Vira, Principal
Private Secretary to the Prime Minister, 19 December 1950, 14/50-Elec I, ECIR. Also
see for a similar request from STs: ECI discussions of two letters from Shri Rajkumar
Lal, Ranchi, on the 'inclusion of Christian aboriginals among the Scheduled Tribes'.
S. no. 23–27, 24 August–23 November 1950, 14/50-Elec I, ECIR.

[150] Letter from Sukumar Sen, Chief Election Commissioner to The Honourable Shri
Jagjivan Ram, Minister of Labour, 23 December 1950, 14/50-Elec I, ECIR.

The Chief Election Commissioner emphasised that an entry in the electoral rolls could not 'under any circumstance be accepted as sufficient or even *prima facia* [sic] proof' that a voter belongs to a SCs.[151]

It can be argued on the basis of the many requests of SC organisations to restore their designated place on the electoral roll that there was, in fact, plenty of appreciation of the constitutional position, and of the political prospect of the right to vote. In a sense, precisely because people from the margins found meaning and a place for themselves in the new polity based on universal adult franchise, they also understood the potential new power of making group identity claims. The SCs and STs turned into voters and could now, under universal franchise, fully partake in the compulsions of electoral politics. The categorisations of community and caste for policy purposes and special minority group rights had been, since colonial time, opened to political negotiations, changing and determined in political struggles.[152] The universal franchise for a mass electorate opened a far broader scope for people to see themselves as minorities, and to enter into political negotiations on that basis.[153]

Thus, the making of universal adult franchise on a basis of a joint electorate, and the bureaucratisation of the principle of procedural equality for all adults for the purpose of authorising their government did not forestall the retention of conservative social structures for the purpose of political representation. Paradoxically, the successful implementation of

[151] Ibid. He noted that the electoral rolls 'have been, and will in future be, prepared mostly by village Patwaris, and it is undesirable and risky to leave it to that class of officials to decide finally whether a particular voter belongs to a Scheduled Caste or not'. Ibid. This form of reply was rehearsed in response to similar queries and grievances at the time. See, for example, draft response of the secretary of the ECI to a Starred question for Parliament (Ministry of Law), No. 4311 (Shri Jangde, 22 January 1951), 13 February 1951, 5/7/51-Elec, ECIR.

[152] See, for example, B. Cohn, 'The Census, Social Structure and Objectification in South Asia', in *An Anthropologist among the Historians and Other Essays*, Delhi: Oxford University Press, 1987, pp. 224–54; Nicholas B. Dirks, *Castes of Mind: Colonialism and the Making of Modern India*, Princeton, NJ: Princeton University Press, 2001; Susan Bayly, *The New Cambridge History of India: Caste, Society and Politics in India from the Eighteenth Century to the Modern Age*, Cambridge: Cambridge University Press, 1999; Christophe Jaffrelot, *India's Silent Revolution. The Rise of the Lower Castes in North India*, London: Hurst & Company, 2003; Ornit Shani, *Communalism, Caste and Hindu Nationalism: The Violence in Gujarat*, Cambridge: Cambridge University Press, 2007, chapter 2; Shani, 'The Politics of Communalism and Caste', in Isabelle Clark-Decès (ed.), *A Companion to the Anthropology of India*, Malden: Wiley-Blackwell, 2011, pp. 297–312; Zoya Hasan, *Politics of Inclusion: Caste, Minorities and Affirmative Action*, New Delhi: Oxford University Press, 2009.

[153] This is suggestive of Pierre Rosanvallon's discussion of the change that occurred in democracies, whereby people see themselves as minorities. Pierre Rosanvallon, *Democratic Legitimacy, Impartiality, Reflexivity, Proximity*. Translated by Arthur Goldhammer. Princeton: Princeton University Press, 2011, pp. 3–4.

universal franchise by the time the constitution came into force enabled the insertion of social identities into the design of political representation. Here lay the seeds of the dynamic caste and identity politics, which have marked the development of electoral politics in India, and which have posited over the years challenges to its democracy. This was demonstrated clearly once electoral politics came into play after the edifice of electoral democracy was institutionalised. The politics of ticket distribution for parliamentary and state Assembly seats ahead of the first elections on the basis of 'a fair deal to the minorities' demonstrated clearly these dynamics.[154] This notion underlay both parties' strategies for ticket distribution before the elections, and the structure of claims for representation that contestants to seats made to political parties.[155] Social and cultural structure that is changeable would shift in major ways in the course of the life of India's democracy with the unfolding possibilities the universal franchise brought for the arena of electoral politics, but will do so in ways that attempt to protect basic interests and only slowly and in the face of political and socio-economic pressures.

Conclusion

The constitutional restrictions on the franchise, and the implications of the Constitution makers' late decisions on the impending questions of citizenship and reserved seats for minorities defined the limits of exclusion. But their long-term trajectories, I suggest, were consequential for the future life of democracy in India. The exclusion from franchise in the North-East, the delimitations on citizenship as defined at the commencement of the constitution, and the possibilities that the universal franchise opened up for community and identity politics more broadly, informed conflicts and challenges that would beset India's democracy.

While the Constitution makers were dealing with the making of India's democracy in the abstract, debating principles and theories, the Constituent Assembly Secretariat was hands-on in the implementation process of core elements of democracy, outpacing notions prescribed by constitutional theory. In doing so, the Secretariat's principal imperative from the outset, as previous chapters showed, was to be inclusive.

[154] See for example, representation of 20 Sikhs before the President of the Central Parliamentary Board, Indian National Congress of 27 November 1951; letter from the Delhi Milkmen Association, Sikandrabad Western Constituency to the President, All India Congress Committee (undated), f. 4351 All India Congress Committee (AICC) papers, Nehru Memorial and Museum Library (NMML), New Delhi.

[155] For a detailed study see Ornit Shani, 'Embedding Democracy: The Social History of India's First Elections' (forthcoming).

In putting universal franchise into action they found ways of enrolling refugees who did not qualify according to the draft provisions, and they made sure to include servants sleeping on balconies and staircases, and vagrants living in illegally erected huts. As a member of the CAS noted: 'As the fresh elections are to be conducted on adult franchise basis such persons cannot be deprived of their franchise.'[156]

The large-scale inclusion and the creation of a mass electorate became tangible as fortnightly reports from the provinces and the states containing the summary of the number of voters enrolled began arriving at the CAS in late 1949. The flow of numbers, which ultimately added up to more than 17 Crores pushed through the frontiers of the world's democratic imagination, and gave birth to its largest democracy.

Appendix 6.I

Part II Citizenship (Article 5 in the Constitution of India 1949)

Note: Available at http://indiankanoon.org/doc/237570/ (accessed 21 March 2015).

5. Citizenship at the commencement of the Constitution At the commencement of this Constitution every person who has his domicile in the territory of India and
   (a) who was born in the territory of India; or
   (b) either of whose parents was born in the territory of India; or

---

[156] S. no. 88, 26 March–9 April 1949, CA/1/FR/49-I, ECIR. Despite the CAS's imperative to be inclusive, various forms of administrative disenfranchisement occurred. As already mentioned in Chapter 1, despite the efforts to register women in their own name and to secure their place in the electoral rolls, a large number of women did not register as individuals, by their name and were ultimately excluded from voting in the first elections. The CEC estimated that out of a total of nearly 80 million women voters in the country, nearly 2.8 million eventually failed to disclose their name, and the entries relating to them had to be deleted from the rolls. *Report on the First General Election in India*, p. 73. There were other defects with the first electoral roll. A notable one came to light in 1951 in Rajasthan. The Government of Rajasthan informed the ECI at the time of the preparation of the supplementary rolls that 'a number of villages had been left out of enumeration'. But the commission decided that 'there was no sufficient time for the completion of the revisions of the roll before the commencement of the poll in the state' in accordance with clause (a) of section 25 of the Representation of the People Act, 1950. See note by the Secretary of the Election Commission of India to the Ministry of Law, 19 February 1952, 1/22/51, ECIR. According to some of the correspondence there were a few hundred missing villages in Rajasthan. The ECI instructed the Rajasthan government to include the 'missing villages' on the rolls during the annual revision of the electoral roll in 1952. Ibid. Also see *Report on the First General Election in India*, p. 79.

(c) who has been ordinarily resident in the territory of India for not less than five years preceding such commencement, shall be a citizen of India.

6. Rights of citizenship of certain persons who have migrated to India from Pakistan Notwithstanding anything in Article 5, a person who has migrated to the territory of India from the territory now included in Pakistan shall be deemed to be a citizen of India at the commencement of this Constitution if

(a) he or either of his parents or any of his grand parents was born in India as defined in the Government of India Act, 1935 (as originally enacted); and

(b)

(i) in the case where such person has so migrated before the nineteenth day of July, 1948, he has been ordinarily resident in the territory of India since the date of his migration, or

(ii) in the case where such person has so migrated on or after the nineteenth day of July, 1948, he has been registered as a citizen of India by an officer appointed in that behalf by the Government of the Dominion of India on an application made by him therefor to such officer before the commencement of this Constitution in the form and manner prescribed by that Government: Provided that no person shall be so registered unless he has been resident in the territory of India or at least six months immediately preceding the date of his application.

7. Rights of citizenship of certain migrants to Pakistan Notwithstanding anything in Articles 5 and 6, a person who has after the first day of March, 1947, migrated from the territory of India to the territory now included in Pakistan shall not be deemed to be a citizen of India: Provided that nothing in this article shall apply to a person who, after having so migrated to the territory now included in Pakistan, has returned to the territory of India under a permit for resettlement or permanent return issued by or under the authority of any law and every such person shall for the purposes of clause (b) of Article 6 be deemed to have migrated to the territory of India after the nineteenth day of July, 1948

8. Rights of citizenship of certain persons of India origin residing outside India Notwithstanding anything in Article 5, any person who or either of whose parents or any of whose grand parents was born in India as defined in the Government of India Act, 1935 (as originally enacted), and who is ordinarily residing in any country outside India as so defined shall be deemed to be a citizen of India if he has been registered as a citizen of India by the diplomatic or consular

representative of India in the country where he is for the time being residing on an application made by him therefor to such diplomatic or consular representative, whether before or after the commencement of this Constitution, in the form and manner prescribed by the Government of the Dominion of India or the Government of India

9. Person voluntarily acquiring citizenship of a foreign State not to be citizens No person shall be a citizen of India by virtue of Article 5, or be deemed to be a citizen of India by virtue of Article 6 or Article 8, if he has voluntarily acquired the citizenship of any foreign State

10. Continuance of the rights of citizenship Every person who is or is deemed to be a citizen of India under any of the foregoing provisions of this Part shall, subject to the provisions of any law that may be made by Parliament, continue to be such citizen

11. Parliament to regulate the right of citizenship by law. Nothing in the foregoing provisions of this Part shall derogate from the power of Parliament to make any provision with respect to the acquisition and termination of citizenship and all other matters relating to citizenship.

Conclusion

A 17 Crore and 220 Yard Democracy

I was myself calculating one day the thickness of the volume of the electoral roll for all the Provinces and I found that it will come to nearly three-fourths of a furlong [220 Yard].

(Rajendra Prasad, *Constituent Assembly Debates*, 7 October 1949)[1]

'[B]ut is it realized that you have drawn up a Constitution for 340 millions of people? Look at the magnitude or the size of your State and its people. Has it any parallel in the world? Has any other country, and other State in the world got such a municipality [sic] of problems, of such complexity and diversity as we have got'

(Lakshmi Kanta Maitra, *Constituent Assembly Debates*, 18 November 1949)[2]

[I]n many respects, the political imagination is a reality unto itself, a self-creating reality that can supersede other realities, thus constituting a major part of the political universe.

(Yaron Ezrahi, *Imagined Democracies*)[3]

From October 1949 onwards the CAS received reports from across India on the final number of voters registered on the first draft electoral rolls. The Government of Bihar reported that 'the *provisional* total number of electors' enrolled was 19,682,852.[4] The Government of West Bengal registered 11,657,767 voters.[5] In Madras nearly 26,000,000

---

[1] *CAD*, 7 October 1949. Available on http://parliamentofindia.nic.in/ls/debates/vol1p5.htm (accessed 15 December 2016) All references to the *CAD* hereunder are taken from this source.

[2] *CAD*, 18 November 1949.

[3] Yaron Ezrahi, *Imagined Democracies: Necessary Political Fictions*. Cambridge: Cambridge University Press, 2012, p. 170.

[4] Letter from the Chief Secretary to the Government of Bihar to the Joint Secretary of CAS, 3 December 1949, 2/50 Elec, ECIR. Their letter noted that the actual total would be known after the completion of the preparation of fair copies of the rolls for the press. The final size of the electorate in Bihar after the ultimate preparation of supplementary lists and the revisions after the filing of claims and objections was 18,080,181. See Election Commission of India, *Key Highlights of General Elections, 1951 to the First Lok Sabha*, Election Commission of India, New Delhi, p. 4.

[5] Letter from the Joint Secretary to the Government of West Bengal to the Joint Secretary of CAS, 24 January 1950, 2/50 Elec, ECIR. The final size of the electorate was 12,500,475. *Key Highlights*, p. 4.

voters were enumerated.[6] In the Central Provinces and Berar the total number of voters was 11,572,444.[7] The Government of Orissa provided an estimate of 7,500,000 voters.[8] It reported in early January 1950 that the nine printing centres across the province already produced 82,130 pages of electoral rolls out of the 132,206 pages to be printed, which formed 62.1 per cent of the province's rolls.[9] 15,000,000 voters were reported from Bombay.[10] In Mysore, the total number of persons enfranchised reached 3,701,920.[11] The East Punjab Government reported a total of 5,861,423 electors.[12] The United State of Saurashtra estimated an enrolment of approximately 1,628,377 voters.[13] The Government of Madhya Bharat enumerated 3,836,763 electors.[14] Some states sent the statements of the number of voters they enrolled shortly after the

---

[6] This was the case already in May 1949. Letter from the Additional Secretary to the Government of Madras to the Secretary to the Government of India, Ministry of Law, 25 May 1949, CA/18/FR/49, ECIR. The final size of the electorate was 26,980,961. *Key Highlights*, p. 4.

[7] Report from the Government of Central Provinces and Berar on the progress of preparation of electoral rolls, 22 December 1949, CA/1/FR/49-IV, ECIR. The final size of the electorate in then Madhya Pradesh was 11,075,140. *Key Highlights*, p. 4.

[8] Letter from the Government of Orissa, Home (Election) Department to the Joint Secretary of CAS, 3 September 1949, CA/1/FR/49-III, ECIR. The final size of the electorate was 7,708,161. *Key Highlights*, p. 4.

[9] Letter from the Government of Orissa, Home (Election) Department to the Joint Secretary of CAS, 3 January 1950, CA/1/FR/49-IV, ECIR.

[10] 'Bombay's Electoral Rolls Ready', *The Hindustan Times*, 14 January 1950, p. 9. The final size of the electorate in Bombay was 16,789,609. *Key Highlights*, p. 4.

[11] Letter from the Legal Remembrancer and Secretary to Government, Law Department Mysore to the Joint Secretary of CAS, 29 November 1949, 2/50-Elec, ECIR. The letter included an eight-page statement of the number of persons brought on the rolls according to districts and for each district for town and urban areas. The numbers were in reference to 1 January 1948 for the age of voters. The Mysore Government was in the process of revising the rolls with reference to 1 January 1949. The final size of the electorate was 3,969,735. *Key Highlights*, p. 4.

[12] Letter from the Election Commissioner, East Punjab to the Joint Secretary of CAS, 19 October 1949, CA/1/FR/49-IV, ECIR. In April 1950 the Election Commissioner, Punjab sent a detailed revised table of number of voters by Districts and Thana. The final size of the electorate in Punjab after thorough revisions was 6,718,345. *Key Highlights*, p. 4.

[13] Letter from the Chief Secretary, United State of Saurashtra, to the Joint Secretary of CAS, 30 November 1949, (CA/3/FR/49) in 2/50 Elec, ECIR. The final size of the electorate was 1,838,880. *Key Highlights*, p. 4.

[14] Letter from the Deputy Secretary to the Government of Madhya Bharat to the Joint Secretary of CAS, 29 November 1949, (CA/3/FR/49) in 2/50 Elec, ECIR. The final size of the electorate was 4,090,857. *Key Highlights*, p. 4. The Chief Commissioner of Coorg reported that they brought a total of *91,807* electors on the draft roll. Letter from the Chief Commissioner Coorg to the Joint Secretary of CAS, 17 December 1949, 2/50 Elec, ECIR. The final size of the electorate was 94,593. *Key Highlights*, p. 4. In Bhopal, the Chief Commissioner wrote, *416,458* voters were enrolled, but the preparation of electoral rolls of displaced persons was not yet completed. Letter from the Chief Commissioner Bhopal to the Joint Secretary of CAS, 26 December 1949, 2/50 Elec, ECIR. The final size of the electorate was 419,970. *Key Highlights*, p. 4.

commencement of the constitution. The Government of Assam enrolled 3,426,351 voters.[15] In Patiala and East Punjab States Union (PEPSU) 1,562,587 voters were enrolled, excluding the enclaves transferred from Punjab or Himachal Pradesh.[16] In Delhi a total of 663,804 voters were enrolled.[17] The Travancore-Cochin Government enrolled 4,114,329 voters.[18] In Hyderabad 8,797,828 voters were enumerated.[19] The report on the United Provinces electorate, which ultimately reached 31,770,309, was spread over 51 district-wise statements.[20]

The numbers of voters were presented in tables that showed the electors in each district, divided by smaller administrative units like talukas, tehsils, thanas (or police stations), zails, municipalities and towns. The magnitude of the electorate that emerged out of the mounds of tables from across India made real the colossal scale of the franchise. Once tallied, the total number of voters on the electoral rolls came to an estimate of more than 17 Crores, 170 million voters. This figure and the size of the first all-India electoral roll were difficult to fathom. Rajendra Prasad commented in the Constituent Assembly that the 'mere act of printing this is [such] a big and tremendous job that the governments are being hard put to it, to find the presses, which will under take this big job. I was myself calculating one day the thickness of the volume of the electoral roll for all the provinces and I found that it will come to nearly three-fourth of a furlong.'[21] A few months later, in a programme on All India Radio, the metaphor of electricity and its infrastructure was used to convey the importance and magnitude of the undertaking. 'The electric

[15] Letter from the Reforms Commissioner of Assam to the Secretary, Parliament Secretariat, 10 February 1950, 2/50 Elec, ECIR. These figures at that stage did not include the number of voters of the Khasi states that merged at the time to Assam. The final size of the electorate was 4,141,720. *Key Highlights*, p. 4.

[16] S. no. 34, copy of letter from Deputy Secretary to the Government of Patiala and East Punjab State Union to the Secretary, Election Commission, India, 9 February 1950, 2/50 Elec, ECIR. The final size of the electorate was 1,763,531. *Key Highlights*, p. 4.

[17] Letter from Home Secretary to the Chief Commissioner Delhi to the Secretary, Election Commission, 23 February 1950, 2/50 Elec, ECIR. The figures for the Delhi Cantonment were not available

[18] Letter from the Secretary to the Government Travancore-Cochin to the Election Commission of India, 4 May 1950, 2/50-Elec, ECIR. The final size of the electorate in Travancore-Cochin was 4,210,244. *Key Highlights*, p. 4.

[19] Letter from the Election Commissioner, Hyderabad to the Secretary of the Election Commission, 27 April 1950, 2/50-Elec, ECIR. This was based on the preparation for elections for the Hyderabad Constituent Assembly on the basis of adult franchise with reference to 1 January 1948 as the qualifying date. The final size of the electorate in Hyderabad was 9,032,229. *Key Highlights*, p. 4.

[20] Letter from the Additional Deputy, Government of the United Provinces to the Election Commission of India, 28 April 1950, 2/50-Elec, ECIR; *Key Highlights*, p. 4.

[21] *CAD*, 7 October 1949. Also see 'Temporary Provisions in the Draft Constitution of India', *TOI*, 8 October 1949, p. 13.

posts are there, there are the cables and the copper, the bulbs are there', and these were now awaiting for the switch, that is the act of voting, to be turned on and instantaneously run the current: 'what the switch is to the electric power the vote is to political power... Give the citizen the vote, there is light, breeze and sound everywhere.'[22]

The spectacle of numbers emerging of the lists of voters gave democracy in India its first real appearance.[23] The electoral rolls on the basis of universal franchise constituted the institutional infrastructure for the notion that sovereignty resided with the people. The production of that register of more than 170 million people that were bound together as equal citizens for the purpose of authorising their government also rendered existent the idea of 'the people'; even before they became 'We the People of India' with the enactment of the constitution. The all-encompassing national identity of Indians on the eve of the commencement of the constitution was that of being equal voters. Indians were voters before they became citizens.

In making concrete their democracy through the preparation of the first draft electoral roll over the two years that preceded the enactment of the constitution, Indian bureaucrats and the people did not make a leap to catch up with Western democracies. To use Dipesh Chakrabarty's construction and idea, they 'provincialized Europe'.[24] They did so in terms of the scale of the electorate and the magnitude of work that producing it required, which surpassed any previous democratic historical experience. The measure and tenacity of inclusion that drove the making of the universal franchise in India at the inception of establishing its edifice of electoral democracy, against the partition and the exclusionary policies and discourses it wrought, was also unsurpassed. Moreover, the implications of the preparation of the electoral rolls for the institutionalisation of democracy and for the democratisation of the Indian popular imagination explained in this book suggest that what made Indian democracy – citizenship and electoral democracy – real was the actual process of implementing it.

It was not just the idea of India, democracy, or the idealism of nationalism that mattered, but the considered attempt to see how it could

---

[22] 'The New Franchise', *Indian Listener*, Vol. XV, no. 22, 28 May–3 June 1950, p. 1, All India Radio (AIR), Prasar Bharati Archive, New Delhi.

[23] For the formation of a reality effect of democracy see Ezrahi, *Imagined Democracies*. For a discussion of the productions of spectacles that affirm and re-affirm the imagination of the state and its authority see Srirupa Roy, *Beyond Belief: India and the Politics of Postcolonial Nationalism*, Durham: Duke University Press, 2007, particularly chapter 2.

[24] Dipesh Chakrabarty, *Provincializing Europe: Postcolonial Thought and Historical Difference*, Princeton: Princeton University Press, 2000.

operate. In doing so, Indians produced an 'Indian way' of making democracy. Constitution makers determined that India should be a democracy based on universal adult franchise, and that it should be a strong united federal state. But the Constituent Assembly Secretariat, the non-partisan executive branch of the Assembly, led by B. N. Rau, in anticipation of the constitution being finally framed and approved, began, over quite an extended period, not to consult in the abstract about it all but to assume it would be implemented along the lines indicated. They undertook the practical steps needed to prepare for the eventuality. Indeed, the Secretariat's request of all the governments of the provinces and the states in November 1947 to imagine what the preparation of electoral rolls on the basis of adult franchise would entail, and their March 1948 instructions, were posited as an administrative task and written in a dispassionate bureaucratic style. No reference was made to the revolutionary nature of this undertaking, nor to the grand dream of nationalism and independence it meant to fulfil.

Embarking on the preparation of the electoral rolls had the effect of tackling a lot of issues, large and small, ahead of the constitution. That led, in incremental ways to rulings about them, and would, in consequence embed the high principles – universal franchise, the right to vote, and citizenship – firmly into the society. If all this had come up later, after the approval of the Constitution, it is likely that many of the issues that surfaced during the preparation of the first draft electoral rolls would have been politicised in ways that would have adversely effect the making of the universal franchise and the establishment of an electoral democracy.[25]

While the details of India's constitution were formulated by the Constituent Assembly, democracy was made on the ground not from a formal abstract consultation, but from wrestling with practical problems of implementing the registration of all adults would be citizens as voters. This entailed numerous interactions between bureaucrats at all levels, people, and various social associations across the country. The Secretariat's team was responsive to the problems and confusions that arose, and consultative and consensual in dealing with them. They

---

[25] The debate that arose in the Constituent Assembly in January 1949 about the registration of partition refugees during the motion on the preparation of rolls, ten months after the work was undertaken, and therefore in principle to no effect, forms one example that attests to that. See Chapter 5. This became more evident in relation to the process of the delimitation of constituencies and the enactment of the Representation of the People Act after the commencement of the constitution. At that time these aspects of the electoral system became more politicised. See Ornit Shani, 'Embedding Democracy: The Social History of India's First Elections' (forthcoming).

engaged public officials, people and citizens' associations in the details of voter registration and citizenship, mentoring them into both the abstract principles and practices of electoral democracy. Indeed, people and administrators began using the draft constitution to pursue their citizenship and voting rights; and they linked its abstract text to their everyday lives. Officials at all levels were testing some constitutional principles as they worked on their implementation. As a result of all these interactions there was significant input into constitution making from administrators, associations and private individuals. These feedbacks, and the lessoned learnt from putting into action draft constitutional provisions for electoral democracy, drove the Secretariat to initiate some revisions to the constitution, while there was still time to improve it before it was approved. Some of India's finest democratic faculties, in particular the emergence of an autonomous Election Commission, independent of any ministry, and responsible for the oversight of elections, thus reinforcing the unification and democratisation processes of the country as a whole, originated from the inputs to constitution making from below.[26]

The Secretariat's answerability and responsiveness empowered individuals and communities. It created the scope for people to sense the meaning of the right to vote, the notion of rule by the people, and their potential to become influential. The narrative-story about the preparation of the electoral rolls that the Secretariat authored and that shortly became like a serialised epic was about the people, who thus found meaning in it. They inserted themselves into the narrative. They saw their stake in the new polity of the universal franchise and exhibited

---

[26] While it is unrealistic to argue that the Election Commission is ever and always immune from politics, the fact remains that its ethos is that it is, and that continues to count for a great deal, even seventy years on. Indeed, the Election Commission is one of the most trusted public institutions in India. Survey data of the last two decades suggest that about 50% of the Indian electorate has a 'great deal' of trust in the Election Commission. See, for example, Alfred Stepan, Juan J. Linz, and Yogendra Yadav, *Crafting State-Nations: India and Other Multinational Democracies*, Baltimore: Johns Hopkins University Press, 2011, p. 77: data for 2005 shows that 51% of the respondents said that they had a 'great deal', or quite a lot of trust' in the Election Commission. Also see Subrata K. Mitra, *The Puzzle of India's Governance: Culture, Context and Comparative Theory*, London: Routledge, 2006, pp. 75–6: according to the National Election Study 1996 a total of 46% (48% of Muslim) respondents had a 'great deal ' of trust in the Election Commission. The Election Commission of India superintends, direct and control the elections to Parliament, state legislatures, the office of the President and the Vice-President. Elections for institutions of local self-government of Panchayats and Municipalities are conducted, in accordance with the Constitution (Seventy-third Amendment), Act, 1992, and the Constitution (Seventy-fourth Amendment) Act, 1992 by the state Election Commission, appointed by the state governments. See V. S. Devi and S. K. Mendiratta, *How India Votes: Election Laws, Practice and Procedure* (Second Edition, S. K. Mendiratta), New Delhi: LexisNexis, 2017, pp. 1282-88.

commitment to it. Once people personalised the universal franchise it also captured their imagination. Their experiences with the forms and core principles of democracy of draft constitutional provisions down to the fine details turned the notion of democratic citizenship and adult franchise for India's masses – the poor, the illiterate, refugees, vagrants, and the passage and staircase dwellers – into a convention. The story of the preparation of the first draft electoral roll became the true epic of the constitution, which grounded its democratic principles in its undemocratic soil.

The democratic drive to implement universal franchise in anticipation of the constitution also facilitated the formation of a strong unitary federal state. Achieving this was not an inevitable outcome in the face of princely states with a firm identities of their own, that were still largely sovereign entities, and that were not, as has commonly been assumed, passive opponents of integration and Indian unity. The preparation of the electoral rolls across the country became a mechanism for the integration into a Union of the provinces and the princely states. This process enabled the centre that was in the making to override, for example, 'states' rights', or local interpretations of who was and was not a citizen, and forge, in turn, a uniform notion of being Indian.[27] Just as with the institutionalisation of an electoral democracy, the disciplining of the federal structure did not rely on beliefs in an Indian nationalism. It was a result of the preparation of a joint list comprised of all India's adults that covered the entire territory over which the Indian state was to exercise authority. In this process the new Union was operationalised and firmly grounded in practical ways that would become very difficult to unravel. Paradoxically, building a state with a strong centre through this democratic drive also reproduced inbuilt colonial legacies in the new democratic Constitution.

As a result of the preparation of the first draft electoral roll on the basis of universal franchise Indians produced the largest democracy in the world. They did so against many odds. The way Indians made their democracy did not necessarily mean that India would become better than other democracies, nor immune from the problems that have beset democracies elsewhere. Indeed India's democracy fell short of its constitutional promises, for example to promote social and economic equality.[28] From the 1980s, episodes of state violence, and the rise of belligerent Hindu nationalism, in particular, have beset its democratic

---

[27] See, for example, the case of Travancore discussed in Chapter 5.
[28] For important analyses of the unfulfilled promises of India's democracy see Pratap Bhanu Mehta, *The Burden of Democracy*, New Delhi: Penguin Books, 2003; Sudipta

public life and institutions. This challenge has been looming larger since 2014. Moreover, the institutionalisation of electoral democracy did not transform the particularisms of society and region. Some of these even gained strength with the advent of full electoral democracy and in the face of the changing political, social and economic circumstances. That these social structures sometimes gained strength was also an expression of democratic deepening. This paradox was inherent to the making of the universal franchise.

Making democracy in India at independence through the considered attempts to operationalise it was extraordinarily significant to its institutionalisation and to the endurance of its constitution. Indeed, the largest democracy in the world is widely recognised after seventy years of its democratic career to be robust. Scholars find it difficult to continue claiming, as was the case for many decades, that it is an anomaly, or an exception. Understanding the way India's democracy and its constitution came about historically and evolved into a sustainable political system, provides a basis, I hope, to think afresh more broadly about our understanding of democracy and democratisation elsewhere. This is particularly important and timely against the dire times for democracies in the world and the profound challenges they face.

When Jawaharlal Nehru moved the resolution on the Aims and Objects of the Constituent Assembly just as it began the process of constitution making in December 1946, he declared: 'Obviously we are aiming at democracy and nothing less than a democracy... It will be for this House to determine what shape to give to that democracy, the fullest democracy I hope.'[29] As this book has shown, the origins of how India became democratic in the midst of the partition and the integration of 552 princely states was not merely the logical outcomes of decisions made by its constitution makers. The preparation of the first electoral roll democratised the popular political imagination and fostered its institutional embedding. It was in large measures people of modest means who drove this process as they struggled for their democratic rights in anticipations of the constitution and debated it with bureaucrats at all levels.

On 17 March 1950, shortly after the commencement of the constitution, and two years after the Secretariat instructed that the preparation of electoral rolls should be taken forthwith, S. N. Mukerjee, formerly

Kaviraj, 'The Empire of Democracy: Reading Indian Politics Through Tocqueville', in Partha Chatterjee and Ira Katznelson (eds), *Anxieties of Democracy: Tocquevillean Reflections on India and the United States*, New Delhi: Oxford University Press, 2012, pp. 20–49; Niraja Gopal Jayal, *Citizenship and Its Discontents: An India History*, Cambridge Massachusetts: Harvard University Press, 2013.
[29] *CAD*, 13 December 1946.

the Joint Secretary of the CAS and now the Joint Secretary to the Government of India Ministry of Law, wrote to the governments of all the states of the Union:

I am directed to say that it is the intension of the Government of India – and public statements have been made from time to time – to hold the first general elections under the new Constitution as early as practicable... Some preliminary action was taken by the Constituent Assembly Secretariat as a result of which the gigantic task of preparing electoral rolls on the basis of adult suffrage has achieved varying degrees of progress in the States. Recently the Chief Election Commissioner who for the present will constitute the Election Commission has been appointed and is expected to assume charge on the 21st March 1950. The next step to be taken is the passing by Parliament of the necessary law for the allocation of seats in the House of the People, the States Legislative Assemblies, and (where such councils are to be constituted) the State Legislative Councils, the delimitation of constituencies for the purpose of elections to those Houses, the qualification of voters... the preparation of electoral rolls and other ancillary matters. A tentative draft of a Bill for these purposes, together with an explanatory note, is enclosed. I am to request that the views of the States Government on the points specifically mentioned ... and generally, may kindly be obtained ... *not later than 1st April, 1950.*[30]

This letter marked the dawn of a full electoral democracy in India. There was still, as Mukerjee wrote, work to be done on the rolls.[31] Indeed, the experience of the preparation of the first draft electoral roll set a precedent for universal franchise and democracy as something to relentlessly fight for and defend, rather than something to settle once and for all.[32] In the final administrative account from a province this was felt as well. Writing to the CAS in December 1948 to inform them that the preparation of the roll in manuscript form was 'now fast nearing completion' in West Bengal, the Deputy Secretary of the Government commented: 'It will, it is hoped, be appreciated that the work can never be completed in a final sense...'[33]

---

[30] Letter No. F.8/50-C from S. N. Mukerjee, Joint Secretary to the Government of India, Ministry of Law to the Chief Secretary to the Governments [all state], 17 March 1950, 25/50 Elec, ECIR.

[31] It is noteworthy that the number of voters registered on the first draft electoral rolls on the eve of the enactment of the constitution was quite accurate when compared with the final electorate (after the preparation of supplementary lists) for the first elections in 1951. See Election Commission of India, *Key Highlights*, p. 4; and fns. 3–18 above.

[32] See Ken Hirschkop, *Mikhail Bakhtin: An Aesthetic for Democracy*, Oxford: Oxford University Press, 1999, p. 34.

[33] Letter from Deputy Secretary to the Government of West Bengal to CAS, 14 December 1948, CA/1/FR/48-IV, ECIR. He referred specifically to the imminent expectation that 'fresh claims for enrolment in each electoral area will always arise with fresh individuals and families taking up residence in that area as the result of the continuous movement of people from place to place, especially of refugees'. Ibid.

The completion of the work that was still to be done for the preparation and conduct of India's first election, the largest ever in world history at that time, deserves its own story. The design and the putting up of the machinery – legal, administrative and material – for the operation of the first election, and the popular mass mobilisation that took place ahead of the election on the basis of a full electoral democracy form the sequel to the story of how India became democratic through the making of the universal franchise.[34]

It is difficult to find the pithy prose to describe how far the making of the universal franchise irreversibly transformed the meaning of social existence in India. An excerpt from recollections of B. Shiva Rao who contested a parliamentary seat in the first elections, gives a first-hand account of this watershed experience. His was a rural constituency in Madras, 'on the picturesque, palm-fringed coastline of India'.[35] The majority of the electorate was illiterate. Rao recounted that 'As a preliminary to the start of my campaign I looked at the formidable pile of electoral rolls in front of me. There were 342,000 voters, men and women – but more women than men, as my wife discovered, studying the lists.'[36] Then came the experience of voting day:

Cheerfully the rural voters walked long distances, men and women, formed queues outside the polling booths and waited patiently for 2 or 3 hours and more for their turn to vote. Moslem women, because of their custom of wearing the veil had exclusive booths to themselves. It was in some ways an incredible sight on polling day... Actually a majority of Moslem women went to the polling booths. They walked through the streets in groups of ten or twelve, with a white sheet held over their heads... In my constituency, vestiges of untouchability still persist, especially in rural areas... I did not think the untouchables in the rural areas would attach any great importance to the vote. There again I was in serious error. I visited dozens of polling booths all over the constituency on voting day and found in every queue, whether of men or of women voters, untouchables in considerable numbers. That, I thought, was a good sign; but the sequal [sic] was even more remarkable and for me significant. After the announcement of my success at the polls, I again went round the constituency and addressed nearly a hundred meetings. The experience of standing in the same queue with one's employer, and the consciousness of having the same political right as the

---

[34] Shani, 'Embedding Democracy: The Social History of India's First Elections' (forthcoming).

[35] B. Shiva Rao, 'India's General Elections' (undated), in *B. Shiva Rao papers*, II Inst., Speeches and Writings by him, f. 33, NMML.

[36] Ibid. Rao, reminisced on his 'rural constituency on the picturesque, palm-fringed coastline of India, about four hundred miles south of Bombay'. He compared it to the elections he contested under the Raj in 1926 to the Central Parliament. His constituency was enormous in size but the electorate composed of only 17,000 voters under the restricted franchise, and there were hardly any women amongst them.

high-caste landlord made, I think, a deep impression on many untouchables. To my post-election meetings they came in hundreds and this [sic] sat with the rest of the people.[37]

There was 'an incredible heroic dimension' in making the universal franchise. It reverberated the sense 'that came from the simple putting up of poles for the wires to travel along' in making rural electrification that Richard Brautigan described in a short story: 'Suddenly, religiously, with the throwing of a switch the farmer had electric lights to see by when he milked his cows in the early black winter mornings. The farmer's family got to listen to the radio. It was really a fantastic movie and excited me... I wanted electricity to go everywhere in the world.'[38]

> Similarly, with the universal franchise,
> Even India's rural poor had the right to authorise their government,
> To see and oversee how they were governed,
> And to have real opportunities to authorise a better one.
> The making of the universal franchise was in that sense like putting up poles
> For the generation and regeneration of political hope.
> It was now left for Indians to make their democratic politics.

---

[37] Ibid. Rao won the seat by a margin of only 8,841 votes (4.29%). The voter turnout was just above 60%, and only 500 ballots were invalid. Also see Election Commission of India, *Statistical Report on General Elections, 1951 to the First Lok Sabha*, Volume I, Election Commission of India: New Delhi, p. 169.

[38] Richard Brautigan, 'I Was Trying to Describe You to Someone', in *Revenge of the Lawn*, London: Pan Books, 1974, p. 60. In the story, Brautigan recalls a film he saw as a child about 'rural electrification and a perfect 1930s New Deal morality'. I thank Lucy Rhymer for drawing my attention to this story.

Selected Bibliography

PRIVATE PAPERS

B. Shiva Rao Papers, Nehru Memorial Museum and Library.

OFFICIAL MANUSCRIPT SOURCES

All India Radio (AIR) Prasar Bharati Archive, New Delhi.
Centre of South Asian Studies Archives, Cambridge
Election Commission of India Record Room, Election Commission, New Delhi.
India Office Records, British Library, London.
Maharashtra State Archives, Mumbai.
National Archives of India, New Delhi.
Nehru Memorial and Museum Library, New Delhi.

OFFICIAL REPORTS

Constituent Assembly Debates, Available on http://parliamentofindia.nic.in/ls/debates/debates.htm
Constituent Assembly of India, *Interim Report of the Advisory Committee on the Subject of Fundamental Rights* (presented on 29 April 1947 – date of Report, 23 April 1947), Reports of Committees (First Series) 1947 (from December 1946 to July 1947), New Delhi: The Manager, Government of India Press, 1947.
North-East Frontier (Assam) Tribal and Excluded Areas Sub-Committee, Vol. II (Evidence) Part I (Lushai, North-Cachar, Garo, Mikir And Naga Hills), copy dated 19 December 1947.
North-East Frontier (Assam) Tribal and Excluded Areas Sub-Committee, Vol. II (Evidence) Part II (Margherita, Sadiya Frontier Tract, Balipara Frontier Tract, Khasi and Jaintia Hills and General). A copy dated 16 February 1948.*Report of the Linguistic Provinces Commission*. New Delhi: The Manager Government of India Press, 1948.
Constituent Assembly of India Advisory Committee Tribal and Excluded Areas, *Pamphlet: 'Excluded and Partially Excluded Areas', Parts I & II (General Note and Appendices, Statements and Factual Memoranda of Provinces)*, Constituent Assembly, 26 February 1947.
Election Commission of India, *Key Highlights of General Elections, 1951 to the First Lok Sabha*, New Delhi: Election Commission of India, 1951.

Report on the First General Elections in India 1951–52, Vol. I, New Delhi: Government of India Press, 1955.

Report on the Second General Elections in India 1957, Vol. I, New Delhi: Government of India Press, 1959.

Report on the Third General Elections in India 1962, Vol. I, New Delhi: Government of India Press.

Statistical Report on General Elections 1967 to the Fourth Lok Sabha, New Delhi: Government of India Press, 1968. *Hand Book for Booth Level Officers*, New Delhi, 2011.

Belief in the Ballot: 101 Human Stories from India Elections. Publication Division Ministry of Broadcasting and Information: Government of India, 2016.

Government of Assam, Home and Political Department, *White Paper on Foreigners Issue*, 22 May 2015.

Government of India Ministry of States, *White Paper on Indian States*, New Delhi: The Manager Government of India Press, July 1948.

Report of the Indian States Finances Enquiry Committee 1948–49, Part I, New Delhi: Manager of Government of India Press, 1949.

White Paper on Indian States, Delhi: The Manager Government of India Press, 1950.

Nehru, Moti Lal, *Report of the All Parties Conference (Together with a Summary of the Proceedings of the Conference Held at Lucknow)*, Allahabad: General Secretary, All India Congress Committee, August 1928.

Report of the Committee for the Drafting of a Model Constitution for the Indian States, New Delhi: Manager Government of India Press, 22 March 1949.

Report of the State Reorganisation Commission, New Delhi: Manager of Publications, 1955.

The Drafting Committee, Constituent Assembly of India, *Draft Constitution of India*, New Delhi: The Manager Government of India Press, 1948.

NEWSPAPERS

The Hindu
The Hindustan Times
The Times of India

SECONDARY LITERATURE

Ackerman, Bruce. 'The Rise of World Constitutionalism'. *Virginia Law Review* 83 (1997): 771–97.

'The New Separation of Powers'. *Harvard Law Review* 113, no. 3 (January 2000): 633–725.

Ahuja, Amit, and Pradeep Chhibber. 'Why the Poor Vote in India: "If I Don't Vote, I am Dead to the State"', *Studies in Comparative International Development* 47, no. 4 (2012): 389–410.

Ahuja, M. L. *General Elections in India, Electoral Politics, Electoral Reforms and Political Parties*. New Delhi: Icon Publishers, 2005.

Alam, Javeed. *Who Wants Democracy?* New Delhi: Orient Longman, 2004.

Almond, Ian. *The Thought of Nirad C. Chaudhuri. Islam, Empire and Loss*. Cambridge: Cambridge University Press, 2015.

Ambedkar, Bhimrao Ramji. *Federation versus Freedom*. Jullundur: Bheem Patrika Publications, 1977. Kale Memorial Lecture, Gokhale Institute of Politics and Economics, Pune, 29 January 1939.

Ansari, Sarah F. D. *Life after Partition: Migration, Community and Strife in Sindh, 1947–1962*. Oxford: Oxford University Press, 2005.

Asif, Manan Ahmed. 'Half a Cheer for Democracy in Pakistan'.*The New York Times*, 20 March 2017.

Austin, Granville. *The Indian Constitution: Cornerstone of a Nation*. New Delhi: Oxford University Press, 2006.

Bajpai, Rochana. 'The Conceptual Vocabularies of Secularism and Minority Rights in India'. *Journal of Political Ideologies* 7, no. 2 (June 2002): 179–97.

  Debating Difference: Group Rights and Liberal Democracy in India. New Delhi: Oxford University Press, 2011.

Banerjee, D. N. 'Indian States and the Future Constitution of India'. *The Indian Journal of Political Science* 10, no. 1/2 (1949): 94–100.

Banerjee, Mukulika. *Why Indian Votes?* New Delhi: Routledge, 2014

Baruah, Sanjib. '"Ethnic" Conflict as State–Society Struggle: The Poetics and Politics of Assamese Micro-Nationalism'. *Modern Asian Studies* 28, no. 03 (1994): 649–71.

  'Citizens and Denizens: Ethnicity, Homelands, and the Crisis of Displacement in North East India'. *Journal of Refugee Studies* 16, no. 1 (2003): 44–66.

  'Partition and the Politics of Citizenship in Assam'. In Urvashi Butalia (ed.), *Partition: The Long Shadow*. New Delhi: Zubaan, 2015: 78–101.

Baxi, Upendra. 'The Little Done, the Vast Undone: Some Reflections on Reading Granville Austin's *The Indian Constitution*'. *Journal of the Indian Law Institute* 9 (1967): 323–430.

Bayly, C. A. *Empire and Information: Intelligence Gathering and Social Communication in India, 1780–1870*. Cambridge: Cambridge University Press, 1997.

Bayly, Susan. *The New Cambridge History of India: Caste, Society and Politics in India from the Eighteenth Century to the Modern Age*. Cambridge: Cambridge University Press, 1999.

Bell, F. O. 'Parliamentary Elections in Indian Provinces'. *Parliamentary Affairs* 1, no. 2 (Spring 1948): 20–9.

Beverley, Eric Lewis. *Hyderabad, British India, and the World. Muslim Networks and Minor Sovereignty c. 1850–1950*. Cambridge, United Kingdom: Cambridge University Press, 2015.

Bhargava, Rajeev, ed. *Politics and Ethics of the Indian Constitution*. Delhi: Oxford University Press, 2008.

  'Introduction'. In Rajeev Bhargava (ed.), *Politics and Ethics of the Indian Constitution*. Delhi: Oxford University Press, 2008: 1–42.

Boxall, Peter. *The Value of the Novel*. Cambridge: Cambridge University Press, 2015.

Brautigan, Richard. *Revenge of the Lawn. Stories, 1962–1970*. London: Pan Books (Picador), 1974.

Burra, Arudra. 'The Indian Civil Service and the Raj: 1919–1950,' 11 February 2007. SSRN: https://ssrn.com/abstract=2052658 (accessed 25 June 2017).

Butalia, Urvashi. *The Other Side of Silence: Voices from the Partition of India*. Delhi: Penguin Books, 1998.

Caracciolo, Marco. *The Experientiality of Narrative*. Berlin: De Gruyter, 2014.

Chakrabarty, Dipesh. *Provincializing Europe: Postcolonial Thought and Historical Difference*. Princeton, NJ: Princeton University Press, 2000.

Chakrabarty, Dipesh, Rochona Majumdar, and Andrew Sartori, eds. *From the Colonial to the Postcolonial. India and Pakistan in Transition*. New Delhi: Oxford University Press, 2007.

Chandavarkar, Rajnarayan. 'Customs of Governance: Colonialism and Democracy in Twentieth Century India'. *Modern Asian Studies* 41, no. 3 (2007): 441–70.

Chatterjee, Partha. *The Nation and Its Fragments: Colonial and Postcolonial Histories*, Princeton, NJ: Princeton University Press, 1993.

The Politics of the Governed: Reflections on Popular Politics in Most of the World. New York; Chichester: Columbia University Press, 2004.

Empire and Nation: Selected Essays. New York: Columbia University Press, 2010.

Chatterji, Joya. 'Right or Charity? The Debate over Relief and Rehabilitation in West Bengal, 1947–50'. In Suvir Kaul (ed.), *The Partitions of Memory: The Afterlife of the Division of India*. Delhi: Permanent Black, 2001: 74–110.

The Spoils of Partition: Bengal and India: 1947–1967. Cambridge: Cambridge University Press, 2007.

'South Asian Histories of Citizenship, 1946–1970'. *The Historical Journal* 55, no. 04 (December 2012): 1049–71.

Chaudhury, Sujit. 'A God-Sent Opportunity', *Seminar* 510 (2002): 61–7.

Chiriyankandath, James. '"Democracy" Under the Raj: Elections and Separate Representation in British India', in Niraja Jayal Gopal (ed.), *Democracy in India*. New Delhi: Oxford University Press, 2001: 53–81.

Choudhry, Sujit, Madhav Khosla, and Pratap Bhanu Mehta. 'Locating Indian Constitutionalism'. In Sujit Choudhry, Madhav Khosla, and Pratap Bhanu Mehta (eds), *The Oxford Handbook of the Indian Constitution* Oxford: Oxford University Press, 2016: 1–13.

Choudhry, Valmiki, ed. *Dr Rajendra Prasad: Correspondence and Select Documents*, Vol. 11. New Delhi: Allied Publishers, 1988.

Choudhury, G.W. *Constitutional Development in Pakistan*. London: Longmans, 1959

Clarke, Sir Geoffrey. *The Post Office of India and Its Story*. London: John Lane The Bodley Head, 1921.

Cody, Francis. 'Daily Wires and Daily Blossoms: Cultivating Regimes of Circulation in Tamil India's Newspaper Revolution'. *Journal of Linguistic Anthropology* 19, no. 2 (December 2009): 286–309.

Cohn, Bernard S. 'The Census, Social Structure and Objectification in South Asia'. In *An Anthropologist among the Historians and Other Essays*, 224–54. Delhi: Oxford University Press, 1987.

Copland, Ian. *The Princes of India in the Endgame of Empire, 1917–1947*, Cambridge: Cambridge University Press, 1997.

Coupland, Reginald. *The Indian Problem, 1833–1935: Report on the Constitutional Problem in India, Submitted to the Warden and Fellows of Nuffield College, Oxford*. Part 1, London: Oxford University Press (Third Imprint), 1943.

Cover, Robert M. 'Forward: Nomos and Narrative' in 'The Supreme Court, 1982 Term'. *Harvard Law Review* 97, no. 1 (November 1, 1983): 4–68.

Dahl, Robert Alan. *Democracy and Its Critics*. New Haven: Yale University Press, 1989.

On Democracy. New Haven: Yale Nota Bene Book, 2000.

Dasgupta, Sandipto. '"A Language Which Is Foreign to Us": Continuities and Anxieties in the Making of the Indian Constitution'. *Comparative Studies of South Asia, Africa and the Middle East* 34, no. 2 (2014): 228–42.

Datta, Antara. *Refugees and Borders in South Asia: The Great Exodus of 1971*. London: Routledge, 2012.

De, Rohit. 'Beyond the Social Contract'. *Seminar*, no. 615 (November 2010).

'Rebellion, Dacoity, and Equality: The Emergence of the Constitutional Field in Postcolonial India'. *Comparative Studies of South Asia, Africa and the Middle East* 34, no. 2 (January 1, 2014): 260–78.

The People's Constitution (1947–1964). Princeton: Princeton niversity Press, forthcoming.

Devi, V. S., and S. K Mendiratta. *How India Votes: Election Laws, Practice and Procedure*. Second Edition, S. K. Mendiratta. New Delhi: LexisNexis, 2017.

Dirks, Nicholas B. *Castes of Mind: Colonialism and the Making of Modern India*. Princeton, NJ: Princeton University Press, 2001.

Doctor, Geeta. 'A Toast to Another Age'. *The Hindu*, 28 June 2014.

Doctor, Vikram. 'A Witness to the Birth of a Nation'. *The Economic Times*, 16 August 2011.

Eapen, K. E. 'Daily Newspapers in India: Their Status and Problems'. *Journalism Quarterly* XLIV (1967): 520–32.

Elangovan, Arvind. 'The Making of the Indian Constitution: A Case for a Non-Nationalist Approach'. *History Compass* 12, no. 1 (January 2014): 1–10.

'Provincial Autonomy, Sir Benegal Narsing Rau, and an Improbable Imagination of Constitutionalism in India, 1935–38'. *Comparative Studies of South Asia, Africa and the Middle East* 36, no. 1 (2016): 66–82.

'"The Road Not Taken". Sir Benegal Narsing Rau and the Indian Constitution', in Sekhar Bandopadhyay (ed.), *Decolonization and the Politics of Transition in South Asia*. New Delhi: Orient Blackswan, 2016: 141–59.

A Constitutional Imagination of India: Sir Benegal Narsing Rau amidst the Retreat of liberal Idealism (1910–1950). Unpublished PhD thesis, University of Chicago, 2012.

Ernst, Waltraud, and Biswamoy Pati, eds. *India's Princely States: People, Princes and Colonialism*. London: Routledge, 2007.

Everett, Jana Matson. *Women and Social Change in India*. New Delhi: Heritage, 1981.

'"All the Women Were Hindu and All the Muslims Were Men": State, Identity Politics and Gender, 1917–1951'. *Economic and Political Weekly* 36, no. 23 (2001): 2071–80.

Ezrahi, Yaron. *Imagined Democracies: Necessary Political Fictions*. Cambridge: Cambridge University Press, 2012.

Fisher, Margaret W., and John V. Bondurant. *The Indian Experience with Democratic Elections*. Vol. 3. Berkeley: University of California, 1956.

Forbes, Geraldine Hancock. *Women in Modern India*. Cambridge: Cambridge University Press, 1996.

Foucault, Michel. 'Governmentality'. In Peter Miller, Colin Gordon, and Graham Burchell (eds), *The Foucault Effect: Studies in Governmentality.* Chicago: University of Chicago Press, 1991: 87–104.

Furber, Holden. 'The Unification of India, 1947–1951'. *Pacific Affairs* 24, no. 4 (December 1951): 352–71.

Gadgil, D. R. (Dhananjaya Ramchandra) *Federating India.* Vol. 13. Poona: Gokhale Institute of Politics and Economics, 1945.

Geuss, Raymond. *History and Illusion in Politics.* Cambridge: Cambridge University Press, 2001.

Gilmartin, David. 'A Magnificent Gift: Muslim Nationalism and the Election Process in Colonial Punjab'. *Comparative Studies in Society and History* 40, no. 03 (1998): 415–36.

———. 'Election Law and the "People" in Colonial and Postcolonial India'. In Dipesh Chakrabarty, Rochona Majumdar, and Andrew Sartori (eds), *From the Colonial to the Postcolonial. India and Pakistan in Transition.* New Delhi: Oxford University Press, 2007: 55–89.

Gilmartin, David, and Robert Moog. 'Introduction to "Election Law in India"', *Election Law Journal* 11, no. 2, (2012): 136–48.

Goswami, Manu. *Producing India: From Colonial Economy to National Space.* Chicago Studies in Practices of Meaning. Chicago: University of Chicago Press, 2004.

Gould, William. *Bureaucracy, Community and Influence: Society and the State in India, 1930s–1960s.* Routledge Studies in South Asian History. London: Routledge, 2011.

———. 'From Subjects to Citizens? Rationing, Refugees and the Publicity of Corruption over Independence in UP'. *Modern Asian Studies* 45, no. 01 (January 2011): 33–56.

Gould, William, Taylor C. Sherman, and Sarah Ansari. 'The Flux of the Matter: Loyalty, Corruption and the "Everyday State" in the Post-Partition Government Services of India and Pakistan c. 1946–1952', *Past and Present* 219, no. 1 (1 May 2013): 237–79.

Grill, Genese. *The World as Metaphor in Robert Musil's The Man Without Qualities: Possibility as Reality.* New York: Camden House, 2012.

Groenhout, Fiona. 'The History of the Indian Princely States: Bringing the Puppets Back onto Centre Stage'. *History Compass* 4, no. 4 (2006): 629–44.

Guha, Amalendu. *Planter-Raj to Swaraj: Freedom Struggle and Electoral Politics in Assam 1826–1947.* New Delhi: Indian Council of Historical Research, 1977.

Guha, Ramachandra. 'Democracy's Biggest Gamble: India's First Free Elections in 1952'. *World Policy Journal* 19, no. 1 (2002): 95–103.

———. 'Savaging the Civilized: Verrier Elwin, His Tribals, and India'. In *The Ramachandra Guha Omnibus.* New Delhi: Oxford University Press, 2005.

———. *India after Gandhi: The History of the World's Largest Democracy.* 1st ed. London: Pan Macmillan, 2008 (first published 2007).

———. *Democrats and Dissenters.* New Delhi: Penguin Random House India, 2016.

Gupta, Devyani. *The Postal System of British India, c. 1830–1920.* Unpublished PhD thesis, University of Cambridge, 2016.

Guyot-Réchard, Bérénice. *Shadow States: India, China and the Himalayas 1910–1962.* Cambridge: Cambridge University Press, 2017.

Hannah, Matthew G. *Governmentality and the Mastery of Territory in Nineteenth-Century America*. Cambridge Studies in Historical Geography 32. Cambridge: Cambridge University Press, 2000.

Hasan, Zoya. *Politics of Inclusion: Caste, Minorities and Affirmative Action*. New Delhi: Oxford University Press, 2009.

Heller, Patrick. 'Degrees of Democracy: Some Comparative Lessons from India'. *World Politics* 52, no. 04 (July 2000): 484–519.

'Making Citizens from Below and Above. The Prospects and Challenges of Decentralization in India'. In Sanjay Ruparelia, Sanjay Reddy, John Harriss, and Stuart Corbridge (eds), *Understanding India's New Political Economy. A Great Transformation?* London: Routledge, 2011: 157–71.

'Democratic Deepening in India and South Africa', *Journal of Asian and African Studies* 44, no. 1 (2009): 123–49.

Henkin, David M. *The Postal Age: The Emergence of Modern Communication in Nineteenth-Century America*. Chicago: University of Chicago Press, 2006.

Hirschkop, Ken. *Mikhail Bakhtin: An Aesthetic for Democracy*. Oxford: Oxford University Press, 1999.

'India: An Enigmatic Future'. *The Round Table: The Commonwealth Journal of International Affairs* 38, no. 151 (1948): 690–5.

'India: First Year of Freedom'. *The Round Table* 38, no. 152 (1948): 793–7.

Israel, Milton. *Communications and Power: Propaganda and the Press in the Indian Nationalist Struggle*. Cambridge: Cambridge University Press, 1994.

Jaffrelot, Christophe. *India's Silent Revolution. The Rise of the Lower Castes in North India*. London: Hurst & Company, 2003.

Jayal, Niraja Gopal. *Citizenship and Its Discontents: An India History*. Cambridge MA: Harvard University Press, 2013.

Jeffrey, Robin. ed. *People, Princes and Paramount Power. Society and Politics in the Indian Princely States*. Delhi: Oxford University Press, 1978.

'Culture of Daily Newspapers in India: How It's Grown, What It Means?' *Economic and Political Weekly* 22, no. 14 (1987): 607–11.

'The "Kerala Model" and Portents for Indian Politics: Inferences from the First Universal-Suffrage Elections, Travancore, 1948', unpublished paper.

Kalpagam, U. *Rule by Numbers: Governmentality in Colonial India*. Lanham: Lexington Books, 2014.

Kamran, Tahir. 'Early Phase of Electoral Politics in Pakistan: 1950s'. *South Asian Studies* 24, no. 2 (2009): 257–82.

'Electoral Politics in Pakistan 1955–1969'. *Pakistan Vision* 10, no. 1 (2010): 82–97.

Kaviraj, Sudipta. 'Democracy and Development in India'. In Amiya Kumar Bagchi (ed.), *Democracy and Development. Proceedings of the IEA Conferences Held in Barcelona, Spain*. New York: Palgrave Macmillan, 1995: 92–137.

'A Critique of the Passive Revolution'. In Partha Chatterjee (ed.), *State and Politics in India*. New Delhi: Oxford University Press, 1998: 45–87.

The Imaginary Institution of India: Politics and Ideas. New York: Columbia University Press, 2010.

'The Empire of Democracy: Reading Indian Politics Through Tocqueville'. In Partha Chatterjee and Ira Katznelson (eds), *Anxieties of*

Democracy: Tocquevillean Reflections on India and the United States. New Delhi: Oxford University Press, 2012: 20–49.

Keane, John. *The Life and Death of Democracy*. London: Simon & Schuster, 2009.

Kermode, Frank. *The Sense of an Ending. Studies in the Theory of Fiction. (The Mary Flexner Lectures, 1965.)* New York: Oxford University Press, 1967.

Khan, Yasmin. *The Great Partition: The Making of India and Pakistan*. New Delhi: Penguin Viking, 2007.

Khilnani, Sunil. *The Idea of India*. London: Hamish Hamilton, 1997.

'Branding India', *Seminar*, no. 533, 2004.

'Arguing Democracy: Intellectuals and Politics in Modern India'. Centre of the Advanced Study of India (CASI) Working Paper Series, University of Pennsylvania, 2009.

Khosla, Madhav. *The Indian Constitution*. New Delhi: Oxford University Press, 2012.

Kogekar, Sadanaud Vasudeo and Richard L. Park (eds), *Reports on the Indian General Elections, 1951–52*. Bombay: Popular Book Depot, 1956.

Kohli, Atul, ed. *India's Democracy: An Analysis of Changing State–Society Relations*. Princeton, NJ: Princeton University Press, 1988.

The Success of India's Democracy. Cambridge: Cambridge University Press, 2001.

Kudaisya, Gyanesh. 'The Demographic Upheaval of Partition: Refugees and Agricultural Resettlement in India, 1947–67'. *South Asia: Journal of South Asian Studies* 18, no. Special Issue (1995): 73–94.

Kumar, Chandra Bhushan. *Imaging Arunachal Pradesh: The Indelible Ink of Democracy*. Itangar: Chief Electoral Officer, Arunachal Pradesh, 2016.

Kumar, Virendra. *Committees and Commissions in India: 1947–1973*. Vol. 1: 1947–54. New Delhi: Concept Publishing Company, 2004.

Legg, Stephen. 'An International Anomaly? Sovereignty, the League of Nations and India's Princely Geographies'. *Journal of Historical Geography* 43 (January 2014): 96–110.

'Dyarchy: Democracy, Autocracy, and the Scalar Sovereignty of Interwar India'. *Comparative Studies of South Asia, Africa and the Middle East* 36, no. 1 (2016): 44–65.

Lijphart, Arend. *Democracies: Patterns of Majoritarian and Consensus Government in Twenty-One Countries*. New Haven: Yale University Press, 1984.

'The Puzzle of Indian Democracy: A Consociational Interpretation'. *American Political Science Review* 90, no. 2 (June 1996): 258–68.

Lotus, Magnolia (Manjula Padmanabhan). 'My Dad's Birth Centenary', http://marginalien.blogspot.co.uk/2011/02/my-dads-birth-centenary.html (accessed 29 June 2017).

Luthra, P. N. *Constitutional and Administrative Growth of the North-East Frontier Agency*, Director of Information and Public Relations, NEFA (North-East Frontier Agency Administration), 1971.

Lyngdoh, James Michael. *Chronicle of an Impossible Election: The Election Commission and the 2002 Jammu and Kashmir Assembly Elections*. New Delhi: Penguin Viking, 2004.

Maheshwari, Shriram. *The Census Administration under the Raj and After*. New Delhi: Concept Publishing Company, 1996.

Mann, Michael. *The Sources of Social Power*, Vol. II. Cambridge: Cambridge University Press, 1998.

Manto, Sadaat Hasan. 'The New Constitution'. In Khalid Hasan (ed. and transl.), *Bitter Fruit: The Very Best of Saadat Hasan Manto*. New Delhi: Penguin Books, 2008: 206–15.

McMillan, Alistair. *Standing at the Margins: Representation and Electoral Reservation in India*. New Delhi: Oxford University Press, 2005.

Mehta, Pratap Bhanu. *The Burden of Democracy*. Interrogating India. New Delhi: Penguin Books, 2003.

'What Is Constitutional Morality?' *Seminar*, no. 615 (November 2010).

Mehta, Uday S. *Liberalism and Empire: A Study in Nineteenth-Century British Liberal Thought*, Chicago: University of Chicago Press, 1999.

'Indian Constitutionalism: The Articulation of a Political Vision', in Dipesh Chakravarty, Rochona Majumdar, and Andrew Sartori (eds), *From the Colonial to the Postcolonial. India and Pakistan in Transition*. New Delhi: Oxford University Press, 2007: 22–30.

Menon, V. P. *The Story of the Integration of the Indian States*. New Delhi: Orient Longmans, 1961.

Misra, Udayon. 'Immigration and Identity Transformation in Assam'. *Economic and Political Weekly* 34, no. 21 (1999): 1264–71.

Mitchell, W. J. T. 'Editor's Note: On Narrative'. *Critical Inquiry* 7, no. 1 (1980): 1–4.

Mitra, Subrata Kumar. *The Puzzle of India's Governance: Culture, Context and Comparative Theory*. Routledge Advances in South Asian Studies; 3. London: Routledge, 2006.

Morris-Jones, W. H. 'The India Elections', *The Economic Weekly*, 28 June 1952.

Mukerjee, S. N. 'The Constitution of India – an Analysis'. *The Hindustan Times*. 26 January 1950, p. II.

Musil, Robert. *The Man Without Qualities. London: Picador*, 1995.

Nair, Janaki. *Mysore Modern: Rethinking the Region under Princely Rule*. Minneapolis: University of Minnesota Press, 2011.

Narayan, Uma. 'The Constituent Assembly of India: Recollecting Contributions of Sir Benegal Narsing Rau, the Constitutional Advisor', *International Journal of Legal Information* 44, no. 3 (2016): 225–34.

Newbigin, Eleanor. *The Hindu Family and the Emergence of Modern India. Law Citizenship and Community*. Cambridge: Cambridge University Press, 2013.

Newbigin, Eleanor, Ornit Shani, and Stephen Legg. 'Introduction: Constituti onalism and the Evolution of Democracy in India'. *Comparative Studies of South Asia, Africa and the Middle East* 36, no. 1 (2016): 42–3.

Nigam, Adiya. 'A Text without Author: Locating Constituent Assembly as Event'. *Economic and Political Weekly* 39, no. 21 (May 22, 2004): 2107–13.

O'Donnell, Guillermo A, Philippe C. Schmitter, and Laurence Whitehead, eds. *Transitions from Authoritarian Rule: Comparative Perspectives*. Baltimore and London: Johns Hopkins University Press, 1991.

Pandey, Gyanendra. 'Mobilization in a Mass Movement: Congress "Propaganda" in the United Provinces (India) 1930–1934'. *Modern Asian Studies* 9, no. 02 (1975): 205–26.

Remembering Partition. Cambridge: Cambridge University Press, 2001.

Park, Richard L. 'Indian Democracy and the General Election'. *Pacific Affairs* 25, no. 2 (1952): 130–9.

'India's General Elections'. *Far Eastern Survey* 21, no. 1 (9 January 1952): 1–8.

'The General Election in the City of Bombay, 1952 by M'. *Pacific Affairs* 28, no. 2 (June 1955): 192.

Parulekar, N. B. 'The Power of Your Vote', *The Hindustan Times* (Sunday Magazine), 1 August 1948.

Pillai, Sarath. 'Fragmenting the Nation: Divisible Sovereignty and Travancore's Quest for Federal Independence'. *Law and History Review* 34, no. 3 (2016): 743–82.

Prakash, Gyan, Michael F. Laffan, and Nikhil Menon (eds.), *The Postcolonial Moment in South and Southeast Asia*, New York: Bloomsbury (forthcoming).

Radhakrishnan, S. 'Democracy: A Habit of the Mind (Presidential Address at the Annual Session of Andhra Mahasabha, Madras, September 1938)'. In *Education, Politics and War*. Poona: The International Book Service, 1944.

Raghavan, Srinath. *War and Peace in Modern India*. Basingstoke: Palgrave Macmillan, 2010.

Rajkumar, Nagoji Vasudev. *The Pilgrimage and After. The Story of How the Congress Fought and Won the General Elections*, New Delhi: All India Congress Committee, 1952.

Ramusack, Barbara N. *Indian Princes and Their States*. Cambridge: Cambridge University Press, 2004.

Ranadive, Ramchandra Keshava. *The Legal Rights of the Indian States and of Their Subjects or The Truth about the India States*. Baroda: The Good Companions, 1950.

Rao, Anupama. *The Caste Question: Dalit and Politics in Modern India*. Berkeley: University of California Press, 2009.

Rao, B. Shiva. *The Framing of India's Constitution: A Study*, Vols 1–IV. Nasik: Government of India Press, 1968.

Rau, B. N. *Constitutional Precedents*. New Delhi: The Government of India Press, 1947.

'The Constitution of the Union of Burma', *23 Wash. L. Rev. & St. B. J.*, 288, (1948): 188–300.

India's Constitution in the Making. ed. B. Shiva Rao. Madras: Orient Longmans, 1960.

Rosanvallon, Pierre. *Democratic Legitimacy. Impartiality, Reflexivity, Proximity*. Translated by Arthur Goldhammer. Princeton: Princeton University Press, 2011.

Roy, Anupama. *Mapping Citizenship in India*. New Delhi: Oxford University Press, 2010.

'Identifying Citizens: Electoral Rolls, the Right to Vote, and the Election Commission of India'. *Election Law Journal* 11, no. 2 (2012): 170–86.

Roy, Haimanti. *Partitioned Lives: Migrants, Refugees, Citizens in India and Pakistan*. New Delhi: Oxford University Press, 2012.

Roy, Srirupa. *Beyond Belief: India and the Politics of Postcolonial Nationalism*. Politics, History, and Culture. Durham: Duke University Press, 2007.

Rudolph, Susanne Hoeber, and Lloyd I. Rudolph. 'New Dimensions of Indian Democracy'. *Journal of Democracy* 13, no. 1 (2002): 52–67.

Rushdie, Salman. *Midnight's Children*. London: Vintage Books, 2006.

Sarkar, Sumit. 'Indian Democracy: The Historical Inheritance'. In Atul Kohli (ed.), *The Success of India's Democracy*. Cambridge: Cambridge University Press, 2001: 23–46.

Scott, James C. *Seeing Like a State: How Certain Schemes to Improve the Human Condition Have Failed*. New Haven: Yale University Press, 1998.

Sen, Uditi. 'Developing Terra Nullius: Colonialism, Nationalism and Indigeneity in the Andaman Islands', *Comparative Studies in Society and History* 50, no. 4, 2017.

Shani, Ornit. *Communalism, Caste and Hindu Nationalism: The Violence in Gujarat*. Cambridge: Cambridge University Press, 2007.

'Conceptions of Citizenship in India and the "Muslim Question"'. *Modern Asian Studies* 44, no. 1 (2010): 145–73.

'The Politics of Communalism and Caste'. In Isabelle Clark-Decès (ed.), *A Companion to the Anthropology of India*. Malden: Wiley-Blackwell, 2011: 297–312.

'Making India's Democracy Rewriting the Bureaucratic Colonial Imagination in the Preparation of the First Elections'. *Comparative Studies of South Asia, Africa and the Middle East* 36, no. 1 (January 1, 2016): 83–101.

'Embedding Democracy: The Social History of India's First Elections', forthcoming.

Sherman, Taylor C. *Muslim Belonging in Secular India. Negotiating Citizenship in Postcolonial Hyderabad*. New York: Cambridge University Press, 2015.

Sherman, Taylor C., William Gould, and Sarah Ansari. 'From Subjects to Citizens: Society and the Everyday State in India and Pakistan, 1947–1970'. *Modern Asian Studies* 45, no. 01 Special issue (January 2011): 1–6.

Shulman, David Dean. *More than Real. A History of the Imagination in South India*. Cambridge, Mass: Harvard University Press, 2012.

Siegel, Benjamin. '"Self-Help Which Ennobles a Nation": Development, Citizenship and the Obligations of Eating in India's Austerity Years'. *Modern Asian Studies* 50, no. 3 (2016): 975–1018.

Singer, Wendy. *A Constituency Suitable for Ladies and Other Social Histories of Indian Elections*. New Delhi: Oxford University Press, 2007.

Sinha, Mrinalini. 'Suffragism and Internationalism: The Enfranchisement of British and India Women under an Imperial State'. *Indian Economic and Social History Review* 36, no. 4 (1999): 461–84.

Specters of Mother India: The Global Restructuring of an Empire. Durham, NC: Duke University Press, 2006.

'Totaram Sanadhya's Fiji Mein Mere Ekkis Varsh: A History of Empire and Nation in a Minor Key'. In Antoinette Burton and Isabel Hofmeyr (eds), *Ten Books that Shaped the British Empire: Creating an Imperial Commons*. Durham: Duke University Press, 2014: 168–89.

Stepan, Alfred. 'Federalism and Democracy: Beyond the U.S. Model'. *Journal of Democracy* 10, no. 4 (1999): 19–34.

Stepan, Alfred C., Juan Linz, and Yogendra Yadav. *Crafting State-Nations. India and Other Multinational Democracies*. Baltimore: Johns Hopkins University Press, 2011.

Stoler, Ann Laura. *Along the Archival Grain: Epistemic Anxieties and Colonial Common Sense*. Princeton. NJ: Princeton University Press, 2009.

Suhrawardy, Huseyn Shaheed. 'Political Stability and Democracy in Pakistan'. *Foreign Affairs* 35, no. 3 (1957): 422–31.

Sundar, Nandini. *Subalterns and Sovereigns: An Anthropological History of Bastar, 1854–2006*. New Delhi: Oxford University Press, 2007.

The Burning Forest: India's War in Bastar. New Delhi: Juggernaut, 2016.

Tagore, Rabindranath. *The Post Office (Daak Ghar)*. Translated by Devabrata Mukerjea. London: Macmillan, 1914.

Talbot, Ian, and Gurharpal Singh. *The Partition of India*. Cambridge: Cambridge University Press, 2009.

Tejani, Shabnum. *Indian Secularism: A Social and Intellectual History, 1890–1950*. Indianapolis: Indiana University Press, 2008.

'The Revolution of the Indian States'. *The Round Table: The Commonwealth Journal of International Affairs* 39, no. 153–6 (1948): 36–43.

Tinker, Irene Celeste. 'Representation and Representative Government in The India Republic', PhD thesis, University of London (June 1954).

Tinker, Irene Celeste, and Mil Walker. 'The First General Elections in India and Indonesia'. *Far Eastern Survey* 25, no. 7 (July 1956): 97–110.

T. N. Z, and Z. M. 'The Indian General Elections'. *The World Today* 5, no. 8 (1952): 181–91.

Tudor, Maya. *The Promise of Power: The Origins of Democracy in India and Autocracy in Pakistan*. Cambridge University Press, 2013.

Varshney, Ashutosh. 'Why Democracy Survives?' *Journal of Democracy* 9, no. 3 (1998): 36–50.

Battles Half Won. India's Improbable Democracy, New Delhi: Penguin Viking, 2013

Venkatachalapathy, A. R. 'Reading Practices and Modes of Reading in Colonial Tamil Nadu'. *Studies in History* 10, no. 2 (1994): 273–90.

Washbrook, David. 'The Rhetoric of Democracy and Development in Late Colonial India'. In Sugata Bose and Ayesha Jalal (eds), *Nationalism, Democracy and Development: State and Politics in India*, 36–49. Delhi: Oxford University Press, 1997.

Weiner, Myron. *Sons of the Soil: Migration and Ethnic Conflicts in India*. Princeton, NJ: Princeton University Press, 1978.

'The Political Demography of Assam's Anti-Immigrant Movement'. *Population and Development Review* 9, no. 2 (June 1983): 279–92.

The Indian Paradox: Essays in Indian Politics. Ashutosh Varshney (ed.), New Delhi: Sage, 1989.

White, Hayden. 'Value of Narrativity in Representation of Reality'. *Critical Inquiry* 7, no. 1 (Autumn 1980): 5–27.

Widmalm, Sten. 'The Rise and Fall of Democracy in Jammu and Kashmir, 1975–1989'. In Amrita Basu and Atul Kohli (eds), *Community Conflicts and the State in India*. New Delhi: Oxford University Press, 1998: 149–82.

Wilkinson, Steven I. *Army and Nation: The Military and Indian Democracy since Independence*. Cambridge, MA: Harvard University Press, 2015.

Williams, P. *Everyday Peace? Politics, Citizenship and Muslim Lives in India*. Chichester, UK: Wiley-Blackwell, 2015.

Zamindar, Vazira Fazila-Yacoobali. *The Long Partition and The Making of Modern South Asia: Refugees, Boundaries, Histories*. New York: Columbia University Press, 2007.

Index

Abidi, A.A., 61n. 40, 131n. 38, 172n. 51, 193n. 142, 197, 206–07
Abors (Minyong and Padam), 217
abuses (in voter registration), 56n. 20, 76–78, 106, 106n. 93; of the democratic system;democratic, 106; in the registration of the refugees, 78
Acceding States, 166
Acts and Regulations: Assam Land and Revenue (Amendment) Act, 1947, 175–76; Assam Legislative Assembly Electoral Rules 1936, 39; Baroda Domicile Act, 102; Bihar Legislative Assembly Electoral (Preparation Revision and Publication of Electoral Rolls) Rules,1936, 240; Central Provinces and Berar Act (Refugee Registration and Movement), 62; Cochin Nationality and Naturalisation Act, 172; The Government of India Act 1935, 22, 22n. 6, 32n. 56, 42, 55, 127, 137, 146, 182, 212, 212n. 13, 213n. 18, 246; Indian Independence Act, 122; Negotiable Instruments Act, 27n. 29, 113, 113n. 117; Refugee Registration and Movement Act (of the provincial governments), 62; Representation of the People Act, 233; The Government of India Act 1919, 212; The Government of India Act 1935, 127–28, 212, 214; Travancore Interim Constitution Act, 173; Travancore Naturalization Act 1945, 173
acts and regulations, The Government of India Act 1935, 2n. 5, 3–4, 12
Additional Secretary to the Government of Madras, 78n. 122, 135n. 48, 135n. 49, 135n. 50, 135n. 51, 144n. 93, 144n. 94, 146n. 103, 147n. 107, 152n. 127, 156n. 140, 182–83, 182n. 96, 183n. 101, 183n. 99, 249n. 6

administration, 50, 65n. 61, 67, 144, 157, 192, 212–13, 212n. 12, 216, 219, 221n. 61; central, 124; regular, 215
adult franchise, 4, 4n. 13, 13n. 35, 22–23, 25–32, 46–47, 50–51, 86–89, 97–98, 99–102, 102n. 73, 103n. 79, 104n. 82, 106–09, 113–15, 133–34, 134n. 45, 134n. 47, *also see* universal adult franchise, and universal franchise
adult suffrage, 2–4, 2n. 3, 3n. 10, 23, 91, 97n. 39, 98, 106n. 93, 150, 159, 161n. 5, 167, 167n. 33, 171, 177; assuming, 21; implementing, 31; universal, 42
adult voters, 27, 101, 130, 156
adults, 29, 30–31, 41, 43, 50, 103, 109, 152, 209, 243, 252, 254; eligible, 22; preparing a list of all, 28
Advisory Committee, 2n. 3, 58n. 28, 161n. 5, 189, 192n. 139, 213, 213n. 17, 219n. 52, 238, 238n. 134
age limits, 26n. 25, 91, 108–09; prescribed, 108–09
age of voters; left to the discretion of each province and state, 39; proof of, 25, 39, 243; qualifications used, 39, 49n. 123; and the use of age certificates, 39–41; using an "intelligently frame" in Assam, 39; using 'school certificate or a municipal certificate of birth or horoscope as proof, 39
AICC. *see* All India Congress Committee (AICC)
All India Radio, 250
all-India, 22, 50, 56, 60, 83, 129, 142, 157; and citizenship, 73, 125; and Election Commission, 188–89; electoral roll, 250; and the integration of the princely states, 22, 34, 125, 129; and producing an electoral roll on a scale for, 22, 34; project, 50, 157; and the refugee

all-India (*cont.*)
   problem, 60; and the refugee problem,
      83; and the refugee problem, 56
Amado, Gilberto, 196, 197n. 151
Ambedkar, B.R., 181, 193, 195–96,
   225–26, 233, 235n. 117; and federation
   federation, 124n. 12; and the citizenship
   provisions, 227; and the constitutional
   provisions for elections, 184–85,
   191–92; and federation, 127n. 22, 128n.
   29, 129n. 31; and the motion on the
   preparation of electoral roll, 170–71
amendments, 126n. 20, 169, 170, 174–78,
   176n. 67, 179–82, 179n. 83, 180n.
   88, 184n. 103, 185, 219, 219n. 52,
   225n. 76; consolidated, 225; suggested,
   191, 194
American Constitution, 179, 179n. 83
Andaman and Nicobar Islands, 141, 181n.
   93, 222–23, 222n. 63, 222n. 64, 224n.
   70, 231n. 99
"anna franchise", 43
archives, 7–9
Article (Draft Constitution): article 5,
   32, 40–54, 55n. 12, 57, 59n. 32, 63,
   66, 67, 67n. 72, 75, 76n. 113, 77, 79,
   96, 118, 154, 177, 225–27, 225n. 74,
   226n. 78, 228, 231, 245–48; article 6,
   54, 227, 227n. 82, 228, 229, 229n. 94,
   230, 231n. 99, 232, 246, 247; article 7,
   227, 227n. 82, 229, 229n. 94; article 8,
   227, 247; article 9, 174, 227; article 10,
   227; article 11, 227, 233n. 109; article
   13, 175–76, 176n. 66; article 15, 179;
   article 23, 176–77; article 60, 222n. 63;
   article 67, 154n. 135, 167n. 33, 168n.
   33, 168n. 40, 179, 181n. 93, 182, 182n.
   98, 183, 184n. 102, 222n. 63, 223n.
   65; article 81, 223; article 149, 167,
   167n. 33, 168n. 33, 171, 182, 182n. 98,
   183; article 150, 178, 180, 180n. 88;
   article 151, 178, 180; article 167, 177,
   183; article 172, 179n. 81; article 215,
   181n. 93, 222n. 63; article 235, 144,
   146, 146n. 102; article 242, 238n. 131;
   article 289, 168n. 33, 174, 182, 183,
   184, 185, 185n. 107, 185n. 108, 186,
   188, 189, 190, 190n. 130, 191, 195n.
   146; article 290, 183, 185, 190; article
   291, 178, 183, 185, 190; article 306,
   223; article 392, 238n. 131
Arunachal Pradesh, 221, 222n. 61
Assam, 33n. 60, 36n. 66, 36n. 67, 36n. 68,
   37n. 69, 56n. 20, 57n. 22, 58n. 25, 58n.
   27, 59n. 30, 66–68, 67n. 69, 68n. 75,

69n. 84, 71n. 91, 71n. 92, 72n. 94, 72n.
98, 75n. 110, 76n. 112, 76n. 113, 76n.
114, 77n. 115, 78n. 124, 80n. 130, 80n.
131, 81n. 132, 82n. 134, 118–19, 151n.
122, 151n. 124, 152n. 125, 154n. 133,
192n. 136, 192n. 137, 192n. 140, 195n.
146, 212–15, 212n. 14, 213n. 17, 213n.
18, 214n. 19, 214n. 22, 215n. 24, 216n.
33, 217n. 36, 219n. 50, 219n. 52, 220n.
53, 220n. 54, 220n. 55, 220n. 56, 220n.
57, 221n. 58, 221n. 59, 221n. 61, 228n.
87, 228n. 88, 228n. 89, 228n. 90, 228n.
91, 229n. 94, 230n. 96; Chief Electoral
Officer of, 220, 220n. 53, 220n. 54,
220n. 55, 220n. 56, 221n. 58, 221n. 59;
citizens' organisations in, 65n. 61, 67,
69, 76, 81; procedure for the registration
of refugees, 68; Reforms Commissioner
of, 36n. 66, 36n. 67, 36n. 68, 37n. 69,
38n. 77, 39n. 80, 40n. 85, 57–58, 58n.
25, 58n. 27, 67–68, 67n. 69, 68n. 75,
69n. 84, 71n. 91, 76–78, 76n. 112, 76n.
113, 76n. 114, 77n. 115, 78n. 124, 80n.
130, 80n. 131, 81n. 132, 146n. 103,
147n. 107, 148n. 108, 151n. 122, 152n.
124, 152n. 125, 154n. 133, 228–30,
228n. 88, 228n. 89, 228n. 91, 229n. 94,
229n. 95, 230n. 96
Assam Bengalee Association, 56n. 20, 68–
   69, 68n. 79, 69n. 81, 69n. 82, 69n. 83,
   73n. 103
Assam Citizens' Association Dhubri, 56n.
   20, 64, 64n. 58, 65n. 62, 67n. 73, 69n.
   81, 69n. 83, 70n. 85, 76n. 110, 175–77,
   175n. 61, 176n. 69
Assam Citizens Association Gauhati, 56n.
   20, 68n. 78, 69n. 81, 71n. 91, 175,
   175n. 62, 176, 176n. 65, 176n. 69
Assam Citizens' Association Mangaldai,
   64, 64n. 59, 64n. 61, 72, 72n. 96, 73n.
   102, 76n. 110, 81n. 132, 81n. 134
Assam Citizens Association Nowgong, 71–
   72, 71n. 91, 71n. 92, 72n. 94, 81n. 132
Assam Government, 36n. 66, 44–45,
   44n. 100, 58, 68, 81n. 132, 96, 96n.
   36, 118–19, 146n. 103, 147n. 107,
   151n. 124, 154n. 133, 228n. 88,
   228n. 90
Assam Land and Revenue (Amendment)
   Act, 1947, 175–76
Assam Refugees' Association, 63–64,
   75n. 110

Bahawalpur State, 70
Bakhtin, Mikhail, 87

Balipara Frontier Tract, 212, 212n. 12, 213n. 18, 215, 216n. 33, 217, 217n. 38, 217n. 39, 218n. 45, 220n. 52

Banaras District, 138

Baroda Domicile Act, 102

Baroda State, 93, 101–02, 102n. 68, 122n. 2, 141, 149n. 115

Baster State, 131

Basu, M.M., 75n. 109, 77n. 117, 132n. 40, 151n. 121, 151n. 123, 160, 160n. 4, 178–81, 178n. 77, 179n. 81, 179n. 83, 180n. 87, 180n. 88, 182n. 95

Bengal, 45, 58n. 27, 59, 69n. 80, 70, 70n. 88, 100, 151n. 122, *also see* West Bengal

Bengali Association Dibrugarh, 56n. 20, 69n. 81

Bengali Association, Margherita, 56n. 20

Bengali refugees, 233

Bengali speaking Hindus from East Pakistan, 72

Berar Government, 38, 238, 249

Bhadur, Maharao Sahib (of Kutch), 29n. 37

Bhandari, Gagan Dev, 111

Bhargava, Thakur Das, 177

Bhopal State, 102, 102n. 71, 133n. 44, 134n. 45, 142, 149n. 115, 249n. 14; Consititution of, 133

Bhuj (Kutch) state, 28

Bhushan, Brij, 31n. 49, 188, 188n. 121, 193n. 142, 197, 206–07

Bihar, 61, 66; first elections, 241; Government of. *see* Government of Bihar; house numbering in, 93; preparation of electoral rolls, 141, 240

Bihar Legislative Assembly Electoral (Preparation, Revision and Publication of Electoral Rolls) Rules,1936, 240

Bombay, 92, 101, 101n. 63, 103, 103n. 79, 110–12, 153n. 130, 154n. 133, 208–10, 208n. 1, 209n. 6, 210n. 10, 229n. 95, 230n. 98, 230n. 99, 234–35

Bombay Government, 208, 209

Brautigan, Richard, 258

bureaucracy, 34–35, 34n. 61, 53

bureaucrats, 1, 16, 21–23, 28, 34–35, 41, 50, 151, 152, 180, 252, 255

Cachar District, 38n. 77, 213n. 18, 214

CAD. *see* Constituent Assembly Debates (CAD)

Canada, 188–89, 204

candidates, 33n. 60, 42, 49, 92, 109–10, 155n. 137, 221, 234, 239; contesting

reserved seats for SCs and STs, 242; making caste appeals, 111

CAS. *see* Constituent Assembly Secretariat (CAS)

caste, 28n. 35, 110–12, 112n. 112, 211, 234–35, 235n. 117, 238n. 131, 239, 239n. 135, 239n. 137, 240, 240n. 140, 241, 241n. 144, 242–43, 243n. 152;appeals, 111; column of (on the electoral roll), 111, 234–35, 235n. 117; and the electoral roll, 211, 233–35, 239–41; and identity politics, 244; politics, 211; reservation system, 235

census, 23, 25n. 21, 27, 31n. 47, 36n. 67, 135n. 52, 182, 182n. 98, 235n. 117, 237n. 129, 238n. 133, 240n. 140, 243n. 152; decennial, 24, 25; and divorcing the preparation of the electoral rolls from the, 25; and the electoral roll, 24–25, 33, 51, 64, 204, 235; house-to-house, 138; inaccuracies in, 24; operation, 26; rejection of the proposal to combine with the electoral roll, 24–29

Central and Provincial legislatures, 32, 91, 99, 133, 161n. 5

Central and State legislatures, 99, 140

Central Election Commission, 190

Central Government, 55n. 13, 64, 117, 155n. 137, 169n. 40, 191, 214, 219

Central Legislatures, 144, 144n. 93, 146, 184

Central Provinces and Berar Act (Refugee Registration and Movement), 62

Chief Commissioner, 127, 134n. 47, 136, 136n. 53, 136n. 55, 140–41, 144n. 92, 149n. 115, 152n. 125, 158, 222n. 63, 229n. 95, 236n. 125, 249n. 14; of Delhi, 104, 236, 237n. 126; of Himachal Pradesh, 136

Chief Commissioner's Provinces (8), 140

Chief Draftsman, 201

Chief Electoral Officer of Assam, 220, 220n. 53, 220n. 54, 220n. 55, 220n. 56, 221n. 58, 221n. 59

Chief Justice of India, 144

Chief Minister of Cooch Behar State, 30n. 45, 148

Christian Constituency, 22

citizens, 53–54, 54n. 9, 56–58, 56n. 20, 63–69, 73, 75–77, 79–83, 167–68, 183–85, 224–32, 247, 251; adult, 122, 129, 185n. 107, 186, 210n. 11; democratic, 210; prospective, 74; registering, 63

citizens' associations, 68, 231, 253, *see also* citizens' organisations

citizens' organisations, 66, 71, 81–82, 83, 231, *see also* citizens' associations

citizenship, 6, 52–60, 56n. 20, 57n. 21, 58n. 27, 63–68, 74–75, 118, 167–69, 173–75, 225–33, 225n. 74, 225n. 75, 225n. 76, 226n. 77, 226n. 79, 227n. 83, 231n. 99, 232n. 103, 232n. 107, 233n. 108, 233n. 109, 244–47, 251–53; acquired, 231; anticipatory, 162; articles on, 54n. 5, 73, 166; clause, 54n. 5, 161, 161n. 6, 168; common, 128, 224; contests in roll making, 63–72; declarations for, 64–66, 66n. 66, 74, 76n. 111; demanded by citizens' associations, 231; democratic, 53, 73, 80, 89, 98, 105, 254; democratising, 73; dual, 128; dual (union and state), 128; securing, 64, 82; special law conferring, 233; struggles for, 53, 68, 80, 82–85; temporal, 82

citizenship articles, 82, 154, 167, 194, 211, 225–26, 231–32; detailed draft, 161; final, 227, 232

citizenship provisions, 54, 151n. 121, 227, 230–32; adopted, 228; anticipatory, 53; enacting of draft, 231; final, 225, 227, 227n. 82, 231

citizenship rights, 53–54, 63–66, 70, 73, 75, 82, 164, 246–47

civic organisations, 8, *also see* citizens' organisations

Cochin Nationality and Naturalisation Act, 172

Cochin State, 30, 93, 100n. 52, 102, 102n. 70, 141, 154n. 136, 172, 172n. 51, 174, 174n. 59, 175n. 60

colonial administrators, 2–4, 6, 12

colonial practices, 25, 46, 50–51; administration and administrators, 21, 41–44, 47–48, 212; and the concept of universal franchise and colonial attitudes, 23

colonial rule, 1, 2, 5

colonialism, 3, 15n. 44

Committee for Acquiring Indian Citizenship Jamshedpur, Bihar, 66, 79

Committee of the Constituent Assembly, 7

committees and sub-committees (of the Constituent Assembly of India); Advisory Committee on Fundamental Rights, Minorities and Tribal and Excluded Areas, 58n. 28, 161n. 5, 189, 192n. 139, 213, 213n. 17, 219n. 52, 238, 238n. 134; Fundamental Rights Sub-Committee, 189; Minorities Sub-Committee, 161n. 5, 184n. 103, 189;

North-East Frontier (Assam) Tribal and Excluded Area Sub-Committee, 213; Union Constitution Committee, 180, 180n. 89, 180n. 90, 181n. 92, 181n. 93, 184, 184n. 103, 189, 222

Constituent Assembly, 4n. 15, 7–8

Constituent Assembly Debates (CAD), 123n. 6, 161n. 5, 161n. 6, 165n. 20, 165n. 21, 168n. 34, 169n. 40, 171n. 46, 171n. 47, 176n. 66, 176n. 67, 181n. 94, 182n. 98, 184n. 103, 184n. 104, 185n. 106, 185n. 108, 190n. 130, 191n. 134, 192n. 140, 193n. 143, 195n. 147, 196n. 149, 219n. 52, 221n. 57, 225n. 75, 225n. 76, 226n. 80, 248, 248n. 1, 250n. 21, 255n. 29

Constituent Assembly of India, 7, 106–07, 113–15, 126–28, 128n. 27, 129n. 31, 132n. 40, 133n. 43, 144n. 95, 146n. 102, 148n. 111, 149n. 115, 151n. 123, 162–65, 171–72, 172n. 50, 173n. 52, 175–78, 175n. 61, 176n. 63, 176n. 69, 177n. 71, 178n. 77, 180n. 87, 180n. 88, 181n. 90, 182–85, 182n. 95, 182n. 98, 183n. 101, 197–201, 197n. 154, 203n. 172, 205n. 183, 209n. 6, 212n. 12, 212n. 13;

committees of, 7; debates, 6; debates on the electoral rolls, 123n. 6, 161n. 5, 161n. 6, 165n. 20, 165n. 21, 168n. 34, 169n. 40, 171n. 46, 171n. 47, 176n. 66, 176n. 67, 181n. 94, 182n. 98, 184n. 103, 184n. 104, 185n. 106, 185n. 108, 190n. 130, 191n. 134, 192n. 140, 193n. 143, 195n. 147, 196n. 149, 219n. 52, 221n. 57, 225n. 75, 225n. 76, 226n. 80, 248, 248n. 1, 250n. 21, 255n. 29; decision to adopt universal franchise, 129; Secretariat, 1, 4

Constituent Assembly Secretariat (CAS), 23, 91, 93, 162, 165, 184–94, 196–97, 201, 203–04, 242, 244; administrative deliberations within, 53; direction of instructions for draft electoral roll, 23–24, 162, 243; instructions for compilation of the first draft electoral roll (universal franchise), 24, 93; requests of the provinces and states, 93, 162, 203, 241; Secretary, 162, 203; and shaping of the Constitution, 184–94, 236, 241

Constitution Drafting Committee, 82, 170, 175, 176, 177, 180, 181, 189, 191, 192, 193, 225

Constitution for India, 3n. 10

Constitution of India, 116, 122, 125, 197n. 152, 202n. 168, 203, 203n. 171,

241, 245; draft, 32–33, 54, 63, 67, 75–
77, 143–44, 173–74, 175–78, 180–85,
194–95; making of, 196, 203, 205, 244;
new, 32–34, 36n. 66, 36n. 67, 36n. 68,
37n. 69, 38n. 77, 39n. 80, 40n. 85,
40n. 86, 90–92, 94n. 25, 95n. 29, 97n.
39, 99–100, 140n. 77, 141n. 79, 142n.
89, 148, 159–62, 165–67, 181n. 93,
182n. 96, 183n. 99, 240–41; theories
of, 171–72

Constitutional Adviser, 4, 8, 31, 59n. 30,
60, 62, 64n. 59, 65–66, 161n. 6, 181n.
90, 187n. 114, 187n. 115, 193n. 142,
197–200, 203–04, *also see* B. N. Rau

constitutional citizenship (provisions), 66,
75, 129n. 31, 177

constitutional conversations, 178, 180

constitutional debates, 2, 161, 164,
181, 193

constitutional discrepancies, 137, 143,
148, 173n. 52, 190

constitutional framework, 53, 202, 226

constitutional gaps, 126, 157

constitutional interpretations, 65, 146

constitutional morality, 195–96, 196n. 149

constitutional position, 76, 233,
241, 242–43

constitutional principles, 87, 253

constitutional promises, 254

constitutional provisions, 161, 164, 170–
72, 175, 177–78, 188n. 121, 194–95,
210–11, 225, 238, 253–54

Cooch Behar State, 30n. 45, 148, 148n.
108, 152n. 127, 154n. 136

Coorg, 93, 141, 181n. 93

correspondences, 29, 83, 113–16, 130,
131n. 34, 133, 146–48, 155, 157, 164,
186n. 111, 187n. 117, 213–32, *also see*
letters; of administrators of provinces
and states regarding universal franchise,
202; conducted, 194; prolonged, 44,
130; regular, 140; repeated, 80

costs (of preparation of rolls), 130, 137,
142–50, 148n. 111, 155–56, 157,
170n. 45, 186n. 110, 187, 187n. 116,
189n. 125, 191n. 133; estimated, 103,
137; negligible, 147; recovery of, 144,
144n. 93

covenants (of Union of States), 124, 126,
126n. 18, 127n. 21, 134n. 47

Cover, Robert, 86, 115

Cutch, 141

Cuttack, 134, 134n. 47

Dabeka, 72

Dacca, 22

dangers (of adult franchise), 106–07; of
introducing election ferment, 49; of
unrestricted political power, 107

decennial census, 24–25

declarations, 55, 60–79, 66n. 66, 74n. 107,
76n. 111, 77n. 115, 78n. 124, 81, 96,
117–19, 166–67, 169, 225n. 74, 227–
28, 230; for citizenship, 57, 66, 74; filing
of, 71, 81; husband's, 118; oral, 171;
receiving of, 57; for refugees' registration
as voters, 68; required, 168; requisite,
64, 76n. 113

Delhi, 73n. 99, 75–77, 76n. 112, 104,
104n. 82, 137, 235–36

Delhi Municipality, 104

deliberations, 61, 149, 163, 183;
administrative, 31; constitutional, 194;
final constitutional, 194; informed, 23

Delimitation Committee, 242; of
constituencies, 152, 167, 170, 188, 194,
242, 256

democracy, 1–6, 9–12, 14–15, 89, 107–
08, 127n. 22, 127n. 23, 191–92, 244,
251–55, 251n. 23, 254n. 28, 256n. 32;
establishment of, 5; institutionalisation
of, 251, 254, 255; largest, 1, 245,
254–55; meaning of the term, 5;
parliamentary, 122; problems besetting
Indian, 254; "pucca", 130, 150

democratic cartography for India,
130, 153

democratic citizenship, 5–7, 11, 15–17

democratic constitution, 6

democratic dialogues, 84, 85

democratic dispositions, 35, 50, 85

democratic federal order, 130

democratic institution building, 50

democratic nationhood, 2

democratic politics, 5

democratic republic, 94, 202

democratic state-building processes, 6

democratisation, 34, 54, 85, 89, 127n.
22, 133, 191, 255; of citizenship, 251;
processes, 253; spatial, 130

depressed classes, 112, 238

Devicolam Taluq Travancore, 172, 173–74,
173n. 51, 173n. 53

devolution, principles of, 23n. 10, 33,
42n. 92

Dhebar, U.N., 156

difficulties (in preparation of electoral
rolls), 26, 27–30, 39, 44–46, 70n.
89, 93–94, 136, 155, 220, 237;
administrative, 42, 216; imagined,
29; raised by local authorities, 72;
registration of woman, 42

directives (for enrolment), 32, 38, 76, 80–82, 90, 158; detailed, 32; issued, 100; new, 62, 140, 142
disciplining the new federation, 122, 130, 140, 143, 254
disenfranchisement, 31, 47, 70, 104, 185, 190, 220
displaced persons, 55, 80, 93, 154, 228–31, 249n. 14
disputes, 100, 126–27, 184n. 103, 185n. 105, 194, 232
disqualifications, 32, 32n. 56, 91–92, 149, 161n. 5, 182–83
District Magistrates, 22, 55, 62, 66, 74, 75n. 107, 118, 167, 169, 171
District Officers, 27, 27n. 28, 28n. 33, 35, 36n. 66, 36n. 68, 37n. 69, 39, 45–48, 45n. 107, 45n. 110, 46n. 113, 47n. 115, 58n. 25, 58n. 27, 77–78, 91, 138–40, 140n. 75, 140n. 76
disturbances, 62, 97, 118, 166, 230n. 99
Dominion of India, 66, 126n. 18, 127, 127n. 21, 142n. 89, 246–47, see also India
Dominion Parliament, 144, 149, see also Parliament
draft articles, 32n. 56, 55, 82n. 136, 154n. 135, 169, 181, 184, 225n. 74, 227, 230; final, 161; new, 190n. 130, 192; original, 191
draft citizenship, 52, 54, 66, 160, 227n. 83, 228, 231; clauses, 161; provisions, 164, 169
Draft Constitution, 6
draft Constitution of February 1948, 212
draft Constitution of India, 32–33, 53–54, 62–63, 66–67, 75–77, 125n. 16, 126n. 17, 128n. 30, 129n. 31, 143–44, 173–74, 175–78, 180–85, 194–95
draft Electoral Rolls, 34, 36n. 68, 37n. 70, 37n. 71, 37n. 72, 38n. 76, 38n. 77, 40n. 84, 40n. 87, 47, 48, 49n. 123, 57, 74n. 106, 75n. 109, 77, 92–93, 99n. 45, 101, 148n. 111, 152, 153n. 130, 157, 162, 193, 206; preparation of, 36n. 65, 36n. 66, 36n. 66, 36n. 67, 38n. 73, 38n. 77, 39n. 78, 39n. 80, 40n. 82, 40n. 85, 40n. 86, 46n. 113, 89n. 16
dual citizenship (union and state), 128

East Bengal, 58n. 27, 65n. 61, 66
East Bengal Minority Welfare Central Committee; Calcutta, 57
East Khandesh District Congress Committee, 110, 110n. 107, 111n. 108, 114n. 121, 160, 160n. 3

East Pakistan, 72, 232–33, 233n. 108
East Punjab, 37, 39–41, 59n. 33, 70–71, 70n. 88, 99, 101, 137–39, 141, 237, 238–40
East Punjab Government, 40–41, 59n. 33, 100, 137–38, 154, 249
ECI. see Election Commissioner of India (ECI)
education (and universal franchise), 52n. 2, 83n. 137, 106, 110, 177, 216–18; institutions, 176, 239; rights, 176
Election Commission, 182–84, 184n. 103, 188–89, 189n. 124, 190n. 130, 191n. 133, 192n. 141, 205n. 183, 220, 223n. 69, 231, 232n. 103, 232n. 105, 250n. 16, 250n. 17, 250n. 19, 253n. 26, 256; autonomous, 253; centralised, 190; interim, 190; and the note from the Drafting Committee, 189, 189n. 125; single central, 185
Election Commission of India, 4, 7–9; First Chief Election Commissioner, 4; and opinion notes prepared by members of the CAS, 8
Election Commission of India (ECI), 47n. 116, 48n. 120, 191n. 133, 205–06, 210n. 10, 220n. 53, 220n. 54, 221n. 58, 223n. 67, 231–32, 242n. 149, 243n. 151, 245n. 156, 248n. 4, 250n. 18, 250n. 20, 256n. 31, 258n. 37
Election Commissioners, 70n. 86, 70n. 89, 103, 137n. 59, 138n. 65, 139n. 73, 155n. 137, 237, 237n. 127, 249n. 12, 250n. 19; of East Punjab, 39n. 77, 39n. 78, 40n. 82; of East Punjab, 28n. 33, 29, 29n. 40, 38n. 73, 40n. 86, 41n. 88, 46n. 113, 70n. 89, 76n. 112, 137–39, 235n. 115; for Hyderabad, 102
election laws, 34, 92, 162, 210n. 10
election management bodies, 128, 143, 150, 188, 191, 207
Election Officers, 29, 93, 137n. 58
election provisions, 195; future constitutional, 185
election tribunals, 182, 184n. 103, 185n. 105
electioneering, 49, 107
elections, 2–4, 10, 13, 35n. 65, 36n. 67, 36n. 68, 37n. 70, 37n. 71, 37n. 72, 38n. 75, 38n. 76, 38n. 77, 39n. 79, 40n. 84, 40n. 85, 40n. 87, 101–03, 102n. 71, 102n. 72, 103n. 76, 103n. 78, 103n. 79, 106–07, 106n. 91, 134n. 45, 139n. 68, 155n. 137, 156n. 140, 159n. 149, 161n. 5, 172–74, 182n. 96, 183n. 99, 184–86,

184n. 103, 185n. 105, 185n. 106, 188–
91, 192–93, 241–44; conduct of, 188,
207; first, 4–5, 6, 8, 9, 14, 30, 47n. 116,
53, 103n. 79, 138, 148, 157, 185, 191n.
133, 206, 220n. 52, 233, 233n. 108,
234, 240n. 140, 241, 242, 244, 245n.
156, 256n. 31, 257; free, 102; fresh,
209, 245; municipal, 106; new, 187; in
Pakistan, 29; planned, 102; preparation
for, 99, 143; provincial, 149; and P.S.
Subramanian, 206; in the UK, 188; in
the USA, 188
electoral colleges, 107
electoral democracy, 4, 5, 6, 8, 9–18, 53,
73–74, 80, 83–84, 94, 101, 159, 164–65,
194, 202, 251–55, 256; edifice of, 244,
251; form of, 257; institutions of, 21, 86
electoral institutions, 2
electoral law, 13, 48, 60–62, 117, 143, 151,
157, 159, 162, 170, 225, 230, 241; new,
91–93, 117, 156, 162, 241; pending, 138
electoral politics, 58n. 27, 211,
240, 243–44
electoral roll, and the "religion column",
104n. 82
electoral rolls, 1–5, 6–7, 9, 13–14, 21–28,
30–38, 54, 85–92, 87n. 10, 88n. 12, 89n.
16, 90n. 19, 90n. 22, 94n. 25, 95–107,
95n. 29, 97n. 39, 100n. 58, 101n. 62,
101n. 63, 102n. 68, 103n. 75, 103n. 76,
103n. 79, 132–43, 134n. 45, 134n. 47,
135n. 48, 135n. 49, 135n. 50, 136n. 53,
136n. 55, 137n. 59, 138n. 65, 138n. 66,
138n. 67, 139n. 68, 139n. 71, 139n. 72,
139n. 73, 140n. 77, 141n. 79, 142n.
89, 144–49, 144n. 93, 145n. 100, 145n.
99, 147n. 106, 148n. 111, 149n. 115,
230–37, 238–43, 248–54, *also see* voters
list, and preliminary electoral rolls;
and citizenship, 63–73; colonial, 22;
costs, 103, 130, 137, 144, 144n. 93,
147, 148n. 111, 150, 156, 157, 170n.
45, 186n. 110, 187, 187n. 116, 189n.
125, 191n. 133; and domestic servant,
208, 209, 210; and hotel servant, 208;
and house numbering, 33, 36–38,
41, 92, 95, 135, 137–38; information
concerning, 239; new, 22, 99n. 44,
101n. 62, 101n. 64, 104n. 82; original,
175; provisional, 96n. 36, 118; and
the relations between the centre and
the states, 129, 256; and the "religion
column", 73, 111–12, 111n. 110, 176,
211, 233–36, 239–42, 239n. 135,
241n. 144; reprinting of, 147, 152; and
residency, 55, 169, 174, 231n. 99; set

a precedent for universal franchise and
democracy, 256
electoral system, 31n. 51, 109, 110n. 106,
252n. 25
electoral units, 32–33, 54, 70, 91–92,
94, 129
electorate, 3, 3n. 9, 4, 4n. 13, 12, 13, 30,
33, 42–43, 47–48, 48n. 120, 155–56,
234, 241, 248n. 4, 248n. 5, 249n. 10,
249n. 11, 249n. 12, 249n. 13, 249n.
14, 249n. 6, 249n. 7, 249n. 8, 250–51,
250n. 15, 250n. 16, 250n. 18, 250n. 19,
257, 257n. 36; enlightened, 122; female,
43; joint, 102, 111, 161n. 5, 185n. 107,
241, 243; large, 42, 50; mass, 243, 245;
restricted, 22
enactment of the constitution, 5
enfranchisement, 24, 43n. 95, 48–49,
210n. 10, 214, 217–19, 224
enfranchising, 50, 233
enlistment process, 29, 41, 101
enrolment, 27, 50, 53–54, 59, 62, 67–70,
73–74, 78, 96n. 36, 100n. 57, 117–19,
148–49; instructions for, 54; procedures,
186; process, 80
enrolment (of voters), 4, 6
enumeration, 26, 28n. 36, 32–33, 50, 77n.
118, 81, 82n. 134, 101, 101n. 64, 104n.
82, 112–13, 156; complete, 24; forms,
156; house to house, 155
enumerators, 28n. 36, 37, 40, 69, 77,
81n. 134, 101, 104n. 82, 112, 129,
168, 234–36
equality, 26, 29, 74, 163n. 17, 179;
economic, 254; procedural, 31, 34, 41,
51, 85, 210, 243
ethno nationalist attitudes, 72, 79
evacuees, 55n. 13, 59, 80
expenditure, 129, 144–47, 150, 156, 156n.
140, 170, 186, 190; incurring heavy,
156; large, 145
Ezrahi, Yaron, 142n. 88, 248, 248n. 3

federal scheme, 122, 127n. 22, 128,
129, 200
federal state, 254; building process, 142;
strong united, 252
federal structure, 122, 254; democratic,
129; emerging, 129; forming, 132; new,
117, 153
federalism, 122
federation, 116, 122–23, 124n. 12, 125–
30, 127n. 22, 128n. 29, 133, 143, 148,
156–57, 191, 198; forming, 133, 140,
142, 159; Indian, 127, 142, 156–57;
new, 130, 136

Federation of India. *see* Indian federation
female voters, 39, 45n. 110, 46–47,
    46n. 113
Fifth Schedule (of the Draft), 22n.
    6, 181–82
First World War, 3, 60
floods, 39, 138, 139n. 72, 141
footpaths (dwellers), 208–10
Foucault, Michel, 26n. 23
framework, legal, 3, 12–14
The Framing of India's Constitution,
    161n. 5, 176n. 63, 176n. 68, 177n. 70,
    181n. 90, 184n. 103, 189n. 124, 189n.
    126, 192n. 141, 212n. 14, 213n. 17,
    214n. 22, 214n. 23, 219n. 50, 219n. 52,
    222n. 62, 223n. 68
franchise, 1, 2–7, 9, 13, 89, 101, 113, 116;
    branch, 113, 205; democratic, 73;
    education and gender qualifications
    under colonial rule, 3; expansion of
    the, 42, 42n. 93; and illiteracy, 42, 254;
    limited, 2, 28; making universal, 26, 51;
    provisions, 22; qualifications, 44, 128,
    149–50, 149n. 115, 241; restricted, 3;
    rights, 53, 59, 64, 66–68, 82, 105, 233;
    women's, 44n. 100, 46
Franchise Section, 108n. 98, 109n. 101,
    142n. 89, 191n. 133, 193n. 142, 197,
    205n. 183, *also see* franchise branch
Frankfurter, Justice Felix, 196, 200
"Free India" elections, 98, 101, 101n. 63,
    160, 222n. 63
freedom, 29, 124n. 11, 124n. 12, 127n.
    22, 128n. 29, 175–76, 214; movement,
    39; and the protection of certain rights
    regarding, 175
Frontier Tracts (Sadiya, Balipara and
    Tirap), 77n. 115, 81n. 131, 140n. 75,
    215–16, 218–21, 229n. 94, 230n. 96
Fundamental Rights Committee of the
    Constituent Assembly, 23
Fundamental Rights Sub-Committee, 189

Gandhi, M.K., 112, 153
general elections, 48n. 120, 92–94,
    99, 101–02, 108, 221–23, 221n. 61,
    223n. 67; holding fresh, 91, 94; in India,
    99; national, 103
Government of Bihar, 43, 48, 79, 97n. 39,
    147, 147n. 105, 147n. 106, 151n. 123,
    151n. 124, 152n. 125, 152n. 127, 240,
    248, 248n. 4
Government of Bihar and Orissa, 43, 44,
    44n. 101, 47n. 117, 48n. 118
Government of Cochin, 174

Government of India, 47–49, 124n. 10,
    124n. 11, 125n. 13, 125n. 16, 126n. 18,
    131n. 34, 131n. 36, 133n. 43, 134n. 47,
    140n. 78, 142–50, 144n. 92, 144n. 93,
    146n. 103, 147n. 107, 156, 156n. 140,
    158n. 144, 186n. 110, 188n. 119, 200–
    01, 220n. 53, 220n. 56, 221n. 58, 221n.
    59, 237n. 129, 238n. 131, 240n. 140,
    242n. 148
The Government of India Act 1919, 127
The Government of India Act 1919, 44n.
    100, 212–13, 212n. 13
The Government of India Act 1935, 127–
    28, 212–13, 214
Government of India Bill 1935, 43
Government of Orissa, 43, 47–48, 134–35,
    135n. 48, 135n. 49, 135n. 50, 135n.
    51, 144, 144n. 93, 144n. 94, 155, 155n.
    139, 249, 249n. 8, 249n. 9
Government of the Central Provinces and
    Berar, 35–38, 35n. 65, 36n. 67, 37n. 71,
    38n. 75, 39n. 79, 40n. 85, 77, 77n. 119,
    77n. 120, 147n. 107, 150n. 120, 154n.
    136, 156n. 140, 237–38, 237n. 130,
    238n. 131, 249, 249n. 7
Government of Travancore, 30–31, 30n.
    46, 67n. 68, 72n. 98, 172–74, 173n.
    54, 185
Government of West Bengal, 37–40, 37n.
    68, 37n. 70, 37n. 71, 37n. 72, 38n. 76,
    38n. 77, 40n. 84, 40n. 87, 62–63, 66–67,
    73n. 100, 74–77, 74n. 105, 74n. 107,
    75n. 109, 96, 146, 146n. 103, 147n.
    104, 151n. 121, 151n. 122, 151n. 123,
    151n. 124, 153n. 131, 178n. 77, 180n.
    88, 182n. 95
Governor of Assam, 212, 219n. 52,
    220n. 54
Governor's Provinces (9), 140, 181n. 93

Harijans, 90n. 19, 110n. 106, 111n. 109,
    139, 237, 240
health (access to), 216–17
Himachal Pradesh, 136, 136n. 53, 136n.
    55, 141, 154n. 136, 250
Hindus, 22, 28n. 36, 38n. 77, 43n. 95,
    44n. 100, 58n. 27, 97n. 39, 99n. 49,
    100n. 52, 226, 227n. 81, 232–37, 240
Hirschkop, Ken, 87, 116
Hkamtis, 218, 218n. 45
Hojai, 71–72, 71n. 91, 71n. 92
home, 31, 39, 55n. 14, 69, 100, 113;
    adopted, 172; ancestral, 172, 231;
    original, 228
"house census", 138

house numbering, 31n. 47, 33, 36–38, 36n. 67, 41, 92, 94, 95, 135, 137–38
House of Commons, 49
House of Parliament, 179
House of the People, 256
husbands, 43–44, 48, 72, 76, 96, 96n. 34, 109, 113, 118, 169
huts, 208–10, 245
Hyderabad, 53n. 4, 78, 102–03, 102n. 73, 103n. 75, 103n. 76, 103n. 77, 104n. 79, 123n. 8, 124n. 9, 133n. 42, 158–59, 159n. 149, 229n. 95, 250, 250n. 19; and the invasion by the Indian Army, 102, 102n. 73

identity, 43n. 95, 58n. 27, 134n. 44, 134n. 47, 137, 153n. 128, 157, 243–44, 251; political, 156, 244; regional, 153; social, 244
Iengar, H.V. R., 5n. 15
Iengar, H.V.R., 25n. 20, 160, 160n. 2, 180n. 89, 186, 187n. 113, 187n. 114, 197, 197n. 153, 197n. 154, 199, 199n. 159, 203–04, 203n. 172, 204n. 173
illiteracy, 42n. 92, 88, 111, 111n. 108, 135, 167, 171, 254, 257; of rural people, 49; of voters, 49
illustrative form, 33, 45
imagination, 41–42, 81n. 131, 85, 89, 94, 108, 115, 153n. 128, 251n. 23, 254; bureaucratic, 34; democratic, 115, 245; popular, 251
immigrants, 53, 57, 57n. 21, 58n. 27, 65–67, 65n. 61, 67n. 69, 177n. 73
incidents, 186; of abuse in the registration of refugees, 78; of exclusion from registration, 186, 211
income tax, 43, see also tax
independence, 2, 5, 6, 181n. 90, 184n. 102, 184n. 103, 188, 190n. 130, 192, 207, 211–13, 224, 224n. 71, 233n. 109, 252, 255; and the administrative machinery preceding, 124; and colonial rule, 23; and the integration of 552 princely states, 122; safeguarding of, 192; and the signing of the Instruments of Accessions, 123
Indian citizens, 159, 221, 228, 231
Indian citizenship; common, 225; democratic, 73
Indian Civil Service, 160n. 4, 181n. 90, 184n. 102, 198
Indian Constitution, 149n. 115, 150n. 119, 160, 163, 163n. 14, 163n. 15, 163n. 16,

164n. 17, 165n. 19, 193n. 141, 198n. 156, 199, 202, 205
Indian Delimitation Committee, 49, 49n. 126
Indian federation, 127, 142, 156–57
Indian Franchise Committee, 43, 47, 48n. 120
Indian Independence Act, 122
Indian States (Princely), 50, 116, 116n. 131, 117n. 133, 122, 122n. 2, 123n. 4, 123n. 8, 124n. 10, 124n. 11, 125n. 15, 126–27, 126n. 17, 126n. 19, 127n. 22, 128n. 26, 131n. 34, 131n. 36, 133n. 43, 134n. 47, 140n. 78, 158n. 144, 254
Indian Supreme Court, 117, 117n. 134, 127
Indian Union, 7, 59, 73, 75, 111, 118, 124, 125n. 16, 128n. 30, 172, 177, 231
Indian unity, 254
Indian women, 104
individual States (14), 140
instructions, 22–23, 32–39, 36n. 66, 36n. 68, 38n. 73, 39n. 78, 40n. 82, 41n. 89, 50, 61–63, 66–68, 75n. 110, 77n. 115, 78n. 122, 82, 88n. 16, 95n. 31, 139–40, 171–72, 234–35; for compilation of the first draft electoral roll (universal franchise), 24, 93; confidential, 68; detailed, 55, 57; devising, 34n. 61, 46; general, 32, 90–91; government's, 73; initial, 80; interim, 57; local, 35, 41; misconstrued, 74; necessary, 101n. 63, 139, 229n. 95; new, 62; secret, 242
Instrument of Accession, 117, 117n. 133, 123–25, 124n. 10, 126n. 18, 133
integration (of states), 116–17, 116n. 131, 123–24, 123n. 4, 123n. 8, 124n. 12, 125n. 13, 125n. 14, 126–27, 129, 134, 134n. 44, 134n. 47, 136, 142–43, 156–57, 254–55; administrative, 157; challenges of, 122; key mechanism of, 129, 224; national, 130; political, 156; procedures, 128; process of, 101, 123n. 6, 124n. 12, 124n. 9, 157–58; and the Supreme Court, 117

Jaipur Government, 26, 27n. 27, 29–30, 30n. 42, 142, 144n. 92
Jammu and Kashmir, 113n. 117, 158–59, 223
Jat-Pat Torak Mandal (society), 234–35, 234n. 113, 235n. 114, 235n. 115, 235n. 116, 235n. 118, 235n. 119
Jodhpur, 93, 141

joint electoral roll, 22, 26, 122, 185
Jullundur, 104, 124n. 12

Kachins tribe, 216–17
Kerr, Sir John, 43
Khaund, R.R. (Reforms Commissioner of
    Assam), 36n. 66, 36n. 67, 36n. 68, 37n.
    69, 38n. 77, 39n. 80, 40n. 85, 76n. 113,
    220n. 53, 220n. 54, 220n. 56, 221n. 58,
    221n. 59
Kolhapur government, 93, 136, 137n. 58,
    141, 144, 144n. 92
Krishnamachari, T.T., 126n. 17, 128n.
    30, 193
Kurukhshetra, 70

labour unions, 47, 113
Lahore, 29
Lakhimpur, 71, 71n. 91, 213n. 18
language, 33, 38, 53, 66, 73, 92, 95, 163n.
    15, 163n. 17, 181n. 90, 196n. 149;
    abstract, 53, 164; common, 195;
    political, 79; vernacular, 88, 88n. 16
law, 85–86, 91–93, 126–27, 127n. 21,
    144n. 93, 146n. 103, 147n. 107,
    178–79, 183n. 100, 184n. 103, 186–
    87, 186n. 111, 186n. 112, 191n. 133,
    204n. 172, 204n. 174, 205n. 183,
    220n. 53, 220n. 56, 221n. 58, 221n. 59,
    246–47; common, 172n. 51, 173, 202;
    constitutional, 122; evacuee property, 79
legacy of colonial rule, 1, 3
Legal Remembrancer, 198, 249n. 11
legislation, 29–30, 126, 175, 177, 225n.
    74, 227, 233, 233n. 109; auxiliary, 79;
    making of new, 175
legislative assemblies, 146–47, 182,
    182n. 98
Legislative Councils, 44, 149, 178
legislatures, 23–24, 30n. 46, 31n. 51, 33n.
    60, 148–49, 165–66, 170, 174, 177–
    78, 182n. 98, 184n. 103, 185n. 105,
    211, 213; bi-cameral, 178; sovereign, 24
letters, 32, 45n. 110, 130, 133, 145, 158,
    207, 239; of complaint, 56, 56n. 20;
    confidential, 229, 229n. 94, 230n. 96;
    detailed, 23; of instruction, 33, 34, 87,
    91, 131, 136, 138, 158, 162, 235, 239;
    official, 83; report, 136
lists (of voters), 29, 37, 50, 111, 114, 116,
    130–31, 131n. 34, 131n. 35, 133n. 42,
    133n. 43, 142n. 89, 156, 158n. 146,
    237–38; joint, 116, 254; original, 70;
    preliminary, 93; supplementary, 151–53
literacy, 22n. 6, 28n. 35, 43, 45
local administrators, 49, 55

local bodies, 93, 104
local gazette, 237
local governments, 40–41, 44n. 100, 45n.
    105, 63, 76, 81–83, 140, 164, 191
Lord Wavell, 122, 122n. 1, 123n. 5, 200,
    200n. 164
Lothian Committee, 4n. 13, 48
Lower Houses, 36n. 65, 37n. 68, 37n. 70,
    37n. 71, 37n. 72, 38n. 76, 38n. 77, 40n.
    84, 40n. 87, 91, 99, 107, 144, 146, 148

machinery (for election), 111, 168n. 40,
    187–89, 189n. 123, 257; administrative,
    23, 125, 195n. 147; autocratic state, 153;
    centralised electoral, 192; political, 214
MacMahon Line, 215
Madhava, K.B., 24–25, 24n. 14, 24n. 15
Madhya Bharat (also Madhyabharat),
    127n. 21, 141, 149, 150, 249; and
    Constituent Assembly, 149, 149n. 113,
    150n. 117, 150n. 118, 249n. 14
Madras, 27n. 29, 28n. 35, 29n. 41, 92,
    100, 112–13, 122n. 1, 146n. 103, 147n.
    107, 154n. 133, 182–83, 182n. 96,
    183n. 100, 183n. 101, 183n. 99, 196n.
    150, 198n. 156, 234–35
Madras Government, 28n. 35, 29n. 41
Madras Legislative Council, 177, 177n. 74
Maharaja of Cochin, 102
Maharaja of Mayurbhanj, 134, 134n. 46,
    134n. 47, 141
Maharani of Scindia, 105
Mandi State, 136
Manipur State, 30, 30n. 45, 93, 141, 149n.
    115, 149n. 116, 173n. 52
March instruction letters, 36n. 66, 131–32,
    143, 162
matriarchal system, 44
Menon, V.P., 116, 116n. 131, 123n. 4, 123n.
    8, 124, 124n. 12, 124n. 9, 125n. 13, 125n.
    14, 133n. 44, 134n. 47, 174n. 59
mentoring administrators, 73, 83, 202, 253
mergers (of states), 117, 123n. 8, 124,
    126n. 18, 129, 134, 134n. 44, 136,
    143, 157–59; agreements, 124–27;
    gradual, 128
Mewar State, 30
migrants, 75n. 109, 227, 227n. 83, 233,
    233n. 108, 246; refugees, 231
migration, 62, 68, 97, 227n. 81, 228,
    232, 246
Ministry of Defence, 139, 139n. 69,
    139n. 70
Ministry of Home Affairs, 183n. 100, 186,
    187n. 113, 213n. 14, 229–31, 229n. 95,
    237, 237n. 129

Ministry of Law, 144n. 93, 145n. 100,
146n. 103, 147n. 107, 183n. 100, 186–
88, 186n. 111, 186n. 112, 187n. 113,
191n. 133, 204n. 172, 204n. 174, 205n.
183, 220n. 53, 220n. 56, 221n. 58,
221n. 59, 229n. 95, 232n. 104, 233n.
108, 236n. 124, 243n. 151, 245n. 156,
249n. 6
Ministry of Relief and Rehabilitation, 118
Ministry of States, 123n. 6, 124n. 10,
124n. 11, 125n. 16, 126n. 17, 130–31,
130n. 34, 158–59, 159n. 150, 175n. 59,
237, 238n. 131
Ministry of Works, Mines and Power, 148
minorities, 109, 176, 211, 213, 218n.
45, 234, 238, 238n. 134, 241–44,
243n. 153; a fair deal to the, 244;
groups, 176; religious, 211, 238;
reservations for, 111n. 110, 211, 235,
238; setting up sub-committees, 213
Minorities Sub-Committee, 161n. 5, 184n.
103, 189
Mishmis, 218
Mohammadan constituency, 22, 43
motion preparation of electoral rolls, 41,
87, 142, 165, 169, 170–71
Mukherjee, S.N., 70n. 86, 73n. 100, 76n.
113, 77n. 116, 160n. 4, 162n. 11, 164,
170n. 44, 178, 178n. 77, 180–81, 180n.
87, 180n. 88, 182n. 95, 193, 193n.
142, 201
municipal land, 208–10
municipalities, 92, 155n. 137, 248, 250
Musil, Robert, 87n. 7, 95, 95n. 30
Muslims, 33n. 60, 43n. 95, 44n. 100, 58n.
27, 92, 111–12, 137, 226, 227n. 81,
233–35, 236n. 125, 240
Mysore, 24n. 14, 28n. 34, 30n. 42, 93,
102, 141, 158, 159n. 149, 229n. 95, 249
Mysore Government, 28n. 35, 249n. 11

Naga Hills District, 213n. 18, 214
Naga Tribal Areas, 212, 219
names, 44–48, 46n. 113, 47n. 116, 81n.
131, 81n. 134, 97n. 39, 103–04, 106,
112–16, 137, 151–52, 151n. 124,
153n. 130, 153n. 131, 245n. 156;
father's, 45; husband's, 45, 92; new,
112, 170; registration of, 37, 99, 138; of
Scheduled Tribes and Scheduled Castes,
238; spelling of, 38; of voters, 38–40;
woman's, 41–49; woman's, 44
narratives, 85–89, 85n. 1, 86n. 4, 86n.
7, 87n. 10, 95n. 30, 97–98, 113–16,
115n. 128; popular, 86; public, 97
National Planning Committee, 24

national polity, 23, 31
National Register of Citizens, 232
nationalism, 251–52, 254
naturalization, 25, 60
Negotiable Instruments Act, 27n. 29, 113,
113n. 117
Nehru Memorial, 5n. 15
Nehru Report, 3, 3n. 10, 6
Nehru, Jawaharlal, 4n. 15, 6n. 17, 110,
145, 145n. 100, 166, 166n. 22, 168,
171n. 47, 186–87, 186n. 110, 186n.
111, 187n. 115, 187n. 117, 189, 189n.
125, 232, 255
Nicobar Islands, 181n. 93, 222n. 63,
222n. 64, 223n. 65, 223n. 66, 224n. 70,
231n. 99
North East Frontier, 212n. 14, 213–14,
213n. 18, 214n. 22, 215n. 24, 216n. 33,
217n. 36, 220n. 57, 224

officers, 28, 33, 58, 68n. 76, 71n. 91,
81, 81n. 131, 90, 92, 97n. 39, 101n.
63, 246; local, 75, 102; polling, 42,
155n. 137; presiding, 49, 154n. 135,
155n. 137; responsible, 118, 169;
senior ICS, 180; supervision, 77;
"verifying that the declarant is actually
a refuge", 68
officials, 35, 38, 40, 45, 56, 63, 76–
78, 104, 138, 236, 243n. 151, 253;
engaged public, 253; local, 71, 80n.
130; lower level, 50; provincial, 79;
senior, 76
omissions, 135, 153n. 130, 156, 242;
inadvertent, 211; necessary, 152–53
orders, 59–61, 63, 66, 74–75, 79, 95–97,
99, 118–19, 135–36, 187n. 113, 213n.
14, 238n. 131, 239n. 136, 240n. 140;
final, 237; new, 80; original, 96, 118;
political, 84–86; sequential, 88, 94;
unidimensional, 95
ordinances, 58n. 27, 79–80, 80n. 128,
126n. 20, 227
Orissa, 43–45, 49, 131n. 35, 134–35,
134n. 47, 135n. 48, 135n. 49, 135n.
50, 135n. 51, 135n. 52, 144, 144n. 93,
144n. 94, 154n. 133, 155n. 139, 241,
249, 249n. 8, 249n. 9
Orissa Government, 43, 48, 135, 144
Orissa States, 134, 134n. 47
Ottoman Empire, 60

Padmanabhan, K.V., 21, 21n. 1, 25n. 19,
90n. 22, 180n. 90, 193n. 142, 197, 203–
06, 203n. 172, 204n. 173, 204n. 175,
205n. 180

Pakistan, 1, 55–57, 55n. 14, 57n. 21, 58n.
27, 59n. 32, 142n. 89, 226–31, 226n.
77, 227n. 81, 227n. 83, 229n. 94, 230n.
99, 232–33, 246
Panth Piploda, 95, 141, 181n. 93
paper, anticipated shortfall, 29–30, 30n.
42, 103, 129, 148, 151n. 123, 154, 155;
reams of, 30, 148, 154, 155
Parliament, 42n. 90, 42n. 92, 103n. 79,
105n. 88, 179, 185, 223, 231n. 99, 232–
33, 232n. 104, 240, 243n. 151, 247,
256, see also Union Parliament
Parliamentary Elections, 22n. 9, 221, see
also elections
Part B Tribal Areas (Assam), 212n. 12,
216n. 33, 219–21, 220n. 52, 221n. 58,
223, 224n. 70
partition, 1–2, 6, 52n. 3, 58n. 27, 70n. 88,
112, 225–27, 227n. 83, 231–32, 233n.
109, 251, 255; of India and Pakistan, 1;
and refugees, 52–54, 65n. 61, 67, 72n.
98, 85, 200, 211, 225, 225n. 74, 227,
232, 252n. 25; registering refugees, 54–
63; subcontinent's, 1; and violence, 1n.
2, 55, 233
passage and staircase dwellers (and
enrolment), 89n. 17, 97, 116, 189n. 125,
208–10, 245, 254
Patiala and East Punjab States Union
(PEPSU), 102, 102n. 72, 110, 125n. 16,
141, 155n. 138, 242, 250, 250n. 16
Patna State, 27–28, 28n. 31, 131, 143n.
90, 144n. 92
Peermade Taluqs Travancore, 172, 173–74
personalisation of universal
franchise, 85–157
political imagination, 31, 84–86, 87, 142n.
88, 248; bureaucratic, 23; democratic,
23, 26–27, 34, 142; popular democratic,
85–86, 255
political officers (on the Frontier Tracts),
68n. 75, 77n. 115, 140n. 75, 216–18,
217n. 38, 218n. 47, 220n. 54, 220n. 57
political organisations, 56n. 20, 87, 89
political parties, 42n. 92, 155n. 137, 244
political power, 107, 110, 251
political representation, 216, 219, 243–44
polling day, 257
polling stations, 151, 151n. 124, 154n.
135, 155n. 137
population, 42, 48n. 120, 53, 58n. 27, 123,
129, 136–37, 185, 191, 219–20, 223n.
65, 224n. 70, 240n. 140; adult, 26, 35,
106, 157; counting for the new form, 25;
excitable, 49; "extra", 220; floating, 72,

80n. 131; movement, 227; non-resident,
57, 80n. 130, 192; total, 220, 222;
voter, 29
post offices, 70, 85, 85n. 3, 92, 94, 97n.
39, 99, 114, 115n. 126
Prasad, Rajendra, 4n. 15
Prasad, Rajendra, 23–25, 65–66, 106–09,
186–89, 199–200
precedents, 22, 56, 83, 127n. 21, 256;
bureaucratic colonial, 48; explored
international, 60; foundational, 50; legal,
83; new bureaucratic, 34, 199
preliminary electoral rolls, 6–7, 26, 53, 54,
60–61, 64–65, 68, 78, 79, 111n. 110,
112n. 116, 118–19, 129–30, 150–56,
238–41; people making claims of the
state, 164; printing of, 152–53; starting
the preparation of, 26, 95, 98, 130, 133,
158, 256
Preparation of Draft Electoral Rolls for
elections, 36n. 65
Preparation of Draft Electoral Rolls for
elections to the Lower Houses of the
Central and Provincial Legislatures,
36n. 65
preparation of electoral rolls, 24–25, 36n.
66, 36n. 67, 38n. 73, 38n. 77, 39n. 78,
39n. 80, 40n. 82, 40n. 85, 40n. 86, 46n.
113, 89n. 16, 162, see also instructions
for compilation of the first draft electoral
roll (universal franchise); draft roll
on the basis of adult franchise, 24;
proposals to combine with census, 24;
under colonial framework, 49–50
Preparation of Electoral rolls and
citizenship, 57n. 21
"Preparation of Electoral rolls and
citizenship of the Immigrants from
Pakistan", 57n. 21
press, 57, 82, 90, 98, 155; announcements,
108; communiqués, 40, 47, 47n. 116,
90n. 22, 102, 104; comprehensive
coverage, 96
Press Information Bureau, 90, 91n. 23
press notes, 79n. 125, 80–82, 87–91,
88n. 12, 94n. 25, 95, 95n. 29, 96n. 36,
97, 97n. 37, 97n. 39, 100n. 57, 107,
113, 117–18, 119n. 136, 234n. 110,
234n. 111; detailed explanatory, 62, 79;
draft, 90, 95–96; key, 89
Princely States, 22, 28, 98, 116, 122, 123,
124, 125, 128, 143, 157, 254, 255
printing (of the electoral rolls), 129–30,
137, 141–53, 147n. 106, 151n. 121,
151n. 123, 152n. 125, 155–56, 165,

169–70, 171, 228, 240–41, 250; centres, 249; cost of, 144, 146, 148, 153; of electoral rolls, 152–53; reprinting, 147, 152; suggested size of run, 154
problems (with preparation of electoral rolls), 45–46, 56, 59, 93, 95, 97, 104–06, 138n. 66, 139n. 73, 156–57, 169–71, 198–200, 237–38; administrative, 26–29, 27n. 27, 30n. 42, 130, 157; anticipated, 177; envisaged, 30; general, 21; insuperable, 25; practical, 252; redressing, 76, 83; solving, 29, 83
procedural equality, 5
progress (in the preparation of electoral rolls), 27, 34, 38, 93–95, 99–101, 100n. 58, 101n. 62, 111, 117, 132n. 40, 135, 135n. 51, 138–42, 138n. 65, 139n. 72, 139n. 73, 140n. 77, 141n. 79; appreciable, 95, 135; continual, 142; fortnightly reports, 27, 34, 38, 95, 134, 137, 138, 139, 245; reports, 141; of work, 46n. 114, 133, 135–36, 135n. 49, 135n. 50, 138, 138n. 66, 138n. 67, 139n. 71, 139n. 72, 158
propaganda, 89n. 16, 111, 135
property, 22n. 6, 44, 124n. 12, 175–76; immovable, 59; ownership, 44
provinces, 26–34, 35–36, 42–45, 60–62, 90–93, 98–101, 119–35, 127n. 23, 130n. 33, 130n. 34, 142–51, 153–58, 187–90, 248–50; governments of, 239, 239n. 138, 240n. 139; premiers of, 26
provinces and states, 26, 26n. 24, 29, 29n. 39, 62, 90, 93, 95, 99, 119, 145, 168; administrators and enlistment process, 26; asked to operationalize the basic procedural aspect of the notion of equality, 26; correspondence of administrators, 204; and the introduction by the CAS of the uniform definition of a "refugee", 95; and the issues of universal franchise, 29, 31, 62
Provincial Election Commission, 182, 182n. 96, 183n. 99
provincial governments, 35–37, 36n. 67, 47–49, 55–57, 59, 61n. 40, 63n. 53, 79–82, 146, 168, 185–86, 190–92, 219; and consultation about preparing electoral registers, 25; reformed, 212; responsible, 46; Secretariat's instructions by, 185
Provincial Legislative Assemblies, 22
publicity (preparation of electoral rolls), 27, 40, 47–48, 69, 76, 88, 93, 100

Punjab, 43, 70, 136, 232, 249n. 12, 250, *also see* East Punjab
"purdahnashin" women, 39, 69, 69n. 81

qualifications (for franchise), 22n. 6, 43–45, 43n. 96, 44n. 103, 92–93, 148–49, 154, 157, 162, 166, 173–74, 208, 225; detailed, 170; electoral, 35; prescribed residency, 55, 169, 174; uniform, 22

Radhakrishnan, S., 52
Rajasthan, 47n. 116, 141, 238, 238n. 133, 245n. 156
Rajputana, 106, 106n. 92
Rampur State, 142
Rao, B. Shiva, 205, 257
Rau, B.N., 4n. 15, 9n. 22
Rau, B.N. (Rau, Sir Benegal) (Constitutional Advisor and Joint Secretary), 31, 34–35, 49n. 123, 60–61, 60n. 39, 61n. 45, 62n. 47, 62n. 51, 63n. 56, 66n. 64, 122n. 1, 123n. 5, 127n. 22, 148n. 111, 181n. 90, 193n. 142, 196–205, 196n. 150, 196n. 151, 197n. 154, 197n. 155, 198n. 155, 199n. 157, 199n. 158, 200n. 163, 200n. 164
Rau, B.N. (Rau, Sir Benegal) (Constitutional Advisor and Joint Secretary), 196–98
Reforms Commissioner of Assam, 36n. 66, 36n. 67, 36n. 68, 37n. 69, 38n. 77, 39n. 80, 40n. 85, 57–58, 58n. 25, 58n. 27, 67–68, 67n. 69, 68n. 75, 69n. 84, 71n. 91, 76–78, 76n. 112, 76n. 113, 76n. 114, 77n. 115, 78n. 124, 80n. 130, 80n. 131, 81n. 132, 146n. 103, 147n. 107, 148n. 108, 151n. 122, 152n. 124, 152n. 125, 154n. 133, 228–30, 228n. 88, 228n. 89, 228n. 91, 229n. 94, 229n. 95, 230n. 96, *also see* Khaund, R.R.
refugee camps, 59, 70
refugee declarations, 62, 67, 76–77, 96, 96n. 36, 169; forms for completion, 68; submitting of, 81
Refugee Registration and Movement Act (of the provincial governments), 62
refugees, 53–63, 55n. 14, 56n. 20, 58n. 27, 59n. 30, 59n. 33, 60n. 35, 61n. 43, 61n. 44, 65–72, 70n. 87, 70n. 88, 70n. 89, 71n. 92, 73–84, 75n. 109, 75n. 110, 76n. 113, 77n. 115, 77n. 119, 78n. 122, 78n. 124, 80n. 128, 80n. 131, 89–90, 93, 118, 167–71, 227; Assam procedure for the registration of, 68; Bengali, 233; compulsory registration

refugees (*cont.*)
of, 61; declarations, 69, 76; definition
of, 62, 78, 95n. 31; definitions of, 72;
enrolment of, 62, 68n. 74, 77n. 120,
245; female, 72, 96; innocent, 69; and
the introduction by the CAS of the
uniform definition of a "refugee", 62,
79, 95, 95n. 31, 96; large number of,
71, 81, 119, 151n. 121; migrants, 231;
Muslim, 232; and partition, 52–54, 65n.
61, 67, 72n. 98, 85, 200, 211, 225, 225n.
74, 227, 232, 252n. 25; problems, 56,
60; registering partition, 54; registration
of, 61n. 40, 63, 68, 75, 78, 79, 95–97,
115; women, 169
registration of voters, 30, 39–41, 45n.
109, 47n. 116, 63–65, 69–71, 76–80,
83–85, 93–95, 138n. 66, 139n. 73,
169–70, 185–86, 229–30; and the
CAS guidelines, 41; and the confusion
with the explanation to article 5 of the
Draft Constitution on citizenship, 62;
and forms, 28, 33, 43; and the link to
citizenship, 60; and the new forms, 33,
43; on a house-to-house basis, 30; on
the basis of adult franchise as proposed
by the Constitutional Advisor, 31; on
the basis of universal franchise, 41;
and the partition refugees, 53–56, 60;
practice for homeless persons, 210n.
10; process of, 22, 56n. 20, 86, 185,
230n. 96; and the proposal for relaxing
the prescribed period of residential
qualification for refugee, 61n. 43; and
the qualifications for being a voter, 32;
and the refugees, 61
relief camps, 77
religion, and the electoral roll, 73, 104n.
82, 111, 111n. 110, 176, 211, 233–36,
239–42, 239n. 135, 241n. 144
Report on the Principles of the Union
Constitution, 161
representation, 96n. 36, 97n. 38, 119, 212–
15, 217–20, 220n. 53, 221n. 60, 221n.
61, 223, 230n. 99, 231, 233, 244n.
154, 245n. 156; direct democratic, 222;
given, 218; structure of claims for, 244
Representation of the People Act
1950, 233
Republic of India. *see* India
reservations (for minorities), 211, 233,
235, 238
residence (for enrolment), 40, 57–59, 67,
75n. 110, 77–78, 166, 174, 208–09,
208n. 1, 230, 256n. 33; orders, 208;

ordinary, 225; period of, 61, 117, 225n.
74; place of, 32, 32n. 56, 40, 54, 54n. 7,
62, 99, 118, 129, 166, 210n. 10, 230n.
99; proof, 25, 39, 243
residential qualification, 55–57, 59n. 33,
60–61, 61n. 43, 61n. 44, 65, 82–83, 93,
117, 148, 167, 170–71, 225, 230
Rewa State, 28n. 36, 134n. 47, 238n. 133
rights, 72, 82, 110, 116, 172, 175–76,
177, 213, 223, 228, 231, 231n. 100,
231n. 101; civic, 64; democratic, 255;
legal, 122n. 2, 149; special minority
group, 243; struggles for franchise and
citizenship, 54, 66
rolls, 31, 146, 152–55, 155n. 137, 196,
240, *also see* electoral rolls; dominion,
149; final, 47n. 116, 152–53;
manuscript, 93, 141; present, 150;
province's, 249; provisional, 48; unitary,
92, 94, 100
rolls (electoral), 1–5, 6–7, 9, 13–14
Rosanvallon, Pierre, 85, 85n. 2, 105, 105n.
85, 243n. 153
rupee franchise, 43

Sadiya Frontier Tract, 212n. 12, 215–18,
216n. 33
safeguards (for minorities), 64, 65n. 61,
100, 105, 125n. 16, 176, 185, 202,
218n. 45, 241; political, 238, 238n.
134; reservation for caste and religious
minorities, 211
Saurashtra State, 102, 106, 127n. 21, 131,
141, 147n. 107, 154, 154n. 135, 154n.
136, 155n. 138, 156–57, 184n. 102,
249, 249n. 13
scheduled castes, 33n. 60, 49, 49n. 127,
92, 111, 117n. 134, 117n. 135, 126n.
18, 135, 137, 234–40, 236n. 125, 238n.
131, 238n. 133, 239n. 136, 240n. 140,
242–43, 242n. 147, 243n. 151
scheduled tribes, 33n. 60, 92, 111, 111n.
110, 135, 176n. 67, 220n. 53, 234–35,
237–43, 238n. 131, 240n. 139, 242n.
147, 242n. 149
Scott, James C., 25, 25n. 22
SCs. *see* scheduled castes
seats (in legislatures), 22, 92, 110–12,
181n. 93, 182n. 98, 211, 218–23, 221n.
61, 234–35, 239–40, 244, 258n. 37;
allocation of, 240, 240n. 141, 256; extra,
220; parliamentary, 257; reservation of,
33n. 60, 92, 234, 236, 236n. 125, 238,
240n. 139, 240n. 140, 242–44; state
assembly, 244

"seats for women", 22
Secretariat, 23–25, 56, 73–74, 89–91, 93, 95–100, 96n. 36, 108, 114–15, 187, 196–98, 201–04, *also see* Constituent Assembly Secretariat; answerability and responsiveness, 253; and the issuing of press announcemnents, 100; requests to all provinces and states for electoral roll preparation, 252; team responsive to the problems and confusions arising from voter registration, 252
Secretariat of the Constituent Assembly, 1, 4n. 15, 7–9, 9n. 22
serialised epic, 85, 253
Servants of Bengal Society, 66
Seshadri, M., 102–03
Shah, K.T., 23–24, 23n. 10, 24n. 11, 24n. 14, 25n. 21
Shulman, David, 1, 1n. 1
Sikhs; problems in registration, 22, 73n. 99, 99n. 49, 139, 227n. 81, 232–37, 238, 244n. 154; Temples (Gurdwaras), 235
Sixth Schedule (draft constitution), 212–24
sovereignty, 50, 117, 123–25, 123n. 8, 125n. 16, 126n. 18, 251; dominion's, 128; enjoyed internal, 126; new, 142
State Legislative Assembly, 221
State Legislative Councils, 256
State Legislatures, 93–94, 99, 133–34, 140, 141, 149n. 115, 150, 159n. 149, 161, 172–73, 174, 178
States (Princely), 1; independent, 126; integrated, 237–38, 238n. 131; member, 26; merging, 143, 148–49, 190, 223; minor, 131; secular, 112
Stoler, Ann Laura, 35n. 64
STs. *see* scheduled tribes
Subramanian, P.S., 109n. 102, 144n. 96, 151n. 124, 152n. 125, 180n. 90, 191n. 133, 193n. 142, 197, 205–06, 230n. 99, 241n. 144
Sukumar Sen, 206
supplementary lists (of voters), 151–53
Surguja State, 28, 28n. 32, 131

Tahsildars, 28n. 36, 93, 94
territories, 1, 54, 57, 116, 122, 124n. 12, 126, 126n. 18, 129, 153, 157, 159, 222–25, 246; defining India's, 224; forming, 130; integrated, 125; new, 73; present Indian, 67; subcontinent's, 122; unified, 98, 103, 116
The Government of India Act 1935, 2n. 5, 3–4, 3n. 9, 12

Tinsukia Bengali Association, 56n. 20, 65n. 62, 69n. 81, 71, 71n. 91
Tirap Frontier Tract, 212, 216, 220n. 52
Travancore Government, 30–31, 30n. 46, 67n. 68, 72n. 98, 172–74, 173n. 54, 185
Travancore Interim Constitution Act, 173
Travancore Naturalization Act 1945, 173
Travancore plan for implementing adult suffrage, 31, 204
Travancore Representative Body, 174
Travancore Representative Body Electoral Rules, 174
Travancore State, 31, 172
Travancore subjects, 67n. 68, 72n. 98, 173, 173n. 54, 186
Travancore-Cochin Government, 250
tribal areas, 212, 214–15, 218n. 47, 219–21, 219n. 52, 220n. 53, 221n. 58, 224n. 70
tribes, 49, 176, 176n. 66, 214–18, 214n. 23, 216n. 32, 218n. 43, 218n. 45, 218n. 47, 220–22, 238n. 131, 238n. 133, 239–42, 239n. 135, 240n. 140
Tripura, 141, 173

U.S. Supreme Court, 179
Union Constitution, 197
Union Constitution Committee, 180, 180n. 89, 180n. 90, 181n. 92, 181n. 93, 184, 184n. 103, 189, 222
Union Government, 215
Union of India, 147, 173, 212n. 12, 223
Union of Matsya, 131, 141
Union Parliament, 162, 223
Unions of States, 122–24, 126–27, 131–34, 140–41, 143–44, 147, 150, 157–58, 172n. 51, 174n. 59, 184n. 103, 198–99, 239n. 138, 240n. 139; (6), 140; newly formed, 61n. 40, 106
United Provinces (UP), 27, 27n. 28, 28n. 33, 45n. 105, 45n. 106, 45n. 107, 46, 46n. 113, 46n. 114, 47n. 116, 48n. 120, 93, 138–39, 138n. 66, 139n. 67, 139n. 71, 139n. 72, 141, 147n. 107, 151n. 123, 152n. 127, 162n. 10, 162n. 11
United Provinces Government, 21n. 4, 42n. 90, 42n. 91, 46, 49, 49n. 126, 55n. 13, 138
United States of Vindhya Pradesh, 126n. 18, 131, 134n. 47, 141, 158, 158n. 144, 158n. 145
universal adult franchise, 21, 161, 161n. 5, 198, 215, 243, 252, *also see* adult franchise, and universal franchise; anticipated, 105; implementing, 31

universal franchise, 1, 2, 3–4, 5–7, 8, 9,
21–23, 33–34, 50–52, 83–89, 115–16,
129–30, 194, 197–200, 210–11, 243–45,
251–55, 256–58; compared to previous
forms of franchise, 22; concept of and
colonial attitudes, 35; concept of and
colonial attritudes, 50; and designing
the electoral rolls on the basis of, 27–29,
34; equality under, 74; and the limits
of inclusion, 211; 'one woman/man;
one vote' concept, 23; and the practical
implications within the bureaucracy, 34
universal suffrage, 42, 107, *also see*
universal franchise
untouchables, 257–58

vagrants, 208–10, 209n. 3, 245, 254
voters, 1, 2, 4, 5–6, 8, 31–33, 35–39,
51–55, 65–70, 93–95, 106–14, 135–37,
153–56, 169–74, 232–36, 240–43, 248–
51; defining, 2; eligible, 52, 101, 224n.
70; equal, 26, 251; list, 29n. 41, 47n.
116, 80n. 130, 99, 159, 234; number
of, 100, 136, 148, 240, 245, 248, 249,
250; prospective, 6; registration of, 6

voting, 34, 65, 109, 137, 172–74, 233,
245n. 156, 251; areas, 110; direct, 102;
electoral, 85; papers, 49; rights, 57,
66, 172, 175, 176–77, 210, 233, 233n.
108, 253
voting day, 257
voting rights, 5

Walker, G.E.D., 216
West Bengal, 37n. 68, 37n. 70, 37n. 71, 37n.
72, 38n. 76, 38n. 77, 40, 40n. 84, 40n. 87,
59n. 30, 62–63, 62n. 50, 63n. 54, 66–67,
73–77, 73n. 100, 74n. 105, 75n. 107,
75n. 109, 76n. 112, 77n. 116, 151n. 121,
151n. 122, 151n. 123, 151n. 124, 153n.
131, 154n. 132, 178n. 77, 180n. 88,
182n. 95, 239n. 135
Western democracies, 251
women; disenfranchising of, 43, 47, 104;
electors, 46, 135; enrolment of, 41,
45–48, 104; Moslem, 257; names of,
45; "purdahnashin", 39; refugees, 169;
registration of, 44–45, 128n. 24; seats
for, 22; voters, 44, 47, 47n. 116, 245n.
156, 257; workers, 47